The most important date of all:
28 December 1972
W.B. Marsh

Dates worth the keeping:
23 March, 4 May, 19 October and 29 November
Bruce Carrick

W.B. Marsh was born and has lived in New York, as well as Paris, Milan, Helsinki, Madrid, Tokyo, Vienna and Brussels. He and his wife now live in London. A Princeton graduate, he served in the US Marine Corps for two years and worked in advertising for 35 years. He has also worked at the V&A Museum in London. He has been collecting stories for days of the year for 23 years. On his birthday – 26 October – the legendary 'Gunfight at the OK Corral' took place at Tombstone, Arizona, in 1881.

Bruce Carrick has worked in book publishing for many years in New York and London, at Scribners, Doubleday, Macmillan and elsewhere. He and his wife live outside New York City in Somers, NY. He has known W.B. Marsh since they went to school together in New York, and they were friends too at Princeton. On his birthday in 1897 Marcel Proust had a duel with fellow writer Jean Lorrain.

W.B. MARSH & BRUCE CARRICK

GREAT STORIES
FROM HISTORY

365

FOR EVERY DAY
OF THE YEAR

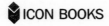

ICON BOOKS

Original edition published in the UK in 2004
This abridged edition published in the UK in 2005
by Icon Books Ltd., The Old Dairy,
Brook Road, Thriplow,
Cambridge SG8 7RG
email: info@iconbooks.co.uk
www.iconbooks.co.uk

Reprinted 2004, 2005, 2006

Sold in the UK, Europe, South Africa
and Asia by Faber and Faber Ltd.,
3 Queen Square, London WC1N 3AU
or their agents

Distributed in the UK, Europe, South Africa
and Asia by TBS Ltd., Frating Distribution Centre,
Colchester Road, Frating Green, Colchester CO7 7DW

This abridged edition published in Australia in 2005
by Allen & Unwin Pty. Ltd.,
PO Box 8500, 83 Alexander Street,
Crows Nest, NSW 2065

Distributed in Canada by
Penguin Books Canada,
90 Eglinton Avenue East,
Suite 700, Toronto,
Ontario M4P 2YE

ISBN-10: 1-84046-675-8
ISBN-13: 978-1840466-75-1

Typesetting by Hands Fotoset

Printed and bound in the UK by Cox and Wyman Ltd

Contents

CONTENTS

CONTENTS

Preface

SOME DATES in the calendar resonate with history. Most people associate 5 November with Guy Fawkes's failed attempt to blow up Parliament, 14 July with a Paris mob storming the Bastille, and 4 July with America's declaration of its independence from Great Britain. The more historically knowledgeable might connect 15 March with the Ides of March and Julius Caesar's assassination, 30 January with the beheading of King Charles, and 18 June with the Battle of Waterloo.

But most calendar dates are not so easily linked with the past. Indeed, some dates that were once synonymous with great historical events have disappeared from our modern calendar. How many of us remember that 24 May was Queen Victoria's birthday? Nevertheless, it is our contention that something worth noting in history occurred on every day of the year. This book is based on that idea.

We attempted to go further than simply connecting events with every date in the calendar. We tried to give some background and colour to each story we selected, to say why it happened, and to describe the sometimes surprising results. Because we have concentrated on portraying the individuals involved, the articles are often as much about men and women – and sometimes children – in unusual circumstances as about the historical events themselves.

Our selection of events is inevitably arbitrary owing to the vast array of history from which to pick and to the practical limitation on the number that could appear in a printed book. The stories we relate here are drawn in the main from British, European and American history but also in smaller number from Japan, India, China, Canada and elsewhere. The article with the earliest date, 25 June 1229 BC, concerns the day the great Pharaoh Ramses II took power in Egypt. Because we decided to regard anything occurring in the past half century or so as a matter of current events rather than history, the most recent event in the book is the conviction for treason of the American spies Julius and Ethel Rosenberg, which happened on 29 March 1951.

Whatever their dates, we selected events we thought were important, with impact on their time (and maybe on our own as well). They include births, deaths, marriages, funerals, coronations, assassinations, convocations, scandals, executions, battles, publication dates, duels and treaties. Often the events involve a famous figure, like Horatio Nelson or Lorenzo the Magnificent or Robespierre or Dante. Sometimes, however, they are simply fascinating bits of historical trivia, such as how the English dynastic name Plantagenet derived from a French noble's habit of adorning his hat with a sprig of yellow gorse, with the name *planta genista*.

Regarding historical 'truth', we have made every effort to be as accurate as possible, but we have seen that historians often disagree even about facts, let alone interpretations. And, in the spirit of offering an entertaining narrative, we have on occasion included reported historical detail that today may not seem altogether credible, such as the 'fact' that Mary, Queen of Scots' lips continued to move for ten minutes after her decapitation.

At one point in the writing we asked ourselves who we thought would constitute the audience for such a book. The response was simple: people like us, of course. That is, anyone who has even a passing interest in the events of the past, who relishes the human dramas that have shaped our civilisation, who enjoys a good tale or an ironic detail or a historical quirk, who is amused by the foibles of great people in all ages, and – above all – who wants to know what else of importance happened on his wife's birthday.

For such an audience, it seems appropriate to end this preface with the same words John Locke used to begin another in 1690:

Reader, I Here put into thy Hands, what has been the diversion of some of my idle and heavy Hours: If it has the good luck to prove so of any of thine, and thou hast but half so much Pleasure in reading, as I have had in writing it, thou wilt as little think thy Money, as I do my Pains, ill bestowed.

1 January

Samuel Pepys starts his diary

1660 'Jan. 1 (Lord's Day). This morning (we living lately in the garret) I rose, put on my suit with great skirts, having not lately worn any other clothes but them. Went to Mr. Gunning's chapel at Exeter House, where he made a very good sermon ...'

So begins the first entry of Samuel Pepys's diary, which he kept faithfully for nine years and five months. After chapel, Pepys returned to the rooms he leased in Axe Yard to dine on leftover Christmas turkey with his wife Elizabeth, who had burned her hand in the preparation of the meal. He spent the afternoon going over accounts. In the evening he and Mrs Pepys ate dinner at his father's house in Salisbury Court, 'where in came Mrs. The. Turner and Madam Morrice, and supt with us. After that my wife and I went home with them, and to our own home.'

When he began the diary, Pepys was 26, the ambitious son of a poor tailor but lucky in his influential cousins. He was also a graduate of Magdalene College, Cambridge, already married for five years, and at the beginning of what would turn out to be a long and successful career as a servant of the crown. He maintained the diary, with most of its contents obscured by his use of shorthand, until 31 May 1669, when failing eyesight forced him to desist. The diary touches on many of the great events and figures of the day – King Charles II, the Great Fire of 1666, the plague, the court, Restoration politics and the naval war against the Dutch – but these serve as background for the main subject, drawn with such remarkable candour, which is Pepys himself, 'that entrancing ego of whom alone he cared to write', in Robert Louis Stevenson's phrase.

Pepys's diary was a secret during his lifetime. After his death in 1703 its six leather-bound volumes remained unnoticed among his library and papers for over a century. It was first published in 1825, in a heavily bowdlerised version that excised many passages dealing frankly with the delicate matters of politics and Pepys's own sexual conquests. Despite the editorial damage done to it, the diary was recognised as a work of genius. Expanded editions followed, but the full diary as Pepys wrote it was not published until 1970. His biographer Claire Tomalin summed up the diarist's accomplishment this way:

> 'The most unlikely thing at the heart of his long, complex and worldly life is the secret masterpiece ... The achievement is astounding, but there is no show or pretension; and when you turn over the last page of the Diary you know you have been in the company of both the most ordinary and the most extraordinary writer you will ever meet.'

Also on this day

1431: Roderigo Borgia (Pope Alexander VI) is born * 1449: Lorenzo de' Medici (the Magnificent) is born * 1729: British statesman Edmund Burke is born * 1735: American revolutionary Paul Revere is born * 1863: The Emancipation Proclamation becomes law, freeing 4 million American slaves * 1901: The Australian commonwealth is established

2 January

Ferdinand and Isabella capture the last Moorish stronghold in Spain

1492 'They are yours, O King, since Allah decrees it', said Boabdil, ruler of Granada, as he handed the keys to the city to King Ferdinand of Aragon after a virtually bloodless siege that had lasted nine months.

So on this day over five centuries ago the last Moorish stronghold in Spain surrendered to the crusading might of the Catholic Monarchs, Ferdinand and Isabella. The Moors, who had arrived in Spain almost 800 years earlier in 711, were finally defeated. The gates of Granada were thrown open and Ferdinand entered, bearing the great silver cross he had carried throughout the crusade of eight years.

Mortified by his capitulation, Boabdil rode out through the gates of the city with his entourage, never to return. Reaching a lofty spur of the Alpujarras, he stopped to gaze back at the fabulous city he had lost. As he turned to his mother who rode at his side, a tear escaped him. But instead of the sympathy he expected, his mother addressed him with contempt: 'You do well to weep like a woman for what you could not defend like a man.' The rocky ridge from which Boabdil had his last look at Granada has henceforth been called El Ultimo Suspiro del Moro (The Last Sigh of the Moor).

The fall of Granada provoked intense and joyful celebration across all of Christian Europe, much as the fall of Jerusalem to Christian crusaders had almost four centuries earlier. Nowhere was the joy greater than in Spain itself, which, during the process of conquering the Moors, had at last become a truly unified nation.

Also on this day

AD 17: Roman poet Ovid and Roman historian Livy die * 1635: Cardinal Richelieu establishes the Académie Française

3 January

François Villon vanishes

1463 A habitual criminal, the great French poet François Villon had been sentenced to be 'pendu et etranglé' (hanged and strangled) for participating in a bloody fracas in the streets of Paris, but today the French Parlement reduced the penalty to banishment for a period of ten years, and he hastily left the city.

Villon (whose real name was François de Montcorbier) was born in Paris in 1431, but he spent his life as a roving poet who travelled with a gang of thieves and murderers. In 1455 he was convicted of killing a priest with his sword during a drunken brawl in the cloisters of Saint-Benoît, but he was eventually pardoned by the King.

We know that Villon was imprisoned at least three times after that, but despite his unruly life, he produced some of France's most beautiful poetry, including the famous 'Ballade des Dames du Temps Jadis' (Ballad of the Ladies of Old) with its haunting refrain 'Mais où sont les neiges d'antan?' (But where are the snows of yesteryear?).

Villon's banishment from Paris on 3 January is our last glimpse of him. We do not know where or when he died.

Also on this day

106 BC: Roman statesman Marcus Tullius Cicero is born * 1521: Pope Leo X excommunicates Martin Luther * 1777: George Washington defeats General Cornwallis's forces at the Battle of Princeton * 1833: Britain seizes control of the Falkland Islands

4 January

Birth of the father of fairytales

1785 The first of six children, Jacob Grimm was born today in Hanau. His lasting fame of course stems from a three-volume work entitled *Kinder- und Hausmärchen* that he published with his brother Wilhelm when both were still in their 20s. More familiar to us under the title of *Grimm's Fairy Tales*, literally translated it means 'Children and House Tales', suggesting that the book was intended for adults as well as children. The brothers believed that folktales were important to everyone because they expressed the universal dreams, fears and joys of mankind.

Considered the greatest anthology of fairytales ever put together, the collection includes stories not just from Germany but from all over Europe from as far south as Spain to as far north as Finland. Among the most famous are *Snow White*, *The Frog Prince*, *Hansel and Gretel*, *Rumpelstiltskin*, *The Bremen Town Musicians*, *Cinderella*, *The Brave Little Tailor*, *The Wolf and the Seven Little Kids* and *Sleeping Beauty*.

In his time Jacob was known for much more serious work. The master of seven languages, during his peripatetic lifetime he was secretary to the war office in Kassel, private librarian to King Jérôme of Westphalia, a librarian and lecturer at the University of Göttingen, a delegate to the Congress of Vienna and a professor in Berlin invited personally by the King of Prussia. He was a leading expert in German and wrote a book that related the early history of the German people to the growth of the language.

Of all his works, Grimm considered his major achievement to be a massive German dictionary that included the etymology of the words. Sadly, when he died at 78 he was still working on the letter F. (His brother Wilhelm had predeceased him, dying at the letter D.) The dictionary, however, was not abandoned, and was finally completed a mere 97 years later.

Also on this day

1797: Napoleon defeats the Austrians at the Battle of Rivoli * 1809: Louis Braille, French deviser of an alphabet for the blind, is born

5 January

England's only saintly king meets his maker

1066 On this day died Edward the Confessor, the only English king who ever became a saint. Kindly and pious, he spent hours each day in prayer and was reputed to have performed miracles of healing. With his prematurely white and flowing beard, he looked more like an ascetic prophet than a ruling monarch. He reigned for 24 years.

Edward was the son of King Ethelred II (the Unready), who died when Edward was only thirteen. By this time the Danes were ruling the country, and Edward was forced to flee to Normandy with his mother Emma. Emma, however, soon returned to England and married the Danish/English King, Canute, who was anxious to consolidate his hold on his English subjects. Two years later a son arrived, whom they christened Hardecanute.

In 1035 King Canute died, and his bastard son Harold claimed the English crown because Canute's legitimate son, Edward's half-brother Hardecanute, was too busy running Denmark to move to England. Meanwhile Edward continued to live in exile in Normandy. But in 1040 Harold died and Hardecanute became English king. A year later he invited Edward to return to his native land as heir to the throne.

Edward was a weak and ineffectual king who permitted the powerful Godwine family virtually to rule in his name. He even married a Godwine daughter, but the marriage was never consummated and foundered after six years. In all his long life Edward never had a sexual relationship with a woman, but the theories explaining why are legion. Some believe that he was homosexual and others that he was impotent, while the more trusting give credence to the report that he had taken a holy vow of chastity. Unsurprisingly, he had no children.

Edward was 63 when he died, and his death let loose the rivalry between his Norman cousin William the Conqueror and his successor on the English throne, his brother-in-law Harold Godwine, who as Harold II became England's last Anglo-Saxon king.

Edward left two enduring reminders of his reign. The first is the so-called St Edward's sapphire, a rose-cut stone once in his coronet, now in the imperial state crown of England. The other is Westminster Abbey, which he founded.

Also on this day

1477: Charles the Bold of Burgundy is killed in battle near Nancy * 1585: Walter Raleigh is knighted * 1589: Catherine de' Medici dies * 1592: Shah Jahan, the man who built the Taj Mahal, is born

6 January

The man who would command the tides becomes king

1017 On this day Canute, the king who we all know ordered the tide not to come in, was crowned at the old St Paul's Cathedral in London.

Canute had first come to England from Denmark with his father's conquering army in 1013. Over the next three years he tricked, conquered or destroyed all local opposition and finally obtained the crown of all of England on the death of Edmund Ironside.

At first Canute ruthlessly murdered any who resisted him, but over time he came increasingly to rely on his English barons, slowly easing out his Danish ministers to replace them with English ones.

Canute's rule was fair and effective; he even became a strong supporter of the Church and made a pilgrimage to Rome. By modern standards, however, his legislation was sometimes excessively stern; his Law 53 ruled that if a woman committed adultery, her husband was entitled to all her property and 'she is to lose her nose and ears'.

But Canute never forgot his Scandinavian origins, inheriting the throne of Denmark in 1019 and that of Norway in 1028, making him King of three countries simultaneously. He was an equally just sovereign in Scandinavia, famous for instructing, 'I want no money raised from injustices.'

Canute died in 1035, and his legitimate son Hardecanute became King of Denmark while his illegitimate son Harold claimed the English throne. Five years later Harold died and Hardecanute became English King.

If you doubt that such a successful monarch would be so foolish as to command the tide, you would be correct. The true story concerns Canute's dislike of fawning courtiers ever praising his supposedly infinite powers. One day he ordered his throne brought to the seashore and then bid the sea, 'Ocean! The land where I sit is mine, and you are part of my dominion. Therefore rise not – obey my commands and do not presume to wet the edge of my robe.'

His sycophantic retainers waited for the sea to comply, but obstinately it continued to roll in. When waves had wet his shoes Canute addressed his courtiers: 'Confess ye now how frivolous and vain is the might of an earthly king compared to that great Power who rules the elements.'

Also on this day

1412: Joan of Arc is born in Domrémy, France * 1838: Samuel Morse gives the first public demonstration of his invention, the electric telegraph * 1919: American president Theodore Roosevelt dies

7 January

The last English stronghold in France

1558 For centuries English kings considered parts of France their own, starting with William the Conqueror, who was still Duke of Normandy after he seized the English crown.

In spite of the success of French kings like Philippe Augustus in clawing back French lands, English monarchs continued to lay claim to large tracts of France. In 1345 England's Edward III launched the Hundred Years' War to regain territory that he thought should be his, and in 1346, in an eleven-month siege, he starved the French port of Calais into submission and added it to his holdings.

And so Calais remained English for over two centuries, the last English possession in France, until King Henri II determined to throw the English out for good.

Henri selected his greatest general, François de Lorraine, second duc de Guise, and ordered him to besiege Calais. Guise was a robust and athletic warrior of 39 who had been fighting for French kings all his adult life. His face carried a deep scar from a battle wound suffered when he was 26, resulting in his nickname, *le Balafré* (Scarface).

At the beginning of January 1558 Guise and his small army launched an assault against the English garrison at Calais, and on this day, after only six days of fighting, the English were forced to yield. And so, after five centuries, England had finally been swept clean out of France.

Among the French, the region around Calais became proudly known as *le Pays Reconquis*, but back in England, bloody Queen Mary lamented the loss with the only quotable comment of her reign, 'When I am dead and opened, you shall find "Calais" lying within my heart.'

Also on this day

1536: Henry VIII's first wife Catherine of Aragon dies * 1776: Thomas Paine's *Common Sense* is first published

8 January

Andrew Jackson wins a peacetime battle

1815 Today the United States badly mauled their British enemies at the Battle of New Orleans – even though, unbeknownst to the combatants, peace had been signed in December of the previous year.

The War of 1812 was the result of what Americans considered unjust and intolerable British conduct at sea during Britain's titanic struggle with Napoleon. Although France had finally agreed not to interfere with American shipping, the British, with the world's most powerful navy, had blockaded all French ports, making it difficult or impossible for Americans to trade. Worse, under the pretence that many American seamen were really disguised British deserters, the Royal Navy blithely stopped American ships and impressed their crews. In June 1812 American President James Madison declared war.

The war was a desultory affair, enlivened principally by the British burning of Washington. Weary of fighting, the two adversaries formally ended the conflict by the Treaty of Ghent signed on 24 December 1814, but communications at the time were so slow that two weeks later the two armies facing each other at New Orleans thought they were still at war.

Commanding the British was Major General Sir Edward Pakenham, the brother-in-law of the Duke of Wellington. He anticipated no trouble in taking New Orleans, as his forces outnumbered those of defender Andrew Jackson by three to one. Hoping he could frighten the Americans into submission, under flag of truce he sent in a letter threatening, 'If you do not surrender, I shall destroy your breastworks and eat breakfast in New Orleans Sunday morning.'

Enraged rather than intimidated, Jackson replied, 'If you do, you will eat supper in hell Sunday night.'

The British promptly attacked, but Jackson's men were sheltered behind bales of cotton. His Tennessee and Kentucky riflemen cut down whole ranks of the advancing enemy, while his pirate-trained cannoneers devastated the enemy with grapeshot, killing 2,000, including General Pakenham. The Americans suffered only seven killed and six wounded. The entire battle lasted only 30 minutes.

This was the last serious fighting in the War of 1812. From his victory at New Orleans Andrew Jackson became a hero, who, despite having won a battle during 'peacetime', used the fame he earned there to launch a political career that culminated in the presidency fourteen years later.

Also on this day

1337: Italian painter Giotto dies * 1499: Louis XII marries Anne de Bretagne, putting Brittany under the control of the French crown * 1642: Italian astronomer, mathematician and physicist Galileo Galilei dies in Arcetri, Tuscany * 1713: Italian composer Arcangelo Corelli dies

9 January

The British abandon Gallipoli

1916 At 3.45 this morning, with a half gale blowing, boats shoved off from W Beach at Cape Helles carrying the last 200 British soldiers from the Gallipoli peninsula, south-west of Constantinople. Ten minutes later the ammunition dumps on shore erupted in a savage roar, bringing to a noisy and unhappy conclusion the greatest amphibious operation the world had ever seen. It could have been a forerunner of D-Day; instead it was the herald of Dunkirk.

In early 1915 Gallipoli had held great strategic promise: by seizing the peninsula and sending a naval force through the fortified Dardanelles straits into the Black Sea, Britain and France could have knocked Germany's war partner Turkey out of the war, opened up a critical supply line to their ally Russia, and moved up the Danube against Austria. Success might have shortened the First World War by three years.

But in ten months of struggle and at the cost of some quarter of a million casualties – British, French, Australian and New Zealand – the Allies came very close but ultimately failed either to get their warships though the straits or to advance their army up the well-defended peninsula. It was not an operation for the faint-hearted, the inconstant or the unimaginative, all of which types were well represented in the highest levels of British civilian and military leadership. Gallipoli needed a Nelson or a Lee or a Rommel.

In Parliament the setbacks at Gallipoli threatened to bring down the government. Needing a scapegoat for the failure, the Cabinet found one in Winston Churchill, a staunch supporter of the operation. He lost his job as First Lord of the Admiralty. Later, the Army commander was sacked. There were calls for reinforcements and a renewal of attacks, but by now there was a shortage of artillery shells and troops were sent to other fronts. By October the government had decided on evacuation.

The next year a Parliamentary commission investigating the

failure cleared Churchill of mismanagement for his part in the operation. He took the occasion to deliver this judgement, which time has proved the right one: 'The ill-supported armies struggling on the Gallipoli peninsula, whose efforts are now viewed with so much prejudice and repugnance, were in fact within an ace of succeeding in an enterprise which would have abridged the miseries of the World ... It will then seem incredible that a dozen old ships, half a dozen divisions, or a few hundred thousand shells were allowed to stand between them and success. Contemporaries have condemned the men who tried to force the Dardanelles. History will condemn those who did not aid them.'

Also on this day

1522: Adrian of Utrecht is elected Pope Adrian VI, the last non-Italian pope until John Paul II from Poland in 1978 * 1799: British Prime Minister William Pitt the Younger introduces income tax, at two shillings in the pound, to raise funds for the Napoleonic Wars * 1828: The Duke of Wellington becomes Prime Minister * 1873: French Emperor Napoleon III dies in exile in England

10 January

Caesar crosses the Rubicon

49 BC Today Julius Caesar led one of his legions across a small stream called the Rubicon, thus defying the Roman Senate and breaking the *Lex Cornelia Majestatis* that forbade a general from bringing an army out of the province to which he was assigned. Turning to his lieutenants just before he crossed, Caesar remarked bitterly, 'Jacta alea est.' (The die is cast.) It was a de facto declaration of war against the Roman Republic.

The Rubicon is a narrow river south of Ravenna that marked the border between the Republic and its province of Cisalpine Gaul, now northern Italy. For the past nine years Caesar had been governor there and also of Transalpine Gaul, most of today's

France and Belgium. There he had waged ferocious war on the primitive local tribes, subduing them in the name of Rome. It was said that he had conquered 800 towns while defeating enemy armies totalling 3 million men, of whom a third were killed and another third sold into slavery.

But now the Roman Senate, jealous of Caesar's success and fearful of his ambitions, were determined to bring him to heel. They demanded that he give up command of his legions and report back to Rome as an ordinary citizen. Caesar knew that, despite his enormous achievements, a small clique of senators were not willing to concede to him the honours he thought he deserved, even wanted to destroy him. He believed, almost certainly correctly, that, once he had relinquished his power, his enemies would trump up charges against him and then ruin or even execute him.

Some credit Caesar with loftier motives – the urgent need to rehabilitate the creaking Roman state that was badly misgoverned by a fractious and self-serving nobility. Most agree that he had no desire to start a war, let alone create a dictatorship, but his *amour propre* demanded that the ungrateful senators recognise his achievements and reward him as they had so many other great generals in the past.

When Caesar crossed the Rubicon, the die really was cast. Not only did his action initiate a three-year civil war but it also led to the end of the Republic and the age of Roman emperors. Many historians consider it the most extraordinary achievement in human history. One man, armed only with a few legions, his own military genius and what Pliny the Elder called 'the fiery quickness of his mind', took over the largest and most advanced empire the world had known.

Also on this day

1645: William Laud, Archbishop of Canterbury, is executed * 1769: French marshal Michel Ney is born * 1941: President Franklin Roosevelt proposes the Lend Lease programme to Congress, under which America will 'lend' destroyers and other military equipment to Great Britain

11 January

Birth of a British bastard who became an American hero

1755 Today is the birthday of Alexander Hamilton, hero of the American Revolution, member of the Continental Congress and first Secretary of the Treasury of the nation he helped found.

But before his brilliant trajectory began, he was born on the volcanic island of Nevis in the Leeward Islands in the West Indies in unpromising circumstances that might have inspired a novel by Dickens. Some years earlier, his mother, with well-to-do planter connections, had deserted an unsatisfactory marriage, abandoning an outraged husband and an infant son. She took up with James Hamilton, the feckless fourth son of a Scottish laird come to the West Indies to make his fortune. They lived together for eight years, during which she bore him two illegitimate sons – Alexander was the second – while he dissipated her money. In 1765 James Hamilton deserted the family to seek prosperity elsewhere, forcing the mother to run a store to make ends meet. Three years later she died of fever, leaving Alexander an orphan at the age of eleven.

Despite his situation, Hamilton was an outstanding youth: largely self-educated, hardworking, precocious, bold beyond his years, and absolutely determined to make his way – cut a swathe, he might have said – in the larger world. In 1769 he wrote revealingly to a friend: 'My ambition is [so] prevalent that I contemn the groveling condition of a clerk and the like, to which my fortune, etc. condemns me, and would willingly risk my life, though not my character, to exalt my station.'

Fortune smiled. In the tight island society of St Croix, his talents and potential were recognised, not only by the merchant employer for whom he clerked but also by a Scottish Presbyterian minister, educated at the College of New Jersey, who saw that the boy's future, whatever it might be, was better found in North America than in the West Indies. The Reverend Hugh Knox arranged for Hamilton's passage to America, where he arrived, as one biographer put it, 'like a seed blown by happy chance onto perfect ground'. It was May of 1773, revolution was in the air, and Alexander Hamilton was eighteen years old.

Also on this day

1449: Italian painter Domenico Ghirlandajo is born * 1879: The Zulu War breaks out * 1891: French city designer Georges Haussman dies in Paris * 1928: British novelist Thomas Hardy dies * 1935: American aviatrix Amelia Earhart becomes the first woman to fly solo across the Pacific

12 January

The man who married Austria into a great power

1519 'Bella gerant fortes: tu, felix Austria, nube. Nam quae Mars aliis, dat tibi regne Venus.' (The strong make war, but you, happy Austria, make marriages. What Mars grants to others, Venus gives to you.) So wrote a 16th-century monk, and it fitted no one so well as that ebullient Austrian Habsburg, Emperor Maximilian I.

Maximilian had been born noble but poor and had himself made the first great dynastic marriage in the family, to Mary of Burgundy, heiress to the fabulous dukedom that included most of modern Belgium and Holland and bits of France. Subsequently Maximilian arranged for his son Philip to wed Juana of Spain, that insane princess who would inherit most of the Iberian Peninsula from her parents Ferdinand and Isabella. Philip died young, leaving two sons. The younger brother Ferdinand would, again through the arrangement of grandfather Maximilian, marry Princess Anne of Hungary, thus sowing the seeds for eventual Habsburg domination of the Balkans. The older brother Charles was to be the greatest emperor in history, ruling Austria, Germany, Belgium, parts of Italy, the Netherlands, Spain and all its vast territories in the New World.

The man who started it all, charming, diffident, ambitious Maximilian, died this day at the age of 60. He changed history by marrying Austria into an empire, parts of which lasted until the First World War. He also founded the Wiener Sängerknaben or Vienna Boys' Choir, which included Haydn and Schubert among its singers and which is still going strong.

Also on this day

1519: Spanish conquistador Vasco Núñez de Balboa is beheaded * 1625: Jan Bruegel the Elder, Flemish painter, dies * 1856: American painter John Singer Sargent is born in Florence * 1882: Wagner's *Parsifal* is completed in Palermo, Sicily

13 January

'J'accuse'

1898 This afternoon 300,000 copies of the newspaper *L'Aurore* hit the Paris newsstands with the force of an explosion. On its front page it ran an article that was the news story of the century. Under the title 'J'accuse', the article accused the leaders of the French Army of framing an innocent Army captain on a charge of treason in 1894, and then, four years later, of covering up their misdeed by arranging the acquittal of a second officer whom they knew to have been the guilty party.

The unlucky captain was, of course, Alfred Dreyfus, the only Jew on the Army's general staff. Convicted as a spy who had passed on French artillery secrets to Germany, he had been sentenced to life imprisonment on Devil's Island. The man who joined his cause with 'J'accuse' was the great French writer Emile Zola.

The Army reacted quickly to 'J'accuse' and put Zola on trial for libel. He was found guilty, and seeing that his appeal would fail, fled to the safety of England. Zola was not the first Dreyfusard, but the Dreyfus case – *l'affaire*, as it became known in France – gained enormous publicity when he took it up so dramatically. With him were men like Georges Clemenceau, Jean Jaurès and Anatole

France. Together they and the other Dreyfusards faced a public sentiment, laced with anti-Semitism, that believed in the Army's rectitude and the captain's guilt.

In a nation divided to its very core, it took a long time for justice to be done. Before it was, Zola died in 1902, asphyxiated by fumes from a faulty chimney (some maintained that anti-Dreyfusards had stuffed the flue). But by then the cause he championed had gained great strength.

Dreyfus was granted a second trial in 1899. He was pronounced guilty once again, but because of 'extenuating circumstances' he was sentenced to just ten years in prison. Many in France now understood that what was extenuating in the case was Dreyfus's innocence. In very poor health, he accepted a pardon from the President of France. In time the guilty officer confessed his role. In 1906 Dreyfus was cleared of all charges by a French court. He was restored to the Army, promoted to the rank of major and given the Legion of Honour. He served in the First World War as a lieutenant colonel.

Also on this day

86 BC: Roman general and consul Gaius Marius dies insane * 1599: English poet Edmund Spenser dies * 1625: Flemish painter Pieter Bruegel 'the Elder' dies * 1628: Charles Perrault, French author of *Mother Goose*, is born * 1898: Lewis Carroll (Charles Dodgson), writer of *Alice in Wonderland*, dies

14 January

Murder triggers the Albigensian Crusade

1208 Of all the cruel and senseless persecutions inflicted in the name of religion, few have been as ferocious as the medieval Church's crusade against the Cathars in south-west France. It was triggered today by the murder of the Pope's representative.

The word 'Cathar' comes from the Greek *katharos* (pure),

which is what believers attempted to be. Cathars thought that the material world was evil and man's task was to free himself from it. The most devout renounced life's pleasures, including meat and sex, in an attempt to find communion with God.

The Church in Rome could hardly find fault with such asceticism, but other Cathar doctrines were anathema. Cathars refused to accept the divinity of Christ, and, worse, sternly criticised the Church for its nepotism, greed and corruption. Perhaps the most terrible crime of all was the Cathars' refusal to contribute financial support to Rome.

The Cathar cult was particularly strong around Toulouse and Albi (hence the name of the crusade, the Albigensian), and Count Raymond of Toulouse was such a defender of the Cathars that an investigating papal legate, Pierre de Castelnau, was sent to threaten him with excommunication for his failure to suppress the heresy. The Count quietly submitted and swore his allegiance, so, his mission accomplished, Castelnau began his journey back to Rome. But when he reached the River Rhône, a knight in the Count's service, but perhaps not on his orders, stabbed the legate to death with a hunting spear. It was a deed with terrible consequences.

Incandescent with rage when he heard the news, Pope Innocent III immediately launched the Albigensian Crusade, offering participants full absolution for all sins if they served for 40 days exterminating the heresy.

A minor French noble, Simon de Montfort, was given the task of leading the campaign, spiritually supported by another papal legate, the fanatical Arnald-Amaury, who believed in massacre in the service of God. Together they gathered an army and ravaged southern France, slaughtering and pillaging indiscriminately.

Unlike most of the crusades to the Holy Land (one of which was also launched by Pope Innocent), the Albigensian Crusade eventually succeeded in its aims by besieging and destroying city after city in southern France, among them Carcassonne, Albi, Toulouse, Mont Ségur and finally, in 1255, the very last Cathar stronghold, the Castle of Quéribus. With some poetic justice, Montfort himself was killed by a boulder thrown from a trebuchet mounted on the ramparts of Toulouse. The few surviving Cathars fled where they could – Spain, Lombardy, England and Germany – or went underground. Three centuries later, the Midi, particularly the area around Toulouse, proved fertile territory for the Protestant Reformation.

The Church's experience with the Cathars had wider repercussions. Innocent died in 1216, but his nephew gained the papal throne as Gregory IX. Fully aware of the dangers of heresy, in 1231 the new Pope launched the Inquisition, which lasted in one form or another until 1908.

Also on this day

1742: Astronomer Edmund Halley dies * 1867: French painter Jean-Auguste Ingres dies * 1875: Alsatian-German theologian, philosopher, organist and mission doctor Albert Schweitzer is born

15 January

What ever became of Emma Hamilton?

1815 History sentimentally remembers Emma Hamilton as the great love of the illustrious English Admiral Horatio Nelson, and portraits of her as a young woman show a beguiling beauty with large, luminous eyes and splendid chestnut hair.

She was born Emma Lyon on 26 April 1765, the daughter of a blacksmith who died when she was two. By all accounts a stunning beauty, her first jobs were as maids. But by age sixteen she was already a kept woman, bearing a child to Sir Harry Fetherston-haugh. Later, after some time as a sort of *poule de luxe*, she moved in with Charles Greville, who claimed 'a cleanlier, sweeter bedfellow did not exist'. Greville subsequently passed her on to his uncle, Sir William Hamilton, the 62-year-old British minister to the Kingdom of Naples. Emma was then still only 21. After living together for five years she and Sir William married.

When Emma started her famous affair with Nelson she was already in her 30s and on the way to becoming immensely fat.

Though still beautiful, she was a vain and silly woman. She seems to have been as truly besotted with Nelson as he was with her, and they lived in a *ménage à trois* with the complaisant Sir William, even when she bore Nelson a daughter.

After Sir William died in 1803, Emma and Nelson (who was still married but had left his wife) set up house in England, becoming something of a national joke and scandal. Although the public adored the admiral, his equals noted his pretensions and evident self-satisfaction. As Admiral St Vincent said of him at the time, 'Poor man, drowned with vanity, weakness and folly, strung with ribbons and medals.'

When Nelson was killed at Trafalgar, Emma was left little money by either husband or lover. She nonetheless continued her extravagant ways, forever hoping for a government pension for her daughter, the only offspring of the great admiral.

Emma moved to progressively cheaper lodgings in London and finally fled to Calais, where she spent much of each day consuming as much wine as her meagre funds could provide. It is there that she died on this day at the age of 50.

Also on this day

1559: Queen Elizabeth I is crowned * 1622: French playwright Molière (Jean-Baptiste Poquelin) is born * 1759: The British Museum is opened at Montague House, Bloomsbury, London

16 January

Sir John Moore falls at La Coruña

1809 Today in the Spanish port of La Coruña, in the final act of his outnumbered army's arduous retreat, the British General Sir John Moore fell from his horse, mortally wounded by a French cannonball that had shattered his left shoulder and collarbone. He died later in the day, but he had already managed to lead his command – battered but intact – to the safety of evacuation by a British fleet.

In October, Moore had taken command of Britain's only field army on the continent of Europe. He had led it out of Portugal into Spain to face an enormous invading French army now commanded by the Emperor Napoleon himself. The Spanish army was in disarray, and when the capital Madrid fell on 4 December Moore's forces were left isolated in the north-west of the country. His first instinct was to retreat to Lisbon, but after learning that Spanish resistance to French occupation had broken out in Madrid, he decided instead to move against the French line of communications.

Thus, his army became, to use Sir Charles Oman's phrase, the matador's cape that distracted the Gallic bull from its main intention of conquering the rest of Spain and then Portugal. Surprised at trouble from this quarter, Napoleon detached significant forces to pursue Moore and postponed his advances south and west. 'If the English are not already in full retreat, they are lost,' the Emperor wrote to his brother, 'and if they retire they will be pursued right up to their embarkation and at least half of them will not get away ... Put it in the newspapers and have it spread everywhere that 36,000 Englishmen are surrounded ...'

In their 250-mile retreat to La Coruña, over mountains and in fierce winter weather, the British army became a rabble. Nevertheless, with strong rear guard actions and by dint of personal leadership, Moore was able to keep his forces together and ahead of their pursuers, now commanded by Marshal Nicolas Soult. Reaching La Coruña on 11 January, Moore formed his lines of defence. Throughout the fighting, strong French attacks were unable to pierce the British positions.

At last, on the 14th the British fleet appeared, and the evacuation, starting with the sick, the artillery and the healthier horses, began. But before it was completed Moore was struck down. At dawn the next day he was buried in the central bastion of the fortress as he had ordered, wrapped in his military cloak with his sword at his side. Only a day later the last British soldier was evacuated to the waiting fleet, and the French occupied the port.

It was perhaps as well that Moore died, like Wolfe and Nelson, in the moment of victory, for when his army was returned to

Britain the first public reaction was one of anger and criticism; many armchair strategists at home believed that instead of retreating, Moore should have attacked. It was many years before his feat was recognised for what it accomplished: a severe disruption of Napoleon's plan to conquer Spain and Portugal and the skilful preservation of a British army that would fight the Emperor another day.

A granite monument erected on the orders of another gallant soldier, his pursuer Marshal Soult, still marks Moore's grave at La Coruña. Almost two centuries later, in January of 2004, the mayor of La Coruña dedicated a bronze bust of Moore at his burial site.

Also on this day

1547: Ivan the Terrible is crowned first Tsar of Russia * 1794: English historian Edward Gibbon dies * 1891: French composer Leo Delibes dies * 1920: The Eighteenth Amendment to the US Constitution is ratified, starting Prohibition

17 January

A tough-minded empress saves her husband's empire

532 Today one of the most remarkable women in history stood firm in the face of bloody insurrection and saved her husband's control of the Byzantine Empire.

The Empress Theodora was hardly born to the purple; she was a prostitute who, according to the contemporary historian Procopius, was sorry that 'God had not given her more orifices to give more pleasure to more people at the same time'.

The daughter of a bear keeper in Constantinople and by all accounts exceptionally beautiful, by her mid-teens Theodora had been kept and discarded by several lovers, by one of whom she bore an illegitimate child. Highly regarded for her voracious sexual appetite, she was an actress (virtually synonymous at the time with prostitute), famous for her role of Leda in which she lay stripped on the stage, her thighs covered with grains of barley, which a live goose playing Zeus-as-swan picked up with its bill.

But by the age of twenty Theodora had met, charmed and married Justinian, who had persuaded his uncle the Emperor Justin to change the law that prohibited a noble from marrying an actress. She was, however, far more than just a superb sexual partner; she was possessed of both an acute intelligence and nerves of steel. After her husband became Emperor in 527, he treated her as a full partner in ruling his realm. An early supporter of women's rights, she also had her own agenda, backing new laws that prohibited the killing of adulterous wives, closing down Constantinople's brothels and outlawing the killing of unwanted children by exposure to the elements.

Justinian's greatest challenge came five years after his ascension, when rioting broke out between the Green and Blue factions at the chariot races in Constantinople's Hippodrome. A city prefect ordered seven hooligans hanged, but during the execution the scaffolding broke, saving two, who fled to sanctuary in a nearby church. When both Greens and Blues petitioned the Emperor for clemency, his refusal provoked a full week of chaos, the two factions combining forces under the slogan 'Nika' (Conquer), the catchword usually shouted during the races. They freed the condemned men, conducted a burning and looting spree throughout the city and demanded that the Emperor dismiss two of his senior officials.

At dawn on Sunday 17 January, Justinian publicly agreed to the rioters' conditions, but it was too late. The hostile mob continued its wanton destruction, proclaimed a noble named Hypatius as Emperor and drove Justinian into his royal palace in full retreat.

The terrified Justinian called together his panicky counsellors, who urged him to flee the city on the ship that was waiting at the garden stairs of the palace. But Theodora would have none of it, addressing her husband and his advisors with a ringing call to defy the rioters: 'If flight were the only means of safety, yet I should disdain to fly ... may I never be seen, not for a day, without my diadem and purple ... I believe in the maxim of antiquity, that kingship is a glorious shroud.'

Inspired by her courage, Justinian regained his nerve and sent his loyal general Belisarius to lead his soldiers to the Hippodrome. There he slaughtered over 30,000 rebels and executed Hypatius, whose body was thrown into the sea. Without Theodora's stirring call to action, Justinian's reign would have ended in shameful flight. As it was, he ruled for another 33 years.

During the rioting an old church had been burned to the ground. Just 45 days after the suppression of the revolt, on Justinian's orders work began on its replacement, the magnificent Hagia Sophia that stands in Istanbul to this day.

Also on this day

1377: The 'Babylonian Captivity' comes to an end, as the papacy returns to Rome from Avignon * 1706: Benjamin Franklin is born * 1751: Italian composer Tomaso Giovanni Albinoni dies * 1773: Captain Cook is the first to cross the Antarctic Circle * 1863: English Prime Minister David Lloyd George is born

18 January

Germany's first emperor is crowned in France

1871 At noon on this bitter cold day, with the smell of smoke in the air from nearby Paris, burning under the Prussian siege and bombardment, a magnificent and fateful gathering took place in the Palace of Versailles. In the Hall of Mirrors King Wilhelm of Prussia was crowned Kaiser of the Germans.

It was a moment for which the Prussian Chancellor Otto von Bismarck had devoted all his craft and considerable energies, the unification of all German states into a single empire led by Prussia. It had taken two wars over six years – first with Denmark in 1864, then with Austria in 1866 – to establish Prussia's dominant position among the German-speaking states and to bring the northern states into a confederation.

In 1870 he produced a third conflict – this one with France – by provoking Emperor Napoleon III into a declaration of war. French aggression, Bismarck calculated, and the resulting need for a collective German defence would have the salutary effect of encouraging the still-independent southern states – principally Wurtemberg and Bavaria – to join the northern confederation.

The combined German armies under Prussian leadership defeated Napoleon's forces with unexpected ease and then embarked on an invasion of France. Even as military operations dragged on longer than expected – stubborn Paris refused to capitulate and guerrilla activities mounted against the German occupation – Bismarck knew the time was right to complete an empire and crown an emperor. He made a variety of concessions to the southern states to overcome their remaining reluctance over the loss of sovereignty to the Prussian confederation. One secret arrangement involved furnishing the mentally unstable King Ludwig II of Bavaria with substantial Prussian funds to reduce the considerable debt he had amassed in his mad castle-building spree.

Standing with Bismarck in the crowded hall waiting for the coronation ceremony to commence was that other architect of victory, the great Prussian General von Moltke, the success of whose war plans had made today's event possible. Others in attendance included General von Roon, the Prussian War Minister; the Kaiser's son the crown prince of Prussia (deemed by his soldiers too tender-hearted for the enterprise of war); the crown prince's own son, almost thirteen (who as Kaiser Wilhelm II would prove far less tender-hearted than his father); and a large collection of kings, grand dukes, princes, landgraves, margraves and lesser ranks of rulers assembled from the various states of Germany.

W.H. Russell described the Kaiser Wilhelm's entrance to the Hall of Mirrors for *The Times*:

> It is twelve o'clock. The boom of a gun far away rolls above the voices in the Court hailing the Emperor King. Then there is a hush of expectation, and then rich and sonorous rise the massive strains of the chorale chanted by the men of regimental bands assembled in a choir, as the King, bearing his helmet in his hand, and dressed in full uniform as a

German general, stalked slowly up the long gallery, and bowing to the clergy in front of the temporary altar opposite him, halted and dressed himself right and front, and then twirling his heavy moustache with his disengaged hand, surveyed the scene at each side of him.

Ten days after the coronation at Versailles, combat operations in the Franco-Prussian War came to an end with the capitulation of Paris. In March, Kaiser Wilhelm returned to Berlin, where standing on the royal balcony with his grandson he was hailed as the conquering hero by rapturous crowds. On 10 May 1871, the Treaty of Frankfurt was signed, by which, in addition to paying an enormous indemnity of 5 billion francs, France was required to hand over to Germany the provinces of Alsace and Lorraine. So, in military triumph, the German Empire was born. It lasted not quite a half-century, ending in 1918 with Germany's defeat in the First World War. Kaiser Wilhelm II abdicated to a modest retirement in Holland, and Germany became for the first time but not the last a republic.

Also on this day

1778: James Cook discovers Hawaii * 1919: The Versailles Peace Conference opens

19 January

Death and the legend of Don Carlos

1568 It is difficult to separate the truth from the legend when it comes to Don Carlos, eldest son of Philip II of Spain. Some reports claim that he was warped in both body and mind, slightly hunchbacked and almost small enough to be a dwarf. Others (more probably) say that he had been a fairly normal boy until at the age of eighteen he fell down a staircase, severely cracking his head in the process. For several days he lay blind and delirious, his head swollen to enormous size, and all despaired for his life.

In a last attempt to save him, his family and doctors called on the intervention of God. In the nearby monastery of Jesús María lay the mummified body of the holy Fray Diego, who had died a century before. Fray Diego's desiccated corpse was placed beside Carlos in bed, and after one night in such company the dying boy started to recover. Soon he was physically well, but all reports agree that before long it became clear that he was mad.

The more extreme stories have him torturing horses, whipping nubile girls and cooking rabbits alive. What is certain is that during the next few years Carlos revelled in sadism and suffered periods of manic and murderous fury. He once attacked the Inquisitor General, shouting, 'A little priest dares to oppose me!' Proclaiming hatred for his father Philip, he tried to escape to Germany.

Finally Philip had no choice but to turn Carlos's room into a prison. Early on the morning of 19 January 1568, the King entered his son's chambers personally to supervise the incarceration: all doors and windows were nailed shut and no one but his jailers was allowed to speak to the Prince. Carlos was never seen again in public.

On 24 July it was announced that Carlos had died. King Philip informed his court that his son had repeatedly attempted suicide, trying everything from self-starvation to lying naked on blocks of ice, to setting his bed on fire. Philip claimed that eventually he had succumbed to fever.

In all probability Carlos died of slow poisoning on his father's orders. The more lurid accounts say that the reason was Philip's fury on learning of Carlos's passion for his Queen, young Elizabeth of Valois, a theory embraced with more gusto than historical probability by Schiller and Verdi. Others claim that Carlos had repeatedly threatened to kill his father. But in all likelihood tough-minded Philip's reason was that only mad Carlos's death could keep him from inheriting the throne of Spain.

Also on this day

1807: Confederate general Robert E. Lee is born * 1809: American writer Edgar Allan Poe is born * 1839: French Postimpressionist painter Paul Cézanne is born

20 January

George V is 'helped' by his doctor

1936 This evening at just past eleven o'clock England's heavy-smoking King George V died of influenza at his mansion at Sandringham, in Norfolk. To this day there remain rumours that the King's doctors, with the understanding of the government, administered a fatal dose of morphine to the dying king so that his death would come in time to be announced in the next day's *Times* rather than in the plebeian tabloids that came out a few hours later.

During his 70 years on earth George V had been a reserved and unbending monarch, bereft of imagination but determined to do his duty. After his death his own biographer wrote that the King was distinguished 'by no exercise of social gifts, by no personal magnetism, by no intellectual powers. He was neither a wit nor a brilliant raconteur, neither well read nor well educated, and he made no great contribution to enlightened social converse. He lacked intellectual curiosity and only late in life acquired some measure of artistic taste.' As such, notes historian Robert Lacey, 'he was, in other words, exactly like most of his subjects'.

By the time George had reached his Silver Jubilee in 1935, however, the British people had developed a certain admiration for him, in spite of his mundanity. As Harold Nicholson wrote, 'In those twenty-five years his subjects had come to recognise that King George represented and enhanced those domestic and public virtues that they regarded as specifically British virtues. In him they saw, reflected and magnified, what they cherished as their own individual ideals – faith, duty, honesty, courage, common sense, tolerance, decency, and truth.'

By the time George became King in 1910, English monarchs had ceded virtually all power to Parliament, in spite of the awe in which they were held by most of their subjects. Nonetheless, George's actions – or lack of them – have left some traces that remain today.

During the First World War, in a moment of high patriotism, George changed the name of the royal family from the Germanic Saxe-Coburg-Gotha to Windsor and ordered all his British relatives to adopt British-sounding names. Thus his cousin Louis of Battenberg simply translated his to Louis Mountbatten. When Germany's Kaiser Wilhelm (who was also George's first cousin) heard of the changes he ridiculed the effort by claiming that henceforth Shakespeare's *The Merry Wives of Windsor* would be known in Germany as *The Merry Wives of Saxe-Coburg-Gotha*.

A different First World War incident concerning yet another first cousin had more serious consequences. On 15 March 1917 Tsar Nicholas II of Russia had been forced to abdicate by the revolt of Petrograd's disillusioned and war-weary soldiers and workers. Although aware that Nicholas was in jeopardy, George refused to grant him and his family asylum in Great Britain for fear of being too closely associated with the autocratic Russian regime at a time when British socialism was raising its head. The Communists subsequently shot Nicholas, his wife and their five children.

More happily, George also set a Christmas precedent that has endured to this day. On the afternoon of Christmas Day in 1932 he broadcast a short radio message to his subjects, the text carefully scripted by Rudyard Kipling (who died two days before King George). Ever since, it has become a tradition for the monarch to broadcast to the nation on Christmas afternoon, although of course now the primary medium is television.

There is still some debate concerning George's last words. According to the high-minded *Times*, as he lay in his bed surrounded by his wife and children, with his final breath he asked, 'How is the Empire?' Another story, however, insists that his last comment was to his doctor. Seven years earlier after a serious illness George had recuperated at the seaside resort of Bognor, which had re-labelled itself Bognor Regis in his honour. Now the doctor tried to soothe his patient with the thought that once again he could convalesce at the same resort, to which the King pithily responded, 'Bugger Bognor!'

Also on this day

1265: The Earl of Leicester Simon de Montfort convenes the first English parliament in Westminster Hall * 1841: Hong Kong is ceded by China and occupied by the British

21 January

Louis XVI goes to the guillotine

1793 Today the king who legalised the guillotine in France himself mounted the scaffold amid the roars of the mob in Paris's place de la Révolution, today the place de la Concorde. He was the well-meaning but fat and bumbling Louis XVI.

The guillotine had been introduced into France as an instrument of kindness and an extension of democracy. It was proposed in the States-General in 1789 by Dr Joseph-Ignace Guillotin, who saw it as a more merciful way of dispatching the condemned and even a gesture of democracy; previously only the nobility had died by decapitation. The guillotine itself was not new. Something very similar was in use in Italy, and the 'Scottish maiden' had anticipated it 200 years earlier in Scotland.

Louis had already been under virtual house arrest for almost two years, and the monarchy had been abolished five months before. Then in December of 1792 Louis had been tried for treason and he was found guilty on 18 January. On the following day the Convention had voted for the death sentence by 380 votes to 310.

And so today ex-King Louis was brought through the streets of Paris in a carriage surrounded by troops in a cavalcade that lasted two hours. At every corner were citizens armed with pikes or guns, a precaution against any demonstration in favour of the King. At last they arrived at the place of execution.

Only 38 years old, the King faced death with courage and composure. He refused to let his jailers bind him and walked resolutely across the scaffold, the surrounding crowd in total silence. Arriving at the foot of the guillotine, he turned to address the throng. His last words were 'I die innocent of the crimes laid to me. I forgive those who have caused my death, and I pray God that the blood you are about to shed may never be visited upon France.' Then the drums drowned out his words and Louis was laid on the plank of the guillotine. The blade swept down, but the King's fat neck prevented it from slicing through instantly and he screamed once before his neck was finally severed. Then, according to his priest, who was an eyewitness, 'The youngest of the guards, who seemed about eighteen, immediately seized the head, and showed it to the people as he walked round the scaffold ... At first an awful silence prevailed; at length some cries of "Vive la République!" were heard. By degrees the voices multiplied, and became the universal shout of the multitude, and every hat was in the air.'

Based on experience gained during the French Revolution, the French considered the guillotine such a success that they kept it in use until a Tunisian murderer named Hamida Djandoubi became the last person ever guillotined in France on 10 September 1977.

Also on this day

1924: Vladimir Ilyich Lenin dies * 1932: English critic and biographer Lytton Strachey dies * 1950: English writer George Orwell (Eric Arthur Blair), author of *Nineteen Eighty-Four*, dies

22 January

An imprisoned emperor dies gazing at the most beautiful building in the world

1666 Today in Agra in north-central India died Shah Jahan, the most cultured and romantic of all Mughal emperors, as he gazed from his fortress prison on the fabulous Taj Mahal he had built in memory of his beloved wife.

Shah Jahan had been born to power, son of the Emperor Jahangir, but in his youth he had rebelled against his father, something his own sons were later to do. Eventually reconciled, he rushed to Agra to seize power when his father died in 1627. After a year of eradicating his rivals he became Emperor.

By this time Shah Jahan had already been married for fourteen years to the beautiful Mumtaz Mahal, whose alliterative name translates as 'Chosen One of the Palace'. Their union was a true love match in which Mumtaz Mahal played a crucial supporting role as his advisor and inseparable companion, accompanying him when he travelled around his empire, even on military operations. Together they established a brilliant court of splendid display and oriental grandeur. Shah Jahan's jewellery collection was possibly the most spectacular the world has seen.

During their years together Mumtaz Mahal bore fourteen children, but died in childbirth with the last during a military campaign when Shah Jahan was still only 38, just three years after he had seized power.

So stricken by grief was the Emperor that his hair and beard turned white in only a few months after Mumtaz Mahal's death. He determined to build in her honour a monument of eternal love, the most beautiful mausoleum in history. He called it a shortened version of her name, Taj Mahal.

Requisitioning over 1,000 elephants for transport, Shah Jahan had white marble and other construction materials brought from all over India. More than 20,000 workers laboured for 22 years to complete the building, at the staggering cost of 32 million rupees.

The Taj Mahal was completed in 1652. Legend has it, probably apocryphal, that Shah Jahan was so enamoured of its splendour that he had the thumbs of all 20,000 workers amputated to prevent them from ever creating another building so beautiful.

Five years later Shah Jahan fell ill, igniting a power struggle among his four sons. The third son Aurangzeb defeated and killed his eldest brother and, on Shah Jahan's unexpected recovery, locked his father away in his own fort within sight of the Taj Mahal. (For good measure, Aurangzeb later had his other two brothers and his nephew executed.)

For the eight years that remained to him Shah Jahan lived in opulent confinement in his fortress prison, wistfully gazing at the magnificent monument he had constructed for Mumtaz Mahal. When he died his body was laid in the vault below the building alongside that of his adored wife.

Also on this day

1561: English writer Francis Bacon is born * 1788: English Romantic poet George Gordon, Lord Byron is born * 1879: Zulus massacre British troops at Isandhlwana * 1901: Queen Victoria dies * 1924: Ramsay MacDonald takes office as Britain's first Labour Prime Minister * 1944: British and American troops land at Anzio on the Mediterranean coast of Italy during the Second World War

23 January

William Pitt the Younger pays for his consumption of port

1806 In Parliament he was incisive, astute and forceful, a brilliant orator with a comprehensive knowledge of the issues of the day. In private he was reserved, withdrawn and arrogant, a man with few friends who never married and was apparently indifferent to women. Such was William Pitt the Younger, Britain's youngest ever Prime Minister, who gained that office at the age of 24 and who occupied it for almost nineteen years. He died today, probably of renal failure and cirrhosis of the liver exacerbated by his heavy consumption of port.

Pitt was the son of William Pitt, now called the Elder, Earl of Chatham, who had twice been Prime Minister for a total of eight years in the 1750s and 60s. The younger Pitt had early showed signs of intellectual brilliance – he had entered Cambridge at fourteen. At 21 he became a Member of Parliament, and his maiden speech was so forceful and eloquent that the British statesman Edmund Burke commented: 'He is not a chip off the old block: he is the old block itself.'

In December 1783 King George III invited Pitt to form a government. On the nineteenth he became Prime Minister but was immediately challenged the following month when his government was defeated on a virtual motion of censure. Despite this reverse, Pitt stubbornly clung to power, backed by the King, who threatened to abdicate rather than allow an opposition coalition of Lord North and Charles James Fox to take over. Although the situation was unprecedented, Pitt hung on, and in March, with the majority against him down to one vote, his government 'went to the country' and retained power, no surprise whatever in a century when no government ever lost a general election. Indeed, Pitt was hardly the people's choice; he had been put in office by King George and stayed there only as long as the King wanted him.

Although serious-minded and hard working, Pitt was extraordinarily insular. He hardly travelled in England, never went to Ireland or Scotland and visited France only once. He showed little interest in either the arts or science.

The greatest test during Pitt's time as Prime Minister was war with France. On 1 February 1793 Republican France declared war, a conflict that was to last 22 years, well beyond his lifetime. Indeed, this war consumed much of Pitt's time and most of his energy, and in spite of Nelson's brilliant victory at Trafalgar in October of 1805, within two months Napoleon had utterly crushed the Austrians at Austerlitz, prompting Pitt's despairing but accurate remark, 'Roll up that map [of Europe], it will not be wanted these ten years.'

By now hard work and too much port were taking their toll. Pitt was clearly ill and looked it. Still he continued to labour, never losing his confidence in a successful outcome to the Napoleonic Wars. 'England has saved herself by her exertions,' he said, 'and will, as I trust, save Europe by her example.' But by 16 January he was too weak to continue and took to his bed in his house in Richmond. For several days he received visits from leading politicians and generals, including the future Duke of Wellington, and made his will. He then lapsed into periods of delirium in which he imagined he was debating in Parliament. On 23 January the young starter became a young finisher at the age of 46.

Shortly after his death English hagiography established Pitt's last words to have been an anguished 'Oh, my country! How I leave my country!' But Disraeli insisted that an aged servant had once told him that his last thoughts were somewhat less high-minded. 'I think', he said, 'I could eat one of Bellamy's veal pies.'

Also on this day

1783: French writer Stendhal (Marie Henri Beyle) is born * 1832: Edouard Manet is born * 1944: Norwegian painter Edvard Munch dies * 1947: French painter and printmaker Pierre Bonnard dies * 1989: Spanish surrealist Salvador Dalí dies

24 January

Frederick the Great is born

1712 Prussia. The word indicates a country but more strongly evokes a state of mind: stern, military, disciplined, orderly, masculine – some of the best but all of the worst of what the world thinks about Germany. Today the greatest Prussian of them all was born, the king who was one of history's generals of genius. He was Frederick II of Prussia, Frederick the Great.

Frederick's military fame comes from a lifetime of generally successful wars – defeating the Austrians and French alternately while carrying on his father's tradition of a well-trained, highly disciplined army. He had no doubts about the importance of military force; he once wrote to his younger brother, 'Don't forget your great guns, which are the most respectable arguments for the rights of kings.'

When Frederick inherited the throne the Prussian army stood at 83,000 men. When he died 46 years later the number had risen to 190,000 – an enormous force in a country whose population was only about 2,500,000, equivalent to Great Britain today having an army of over 4 million. During the Seven Years' War alone (1756–63), Prussia is believed to have suffered 180,000 casualties, almost 15 per cent of the male population.

Apart from his brilliant generalship, however, Frederick himself was hardly what we see today as 'Prussian'. He was an accomplished musician who composed, played the flute and knew Bach personally. He wrote poetry (mostly mediocre), collected art, was a passionate gardener and was probably homosexual. For a king he was a true intellectual, the author of a number of books and patron and friend of Voltaire, with whom he shared a sceptical view of life, once declaring as he looked at himself in the mirror, 'They say kings are made in the image of God. I feel sorry for God if that is what He looks like.' In stark contrast to the German government that followed him two centuries later, Frederick abolished the use of judicial torture.

Frederick was a tolerant if autocratic ruler. 'My people and I have come to a satisfactory understanding', he said. 'They say what they like and I do what I like.' Most surprising of all, he seldom spoke German but both conversed and wrote almost entirely in French.

Also on this day

AD 41: Roman emperor Caligula is assassinated * AD 76: Roman emperor Hadrian is born * 1893: Randolph Churchill dies of syphilis * 1963: Randolph's son Winston Churchill dies

25 January

Al Capone, America's greatest gangster, croaks at last

1947 Today in Palm Island, Florida, Al Capone, the most notorious gangster in US history, died four days after his 48th birthday of an apoplectic stroke complicated by pneumonia. Slow of mind from the ravages of syphilis, he had lived his final eight years in retirement on his Florida estate after eight and a half years in prison.

Raised in Brooklyn of Neapolitan immigrant parents, Capone had left school when he was twelve and had soon become a violent criminal. As a teenager he had murdered at least two men, for which he was never convicted. It was during this time in Brooklyn that he gained the nickname 'Scarface' when he insulted a young woman in a bar-cum-whorehouse named the Harvard Inn and her hoodlum brother slashed his face with a razor.

At twenty Capone moved to Chicago, where he quickly moved up in the gangland hierarchy. Soon he became the city's leading mobster, controlling gambling houses, brothels and racetracks, but his most lucrative business was the illicit sale of alcohol in Prohibition-ridden America. His organisation ran a string of illegal nightclubs, speakeasies and distilleries and generated an income in excess of $100 million a year.

To gain and hold his empire, Capone ruthlessly wiped out all underworld competitors. His most infamous murder was the St Valentine's Day Massacre of 1929, when four of his henchmen, two masquerading as policemen, entered a garage at 2122 North Clark Street in Chicago where the rival bootlegger Bugs Moran kept his headquarters. There they lined up six of Moran's gang plus an unlucky garage attendant against a wall and opened fire with two shotguns and two machine guns. (Moran himself, who was probably the intended victim, was across the street and survived the day, but his rivalry with Capone was over, and he drifted into petty crime, eventually dying in Leavenworth Penitentiary.)

For years Capone seemed immune from prosecution in a city famous for the corruption of both its administration and its police force, and the federal government despaired of bringing him to justice. But finally, ignoring his murders, extortion and other more brutal crimes, the government came up with the idea of prosecuting him for tax evasion, for Capone had never filed a tax return.

In 1931 Capone was indicted for tax evasion and, along with 68 of his henchmen, for violating Prohibition laws. When the trial judge refused to do a deal, Capone tried to bribe the jury, but the judge astutely changed the jury members at the last minute.

On 17 October Capone was convicted on only five of the 23 counts against him, but that was sufficient to earn an eleven-year sentence plus a $50,000 fine.

Capone was still only 33 when he started his term at Atlanta, and he had soon become the kingpin of the prison's inmates and obtained special privileges from the warders. Determined that he should experience a more rigorous regime, the government transferred him to the notorious Alcatraz prison on an island in San Francisco Bay, where he had no contact with the outside world.

While incarcerated at Alcatraz, Capone began to show signs of the dementia caused by tertiary syphilis. He was later transferred to Terminal Island in California and then finally released on 16 November 1939. Now a free man, he moved to his estate in Florida, but his failing mind precluded further mob activity and he lived in slow-witted retirement until his unmourned death.

Also on this day

1533: Henry VIII secretly marries a pregnant Anne Boleyn * 1586: German painter Lucas Cranach the Younger dies * 1759: Scottish poet Robert Burns is born

26 January

Chinese Gordon goes down fighting

1885 He was of medium height with a square jaw, sandy hair and a clipped military moustache. His power of command came through his pale blue and penetrating eyes as well as his somewhat unworldly righteousness. He was Charles Gordon, a British major general known as Chinese Gordon for his daring leadership in helping to put down rebel Chinese warlords in the Taiping Rebellion twenty years earlier.

A man of iron nerve, Gordon was a classic case of Victorian complexity. When not soldiering he spent much time helping orphaned children. He meditated three hours a day with his Bible, was celibate throughout his life and looked forward to death to meet his God. Queen Victoria's secretary referred to him as 'that Christian lunatic'.

In 1884 the British government sent Gordon to the Sudan where a Muslim fanatic called the Mahdi was taking over the country with a large army and threatening British interests in Egypt. Gordon soon arrived in Khartoum where he organised the defending garrison – all Sudanese or Egyptian soldiers except for a handful of British officers.

Soon the Mahdi neared the walled city. Knowing he had no chance of defeating the Mahdi's large army, Gordon still refused to leave. In the meantime Prime Minister Gladstone had at last authorised a relief force, but it seemed beset with incessant delays.

Early on the morning of 26 January the Mahdi ordered the final assault on the doomed city. In rode his fanatical hordes, leaving the streets red with blood. Gordon pulled back to the royal palace and there on an outside staircase he awaited his enemies, unarmed. Tearing open his tunic he faced his attackers and cried out 'Strike! Strike hard!' He finally fell in a rain of spear thrusts.

The relief force arrived two days later, on what would have been Gordon's 52nd birthday, to find they had come too late. Today Chinese Gordon's effigy lies in St Paul's Cathedral in London but not his body, for it was never found.

Also on this day

1788: The first convicts from England land in Australia * 1880: American general Douglas MacArthur is born * 1905: The Cullinan diamond, weighing 114 pounds, is found near Pretoria, South Africa

27 January

Trajan becomes Emperor on the death of Nerva

AD 98 The Emperor Nerva was 62 and looked older when he died of apoplexy on this day in Rome, after a reign of a mere sixteen months. His death brought to power one of Rome's greatest rulers, 44-year-old Marcus Ulpius Traianus, better known to us as Trajan.

A good administrator and 'second man' but not a leader, Nerva had been propelled to the top by the Senate when his malevolent predecessor Domitian had been assassinated. Although hated by the Senate and feared by the population, Domitian had been popular with the army, particularly his Praetorian Guard. So no sooner had Nerva become Emperor than the Guard forced him to execute Domitian's murderers, the very people to whom Nerva owed his throne.

Thus publicly humiliated, Nerva sought to re-establish his authority and regain support in the army by adopting the popular general Trajan. Consequently, when Nerva succumbed, it was Trajan who became the new Emperor.

Trajan was all that Nerva was not – tall, rugged and a first-rate commander who instinctively knew how to win public support. The first time he entered Rome as Emperor he walked among the common people and embraced each senator. But he could also be coldly authoritative; one of his first acts was to summon those guards who had threatened Nerva and order their execution.

Although Trajan came from an Umbrian family, he had been born in Italica, near modern Seville, thus becoming the first Roman emperor born outside Italy. He was to rule for nineteen years, six months and fifteen days, during which time he enlarged the Empire to its greatest extent, conquering parts of Parthia (now Iraq and Iran) and Dacia (now Romania). Even today Romanians claim descent from his occupying soldiers and owe their language to his conquest.

Trajan was also a prodigious builder, some of whose creations like his market in Rome and his famous 100-foot column there can still be admired today. He also implemented Nerva's idea of the *alimenta*, a system of using state funds to support poor children in Italy.

Such was Trajan's popularity that over two centuries after his death the Roman Senate still prayed for each new Emperor to be 'felicior Augusto, melior Traiano' (more fortunate than Augustus, better than Trajan).

Trajan also has a special place in the eyes of the Christian Church, as he was famously lenient with Christians, once instructing his friend Pliny the Younger (then a provincial governor) not to seek them out but to prosecute them only if they disturbed the peace. For this Dante included him in Paradise, unique among pre-Christian emperors, and relates how Pope Gregory the Great prayed for his admission to heaven.

Trajan died of a stroke on 8 August 117, deeply mourned by his people, who saw him as the perfect ruler; indeed, the 2nd-century historian Cassius Dio claims his only vices were wine and young boys.

Also on this day

1756: Austrian composer Wolfgang Amadeus Mozart is born * 1837: Russian poet Alexander Pushkin is killed in a duel * 1859: Kaiser William II of Germany is born * 1901: Italian opera composer Giuseppe Verdi dies

28 January

Death comes to Europe's greatest emperor

814 His language was German, his capital in Aachen, and Germans consider him the first German Emperor as well as the greatest.

The French believe him French, point out that he was King of the Franks, and call his capital Aix-la-Chapelle, named in reference to the lovely octagonal chapel that he built there. They, too, consider him their first Emperor and perhaps their greatest.

In English we call him by his French name, Charlemagne, who conquered vast territories to build an empire that included all of modern France, Belgium and Holland, virtually all of Germany and Austria, half of Italy, part of Hungary and a few north-eastern provinces of Spain. He established the Carolingian dynasty that ruled intermittently until 987, and in several Slavic languages (as well as in Turkish) the word 'king' derives from the German version of his name (Karl), for example *král* in Czech and *król* in Polish. He thus shares a distinction with Julius Caesar, whose name was the origin of the words *kaiser* in German and *tzar* in Russian.

Charlemagne died this day almost 1,200 years ago, probably

from influenza. He was 71. His tomb lies in his chapel in the cathedral at Aachan. It bears the inscription: 'Sub hoc conditorio situm est corpus Karoli Magni et orthodoxi imperatoris, qui regnum francorum nobiliter apliavit, et per annos XLVII felicites rexit.' (Beneath this tomb lies the body of Charles, Great and orthodox Emperor, who led the Kingdom of the Franks with greatness and ruled it successfully for 47 years.)

Although Charlemagne had been a loyal supporter of the Church and spreader of the faith, he was canonised only in 1165 because, in the words of historian Norman Davies, 'the process was obstructed for 351 years by reports that his sexual conquests were no less extensive than his territorial ones'. Sadly for the Great Charles, he never became a proper saint because he was canonised by Paschal III, an anti-pope set up by Holy Roman Emperor Frederick Barbarossa in competition with the legitimate popes of the Catholic Church in Rome.

Also on this day

1457: Henry Tudor, the future King Henry VII of England and first Tudor king, is born * 1521: The Diet of Worms opens, at which Martin Luther is outlawed by the Church * 1547: Henry VIII of England dies * 1921: American painter Jackson Pollock is born * 1935: Iceland becomes the first European country to legalise abortion

29 January

Napoleon III takes a beautiful Spanish bride

1853 She was 26, Spanish and strikingly beautiful. He was 44 and attractive through his power; 68 days earlier he had become Emperor of France. On this day they were married by civil ceremony, but still she refused to go to bed with him until after the church service the following day. She was Eugénia María De Montijo De Guzmán (Eugénie in French), a Spanish aristocrat of severe Catholic views. He was Louis Napoleon Bonaparte, the nephew of the great Napoleon, and now officially known as Napoleon III.

It seems likely that on her wedding night Eugénie was glad she had rebuffed his advances the day before, for Louis apparently attracted women by his energy, intelligence and great family name, not by his prowess in bed. One of his conquests, the marquise de Taisey-Chatenoy, recalled that the experience was brief and unsatisfying, and his heavy breathing had caused the wax on his moustache to melt.

Although Eugénie bore Louis a son in 1856, she was unenthusiastic about her conjugal obligations, and he was no more monogamous during marriage than he had been before. As is the way in dynastic unions, the couple stayed together despite his philandering. After the disastrous French loss to Bismarck's Prussia at Sedan in 1870, they were exiled to England, where Louis died in 1873. But Eugénie continued in the role of the *grande dame* of Napoleonic politics until her death at the great age of 94 in 1920.

Also on this day

1327: Edward III of England is crowned * 1737: Political essayist Thomas Paine is born * 1813: Jane Austen publishes *Pride and Prejudice* * 1856: The Victoria Cross is established

30 January

Double suicide at Mayerling

1889 At some quiet hour after midnight at the royal hunting lodge in Mayerling, Archduke Rudolf, only son of the Emperor Franz Joseph and heir to the throne of Austria-Hungary, composed a despairing letter to his mother ('I know that I am unworthy to be your son') and a brief note to his wife with the equivocal phrase, 'I am going calmly to my death which alone can save my good name.' He then placed a pistol to the temple of his seventeen-year-old mistress lying next to him in bed and pulled the trigger. Some hours later he turned the gun on himself. In the morning servants discovered the shocking scene, and word was sent post haste to Vienna.

Rudolf had been strictly raised by his unaffectionate father and, although he was well educated and intelligent, his father denied him any role in government. His arranged marriage to a Belgian princess had produced one daughter but no happiness, and he turned to mistresses for consolation.

In 1887, when Rudolf was 29, he met Baroness Maria von Vetsera at a ball in the German embassy. Although Maria was only sixteen at the time, she and the unhappy prince were soon enmeshed in a passionate affair.

When Franz Joseph heard of his son's liaison he determined to put a stop to it. On 28 January he summoned Rudolf and rebuked him for his conduct, taking the opportunity to tell him that the Pope had refused his plea to have his marriage annulled. The Emperor strongly voiced his own opposition to any divorce.

The next day an anguished Rudolf took Maria to the hunting lodge where he persuaded this seventeen-year-old innocent to join him in suicide, his only solution for their problems.

Wishing to hush up Maria's murder, Franz Joseph immediately dropped a veil of secrecy over the affair and had her body secretly buried. Then the imperial court issued a series of unconvincing lies that served only to inflame public curiosity and generate ever more bizarre rumours about what had actually happened: Rudolf and Maria had committed suicide because she was pregnant; Rudolf had been assassinated by Austrian republicans; Rudolf had committed suicide after killing Maria because she had emasculated him; Rudolf had shot himself after having been caught plotting against his father; Rudolf had killed them both because he had discovered that Maria was his half-sister; Rudolf was murdered in a love triangle duel with another noble. As recently as 1982 the family continued to leave false trails when former Empress Zita told a newspaper that Rudolf had been murdered for unspecified but mysterious 'political reasons'.

Rudolf's death at Mayerling made his cousin, Archduke Franz

Ferdinand, the next in line to inherit the throne of Austria-Hungary. Twenty-five years later Franz Ferdinand and his wife also met their deaths by pistol fire, but this time there was an assassin, and the place was Sarajevo.

Also on this day

1649: English King Charles I is beheaded, the only English king ever publicly tried and executed as a traitor, tyrant, murderer and public enemy * 1882: American President Franklin Delano Roosevelt is born * 1933: German dictator Adolf Hitler assumes power

31 January

The German Sixth Army surrenders at Stalingrad

1943 Today, the day after the tenth anniversary of his coming to power, Adolf Hitler raised four of his generals to the rank of Field Marshal. At that very moment, one of those newly created marshals was in the process of surrendering his army to the enemy. For Field Marshal Friedrich Paulus and his Sixth Army, and for Hitler and Nazi Germany as well, the tide of Operation Barbarossa, the German army's invasion of Russia, had turned. The high water mark was at the city of Stalingrad.

Not many months earlier, believing that the Red Army was on its last legs and possessed no sizeable reserves with which to mount a counter-attack, the German high command determined to deal its foe a knockout blow before winter set in. Hitler wanted Stalin's city taken, no matter what. In this spirit German ground commanders ignored intelligence reports of large enemy forces building up around the Stalingrad position.

So it was that, beginning on 12 September, when Paulus launched what was supposed to be the final attack, Sixth Army found itself facing the fiercest sort of close-quarter resistance, as it attempted to claw its way through the rubble of the ruined city, block by block, building by building, even floor by floor. When the offensive petered out in late October, the centre of Stalingrad still lay in Soviet hands.

Snow began falling on 12 November. It was followed by heavy Soviet attacks driving through the flanks of the long German salient stretching back west and south of Stalingrad. Suddenly, on 22 November, Sixth Army, 290,000 strong, found itself cut off and surrounded. In the weeks that followed, the Russians hammered in the sides of the German-held pockets. Supplies had to be flown in now, but the Luftwaffe's available air capacity could bring in less than half of what the army needed to keep functioning. From his headquarters in East Prussia, Hitler proclaimed 'Fortress Stalingrad' and forbade any attempt to break out for the safety of the German lines to the west. Men died by the thousands, from wounds, exhaustion, exposure and starvation. Just before Christmas, a rescue mission was fought to a standstill 35 miles short of Sixth Army's lines.

On Christmas Day the temperature was –25° Fahrenheit. On New Year's Day Hitler sent this message to Paulus and his command: 'You and your soldiers ... should enter the New Year with the unshakeable confidence that I and the whole German *Wehrmacht* will do everything in our power to relieve the defenders of Stalingrad ...' It was not to be. Sixth Army had been abandoned.

Surrender discussions began on 31 January. Sick and demoralised, Paulus at one point refused to order the holdout XI Corps to join his surrender, but it made no difference. By 4.00 a.m. on 2 February, the last signs of resistance had flickered out. All that remained of the German Sixth Army – 91,000 soldiers, including 22 generals – was marched away to the Soviet lines. Foreign correspondents witnessing these trophies of the great Soviet victory noted how healthy the German generals appeared compared with their undernourished troops. Of the German soldiers captured at Stalingrad, 95 per cent died in POW camps. Those who survived, around 5,000, were released after the war, the last 2,000 of them in 1955.

Also on this day

1543: Tokugawa Iayasu, founder of the Tokugawa shogunate in Japan, is born * 1606: English terrorist Guy Fawkes and three others are hanged, drawn and quartered * 1797: Austrian composer Franz Schubert is born * 1919: Jackie Robinson, the first black baseball player in the major leagues, is born

1 February

The Bohemian behind La Bohème

1896 Henri Murger was one of the few struggling poets of 19th-century Paris who turned his Left Bank experiences to profitable account.

Born in Paris in 1822, Murger was the son of a tailor and a concierge, and his formal education stopped at the age of thirteen. His early work was undistinguished, and he often lived in poverty with deteriorating health, but the romance and gaiety of 19th-century Paris enthralled him. When he was in his early 20s he started writing serialised stories about Bohemian life in the mid-1840s. Here were the radicals, the rebels and above all the artists who rejected all bourgeois values, choosing instead what they saw as the honesty of artistic creation and the suffering and privation that often went with it, determined to follow a life of independence, work and pleasure. He called the Bohemian life 'la préface de l'Académie, de l'Hôtel-Dieu ou de la Morgue' (the foreword to the [French] Academy, the hospital or the morgue).

If you are an opera fan, one of Murger's stories will sound familiar: 'During that time, the great philosopher Gustave Colline, the great painter Marcel, the great musician Schaunard, and the great poet Rudolphe, as they referred to each other among themselves, regularly frequented the café *Momus*, where they were known as the four musketeers because they were always seen together. In fact, they came together, left together, played together and sometimes didn't pay for their drinks together, always with a harmony worthy of the Conservatory Orchestra.' Rudolphe, of course, was a portrait of Murger himself.

Murger's tales became so popular that he eventually pulled some together into a play called *La Vie de Bohème*, an instant hit of the day. He was celebrated by Victor Hugo, lauded by Louis Napoleon and awarded the Légion d'Honneur. But he enjoyed fame and fortune only briefly. Within a decade he was dead at the age of only 39.

Sadly, Murger did not live to the evening of 1 February 1896 when Giacomo Puccini's opera *La Bohème*, based on Murger's play, was first performed in Turin. More than a century later, *La Bohème* remains the most often produced and most popular opera ever written.

Also on this day

1328: King Charles IV of France dies, ending the Capetian dynasty after 341 years, and starting the Valois dynasty with Philip VI * 1650: French philosopher René Descartes dies in Stockholm * 1793: Britain declares war on France, to last for 22 years

2 February

Birth of a 'bold merry slut' destined to become a king's mistress

1650 Born today in an alley off Drury Lane in London was one of history's most beguiling mistresses, Nell Gwyn, the petite, exuberant brunette who was kept for seventeen years by England's King Charles II.

By her own account, Nell had been born in a bawdyhouse run by her mother. Her father died in debtors' prison when she was still an infant. When she was a young girl her mother had enlisted her help 'to fill strong waters [serve brandy] to the guests' at the brothel, and she later sold oranges in Drury Lane. By the time she was fifteen she had switched to a career on the stage – and in the beds of her lovers. The first was an actor named Charles Hart, and a subsequent one was Charles Sackville, prompting her later to refer to Charles II as '*my* Charles III'.

When Nell was nineteen she came to the attention of the King, who was then 39, and soon became his mistress. 'Pretty witty Nell', as Samuel Pepys called her, charmed Charles not only by her pert good looks and exceptional legs but also by her high spirits and even temper. Once installed as the King's favourite (or at least one of them), she neither meddled in public affairs nor demanded money, although Charles treated her generously. Unlike some of his mistresses (and unlike Charles himself), from the time she joined him she remained faithful.

Famous for her quick wit, Nell once had occasion to use it to save herself from a violent mob. England at the time was rabidly anti-Catholic, and when Nell was riding in her carriage she was mistaken for Louise de Kéroualle, another of Charles's mistresses and a Catholic. As some drunken louts approached the carriage hefting iron bars, she poked her head out the window and called out, 'Pray, good people, be civil, for I am the *Protestant* whore.'

Nell had borne the king two sons and was 35 when Charles died in 1685. On his deathbed he entreated his brother James, 'Let not poor Nelly starve.' Honouring Charles's request, James gave her a pension of £1,500 a year. Two years later, on 14 November 1687, that 'bold merry slut' (Pepys again) died in London of a stroke.

Also on this day

1525, 1594: Italian composer Giovanni di Palestrina is born and dies * 1626: Charles I is crowned King of England * 1882: Irish writer James Joyce is born in Dublin

3 February

How the butcher of Cesena started the Papal Schism

1377 In 1308 the French Pope Clement V had moved the papacy from Rome to Avignon, principally as a political favour to Europe's most powerful king, Philip the Fair of France. One of the results of this so-called 'Babylonian Captivity' was a revolt of the Papal States in Italy, led by the Guelphs of Florence. But Pope Urban VI was disinclined to let Italy free from his control, and he ordered his legate there, Cardinal Robert of Geneva, to bring the Papal States to heel, if need be by force of arms.

Robert of Geneva was a young man (34) of high cultivation and sophistication. Although both lame and fat, he was also a cousin of the King of France. His manner was highly autocratic and his methods entirely ruthless.

Quickly hiring a band of mercenaries led by a renegade English knight named Sir John Hawkwood, Robert immediately attacked the city-states in revolt. He was at first unsuccessful but then came to the town of Cesena, near the Adriatic coast between Ravenna and Rimini.

To persuade Cesena's citizens to open their city gates, Cardinal Robert promised clemency by holy oath. But once inside the town he summoned his mercenaries and called for 'sangue et sangue' (blood and blood). Beginning on 3 February 1377, the soldiers butchered the town's inhabitants for three days and nights. Women were raped, men slaughtered and hundreds drowned in the moat outside the walls while trying to escape. Almost 5,000 in all were slain, and Cesena was put to the torch.

Cardinal Robert's services to the papacy at Avignon were considered so valuable that in September of the following year he was elected Pope as Clement VII, although there was already another pope on St Peter's throne in Rome. Thus this noble murderer became the first anti-pope in the papal schism that was to tear Christendom apart for 71 years.

Also on this day

1809: German composer Felix Mendelssohn is born * 1913: The 16th Amendment to the US Constitution, authorising the collection of income tax, is ratified * 1924: Twenty-eighth US President Woodrow Wilson dies

4 February

Yet another disaster for the House of Stuart

1716 Today James Francis Edward, the last Stuart ever born on British soil, kept family tradition alive with yet another Stuart calamity.

For a family that had the good fortune to become kings at all, the Stuarts of Scotland (and later of England) were certainly dogged by bad luck – or at least by their own persistent incompetence. During the four centuries after the first Stuart became King of Scotland, two royal Stuarts were killed in battle, two were murdered, two were executed and three went mad or were too incompetent to rule.

In the 12th century the Stuart family, which had originally been called the Fitzalans, became hereditary High Stewards of Scotland, taking on the name 'Steward' in the process. (Sometime during the 16th century, due to French influence, the name was respelled because there was no 'w' in the French alphabet.)

The first royal Stuart, Robert II, was heir presumptive to the Scottish throne for more than 50 years. He is mostly remembered for his unsuccessful rebellion against his kingly cousin, David II, and the number of his children. He had nine bastards, later legitimised when he married his mistress, and four more by his second wife, and he sired at least eight other illegitimate children on the side for a grand total of 21.

In 1371 Robert was 54 when he finally inherited the throne. By the time he had reached 65 he had become so incompetent that he turned over control of his realm to his son John.

Imprisoned for helping his father in the abortive revolt against King David, John changed his name to Robert when he succeeded but was soon disabled by being kicked by a horse. Hence during his sixteen years as king he never ruled his nation, leaving power in the hands of his brother.

Robert's son, James I, continued the family custom of misfortune when he was murdered in 1437. Then an exploding cannon killed his son James II while he was defending Roxburgh from the English. The next in line, James III, was murdered while running away from a battle at Sauchieburn.

James III's son, predictably named James IV, was yet another war death, unhorsed and killed at the Battle of Flodden in 1513. Then his son James V died insane shortly after another defeat by the English, and James V's daughter Mary (Queen of Scots) died under the axe of England's Queen Elizabeth.

Mary's son James VI – who became James I of England – defied tradition by dying in bed, but his son Charles I was famously beheaded for his dogged insistence on the Divine Right of Kings.

Charles I's son Charles II was the true exception to the Stuart custom of disaster, and he became only the second kingly Stuart to die peacefully and in full control of his faculties. His brother James II also passed away from natural causes, but his life was calamitous nonetheless, for he lost the throne of England through his unremitting pigheadedness.

Through no fault of James II's, the crown stayed in the family, going to his daughter Mary and her husband William of Orange – but poor Mary reigned for only five years, dying of smallpox at just 32. Then Mary's sister Anne inherited the crown after William of Orange's demise. Her particular misfortune was her inability to have children. Pregnant eighteen times, only four of her children were born alive, of whom only one survived infancy, and he predeceased his mother.

On this date it was the turn of James (Francis) Edward, son of the banished James II and brother of Mary and Anne, to find calamity instead of triumph.

James Edward never relinquished his claim to the thrones of England and Scotland even though he had been taken to France at the age of six months. When his father died in 1701 he gained the support of Louis XIV and styled himself James III of England and James VIII of Scotland.

When he was twenty James Edward made his first attempt to reconquer Scotland but never reached the shore, as British ships forced him to turn tail and return to France.

Seven years later he made one final effort to regain his kingdom by force of arms, landing at Peterhead near Aberdeen on 22 December 1715. Sadly, although a decent and honourable man, the Old Pretender, as James Edward is known in history, was neither warrior nor leader. His troops were too few, his money too little, and just 44 days after his landing, his incursion had become a withdrawal. On this day he hurriedly set sail for the Continent on the *Marie Thérèse*, his invasion a total fiasco. As he abandoned Scotland for ever, he coined the memorable phrase, 'Nous recoulons pour mieux sauter.' (We pull back in order to jump forward better.) Typical of this man who thought he should be King of England, his one famous remark would be made in French.

The Old Pretender spent the remainder of his life in exile in Rome. His son, the romantic Bonnie Prince Charlie, made a final futile attempt to regain the Stuart crowns in 1745 and then died without legitimate offspring, at last putting the House of Stuart out of its misery on 31 January 1788.

Also on this day

1789: George Washington is elected president of the United States * 1861: Seven secessionist southern states form the Confederate States of America, in Montgomery, Alabama * 1945: American, British and Soviet leaders meet in Yalta in the Ukraine to make agreements for post-war Europe

5 February

Birth of the man who gave birth to the Conservative Party

1788 Born today, Robert Peel, the shy, proud man who served as British Prime Minister for over eight years and founded the Conservative Party.

Peel was the grandson of a Lancashire farmer who had set up a calico-printing firm. This eventually provided enough wealth to employ 15,000 people and to buy both a baronetcy and a seat in Parliament for Peel's father, not to mention an education at Harrow and Oxford for Peel himself.

A brilliant student, on graduation Peel followed his father into Parliament and became an under-secretary a year later. Shortly after, he was appointed chief secretary for Ireland, but his involvement failed to lessen his strong anti-Catholicism, and he fought the idea of allowing Catholics to serve in Parliament.

Chosen as Home Secretary at only 34, within five years he had resigned his post rather than agree to Catholic emancipation. By the time he was 40, however, he had come to see the necessity (and the justice) of permitting the election of Catholics and their appointment to most public offices, and he incurred the enmity of many of his political allies by his volte-face.

Peel first became Prime Minister in 1834, and it was then that he formed the Conservative Party, a more liberal version of the old Tory Party. But his Conservatives stayed in power for just over two years, eventually defeated by a coalition.

At the age of 53 Peel once again became Prime Minister and over the next six years transformed British law and government. He repealed the restrictive Corn Laws that prevented the import of cheap corn, abolished hanging for most crimes, legalised trade unions and reformed the central bank and the economy. (He also reintroduced a less popular institution that has been with us ever since when he re-established the income tax, originally set up during the Napoleonic Wars as a temporary measure.)

In spite of his achievements, his peers did not love Peel; his title was too new for the true aristocracy and his manner too superior for the rest. His great enemy Disraeli claimed that his bright smile was 'like the fitting on a coffin'.

Robert Peel died on 6 June 1850 after being thrown from his horse. He is still considered by many historians to be Britain's greatest peacetime Prime Minister. For most of us, however, he is remembered for only one of his achievements, the creation in 1829 of the London metropolitan police force, still affectionately called 'bobbies' in his honour.

Also on this day

1881: Scottish historian Thomas Carlyle dies in London * 1897: French novelist Marcel Proust fights a duel with fellow writer Jean Lorrain

6 February

'I have been a most unconscionable time dying; but I hope you will excuse it.'

1685 According to tradition, it was with the words above that England's King Charles II apologised to the courtiers surrounding him shortly before he died on this day, after six days of hovering on the brink.

King for almost a quarter of a century, Charles is one of history's most appealing monarchs, a man of wit, courage and generosity who sincerely cared for his subjects. An all-round sportsman, he loved tennis, hunted, hawked and shot, enjoyed long walks, swimming and rowing, and was an enthusiastic sailor. But the sport that perhaps he enjoyed the most was gallantry; he fathered at least fourteen bastards by various mistresses and was a keen visitor to London's stews. As Pepys observed, 'He is at the command of any woman like a slave, though he be the best man to the Queene in the world, with so much respect and never lies a night from her; but yet cannot command himself in the presence of a woman he likes.' For all of this he was called the Merry Monarch.

Returning from exile to become King after the eleven harsh Puritan years of Cromwell that followed his father's execution, Charles was welcomed by his citizens on his return and mourned by them at his death. As historian Hesketh Pearson has written, 'Lacking [political] passion, he stood for toleration. Having no malignity, he typified charity. Hating retribution, he desired reconciliation.'

Charles first fell sick on Sunday 1 February in Whitehall in London. At 54, he had been in excellent physical condition, troubled only by gout and a running sore on his leg. On that morning he awoke feeling out of sorts, his leg bothering him so much that he forwent his usual walk, taking a carriage ride instead.

The following day he woke 'pale as ashes', his speech slurred and hesitant. Suddenly at breakfast he gave a great shriek and fainted.

Later he was attacked by convulsions and fever. It was clear to all that he was seriously ill, and so began the torments to which he was subjected by an array of physicians determined to make him well.

During the next four days the doctors repeatedly bled him, even opening his jugular vein, gave him purgatives, emetics and enemas of rock salt and syrup of buckthorn, branded his shaven head and feet with hot irons, applied blistering agents to his skin and in the end even made him drink spirit of human skull taken from a person who had died a violent death. In all it has been calculated that he was subjected to 58 different treatments by fourteen different doctors.

Charles suffered these tortures stoically, but his condition continued to worsen. On the evening of 5 February, with Charles's permission, his brother James (about to become James II) cleared the room of all but two courtiers and surreptitiously introduced the Catholic priest Father Huddleston, who had once helped Charles in his fugitive days when Cromwell was in power. Now Catholicism was despised and virtually illegal in England, but the fervent James was intent on what he saw as his beloved brother's salvation. The King received the last rites and became a Catholic less than a day before he died.

Charles awoke weak but lucid at six on Friday morning, 6 February. 'Open the curtains that I may once more see day', he whispered, and the curtains were drawn back. Half an hour later he had lost his speech and then fell into a coma. He died at noon.

The debate about exactly what killed Charles raged for many years. In his time it was attributed to 'apoplexy', and of course there were the usual rumours of poison. Later many thought his doctors' administrations had done him in. Still later the most popular theory was a stroke, but today most believe it was some form of kidney failure.

Also on this day

1286: Philip IV (the Fair) of France is crowned * 1508: Maximilian I becomes Holy Roman Emperor * 1564: English writer Christopher Marlowe is born * 1911: Fortieth US President Ronald Reagan is born

7 February

Charles Dickens – 'the cheerfullest man of his age'

1812 Today in Portsmouth was born the greatest – or at least the most prolific – of the great 19th-century novelists, Charles Dickens. Lionised when alive, still venerated almost two centuries later, he penned a whole pantheon of works so unique in their style and ability to portray character and caricature that we still use a derivation of his name – Dickensian – to describe both squalid living conditions and humorous if sometimes repulsive people.

Although of a middle-class family, Dickens was withdrawn from school and put to work in a shoe blacking warehouse when he was twelve because his father had squandered his money and been imprisoned for debt. He later returned to school but at fifteen abandoned all formal education to become a solicitor's clerk, then a court stenographer and at seventeen a newspaper reporter.

By the time he was 24, however, Dickens had already started to make his mark as a writer, with the publication in instalments of *The Pickwick Papers*, which was a huge success with the public. The same year, he married Catherine Hogarth, who would bear him ten children. From that time onwards, outwardly at least, Dickens was the successful and contented author living the respectable Victorian life (Victoria having assumed the throne in 1837).

Indeed, by all accounts Dickens had both wit and charm. In one house he had a secret door to his study that was disguised to look like a bookcase, with painted shelves and the spines of books bearing fictitious titles. One set bore the title *The Wisdom of Our Ancestors* and included individual volumes on ignorance, superstition, the block, the stake, the rack, dirt and disease. Beside them sat a single slim companion book entitled *The Virtues of Our Ancestors*, so thin that the title on the spine had to be printed vertically.

After the success of *The Pickwick Papers*, Dickens continued to turn out long, successful novels – *Oliver Twist* followed by *Nicholas Nickleby* and *The Old Curiosity Shop*, a book adored by the public particularly for its sentimental handling of the death of Little Nell. (Not everyone has found it so touching, however. Oscar Wilde once remarked, 'One would have to have a heart of stone to read the death of Little Nell ... without laughing.')

In 1843 Dickens published his most syrupy work, *A Christmas Carol*, which was an immediate success. His own favourite, the partly autobiographical *David Copperfield*, came out in 1850, followed during the next four years by two novels of social protest, *Bleak House* and *Hard Times*. An enthusiastic public eagerly awaited almost all of these, and Dickens became a national figure.

Suddenly, in May of 1858, when Dickens was 46, his wife Catherine moved out, although nothing was said to the outside world. The reason? Ten months before, Dickens had met and fallen in love with an attractive actress named Ellen (Nelly) Ternan, who was 27 years his junior. Two months prior to the collapse of his marriage Dickens had written to a friend, 'The domestic unhappiness remains so strong upon me that I can't write.'

After his wife's departure, however, Dickens evidently regained his creative flair, turning out such masterful novels as *A Tale of Two Cities*, *Great Expectations* and *Our Mutual Friend*. Meanwhile his sister Georgina came to live with him, caring for his younger children and taking care of the household.

As he grew older, Dickens seems to have become inwardly sad and preoccupied although outwardly as ebullient as ever. His American publisher called him 'the cheerfullest man of his age'. He now increased his workload, contributing to magazines and scheduling public readings of his works around Great Britain and in the United States. He undertook another tour of England in 1869, but abandoned it in April when he collapsed. Even then he continued to work, starting *The Mystery of Edwin Drood* and giving readings in London. Then, suddenly, on 9 June 1870 he died at his country house, Gad's Hill in Kent. So revered was he by the nation that he was buried in Westminster Abbey.

Also on this day

1478: English statesman and Catholic martyr Thomas More is born
* 1807: Napoleon defeats the Russians and Prussians at the Battle of

Eylau * 1950: The United States recognises Emperor Bao Dai of
Vietnam rather than Ho Chi Minh, who is recognised by the Soviets

8 February

Mary, Queen of Scots, is beheaded

1587 Mary Stuart, Queen of Scots: once Queen of France, then the
reigning Queen of Scotland, but for the past nineteen years a
prisoner in gentle confinement in England. She was a fiery and
beautiful woman, proud but essentially stupid, brave but vain and
astonishingly foolish.

Twenty years earlier she had been driven from Scotland for
conspiring in the death of her husband and marrying his murderer.
Since fleeing to England she had not ceased from her plotting to
regain her freedom and to seize the English throne from the jailer
whom she had never met, Queen Elizabeth. (Although two
centuries later the German poet Friedrich von Schiller had the two
meet once outside Mary's prison in his play *Maria Stuart*, this was
for reasons of drama rather than history.)

Now at Fotheringhay Castle a great platform was erected in the
main hall. Here Mary was to die, convicted of plotting to kill the Queen.

Proudly she entered, dressed entirely in black, her reddish black
hair impeccably coiffed. Crucifix in hand, she signalled for her
black cloak to be removed. The 300 nobles in attendance gasped as
they saw that underneath she was clad entirely in velvet the colour
of blood. Thus she knelt to die.

Shaken, the masked executioner needed three blows of the axe
to sever her neck, and then the once beautiful head of the 44-year-
old queen rolled across the scaffold. The headsman stooped to
pick it up, and suddenly it slipped from his grasp, and he was left
holding a dark red wig. The beautiful Mary's real hair was short-
clipped and grey, that of an old woman.

According to some sources, the dead queen's lips continued to
move for ten minutes.

9 February

A queen connives in her husband's murder

1567 Henry Stewart, Lord Darnley had been the worst of husbands – vain, stupid, indolent and drunken, with an insatiable desire to wield the full power of a king through his wife. Darnley's wife of course was 25-year-old Mary, Queen of Scots, who had no intention of sharing her power with anyone, least of all with her detested and quite detestable husband who was still only twenty.

Unfortunately for Darnley, Mary was also passionately in love with a Scottish adventurer named James Hepburn, the Earl of Bothwell, who would execute the murder that Mary so much desired.

On 9 February 1567 Mary rushed to join her husband in his house at Kirk o'Field, outside the gates of Edinburgh. Darnley was there convalescing from either smallpox or venereal disease, and Mary, playing the caring wife, showed her concern. In truth, her purpose was simply to ensure that he would be at home that night.

In the middle of the night the Queen suddenly remembered that she had promised to attend a ball following the wedding of one of her maids-in-waiting that very evening. Giving her husband a last kiss, she departed smiling.

A few hours later a tremendous explosion was heard throughout Edinburgh. Bothwell had moved a barrel of gunpowder to the room directly below Darnley's bedroom and had set it off. Darnley subsequently was found naked and dead in the street outside, apparently strangled, whether caught as he fled or throttled in his room and blown onto the street no one could say. Three months and six days later Mary married Bothwell.

Also on this day

1408: Henry IV defeats and kills Henry Percy, Earl of Northumberland at Bramham Moor * 1881: Russian novelist Fyodor Dostoevsky dies in St Petersburg

10 February

Victoria marries Albert

1840 Today marks the wedding of twenty-year-old Queen Victoria to her German cousin, Prince Albert of Saxe-Coburg-Gotha, in the Chapel Royal of St James's Palace in the heart of London's West End.

In October of the previous year Albert had visited Victoria at Windsor, sweeping her off her feet by his serious demeanour and good looks. After only four days together, the Queen had come to her decision. Albert was the man she wanted to marry, and royal protocol demanded that she do the proposing. As she later recorded in her diary, 'After a few minutes I said to him that I thought he must be aware *why* I wished them [Albert and his brother] to come here – and that it would make me *too happy* if he would consent to what I wished (to marry me).' Then, 'we embraced each other, and he was *so* kind, *so* affectionate.'

Although the Queen was clearly enamoured, Albert married primarily to find a larger, more influential place for himself in the world than would have been possible had he remained at home, the second son in the tiny German principality ruled by his father. In the end, however, the marriage proved to be one of the few true royal love matches. Victoria was besotted from the beginning, and over the years he came to love her deeply – and faithfully, a rarity among aristocrats.

Not that the marriage was without problems. Victoria had strong views about her position and the precedence of a queen over her consort, but Albert wished to participate in royal councils and play the traditional role of the husband. One famous story, perhaps apocryphal, illustrates the dilemma.

Annoyed with Victoria for excluding him yet again from an important state decision, Albert retreated to his room and locked the door. Soon Victoria sought him out, knocking loudly and demanding entrance.

'Who is there?' asked the prince from within.

'The Queen of England', came the reply. But the door remained closed.

Once again Victoria knocked, once again Albert asked who was there, and once again the response was 'The Queen of England'. The door remained resolutely shut.

Victoria knocked a third time and Albert again asked, 'Who is there?'

'Your wife, Victoria', came the answer, after which Albert immediately opened the door and welcomed her in.

Eventually Albert became Victoria's prime advisor and confidant, without whose advice she took no decisions. Hardworking, earnest and somewhat priggish, Albert also set for the British public the example of what we would call the Victorian code of conduct.

Victorian morality may long have vanished, but one of Albert's introductions to British culture is with us still: the Christmas tree, an old German tradition he popularised in Britain in 1841 when he gave one to Victoria as a Christmas present.

Also on this day

1258: The Mongols destroy Baghdad * 1482: Italian sculptor Luca della Robbia dies * 1775: English essayist Charles Lamb is born in London

11 February

The long life of America's greatest inventor, Thomas Edison

1847 Today in Milan, Ohio, was born a man who would register 1,093 US patents, the last at the age of 83. He was Thomas Alva

Edison, the greatest practical genius America has ever produced, who claimed he 'never waste[d] time inventing things that people would not want to buy'.

Almost deaf since childhood, Edison became a diligent worker who maintained that 'genius is one per cent inspiration and ninety-nine per cent perspiration. Accordingly, a genius is often merely a talented person who has done all of his homework.'

Edison's first invention was an electric vote-recording machine that was immediately rejected by the Massachusetts Legislature, probably because it restricted politicians' ability to rig the vote. Later creations include the first commercially viable mimeograph, the dictaphone and the electric storage battery, as well as the first successful system for generating and distributing electricity.

But Edison's greatest fame came from three inventions that totally changed the world in which he lived. He invented the phonograph in 1877, the incandescent electric light bulb in 1879 and early in the next century the 'kinetiscope', which was used for the first silent film – although the film wasn't projected; the viewer had to see it through a peephole.

Edison claimed that 'My principal business is giving commercial value to the brilliant – but misdirected – ideas of others.' His light bulb is the perfect example; back in 1801 the British scientist Sir Humphry Davy had first used electricity to heat platinum strips to incandescence. Edison's development of a practical bulb for general public use came 78 years later.

Edison died at 9 p.m. on 18 October 1931, on the anniversary of his invention of the light bulb.

Also on this day

1732: America's first President George Washington is born (when the Gregorian Calendar is introduced in Britain and its colonies in 1752, February 11 becomes February 22) * 1879: French caricaturist Honoré Daumier dies

12 February

Lady Jane Grey mounts the scaffold

1554 Today in the Tower of London a beautiful and intelligent sixteen-year-old girl was beheaded for treason. She was Lady Jane Grey, a pawn manipulated and controlled by her weak but ambitious father and her power-hungry and devious father-in-law, the Duke of Northumberland, because they thought she should be – and could be – Queen.

By early 1553 it was clear to all that Jane's cousin, the young and sickly Edward VI, could not long survive. Northumberland and his allies persuaded the dying boy-king to put aside his sisters, Mary and Elizabeth, and designate Jane as his heir. As a devout Protestant and great-granddaughter of King Henry VII, she seemed the perfect replacement, especially for those who feared Mary's morbid Catholicism and her desire to marry Spain's equally Catholic heir to the throne, the future Philip II.

Edward died on 6 July 1553, and four days later Northumberland and his followers proclaimed Jane Queen, while Mary Tudor fled to Norfolk. But it was almost instantly clear that the country would not support this substitution – Mary was, after all, Edward's sister and the legitimate daughter of King Henry VIII. Jane's support soon withered away, and she was easily persuaded to abandon her claim after a 'reign' of a mere nine days. She and her father were incarcerated in the Tower of London, but he was soon pardoned.

It seems likely that Jane, too, would eventually have been spared, but her father seemed incapable of leaving well enough alone. By the end of the year he had joined another plotter, Sir Thomas Wyat, who raised an army to depose Mary by force. On 3 February 1554, Wyat and some 3,000 fellow rebels advanced on London, but soon disbanded in despair when the local populace bolted their doors and refused to join them.

Wyat's revolt – and Jane's father's support of it – was the last straw. Jane was condemned to death.

On 12 February Jane watched from her window in the Tower as first Northumberland was led to the block, and then her young husband Guildford. One hour later the queen-pretender herself was taken to the axeman. Bravely and willingly she went; just five days earlier she had written to her father, 'Yet can I patiently take it, that I yield God more hearty thanks for shortening my woeful days.'

Also on this day

1804: Prussian philosopher Immanuel Kant dies * 1809: British naturalist Charles Darwin is born * 1809: Abraham Lincoln is born

13 February

The bombing of Dresden

1945 Dresden lies in the broad basin of the Elbe just 100 miles south of Berlin. In the late 17th and 18th centuries three electors of Saxony, Augustus I, II and III, turned it into a Baroque bijou whose only rivals in beauty were Vienna and Prague. Exquisite buildings like the Zwinger, the Japanese Palace and the Hofkirche were built, and the electors also assembled outstanding collections of paintings and objets d'art. So brilliant was the city that it earned the nickname of 'Florence on the Elbe'.

That all changed for ever on the night of 13 February 1945 when the first of 773 British Avro Lancaster bombers released its bombs over the city centre. Before the night was over the British had dropped over 2,500 tons of high explosives, of which two-thirds were incendiaries filled with highly combustible chemicals such as magnesium and phosphorus. This firebombing created a self-sustaining firestorm with temperatures over 1,500° centigrade. Almost 90 per cent of the inner city's 28,000 houses were destroyed, including 22 hospitals. Three centuries of architectural magnificence were incinerated in a single night. During the following two days over 500 American bombers joined the attack, although their target area was restricted to the railway yards.

There is still debate on the number of civilians killed. Before the war Dresden's population was about 650,000, but by 1945 the city was teeming with refugees fleeing from the advancing Russian army, bringing the total closer to 1,000,000. Although Nazi propaganda claimed a quarter of a million had died, modern estimates suggest a lesser figure of some 135,000, still the largest number of casualties ever inflicted in a bombing raid, dwarfing the 70,000 deaths at Hiroshima and almost triple the 51,509 British civilians killed by German bombing during all of the Second World War.

The primary instigator of the attack on Dresden was the head of RAF Bomber Command, Air Marshal Arthur Harris, who derided the type of precision bombing advocated by the US Airforce. Harris insisted that night-time firebombing raids would undermine civilian morale, in spite of the evidence within his own country that indiscriminate German bombing of civilians at Coventry and London simply stiffened British resolve.

The first German cities to suffer from Harris's tactics were Lübeck, Hamburg, Berlin and Cologne, but Dresden remains a special case because it quartered few German troops, had little war-related industry and was virtually undefended by anti-aircraft guns.

Two months after Dresden British Prime Minister Winston Churchill ordered Harris to end the firebombing of German cities 'simply for the sake of increasing the terror' and wrote to the Air Staff, 'The destruction of Dresden remains a serious query against the conduct of Allied bombing.' After the war he conspicuously omitted Harris's name from the list of new peerages, although he awarded them to many less important generals. But perhaps Churchill was a bit disingenuous; there is some evidence that he agreed to Harris's proposed attack in order to intimidate the Russians with the power of Bomber Command.

Although firebombing civilians was Harris's own invention ('The primary objective of your operations should now be focused on the morale of the enemy civil population and in particular of the industrial workers', he briefed his men), he tried to pass the blame upwards, writing in his memoirs, 'Here I will only say that the attack on Dresden was at the time considered a military necessity by much more important people than I.' Nevertheless, post-war criticism was so strong that in 1945 he moved to South Africa. In the end, however, perhaps he was lucky. He was never indicted for war crimes or breaches of the Geneva Convention. Indeed, despite the fervent protestations of the German government, over half a century after Dresden's destruction, Elizabeth, the Queen Mother, led the ceremonies in London at the unveiling of a statue honouring 'Bomber' Harris.

Also on this day

1542: English Queen Catherine Howard is beheaded at the age of 22 * 1571: Italian sculptor and jeweller Benvenuto Cellini dies in Florence * 1754: French diplomat Charles-Maurice de Talleyrand is born in Paris * 1867: Austrian composer Johann Strauss the Younger's waltz the 'Blue Danube' is played publicly for the first time in Vienna * 1883: German composer Richard Wagner dies

14 February

The mysterious death of Richard II

1400 No one really knows how England's King Richard II met his death, and even the exact date is in dispute, but many historians believe that it happened during the night of 14 February at Pontefract Castle in Yorkshire in the year 1400.

Richard had shown a flash of mettle as a fourteen-year-old king when he faced down the Peasants' Revolt, but during most of his time in power he relied on his uncle John of Gaunt to keep England's greedy and ambitious nobles under control. But after Gaunt died in February of 1399, Richard made two grave errors. First he sent Gaunt's son Henry Bolingbroke into exile, and when

Gaunt died shortly after, he confiscated Henry's inheritance. Richard's second mistake was to go abroad to Ireland. While he was gone Bolingbroke invaded England and persuaded other powerful barons to join him. Richard returned to find himself outnumbered, isolated and without hope. He surrendered without a fight and was incarcerated in the Tower of London. There, terrified for his life, on the last day of September he abdicated before Parliament, and on 13 October Bolingbroke was crowned King Henry IV.

Richard was now an ex-king at the age of 33, without even his freedom, this ruler who had once declared, 'I am the law.' But even languishing enchained in prison he remained an intolerable threat, a possible centre for conspiracy and revolt by ambitious barons. Parliament now determined that he should be locked away in secret so that he could never be found or rescued. Forced into disguise to leave the Tower, he was moved from castle to castle and eventually imprisoned in Pontefract Castle in Yorkshire. There he was kept in chains.

In January of 1400 the Earl of Salisbury and a group of Richard's former courtiers conspired to free him and restore him to the throne. For Henry IV this was proof enough that Richard was too dangerous to live.

What happened next is debated. Shakespeare tells us that Richard was attacked in his cell by Henry's henchmen, but rose to defend himself, wrenched a sword from one of his executioners' hands and killed two attackers. But creeping up behind him, his jailer, Sir Pierce of Exton, leaped on a chair and felled him with an axe blow to the back of the head. In the 17th century, however, Richard's body was exhumed, and no marks were found on his skull consonant with the blow of an axe. Other sources claim that, depressed by the hopelessness of his situation, Richard starved himself to death, but most contemporaries thought that his jailers, on orders from the new King Henry, simply cut off his food supply.

However he met his end, two weeks after his death Richard's corpse was taken south on a posthumous royal procession for all to see that he was actually dead. After two days of lying in state at St Paul's, he was quietly interred at the Dominican church at King's Langley, but during the reign of Henry IV's son Henry V, the body was transferred to Westminster Abbey.

Richard was the eighth and last of the direct Plantagenet kings of England (although there were six more indirect Plantagenets from the Houses of Lancaster and York), and the third of his house to die by violence.

Also on this day

1776: English economist Thomas Malthus is born * 1779: Captain James Cook is killed by natives on Hawaii * 1929: The St Valentine's Day Massacre: Al Capone's gang machine-guns seven members of Bugsy Moran's gang in a warehouse in Chicago

15 February

The sinking of the battleship Maine triggers the Spanish–American War

1898 Relations between Spain and the United States had been dangerously soured by the continued revolt in Spanish-owned Cuba and the lamentable conditions of the colonised Cubans. Eventually President William McKinley ordered the battleship USS *Maine* to Havana to reassure Americans living there.

At just past nine on the evening of 15 February the *Maine* swung quietly at anchor, most of the crew already gently sleeping in their hammocks while Captain Charles Sigsbee sat quietly in his cabin writing a letter. Then, he later recalled, 'I laid down my pen and listened to the notes of the bugle [playing taps], which were singularly beautiful in the oppressive stillness of the night. ... I was enclosing my letter in its envelope when the explosion came. It was a bursting, rending, and crashing roar of immense volume, largely metallic in character. It was followed by heavy, ominous metallic sounds. There was a trembling and lurching motion of the vessel, a list to port. The electric lights went out. Then there was intense blackness and smoke.'

An enormous explosion had engulfed the front half of the ship, right where most of the men were billeted. The *Maine* settled to the bottom of Havana harbour; of the 350 men on board, 260 died with the ship. The next morning only the ship's charred and twisted stern and bridge could still be seen above the gently lapping waves of the harbour.

Although no one knew who had detonated the blast, the unscrupulous press baron William Randolph Hearst had no scruples about inflaming American public opinion by blaming the Spaniards. His New York *Journal* was in a fierce circulation war with competitive newspapers, and Hearst believed a war against Spain was just what was needed to build readership. The *Journal* even published drawings purporting to show Spanish saboteurs clamping an underwater mine to the *Maine's* hull. Soon most Americans came to believe that the iniquitous Spaniards had blown up the battleship in a gesture of arrogant contempt for America.

Hearst then urgently dispatched writers and the artist Frederick Remington to Cuba to cover a so-called war between the dastardly Spanish and heroic Cuban rebels. Finding no trace of combat, Remington cabled Hearst: 'There is no war. Request to be recalled.' Hearst's answer was to the point: 'Please remain. You furnish the pictures, I'll furnish the war.'

Hearst was true to his word. Driven by the public's great patriotic fervour, the American Congress soon demanded Spanish withdrawal from Cuba, and by April the Spanish–American War had begun. The United States won a pathetically one-sided contest, in only eight months forcing Spain into a peace treaty by which the United States acquired Guam, Puerto Rico and the Philippine Islands.

In the pride of victory, the public began to forget about the *Maine*. Also forgotten was the fact that for many years no one really knew why she had blown up or who was responsible. But in 1976 a study by the US Navy indicated that the most likely cause was an accidental detonation in the ship's coalbunker, entirely the fault of the *Maine* herself and her crew.

Also on this day

1564: Italian astronomer, mathematician and physicist Galileo Galilei is born in Pisa * 1944: Allied planes destroy the ancient monastery at Monte Cassino in Italy

16 February

The Royal Navy captures the Altmark

1940 Tonight in a remarkable feat of naval derring-do, a British destroyer operating under Admiralty instructions intercepted a German supply ship making her way home along the coast of Norway. With searchlights blazing on her target, HMS *Cossack* pursued the *Altmark* into a narrow fjord where the supply ship ran aground. A boarding party killed seven German defenders, then opened the hatches to get at the cargo in the holds. The *Altmark's* cargo was 300 sailors of the British Merchant Navy, the captured crews of nine merchant vessels sunk the previous autumn by the German raider *Graf Spee*. By midnight *Cossack* was out to sea again, heading with her rescued cargo for the Firth of Forth.

It was, of course, a notable achievement by the Royal Navy and one greatly welcomed by a British public looking for purposeful engagement with the enemy during that trancelike opening period of the Second World War that came to be called the Phoney War or the Sitzkrieg. But the *Altmark* incident had the effect of putting the fat in the fire.

Neutral Norway vehemently protested the British violation of its territorial waters in vain. To Germany the incident demonstrated that Great Britain was willing to violate Norwegian neutrality and that Norway was unable or unwilling to prevent such action. The state of affairs threatened Germany's supply of Swedish iron ore, so vital to the Third Reich's heavy industries and much of it shipped through Norwegian waters. On 21 February Hitler ordered Exercise *Weser* – his planned invasion of Norway and Denmark – moved to the highest operational priority, ahead of Case Yellow, the invasion of France and the Low Countries.

In their reporting of the *Altmark* incident some British newspapers included this description from a *Cossack* sailor's account of the boarding: '... Meanwhile our boys were opening up the hatches. One of them shouted: "Are there any English down there?" There was a yell of "Yes!" You should have heard the cheer when our men shouted back: "Well, the Navy's here."' Some days later in London the First Lord of the Admiralty Winston Churchill appropriated this phrase to good effect addressing a large audience at the Guildhall: 'To Nelson's immortal signal of 135 years ago, "England expects that every man will do his duty," there may now be added last week's not less proud reply, "The Navy's here."'

During the night of 6 April 1940, German naval forces and troop ships left their north-German ports and sailed for Norway. The Phoney War was almost over. The real war was about to begin.

Also on this day

1822: English scientist and founder of eugenics Francis Galton is born * 1862: General Ulysses S. Grant wins the first major Union victory of the American Civil War when Fort Donelson on the Cumberland River in Tennessee surrenders with about 15,000 troops

17 February

Molière's last act

1673 'On ne meure qu'une fois, et c'est pour si longtemps!' (You only die once, and it's for such a long time!) So wrote France's greatest comic dramatist, Molière, who tonight collapsed on the stage at the Palais Royale in Paris to die at home a few hours later at the age of 51.

Molière was born Jean-Baptiste Poquelin but adopted the stage name Molière when he was a 22-year-old actor. By the time he was in his 30s he was not only writing plays but directing them as well, while simultaneously managing a travelling company of actors.

When he was 36 Molière first performed one of his own plays before King Louis XIV, who eventually backed Molière's players and they became the Troupe du roi (the king's troop).

Although Molière was brilliantly original, like Shakespeare he had no compunction about adapting other people's ideas to suit his own purposes. 'Je prends mon bien où je le trouve' (I take whatever belongs to me wherever I find it), he said. He also had little fear of the all-powerful authority of the Church, writing several plays, notably *Tartuffe* and *Don Juan*, that attracted ecclesiastical censure.

By 1673 Molière was at the height of his fame but had become seriously ill. Nonetheless he refused to relinquish his position as star actor in his own works. Today, just before the final curtain of his play *La Malade Imaginaire*, in which he was playing the lead role of the hypochondriac, he collapsed on stage and was rushed to his house, situated in what is now number 40, rue de Richelieu in Paris.

Molière quickly went to bed but soon was haemorrhaging blood. 'Don't be frightened,' he said to a friend at his bedside, 'you've seen me bring up more than that. But you'd better go and tell my wife to come up.' He died an hour later.

Even in death his troubles with the Church were not over. It took the intervention of the King for him to be buried in holy ground, with Church insistence that the burial take place in the dead of night.

Molière's heritage is still with us today. He continues to be one of France's most performed playwrights, and after his death the company he founded went on to become the Comédie Française, of which he is considered the 'father'.

Also on this day

1653: Italian composer Arcangelo Corelli is born * 1776: English historian Edward Gibbon publishes *The History of the Decline and Fall of the Roman Empire* * 1909: Apache leader Geronimo dies

18 February

The Duke of Clarence is drowned in a butt of Malmsey

1478 Malmsey is a sweetish wine from Greece that was much favoured by the English nobility in the 15th century. One of its most ardent consumers was George, Duke of Clarence, younger brother of that handsome and calculating monarch, Edward IV.

Unfortunately George had few of his brother's virtues but many vices of his own, of which the worst were blind ambition and disloyalty. Throughout his brother's reign George plotted with one enemy after another to snatch the crown and make himself King.

Finally Edward had had enough. In January of 1478 George was tried before the Lords of Parliament and condemned to death for treason.

Edward hesitated, loath to execute his own brother, but Parliament urged a speedy end. Legend has it that George, terrified of the pain of the axe, requested that he be drowned in his favourite drink. And so it was that, on 18 February 1478, George, Duke of Clarence, was gently lowered into a vast butt of Malmsey, to die with a sweet taste in his mouth.

Also on this day

1455: Florentine painter Fra Angelico dies * 1546: Martin Luther dies * 1564: Roman sculptor and painter Michelangelo Buonarroti dies

* 1678: John Bunyan's *Pilgrim's Progress* is published * 1861: Victor Emmanuel is proclaimed King of a united Italy at the first meeting of the Italian parliament

19 February

American Marines land on Iwo Jima

1945 Iwo Jima was nobody's idea of prime real estate – five miles end to end, three miles at the widest point, a low hump of island 700 miles south of Tokyo, covered by rock, sand and volcanic ash, its southern tip dominated by an extinct volcano, 556 feet above sea level, named Mount Suribachi. Taking his first look at it, a young US marine pronounced it 'not worth fifty cents at a sheriff's sale'. But considering the price paid in blood to gain possession of it, Iwo Jima had to be one of the most costly places on Earth.

Within its forbidding terrain, the island held three airstrips and a Japanese garrison of 21,000 troops. One observer said it 'bristled with concealed gun emplacements, pillboxes, mine fields, and an elaborate system of underground caves and shelters'. Artillery pieces and mortars were expertly sited to cover not only the beaches but also virtually every square foot of the interior. For the Japanese, Iwo's strategic value was as part of the home islands' defence cordon; for the Americans it would be as a forward base for B-29s and their fighter escorts taking part in the air offensive against Japan.

Everybody knew Iwo would be tough. Two days before the landings, as US battleships opened up with their pre-invasion bombardment of land targets, rocket-firing minesweepers and gunboats swept close in to scout the beaches where the landings would take place. The tempo of the preliminary operation was so high that the Japanese commander concluded actual landings were underway, and he sent out a communiqué to that effect. That night Radio Tokyo proudly misinformed its audiences that the enemy's first invasion attempt had been repelled.

At 0859 today – one minute ahead of schedule – the first wave of marines hit Red Beach One from landing craft. One battalion came across a small sign erected in the sand reading 'Welcome to Iwo Jima'. It was a thoughtful gesture left by Navy Seals two days earlier as they probed the landing area for shoals, reefs, mines and underwater defences.

Two entire Marine divisions went ashore this day. A third would follow. Eventually, there would be 60,000 marines on the island. Mount Suribachi fell on D+4 (23 February), and the first flag went up at 1035. From the crowded beaches below came cheers. Staring at the tiny figures high up on the summit, one marine said, 'Those guys ought to be getting flight pay.' The immortal photograph of the flag-raising ceremony was taken three hours later.

Suribachi was only the beginning. The Marines' advance up the island was bloodily contested every foot of the way. On the tenth day of combat they held less than half the island. Behind every dune, ridge or gully, defenders lay in deadly wait. Iwo Jima was not secured until D+26, and the final act of resistance – a pre-dawn suicide charge – was not quelled until D+35 (26 March). When the Navy released casualty figures for the first three days of combat, press reaction back home was one of shock. In a front-page editorial for the San Francisco *Examiner*, William Randolph Hearst Jr questioned the heavy price in lives lost.

The price was heavy indeed. Among total casualties of almost 26,000 marines and Navy personnel, there were some 6,000 deaths. Of the Japanese, fewer than 1,000 survived to be taken as prisoners. But even before combat was over, a B-29, low on fuel returning from a bombing mission over Japan, made an emergency landing on one of the landing strips. It was the first of 2,400 B-29s to make use of Iwo during the remaining months of the war. Afterwards, Admiral Nimitz characterised the American effort at Iwo Jima as one in which 'uncommon valor was a common virtue'.

Also on this day

1405: Mongol conqueror Tamerlane the Great dies * 1717: English actor David Garrick is born * 1743: Italian composer Luigi Boccherini is born in Lucca

20 February

Execution of an Austrian patriot

1810 Andreas Hofer looked very much the innkeeper that he was – round-faced, bearded and somewhat roly-poly. But beneath his genial exterior beat the heart of a true Austrian patriot, a man who loved his Emperor but wanted no truck with either Bavarians or Frenchmen, who were intent on claiming his homeland, the Tyrol in western Austria.

In 1809, when Hofer was 46, under pressure from Napoleon, Emperor Franz I ceded the Tyrol to Bavaria, but Hofer led a local insurrection to return the province to Austrian control. After decisively crushing the Bavarians at Berg Isel, he set himself up in Innsbruck as commander in chief of the Tyrol, under the protection of Emperor Franz. In October of that year, however, Franz once again bowed to French pressure and once more relinquished the Tyrol.

Still defiant, Hofer continued to resist the French, causing Napoleon to put a price on his head and dispatch a column of troops to capture him.

Evading his enemies, Hofer fled to the mountains, where he holed up in a deserted herdsman's hut, but his pursuers soon tracked him down, brought him barefoot through the snowy mountain passes and took him to French-controlled Mantua.

There Hofer was subjected to a kangaroo court-martial, convicted of treason and sentenced to death. Even though Franz made no effort to save him, he still might have escaped the ultimate penalty had Napoleon not sent a direct order by heliograph from Milan demanding to know the date of execution.

On this day Hofer was led to the city walls to face the firing squad. Refusing a blindfold, he addressed his executioners with the farewell comment, 'Good-bye, wretched world, this death is easy!' Then he ordered the guns, 'Fire!'

Thirteen years later Hofer's remains were brought back to Austria and interred in Innsbruck. For many years a play celebrating his patriotism was performed each year in Merano, in the Tyrolean part of Italy, and a poem about him was adapted as the Tyrolean anthem.

Also on this day

1437: James I of Scotland is murdered * 1872: The Metropolitan Museum of Art opens in New York

21 February

The Battle of Verdun

1916 At 7.00 a.m. German artillery began a bombardment of the French-held salient north of the historic fortress city of Verdun. It was the deafening prelude to the longest and one of the bloodiest battles of the First World War. Erich von Falkenhayn, the German Chief of Staff and War Minister, chose Verdun for the killing ground because it would compel the enemy into costly counter-attacks from which, he promised an appreciative Kaiser, 'the forces of France will bleed to death'.

The shelling from 1,200 artillery pieces paused at 4.00 p.m., as groups of German infantry edged out of the winter gloom to probe the devastated French forward positions. The battered and deafened defenders just managed to hold on until darkness brought an end to the first day's fighting. Then the bombardment resumed.

And so it went, day after day, savage artillery fire followed by infantry attacks, the French, outgunned and outnumbered, slowly giving way. On the 25th, impregnable Fort Douaumont, the linchpin of the entire French position in the salient, fell to the Germans. Supply routes into Verdun came under fire and were almost severed. Withdrawal to more defensible positions across the Meuse would have been the best military option, but for France, with national honour at stake, withdrawal was unthinkable. Someone would have to organise the defence of Verdun.

The organiser turned out to be Philippe Pétain, an unsung major general who had a talent for defensive warfare and the confidence of the *poilus* that he would not send them out to useless slaughter. He paid special attention to his artillery, co-ordinating its operation into an instrument of punishment for the enemy. He rebuilt and maintained the supply routes, assembling 3,500 trucks that operated day and night bringing in vital supplies and reinforcements for the Verdun garrison. He restored the fighting value of his troops by rotating his divisions in and out of the line. In time, these prudent measures turned the German tide. The 23rd of June saw the farthest extent of the German advance, almost – but not quite – to Verdun itself. Now, reaching the limits of its reserves, German strength began to ebb. Under French counter-attacks, the front line edged back northward. On 24 October Fort Douaumont was retaken. In December the fighting subsided into the ordinary, sporadic rhythm of trench warfare.

Verdun bled both armies white. In ten months of battle, the total casualties numbered over 700,000 dead, wounded and missing. For the French it was an act of stubborn heroism, and they hailed it as a great victory, but in truth, as Alistair Horne wrote, 'Neither side "won" at Verdun.' Among its many consequences were these: General von Falkenhayn was replaced as Germany's Chief of Staff in August after it became painfully clear that his campaign would never prevail; the French Commander-in-Chief General Joffre was sacked in December, in part for having neglected Verdun's defences; General Pétain, beloved by his troops, was replaced in May as army commander by a more offensive-minded general, but the next year, in even grimmer military circumstances, France turned once again to her 'architect of victory' and this time made Pétain Commander-in-Chief of the French Army; and a young company commander in the 33rd Infantry Regiment, Captain Charles de Gaulle, was captured on 1 March 1916, and spent the rest of the war in a German prison camp.

Also on this day

1431: Joan of Arc's trial begins in Rouen * 1613: The Romanov dynasty begins: Michael Romanov, son of the Patriarch of Moscow, is elected

Russian Tsar * 1940: The Germans begin construction of a concentration camp at Auschwitz

22 February

Etienne Marcel terrifies the Dauphin

1358 When the English army destroyed the forces of France at the Battle of Poitiers in 1356, one of the trophies they captured was the feckless and pleasure-loving French King, Jean II, called the Good. Deprived of leadership, France fell into anarchy. Of that calamitous time Petrarch wrote: 'On every hand I witnessed a terrible solitude. Fields were abandoned and buildings in ruins. Even near to Paris there were the same signs of fire and desolation. The streets were deserted and grass grew in the high roads. It was as though France had died.'

It was under these tragic conditions that the provost of merchants in Paris, Etienne Marcel, took charge of the city. Walls were repaired, provisions arranged for. Marcel and his followers forced the Dauphin Charles (the future Charles V) to grant reforms, summarised in the Great Ordinance of 1357.

Early in 1358, however, Charles broke his promise by debasing the coinage. Assembling his followers on 22 February, Marcel entered Charles's apartments in the royal palace (today's Palais de Justice). In the Dauphin's presence, without discussion or trial, the mob struck down two of Charles's noble advisors, who fell at the prince's feet, splattering him with blood. Marcel then placed his own cap upon the Dauphin's head, assuring him of protection if he carried out his pledged reforms.

It has been said that this revolt and triumph of the bourgeoisie was the first small step towards liberty and democracy. If so, it was a particularly short-lived one, as Marcel himself was murdered only five months later.

Also on this day

1788: German philosopher Arthur Schopenhauer is born * 1819: Spain cedes Florida to the USA * 1857: English soldier and founder of the Boy Scout movement Robert Baden-Powell is born

23 February

Emperor Diocletian persecutes the Christians

AD 303 Nicomedia lies east of what is now Istanbul in Turkey, today hardly a memory but at the beginning of the 4th century the de facto capital of the Roman Empire and residence of that fearful oppressor of the Christians, the Emperor Diocletian. It was here on this day that the Christian persecutions began when at dawn soldiers and city magistrates broke into the city's most important church and, finding no idols to destroy, burnt the Holy Scripture and then levelled the building to the ground. The next morning Diocletian issued his famous edict ordering the destruction of churches throughout the Empire.

Diocletian's unwavering objective throughout his 21-year reign was to consolidate his enormous territories under central imperial authority. Although in private hardly a religious man, he had reinstituted the ancient Roman gods as a way to give central focus to his authority as Emperor and had transformed himself into a sort of living god, the son of Jove, whom ordinary mortals could approach only prostrate and supine, to kiss the hem of his robe.

Christianity proved a problem in that its adherents refused to worship the Emperor and thus, Diocletian thought, weakened the state. In addition, squabbles among various Christian sects were a threat to public order, and many considered Christianity to be an attempt to establish a separate state within a state. Finally, Christians were exceedingly unpopular among certain elements of Roman society. As the incomparable Gibbon describes it, 'The Pagans [i.e. ordinary Romans] were incensed at the rashness of a recent and obscure sect, which presumed to accuse their countrymen of error, and to devote their ancestors to eternal misery.'

Within two weeks of Diocletian's first edict, the Emperor's palace was twice set alight, and Christians were the prime suspects. Christian resistance was reported from various places in the Empire. Diocletian vowed that his proscriptions would be effected without bloodshed, but that soon became a promise impossible to fulfil, as many of his governors were even more draconian than he. As the conflict grew, the Emperor issued three more edicts, each harsher than the last. Leading Christians were punished, and the entire clergy was ordered imprisoned, to be released only after sacrificing to the Roman gods. Finally, in April 304, Diocletian commanded all Christians to worship the Roman gods on pain of death, and Christian refusal led to an atrocious slaughter, including feeding believers to the lions.

Only a year later, prematurely aged through ill health, Diocletian stunned the Roman world by announcing his abdication and retirement. After a short stay in Nicomedia he moved to his birthplace in what is now Split in Croatia to live in his magnificent palace until his death in 316. Ironically, the mausoleum in which he was buried is now a Christian church.

Also on this day

1633: English diarist Samuel Pepys is born * 1792: English painter Joshua Reynolds dies * 1820: The Cato Street conspiracy: Police arrest conspirators who planned to blow up the British Cabinet * 1821: English poet John Keats dies in Rome * 1836: The siege of the Alamo begins under the Mexican general Santa Anna

24 February

Emperor Charles V Day

1500, 1525, 1530 This day belongs to the greatest of all the Habsburg emperors, Charles V. On it he was born at the very dawn of the 16th century in the Flemish town of Ghent. By the time he was nineteen his father and grandfather were dead, his morbidly insane mother was locked up for life in a lonely town in Spain and Charles was the master of more land in Europe than anyone since the Roman emperors, including Charlemagne. As well as wearing an emperor's crown as Charles V, he was also King of Spain as Charles (Carlos) I.

On Charles's 25th birthday, the date 24 February acquired even more significance. Under the command of King François I himself, a French army of almost 30,000 men was besieging the town of Pavia, in northern Italy. To the relief of the city, a slightly smaller Habsburg army arrived to reinforce the 6,000-man garrison within. The French attacked, but just when they seemed to be in the ascendant, 1,500 Spanish harquebusiers devastated the French cavalry and the Habsburg force counter-attacked, annihilating the French. Among the captured was King François himself, who melodramatically wrote to his mother, 'Tout est perdu fors l'honneur!' (All is lost, save honour!). François was taken away to spend over a year in Madrid as a royal prisoner, and from that date forward Spain dominated the Italian peninsula.

The 24th of February was also the date of Charles's coronation, on his 30th birthday (although he had already been Emperor for over ten years). Charles received his crown in the cathedral in Bologna, as Rome was in ruins, sacked by his own troops. Crowning him was Giulio de' Medici, Clement VII, the pope whom Charles had held prisoner during the sack. Charles was the last emperor to be crowned by a pope until Napoleon coerced another one almost 300 years later.

Also on this day

1786: Fairytale writer Wilhelm Grimm is born * 1836: American painter Winslow Homer is born * 1848: King Louis-Philippe flees France, ending the French monarchy

25 February

Renoir is born

1841 For one of France's greatest painters, Pierre Renoir was remarkably unassuming. 'What are paintings for, after all,' he said, 'to decorate walls.' Renoir always underplayed his talent, once denying that he was a great artist on the grounds that he was not syphilitic, homosexual or insane.

Renoir was born today in Limoges, the son of a tailor. During his 78 years he produced over 5,000 oil paintings and, along with Monet, fathered Impressionism. In old age his hands were so crippled with arthritis that the brushes had to be bandaged to them, but still he painted, often the soft voluptuous nudes for which he is famous. But his real attitude towards women was more sentimental than sexual. 'That is what women are so good at,' he once said, 'to make life bearable.'

Renoir died on 3 December 1919 at Cagnes in the south of France.

Also on this day

1309: Edward II of England is crowned * 1601: Robert Devereux, Earl of Essex, is beheaded for treason * 1723: English architect Christopher Wren dies in London * 1841: French Impressionist painter Pierre-Auguste Renoir is born in Limoges

26 February

Napoleon escapes from Elba

1815 'It's better to die by the sword than in this ignoble retirement.' So counselled the Emperor Napoleon's strong-willed mother Letizia, who shared with him his exile on the island of Elba off the Mediterranean coast of Italy.

Less than a year earlier, on 4 May 1814, Napoleon had arrived on Elba, a beguiling island of pastoral hills and scenic bays covering slightly over 75 square miles. His victorious enemies had treated him handsomely (for a man who had kept Europe almost continuously at war for the better part of fifteen years). He was to be considered an independent ruler of the island, he would retain the title of Emperor, and, to the chagrin of the restored Louis XVIII, France would support him with annual payments of some 2 million francs.

But the Emperor was worried. The French government was baulking at paying his yearly stipend, and his agents had learned that many European ministers felt that Elba was too close for comfort, a few mooting the idea of banishing him to some remoter spot. Finally, he missed his wife Marie-Louise, whom he believed his captors were preventing from joining him. (She had in fact no intention of ever seeing him again, as, unbeknownst to the Emperor, she had taken a full-time lover, the fellow Austrian Adam Adalbert, Count von Neipperg.)

So it was that, taking his mother's advice, Napoleon slipped away from his island prison in the dark of the evening of 26 February 1815. The Emperor, 800 loyal soldiers and a few horses boarded a few small sailing boats and a brig with the unfortunate name of *L'Inconstant*. On 1 March they landed in what was then a tiny fishing village called Golfe-Juan, just a few miles from Cannes.

First ashore was General Pierre Cambronne, who handed out tricolour cockades to all who would take them. Up went Napoleon's famous proclamation, 'L'aigle, avec les couleurs nationales, volera de clocher en clocher jusqu'aux tours de Notre-Dame.' (The eagle, with the national colours, will fly from steeple to steeple until it flies from the towers of Notre Dame.) Off to reconquer France, Napoleon marched north towards Paris (you can still drive along his route north from Grasse, proudly labelled the Route Napoléon by the French Ministry of Culture). Hope ran high in the Emperor's camp, but Waterloo was only three months away.

Also on this day

1781: British Prime Minister William Pitt the Younger makes his maiden speech in the House of Commons * 1802: French writer Victor Hugo is born * 1848: Karl Marx and Friedrich Engels publish *The Communist Manifesto* * 1871: Prussia and France sign a peace treaty at Versailles, ending the Franco-Prussian War * 1901: Boxer Rebellion leaders Chi-Hsin and Hsu-Cheng-Yu are publicly executed in Peking

27 February

Fire in the Reichstag

1933 In Berlin this evening, shortly after 9.00, Marinus van der Lubbe struck a spectacular blow for the cause of German workers. With a torch he set fire to the Reichstag building and soon had it blazing well out of control.

For van der Lubbe, a 24-year-old Dutch bricklayer, former Communist and loner with no political affiliation, his act of arson was meant to protest against the rampant injustices of capitalism. Still in the building when the police arrested him, he readily confessed to his deed. 'I considered arson a suitable method. I did not wish to harm private people but something belonging to the system itself. I decided on the Reichstag.'

But for the Nazi leader Adolf Hitler, Chancellor of Germany for less than a month, the fire was an undisguised blessing. 'A God-given signal,' he called it, 'the work of the Communists.' Herman Göring, agreeing with his Führer, claimed the fire was the first act of an uprising intended to disrupt the forthcoming Reichstag elections in which the Nazi Party hoped to return a clear majority.

The morning after the fire, the Reich Cabinet passed an emergency decree – 'the charter of the Third Reich', the historian Ian Kershaw called it – disposing of all the rights Germans had enjoyed under the Weimar constitution, including those of free speech, assembly, press freedom and privacy of communications. There followed over the next few days a violent government crackdown against the Left: Communists, Social Democrats, trade union leaders and intellectuals were beaten, tortured, imprisoned and killed – all in the name of saving Germany from imminent bolshevism. It was a sign of things to come.

The emergency decree and the ruthless measures were welcomed by the German electorate. The 5 March elections, although not resulting in an outright majority for the Nazis, were a solid victory with 44 per cent of the vote and 230 seats in the Reichstag, the best they had ever achieved. Better yet, the fire had brought out first-time voters in record numbers, most voting for the Nazi Party.

A German court found van der Lubbe guilty of the crime to which he had confessed. Tried with him were four Communists, including the head of the German Communist party. But with the lack of any evidence contrary to van der Lubbe's explicit declaration that he acted alone, the court acquitted the co-defendants, much to Hitler's outrage.

The arsonist himself was executed on 10 January 1934. Whether he was part of a Communist conspiracy, as the Nazis claimed, has never been clearly established. Many considered it more likely that the Nazis themselves had set the fire as the pretext for their first step towards total power. Whatever the truth, instead of the rope, van der Lubbe surely deserved some sort of medal from the Nazis for providing such a golden opportunity to begin the establishment of the Third Reich.

Also on this day

AD 274: Roman Emperor Constantine the Great is born * 1807: American poet Henry Wadsworth Longfellow is born in Portland, Maine

28 February

The Republican Party is born

1854 Today a small group of abolitionists, Free Soilers and former Democrats and Whigs met in a church in Ripon, Wisconsin, to join forces in fighting the extension of slavery into American territories. Under the leadership of Alvan Bovay, the participants adopted an anti-slavery resolution and agreed to meet again the following month. From this slight beginning was born the Republican Party of the United States.

Although the American Civil War was still seven years away, slavery was already the great issue of the day, particularly now that the Kansas-Nebraska Act looked certain to be passed by Congress. This act overturned the 1820 Missouri Compromise that had excluded slavery from the Kansas and Nebraska territories, and made it possible that it would be permitted there if supported by popular vote. Abolitionists were outraged at the turnaround and fearful that pro-slavery forces, supported by slave owners from the South, would institute the hateful practice in the territories.

After the first two meetings, the Ripon organisers found their church too small for a major gathering of likeminded people, and scheduled the first official conference of the new party for 6 July in Jackson, Michigan. There the abolitionists formalised the name 'Republican' and positioned themselves as descendants of Thomas Jefferson's Democratic-Republican Party, with its emphasis on equality for all, blithely ignoring the fact that their hero Jefferson had owned 250 slaves.

Two years later the Republicans nominated John C. Fremont for president with the rallying cry 'Free soil, free labor, free speech, free men, Fremont'. Even though they battled against both Democrats and Whigs, they garnered 33 per cent of the vote, considered by Republicans a 'victorious defeat'. In celebration the American poet John Greenleaf Whittier wrote:

Then sound again the bugles.
Call the muster roll anew;
If months have well-nigh won the field,
What may not four years do?

Indeed, four years later Abraham Lincoln was elected the first Republican president.

The Republicans remained in power for all but eight years from 1861 to 1913, including the anomaly of Lincoln's running mate and successor Andrew Johnson, who was a 'war' Democrat who fervently opposed the secession of the Southern states. In total eighteen Republicans have held the nation's highest office since the party's founding, compared with only nine Democrats.

Over the years the Republicans began referring to themselves as the 'grand old party', soon to be short-handed as 'GOP', surely a misnomer in that the Democratic Party (which also took its name from Jefferson's Democratic-Republicans) had been formed in 1832, some 22 years before the Republicans.

Also on this day

1533: French essayist Michel de Montaigne is born in Bordeaux * 1820: John Tenniel, illustrator of *Alice's Adventures in Wonderland*, is born * 1916: American/British writer Henry James dies

29 February

Caesar decrees a new calendar

45 BC Legend has it that the first Roman calendar was instituted by Romulus in 738 BC, but it had only ten months. Then, in the 7th century BC, the Roman King Numa Pompilius added January and February to create a twelve-month year, and the Roman world lived with it for six centuries even though it totalled only 355 days, leading to calendrical chaos.

Finally Julius Caesar stepped in, decreeing a new calendar based on the calculations of Sosigenes of Alexandria, who had worked out that a year should have 365 and a quarter days.

But how to account for that last quarter day? Cleverly, Sosigenes added an additional day at the end of February every fourth year. The new calendar went into effect on 1 January 45 BC and on this day the world celebrated its first Leap Year. Back then, however, they didn't call it Leap Year but *bis-sexto-kalendae*, a term not explainable in fewer than four paragraphs. Luckily, centuries later the Scandinavians coined the term Leap Year, derived from the

Old Norse *hlaupa* ('to leap'). This was based on the observation that during a Leap Year any fixed event leaps forward an extra day, falling two days after the day of the week it fell on the previous year rather than only one day later as in normal years.

If the number of days, the number of months and a *bis-sexto-kalendae* weren't change enough, Caesar also changed the name of one of the months, or at least the Roman Senate did, when it renamed Quintilis 'July' in his honour. (Later another obsequious senate renamed Sextilis in honour of Caesar's successor, Augustus, calling it 'August'.)

One thing Caesar forgot was the week – there were none in his calendar. But in the 4th century the first Christian emperor Constantine introduced the seven-day week, based on the Book of Genesis. And while Caesar's calendar looked accurate, in fact it overestimated the length of the year by eleven minutes and fourteen seconds, a problem resolved only in 1582 when Pope Gregory XIII adjusted Caesar's calendar and re-baptised it the Gregorian Calendar.

Also on this day

1792: Italian composer Gioacchino Rossini is born * 1868: Benjamin Disraeli becomes Prime Minister for the first time * 1880: The St Gotthard railway tunnel through the Alps is completed, linking Italy with Switzerland

1 March

Frédéric Chopin is born

1810 Like his compositions, Frédéric Chopin's life was brilliant in success, wistful in tone and brief in duration. He was born Fryderyk Franciszek Szopen on this day in a village with the unlikely name of Zelazowa Wola, some 29 miles from Warsaw. Despite his name and place of birth, Chopin was Frenchified from the start: his father was a French émigré who sent him to the local French lycée to be educated.

Chopin's genius showed itself at an early age: he gave his first concert at the palace of Polish Prince Radziwill at the age of eight. At twenty the same prince presented him to Paris society at the home of Baron de Rothschild.

Chopin's life was a classic of 19th-century Romanticism: his music, his aristocratic good looks, his final wasting illness and most of all, his doomed affair with George Sand.

By 1836 Chopin, now a celebrated composer and virtuoso, was introduced by his friend Franz Liszt to a Parisian baroness named Aurore Dudevant, who had already become famous under the pseudonym of George Sand for writing about the anguish and exultation of women in love. Six years older than Chopin and still married, she was already the focus of Parisian gossip about her turbulent liaisons with writers such as Alfred de Musset and Prosper Mérimée. Now she fixed upon Chopin and pleaded with him to become her lover. By 1838 he had succumbed to her blandishments, and the two retreated to Majorca, where they lived for two months in an abandoned monastery.

Returning to France, the couple moved first to Sand's country house at Nohant, then to Paris where they lived in the rue Pigalle and later in the square d'Orléans. But by the time Chopin was 37 in 1847, the affair was over, broken by lovers' quarrels and Chopin's deteriorating health.

Free but unhappy, Chopin organised a desultory seven-month tour of Great Britain and then returned to Paris where, four months before his 40th birthday, he died of consumption. He is still considered the greatest composer of piano music in history.

Also on this day

1780: Pennsylvania becomes the first US state to abolish slavery * 1815: Napoleon lands at Golfe-Juan on the Côte d'Azur on escaping from Elba * 1845: The USA annexes Texas * 1896: Ethiopians crush the Italian army at the Battle of Adwa

2 March

Charles the Bold loses his treasure

1476 In all, Swiss pikemen defeated Charles the Bold, Duke of Burgundy, three times, of which the last cost the Duke his life.

The first victory, however, was in some ways the most profitable for the Swiss. On this day the two armies met at Grandson, near the Lake of Neuchâtel. Through expert use of terrain and the element of surprise, some 20,000 Swiss defeated three times that many Burgundians.

What's more, they captured Charles the Bold's chief portable treasures. The Swiss seized Charles's gold dinnerware and twelve exquisite enamel apostles, plus an incredible collection of jewels which included:

The 'grand duc de Toscane', a diamond of 139 carats mounted in gold and pearls;
'Le Sansy', a 100-carat diamond;
'Le Federlin', a brooch of five rubies, four diamonds, 70 pearls and three giant pearls, intended for Charles's hat;
'Les Trois Frères', three rubies of 70 carats;
Two huge pearls called 'Non Pareille' and 'La Ramasse des Flandres';
Charles's necklace of the Order of the Golden Fleece;
Charles's hat decorated with sapphires, diamonds, rubies and pearls.

Apart from these incredible jewels, the Swiss also took over an even greater treasure left behind by the fleeing Burgundians: some 2,000 Burgundian *filles de joie*.

Also on this day

1791: British preacher John Wesley dies in London * 1882: Roderick McClean tries to assassinate Queen Victoria

3 March

Ponce de León seeks the fountain of youth

1513 Juan Ponce de León was one of the hardy explorer-adventurers who opened up the New World for the kings of Spain. He had fought against the Moors at Granada and served with Columbus on his second voyage. Eventually he became governor of what today is Puerto Rico and amassed a fortune, largely in the slave trade.

It was in Puerto Rico that Ponce de León first heard of the wondrous Fountain of Youth, the miraculous source of water one drink of which would guarantee a life without old age or death. The Fountain, he was told, could be found on a fabulous island somewhere to the north.

On 3 March 1513 Ponce de León set sail with three ships on his famous quest. At the time of the Easter Feast he sighted land. Thinking he had found an island, he promptly named it after the holiday, in Spanish Pascua Florida or 'Flowery Easter'. And so Florida received its name.

As for poor Ponce de León, instead of a fountain of youth he found quite the opposite. While exploring Florida in 1521 he was killed by an arrow during an Indian attack.

Also on this day

1847: Telephone inventor Alexander Graham Bell is born in Edinburgh * 1861: Tsar Alexander II frees Russia's serfs * 1875: The first performance of Bizet's *Carmen* is staged at the Opéra Comique in Paris * 1878: The Treaty of San Stefano frees Bulgaria from Turkish rule after almost five centuries * 1931: 'The Star-Spangled Banner' is adopted as the US national anthem

4 March

The great Saladin dies

1193 There is a certain magic to the name Saladin, the legendary Saracen leader who defied Richard the Lion-Heart in his crusade to reconquer Jerusalem (particularly if you know what his name means – 'Righteousness of the Faith, Joseph, Son of Job'). It was Saladin who caused Richard to come on crusade in the first place by destroying Christian power in the Holy Land in the Battle of Hattin in 1187. And although Saladin's armies never bested Richard in open combat, they were in the end too strong for him, and Richard was forced to abandon his crusade without having taken Jerusalem.

Saladin was born in a town called Tikrit in what was then Mesopotamia, today's Iraq. (Eight centuries later, an Arab as despicable as Saladin was admirable was also born in Tikrit – Saddam Hussein.) By all accounts, Saladin was at least as chivalrous as any European knight. Even while battling with Richard he sent him and his captains chilled wine, pears and grapes from Damascus to ease their life in camp. On one famous occasion, when Richard was engaged in combat his horse was killed under him. Saladin saw the English King fall and, instead of ordering his men to finish him off, sent him a fresh horse instead.

Richard gave up his crusade in October 1192. Ironically, Saladin died in Damascus of fever only five months later, on this day in 1193.

Dying, he saw the ephemeral nature of all his triumphs. His last instructions to his followers were: 'Go and take my shroud through the streets and cry loudly, "Behold all that Saladin, who conquered the East, bears away of his conquests".'

Also on this day

1394: Portuguese patron of explorers Prince Henry the Navigator is born * 1461: Edward IV usurps the English throne * 1493: Columbus sails into Lisbon on his return from discovering the New World * 1678: Birth of Italian composer and violinist Antonio Vivaldi in Venice * 1861: Abraham Lincoln is sworn in as the 16th president of the USA

5 March

Colonial rebels drive the British out of Boston

1776 Morning light revealed the surprise that the American rebels had prepared for General Sir William Howe, the British Commander-in-Chief in America. During the night they had constructed a fortified artillery position at the top of Dorchester Heights, across the bay from the city of Boston, and, even more remarkable, they had placed in it a battery of powerful cannon that now commanded not only the harbour, where the British fleet lay, but also the city itself, where 6,500 redcoats had been bottled up by the rebel army since the previous spring.

Unknown to the British, the Americans had acquired the cannon when they captured the British stronghold at Fort Ticonderoga the year before. Then, in an epic of winter logistics planned by Henry Knox, the Boston bookseller turned artillerist, the heavy guns, weighing some 120,000 pounds, were put on sledges and dragged by oxen over 300 miles of frozen terrain to the rebel siege lines around Boston.

Sir William knew the jig was just about up. With artillery in such a position, Boston would be untenable. Because the British guns in the city could not be sufficiently elevated to deliver counter-battery fire on Dorchester Heights, Howe's only hope of dislodging the Americans and capturing their cannon was with a night assault. He ordered an attack for that very evening, but it was first delayed by heavy rains and then cancelled, giving the Americans further time to strengthen their defences.

The next day General Howe consulted his commanders in a

council of war, at which the decision was taken to evacuate the city. In an agreement with General Washington, Howe promised not to burn Boston if his command were allowed to leave without hindrance. And so it was that ten days later the British garrison and 1,000 American Loyalists boarded ships and sailed away to Halifax, Nova Scotia.

With the evacuation of Boston by the British, round one of the American Revolution – the New England round of Lexington, Concord and Bunker Hill – went to the rebels. But it would be a long war, over six years of fighting, and round two would begin in just four months with a large British army landing near New York City.

Also on this day

1696: Italian painter Giovanni Battista Tiepolo is born in Venice * 1933: Hitler and Nationalist allies win the Reichstag majority, the last free election in Germany until after the Second World War * 1953: Soviet tyrant Joseph Stalin dies

6 March

French cunning captures Richard the Lion-Heart's impregnable castle

1204 Through inheritance, marriage, treaty and conquest, Henry II hammered together the Angevin Empire that included all of England plus roughly half of France, from Normandy in the north through Brittany, Touraine and Poitou, down through Bordeaux to Gascony and the borders of Spain. His son Richard the Lion-Heart inherited this great empire and fought to preserve it from his hereditary enemy, King Philip Augustus of France.

Richard's most significant contribution to the defence was the massive Château Gaillard, of which the ruins still stand atop a cliff at Les Andelys, about 55 miles north-west of Paris. 'Gaillard' in French means strong, large and vigorous, and Richard's fortress was aptly named. With its seventeen massive towers, walls eight feet thick and a moat 45 feet deep, it protected the route the French would have to take to invade Richard's northern possessions. 'I should take it if it were made of steel', Philip is reputed to have boasted. 'I should hold it were it made of butter', was Richard's famous reply.

By the year 1203, however, Richard was dead and his cowardly, incompetent brother John was on the throne. It was then that Philip Augustus moved to conquer Château Gaillard at last.

But the mighty fortress looked just as impregnable now as it had when Richard had built it seven years before. For almost six months the French attackers remained camped outside the walls, suffering the daily jeers from the defenders. But while Philip was failing to take the fortress, John was so unsure of his own barons that he could not raise an army to break the siege. It looked like stalemate.

Then Philip learned that the English had over a year's supply of food on hand, so the garrison could never be starved out. Knowing that the only way to victory was by storming the walls, the French King ordered a direct attack.

First the French troops, protected by screens, built a rough path to the moat and promptly filled it with earth and felled trees. Now they could approach the exterior walls, where they mined one of the corner towers, causing its partial collapse.

But still the attackers were unable to force their way in, so the wily Philip sent in a small team of soldiers who entered the fortress through its latrines and quickly lowered the drawbridge leading to the principal keep. Now able to bring in their massive siege machinery, the French hammered a breach in the last remaining walls, compelling the English garrison to surrender on this day in 1204.

The fall of Château Gaillard marks the start of the destruction of the Angevin Empire. By John's death twelve years later, English-held territory in mainland France had been reduced to a few small holdings in the south-west, and Philip had earned his name of Augustus, father of modern France.

1475: Italian sculptor and painter Michelangelo Buonarroti is born
* 1836: The twelve-day siege of the Alamo ends, with only six survivors
out of the original force of 155

7 March

Marcus Aurelius becomes Emperor

AD 161 If ever a man was born to the purple it was the Roman
Emperor Marcus Aurelius. His grandfathers had both been
consuls, his father's sister was married to the future Emperor
Antoninus Pius and one grandmother was heiress to one of Rome's
greatest fortunes. His position was further strengthened when at
seventeen he was adopted by Antoninus, and seven years later
when he married Antoninus' daughter, the beautiful if unfaithful
Annia Galeria Faustina.

It was on the evening of this day that Antoninus died of acute
indigestion brought on by a surfeit of Alpine cheese two days
before. As the 74-year-old emperor lay on his couch, too weak to
move, the tribune of the day asked for the nightly password.
'Aequanimitas' (peace), he murmured, his last word.

Indeed, Antoninus' 23 years as Emperor had been among the
most peaceful and enlightened in Roman history, and with his
customary foresight he had long since designated his adoptive son
Marcus Aurelius as the next emperor, who today succeeded to the
throne.

Marcus was a few weeks short of his 40th birthday when the
reins of power fell into his hands. His first act was to insist that the
Senate make his younger adoptive brother Verus co-Emperor,
although Marcus was clearly the senior partner. Their co-operation
lasted until Verus died of a stroke eight years later.

Early in life Marcus had been fascinated by philosophy, at
twelve adopting the rough cloak of the Greek philosophers and
sleeping on the ground, until his mother convinced him that he

could contemplate the nature of life equally well from a comfortable couch. And, despite nineteen imperial years spent almost constantly and successfully at war against Rome's enemies, it is for his *Meditations* that today he is primarily remembered.

Marcus' *Meditations* were a series of fragmentary musings jotted down over his years as Emperor. It is unclear if he ever intended anyone to read them, as in them he addresses himself and uses them to record his preoccupation with the futility of human life.

Written in Greek, they strongly reflect the Stoic tradition in which Marcus was educated, and once were considered among the greatest of philosophical tracts. Recent historians, however, have been less impressed, noting the Emperor's repeated angst about the transience of man's life and works, especially his own. Furthermore, although expressed in Marcus' own way, the basic ideas put forward are not original but a reiteration of many of the moral precepts of the freed slave and philosopher Epictetus, who taught that the universe is governed by some sort of divine intelligence of which the human soul is a part.

He also held the Stoic belief that men should look on triumph and tragedy with equanimity, and play a constructive role in public affairs. This Marcus did, governing fairly and with moderation (he forbade the execution of any senator and tolerated the troublesome Christians), continually defending the empire from the depredations of Scythians and Germans.

On 17 March 180 Marcus died at 59, possibly of plague, in Vindobona, now Vienna, where today in the historic district you can find a street called Marc Aurelstrasse, named in his honour.

Marcus Aurelius was the last of the 'five good emperors' who ruled Rome for 84 consecutive years, earning the praise of Gibbon who called it 'a period in the history of the world during which the condition of the human race was the most happy and prosperous'. Sadly, this glorious epoch came to a close on Marcus' death when his eighteen-year-old son Commodus (the villain of the film *Gladiator*) inherited the empire.

Also on this day
322 BC: Greek philosopher Aristotle dies * 1274: Christian philosopher St Thomas Aquinas dies * 1875: French composer Maurice Ravel is born * 1876: Alexander Graham Bell patents the telephone

8 March

The first English parliament?

1265 Simon de Montfort is one of the great controversial characters in English history. The bare outline of his achievements is indisputable: de Montfort led a rebellion by English barons against the weak and puerile leadership of Henry III, and after capturing the King at the Battle of Lewes in 1264, Montfort was de facto ruler of the realm. The controversy is whether he was a man ahead of his time, a believer in liberty and some sort of democracy, or whether he was simply another power-hungry noble with an eye to the main chance.

Whatever the verdict on Montfort's character, what is certain is that on 8 March 1265 he gathered together in Westminster Hall some peers of the land, a sprinkling of bishops, two knights from each shire and two to four 'good and loyal men' from each city and borough. This was the first time in history that ordinary citizens had met to discuss the government and to give opinions regarding the laws they were to live under. Historians consider this the first parliament, the start of what is today the House of Commons and, in a broader sense, the start of parliamentary democracy as it now exists.

Also on this day

1702: Anne becomes Queen of England after William III dies in a riding accident * 1855: Charles XIV of Sweden (the former Napoleonic marshal, Jean-Baptiste Bernadotte) dies

9 March

Napoleon marries Joséphine

1796 Today in a civil ceremony the future Emperor Napoleon married his first wife, née Joséphine Tascher de la Pagerie, better known to us as Joséphine de Beauharnais, the name of her first husband who had been guillotined during the French Revolution. Joséphine herself had been briefly imprisoned during the Terror.

In 1796 Napoleon was just at the start of his giddy ascent, only 26 years old and still spelling his name 'Buonaparte'. Joséphine was 32 and beautiful in a highly erotic way, no doubt impressively polished and worldly for this Corsican *arriviste*.

Both the bride and the groom must have had some doubts about themselves, since Napoleon made himself out to be 28 instead of 26 by using his brother's birth certificate, while Joséphine presented herself as 29.

The marriage must have been a real love match, if we can judge by Napoleon's love letter dated only a month after the marriage. Urging Joséphine to join him in Milan, he wrote: 'But of course you're coming. You'll be here beside me, on my heart, in my arms, on my mouth ... a kiss on your heart, and then one a little lower down, much lower down.'

Later, when her husband was campaigning in Egypt, Joséphine started an affair with another army officer, a scandal that almost brought on divorce. But she finally persuaded Napoleon to forgive her and even talked him into a church wedding that took place on 1 December 1804, the day before he was crowned by the Pope.

By 1810, however, the marriage had finally foundered, battered by mutual infidelity and given the *coup de grace* by reasons of state: it had produced no heir. Joséphine departed to lavish retirement in Malmaison, just outside Paris, where she died a month before her 51st birthday.

1074: Pope Gregory VII excommunicates all married priests * 1451: Italian navigator Amerigo Vespucci is born * 1862: The *Monitor* fights the *Merrimac* in the American Civil War, the first battle of ironclad ships * 1932: Eamon De Valera is elected President of the Irish Free State, promising to abolish all loyalty to the British Crown

10 March

The story of the French Foreign Legion

1831 France's King Louis-Philippe needed some hardened but perhaps expendable troops to pacify Algeria, and he met the need by creating a new military unit. On this date in 1831 his Minister of War Marshal Nicolas Soult formed the French Foreign Legion, specifying that it 'should not be employed in the continental territory of the kingdom'.

The Legion's officers were recruited from veterans of Napoleon's army who had been mouldering on half pay since Waterloo. The enlisted men were drawn from all over Europe, often desperate men who could find no employment or were wanted by the law. Within a year, Legion strength was 5,500 officers, NCOs and Legionnaires.

The Legion first saw combat in April 1832, when two battalions of mainly German and Swiss troops stormed a village called Maison Carrée east of Algiers. Since then, Legionnaires have fought in hundreds of wars and brush fires around the world. They were at the siege of Sebastopol during the Crimean War, and supported the puppet Emperor Maximilian during his ill-fated reign in Mexico. Their African conflicts have included Dahomey, Madagascar, Tunisia, Chad, Lebanon and Algeria. They also served in Vietnam, in Bosnia during the civil war there in 1993 and in the first Gulf War.

Over the years, the Legion has boasted some famous names (although not all of them bore those names when they were

Legionnaires). There have been two Napoleons – the Emperor's nephew who was a captain in 1863, and Prince Napoleon, the Bonaparte pretender to the French throne, who served under the name of Blanchard in 1940. Napoleon/Blanchard must have been amused to find a fellow pretender to the throne serving with him – the comte de Paris, who was a direct descendant of King Louis-Philippe, the man who created the Legion. An earlier royal officer was the future Peter I of Serbia, who used the name Kara as his *nomme de guerre* in 1870.

The most illustrious Legion officer undoubtedly was Patrice de Mac-Mahon, who served in 1843–4, went on to lead the French army at the great victory at Magenta in 1859 and rose to be President of the Third Republic in 1873. Two other Legion members have become Prime Ministers of France. Edouard Daladier was Prime Minister for several years in the 1930s (and co-signer with Neville Chamberlain of the Munich Pact with Adolf Hitler's Germany), and Pierre Messmer was Prime Minister under de Gaulle and Pompidou.

The Legion also boasts some cultural lions. The American poet Alan Seeger spent three years in the Legion during the First World War and was killed in action at Belloy en Santerre, and the Hungarian-born English author Arthur Koestler, writer of *Darkness at Noon*, was in service in 1940. Indeed, the Legion's reputation for hard-bitten souls with a chequered past has been seen as so glamorous that even an American *boulevardier* like Cole Porter maintained that he had been a Legionnaire, although historians now universally debunk the claim.

Today the Legion boasts soldiers of fortune from some 99 countries, usually tough, sometimes criminals on the run. There are no Frenchmen in the Foreign Legion except for officers, all of whom are graduates of the French national military academy of St-Cyr. This combination of French leadership and foreign troops has created a formidable fighting force. The British Second World War Field Marshal Viscount Alanbrooke called it 'the grandest assembly of real fighting men that I have ever seen, marching with their heads up as if they owned the world, lean, hard-looking men, carrying their arms admirably and marching with perfect precision'.

The Legion remained stationed abroad for 131 years, until the liberation of Algeria forced it to move, for the first time, to France. Today it boasts between 8,000 and 9,000 men. Each year there are about 500 candidates to join, but less than 10 per cent are accepted.

Should the Foreign Legion's history and glamour tempt you to join, if you're not French you will have to become a Legionnaire, for whom the rules can be daunting:

The minimum term of service is five years
You cannot have a bank account
You are not permitted to live off barracks
You may not own a car or motorcycle
Marriage is forbidden until you attain the rank of sergeant or
    have served for nine years.

Also on this day

515 BC: The building of the great Jewish temple in Jerusalem is completed * 1872: Italian revolutionary Giuseppe Mazzini dies in Pisa

11 March

General MacArthur leaves the Philippines

1942 In the gathering evening darkness, General Douglas MacArthur, commander of United States Forces in the Far East, stepped off Corregidor Island's North Dock onto the deck of PT-41. Minutes later the motor torpedo boat rumbled away on the first stage of a journey that would take him from the Philippines through the Japanese naval blockade to Australia. In Adelaide a week later, he told reporters, 'I came through', then added the phrase that would become famous: 'and I shall return.'

Left behind was a looming defeat whose dimensions were still unknown to the American public. Against a strong Japanese invasion force that landed two weeks after Pearl Harbor, MacArthur had quickly organised his forces in a stubborn, retreating defence.

But he knew, as did his superiors in Washington, that without reinforcements buttressed by air and sea power the defence of the Philippines was a lost cause.

No one would have known the cause was lost from the communiqués issued by MacArthur's headquarters on Corregidor, messages one historian described as 'gripping though often imaginary accounts as to how MacArthur's guile, leadership, and military genius had continuously frustrated the intentions of Japan's armed forces'. For the American public, he became the first hero of the war.

From Washington, President Roosevelt promised MacArthur help. In January, Army Chief of Staff George Marshall radioed: 'President has seen all of your messages and directs navy to give you every possible support in your splendid fight.' But in the five-month siege of the Bataan Peninsula and Corregidor, no planes, no ships, no reinforcements reached the Philippines. There were none to spare.

Now the question was whether to risk MacArthur's almost certain death or capture with his troops, or bring him out. John Curtin, the Australian Prime Minister, helped decide. In late February, facing the increasing threat of Japanese invasion, the Australian government demanded of British Prime Minister Winston Churchill either the return of three Australian divisions now with the British Eighth Army in North Africa, or the appointment of an American general as supreme commander of an expanded Allied force for the south-west Pacific theatre. Churchill, who had earlier expressed his admiration in the House of Commons for 'the splendid courage and quality of the small American army under General MacArthur', used his influence with FDR.

Initially, MacArthur refused the President's order to leave his command, but Roosevelt persisted, and the general finally agreed. Boarding PT-41 with him this evening for the dangerous voyage were his wife and four-year-old son.

On 9 April the Philippine defence force – 10,000 American soldiers and some 60,000 Filipino troops, out of food, ammo and medical supplies – surrendered to the Japanese. A month later

Corregidor – the Gibraltar of the East – fell, adding the Philippines to the lengthening list of Allied defeats, which by now included Dunkirk, Pearl Harbor, Tobruk, Guam, Wake and Singapore.

By then, however, MacArthur, at Allied headquarters in Melbourne, had taken charge and begun to organise the measures that would in time roll back the Japanese tide. After a brilliant series of air and amphibious operations that leap-frogged across the top of New Guinea, he arrived back in the Philippines on 20 October 1944. Wading ashore on Leyte Island, he reminded the assembled press corps: 'I have returned.'

Also on this day

537: The Goths lay siege to Rome * 1507: Italian adventurer Cesare Borgia is killed in battle * 1513: Giovanni de' Medici becomes Pope Leo X * 1905: The Parisian métro is officially opened

12 March

Hitler creates the Anschluss

1938 At 4.00 this Saturday afternoon Adolf Hitler, Chancellor and President of Germany, drove over a bridge across the River Inn and entered Austria at the town of Braunau, where he had been born almost 49 years earlier. The streets were jammed with expectant crowds who cheered his passing motorcade. 'Ein Volk. Ein Reich. Ein Führer' (One people. One state. One leader) they chanted, in celebration of what they hoped the Führer would engineer the next day: the union – *Anschluss* – of their nation with Nazi Germany.

Hitler could scarcely have retained any memory of Braunau itself, for he was not yet three when his father moved the family to Bavaria. Nevertheless, he managed to turn it to good use in 1924 when, in an effort to construct destiny out of chance, he opened *Mein Kampf* with these words: 'Today it seems to me providential that Fate should have chosen Braunau on the Inn as my birthplace.

For this little town lies on the boundary between the two German states, which we of the younger generation at least have made it our life work to reunite by every means possible.'

In 1938 Austria was no longer the leading state of a sprawling, polyglot empire but a small German-speaking republic with a repressive government and an active core of pan-German sentiment. But even in reduced circumstances, it offered a resurgent Germany vital advantages: gold and foreign currency reserves, natural resources, heavy industry, labour, and a standing army to swell the ranks of the Wehrmacht.

It took Hitler five years to bring about the Anschluss, during which time he had indeed used against Austria every means at his disposal, including, when other methods failed, subversion, agitation, provocation, intimidation, and assassination. Within Austria itself his efforts enjoyed the active and disruptive support of the illegal Austrian Nazi party.

Even so, it had been a slow process that required the murder of one Austrian chancellor and the intimidation of his successor. Only three weeks previously, in a meeting with Hitler at Berchtesgaden, the latter had agreed under the harshest duress to measures that would lead to an early takeover of his country by Germany. But then, returning to Vienna, the chancellor had reneged and instead announced his intention to call a plebiscite in just four days – on 13 March – allowing Austrian voters to decide the question of their nation's independence.

This unexpected recalcitrance, and the prospect that the plebiscite's results would not support integration with Germany, forced an impatient Hitler to play his last and strongest card, one threatened but never dealt: invasion. This morning at 5.30, with Nazi mobs rioting in the streets of Austrian cities, German troops marched over the frontier to 'restore order', just ten hours before their Führer passed through Braunau on his way to nearby Linz.

And so it was that two days later, on the glorious spring morning of 14 March, the Führer motored from Linz to Vienna, his progress marked by massive demonstrations of public approval (enforced by savage treatment for dissenters). In the Heldenplatz at midday he addressed a quarter of a million delirious listeners, proclaiming 'the entry of my homeland into the German Reich'. The following evening he flew back to Germany, master of a greater Germany, his eyes now on Czechoslovakia.

Also on this day

1879: The British Zulu War begins * 1881: Turkish leader Kemal Atatürk is born * 1933: President Paul von Hindenburg drops the flag of the German Republic in favour of the swastika and empire banner

13 March

Mata Hari springs full-grown into the world

1905 Before the four-armed statue of Shiva she danced, her arms and calves encircled by bracelets, her breasts covered only by small bejewelled cups. The other dancers snuffed out the candelabra, leaving the stage in the dim light of a flickering oil lamp. Then, with her back to the audience, she threw off her sarong and moved towards the statue, writhing with passion, apparently nude. As she knelt before the statue, another dancer flung a gold lamé cloak over her shoulders. Rising, she turned to face the stunned crowd as the curtain rang down at the Paris cabaret.

Such was the 'birth' of Mata Hari, the notorious dancer and courtesan who made her first stage appearance today under her assumed name, a Malay term for the Sun, literally meaning 'eye of the day'. Twelve years later she would be shot as a spy by a French firing squad.

Mata Hari was born Margaretha Zella, a dark-haired, olive-skinned Dutch girl of middle-class parents. She had been raised in the Netherlands and had later moved to Java with her mean and dissolute husband whose beatings and philandering eventually drove her to divorce.

When M'greet, as she was called, returned from the Far East she was nearly 30. Unable to find either another husband or a suitable job in Amsterdam, she moved to Paris. There she invented a mysterious new identity for herself, claiming that she came from India, daughter of a temple dancer, and had been raised in the service of the god Shiva. Calling herself Mata Hari, she soon landed a role at the Musée Guimet cabaret, where she found instant fame after her début. Shortly she was triumphantly touring Europe, titillating audiences with her risqué routine and taking lovers along the way.

But by the time she was in her late 30s Mata Hari's body was thickening with age, and she progressively earned her keep more as a *demi-mondaine* than as a dancer. Superbly adroit at lovemaking, she found dozens of rich partners, including celebrities such as a Rothschild baron and Giacomo Puccini. At this time, on the eve of the First World War, she also began her career as a spy.

The details and extent of Mata Hari's espionage remain murky. She claimed that she was enlisted by French Intelligence to seduce German officers to learn their secrets, and in at least one case she was successful. But in late 1916 the French intercepted a coded German message referring to her as their 'agent H 21' and were convinced that she had become a double agent.

The French army quickly brought Mata Hari to trial on charges of espionage, and convicted her in a travesty of justice that was held 'in camera' and during which the defence could not cross-examine witnesses. Mata Hari's choice of a 74-year-old corporate lawyer to defend her primarily because he had once been her lover did not help. The jury of six French officers wasted no time in finding her guilty and condemning her to death.

At dawn on 15 October 1917, Mata Hari was led to the internal courtyard of the Parisian prison at Vincennes. There she faced her fate bravely, telling an attendant nun: 'Do not be afraid, sister. I know how to die.' Refusing a blindfold, she faced the twelve riflemen confronting her and blew them a kiss just before the fusillade ended her life.

Such was the finish of the famed Mata Hari, whose body was given to a French medical school so that student doctors could practice their dissecting skills. The last physical trace of her disappeared in 2000 when her mummified head was stolen from the Museum of Anatomy in Paris.

Also on this day

14 March

Admiral John Byng faces the firing squad

1757 The start of the French and Indian War three years earlier had pitted England against France as each attempted to gain control of ever larger slices of North America. Once started, hostilities were hard to stop, and both nations continued to spar with each other in Europe on the eve of the Seven Years' War.

In May 1756 the British feared a French attack on their base in Menorca and sent a small fleet under the command of an indolent and indecisive admiral named John Byng to counter French aggression. But by the time he arrived, the base had fallen.

The irresolute Byng launched an attack but in such a desultory manner that he was soon driven off, at which point he decided that he was facing insuperable odds and sailed off to the British base at Gibraltar, leaving Menorca to the mercy of the French.

On hearing the news back in London, British Prime Minister Thomas Pelham-Holles, Duke of Newcastle, bristled with indignation and resolved to punish Byng for his apparent lack of zeal. Charging the Admiral with dereliction of duty, Newcastle guaranteed a biased court-martial by announcing publicly that 'he shall be tried immediately; he shall be hanged directly'.

Brought back to Portsmouth in disgrace, Byng was tried and convicted on his own flagship *Monarch* and on this day taken on deck and shot by a firing squad of marines.

No other British admiral had ever been executed for such a crime, and all of Europe was bemused by the news. Two years later, Voltaire published his masterpiece *Candide* which includes the celebrated observation: 'Dans ce pays-ci il est bon de tuer de temps en temps un amiral pour encourager les autres.' (In this country [England] it's good to kill an admiral from time to time to encourage the others.)

Also on this day

1492: Queen Isabella of Castile orders the expulsion of 150,000 Jews from Spain * 1804: Johann Strauss the Elder is born in Vienna * 1879: Albert Einstein is born in Ulm * 1883: Karl Marx dies in London

15 March

The Ides of March

44 BC 'Beware the Ides of March!', the augur Spurinna had warned some days earlier, but Julius Caesar had brushed him aside. Was he not, at 55, the most powerful man in the civilised world? For five years he had been dictator, after having decisively defeated the coalition of nobles, including the great Pompey, who had tried to destroy him. Caesar knew there were senators who hated him, who in fact were plotting to kill him, but so sure was he of his position, of the awe (and perhaps, he hoped, the love) in which he was held, that he had even dismissed the troop of Spanish bodyguards that normally escorted him.

So at mid-morning Caesar set off for Pompey's theatre, where the Senate was meeting. En route a friend handed him a note with the details of the assassination plot, but Caesar simply put it with the other letters he was carrying, having no time to read it.

Entering the theatre, he saw Spurinna among the crowd. 'The Ides of March have come', he mocked. 'Yes', replied the augur, 'but they have not yet gone'.

Caesar took his seat, quickly to be surrounded by conspirators who pretended to be paying their respects. One seized him by the shoulder, and Caesar shook him off, but as he turned away one of the Casca brothers central to the conspiracy stabbed him just below the throat. Grabbing Casca's arm, Caesar stabbed it with his stylus and tried to escape the ring of murderers now surrounding him. But suddenly the great man realised it was hopeless. Since Casca's first thrust he had not uttered a word, but when he saw his protégé Marcus Brutus among his assassins, he murmured in Greek, 'You, too, my child?' He then drew the top of his toga over his face while letting the lower part fall so that he would die with both legs covered. The murderers struck out in a frenzied attack, sometimes wounding each other in their eagerness for the slaughter. Twenty-three knife blows struck home as Caesar stood there, defenceless, before he fell dead to the floor.

So died the greatest of all Romans, perhaps, according to Macaulay, the greatest of all men. But he had changed the world. He replaced the corrupt and incompetent rule of the Roman nobility with an autocracy that lasted for half a millennium in the west and 1,500 years in the east, and he gave to France the Latin civilisation that replaced tribal barbarism and that has lasted to this day.

As for the assassins, virtually all were killed within three years of Caesar's murder or, like Marcus Brutus, committed suicide.

History has a special place for Brutus. Caesar had been his mother's lover and had helped him all his life, but nonetheless five years before the assassination Brutus joined Pompey's army against Caesar. Even so, Caesar pardoned him and appointed him governor of Cisalpine Gaul. For his treachery, in his *Inferno* Dante places him in the lowest circle of Hell alongside Judas, hanging from Satan's mouth.

Also on this day

1767: American President Andrew Jackson is born * 1792: King Gustav III of Sweden is shot at a ball and dies twelve days later * 1807: The first performance of Beethoven's Fourth Symphony takes place at the palace of Prince Lobkowitz in Vienna

16 March

Death of Tiberius the tyrant

AD 37 Like so many Roman emperors after him, Tiberius started his reign in glory and slowly descended into despotism, perversion and paranoia. He died today at the age of 77 after 22 years in power.

Tiberius was the son of Augustus' wife Livia by an earlier marriage and thus automatically a power in the land as stepson to the Emperor. As a young man he was a highly successful general who stayed away from Rome, leaving the politics (and the imperial succession) to Augustus' grandsons. He was austere and distant, some said arrogant. So determined was he to avoid the rivalries of power that by the time he was 36 he had retired to Rhodes. Eight years later he returned to the capital, just days before the death of one of Augustus' two grandsons and less than a year before the demise of the other.

Reluctantly, Augustus then made Tiberius his heir, fearing that his slow deliberation and distant manner would ill prepare him for ultimate power. Reportedly, the old Emperor lamented on his deathbed: 'Poor Roman people, to be ground by those slow-moving jaws.'

On inheriting the throne at Augustus' death, Tiberius at 54 became Rome's second emperor. Initially he was a hard-working and productive ruler. He recognised the difficulty of running the empire, comparing it to 'holding a wolf by the ears'. But after thirteen years he abruptly moved to his magnificent villa on Capri. He never visited Rome again, delegating progressively more power to the commander of his guard and leaving the squabbling Senate to its own devices.

As the years passed, Tiberius became increasingly murderous and vindictive. According to Suetonius, 'Every day brought a new execution', some victims hurled off the cliffs of Capri after unspeakable tortures. One senator was condemned to death for having carried a coin with Tiberius' head on it into a public lavatory. The Emperor also collapsed into paedophilia and pederasty, importing a whole troop of young boys and girls to take part in imperial orgies. Suetonius relates that Tiberius 'would put unweaned babies to his member as though to a woman's breast'. Suetonius also reports that 'since tradition barred the strangling of virgins, when little girls had been sentenced to die this way, the executioner raped them first'.

When he was 71, Tiberius made an error that may have cost him his life when he brought his eighteen-year-old great-nephew Caligula to Capri, eventually naming him as heir to the empire. For six years Caligula remained docile and obsequious, although he already showed signs of the sadism that would mark his years as Emperor.

In early AD 37, Tiberius travelled to Campania to take part in military games. There he injured his shoulder throwing the javelin and then became seriously ill. Returning to his villa on Capri, he lapsed into unconsciousness, and the doctors, shocked by his emaciated condition, declared that death was imminent.

Believing Tiberius to be dead, Caligula slipped his seal ring from the imperial finger to show himself to the waiting crowd as the new Emperor. But suddenly Tiberius woke from what was really a coma and demanded food. Caligula was petrified with terror, but his ally Macro, the quick-thinking commander of the Praetorian Guard, rushed in and stifled the old Emperor with a blanket.

Also on this day

1521: Ferdinand Magellan discovers the Philippines * 1802: The US Military Academy is established at West Point * 1898: English illustrator Aubrey Beardsley dies

17 March

'Neither the sun nor death can be looked at steadily'

1680 The man who wrote this perceptive maxim died early this morning, long a victim of ill health resulting from war wounds. He was François, duc de La Rochefoucauld, who breathed his last in Paris at the age of 66.

Today, La Rochefoucauld is known almost exclusively for his trenchant epigrams, but these were never published until he was in his 50s. In his younger days he had served as a soldier for six years, fighting the Spaniards. It was during this period that he was three times wounded, sustaining severe injuries to his throat and face.

La Rochefoucauld's liking for conflict extended to his civilian life, when he ill-advisedly joined the Fronde, a rebellion by French aristocrats against the constantly increasing power of the throne. Richelieu once imprisoned him in the Bastille, if only for six days, and he came to hate that cardinal's successor, Mazarin, with a virulent loathing. He was also constantly embroiled in a series of lawsuits against other members of the aristocracy on the trivialities of precedence.

At 53, La Rochefoucauld had resigned himself to the unbridled power of Louis XIV's monarchy, and settled in Paris. There he joined the new game in fashion in the city's salons, the invention of epigrams on the manners and mores of the time. And here the mocking La Rochefoucauld came into his own.

'You are never as unhappy as you think, nor as happy as you had hoped', he wrote. Acidly, he pointed out that 'we are all strong enough to bear the misfortunes of others'.

An accomplished courtier of the fair sex, he reserved some of his more pointed thrusts for the field of love. 'If you judge love by the majority of its effects', he wrote, 'it resembles hatred more than friendship'. He observed that 'Jealousy is always born with love but does not always die with it', and 'It is more difficult to be faithful to your mistress when you are happy than when you are treated badly'. He also coined one of the all-time great seduction lines: 'If we resist our passions, it is more because they are weak than because we are strong.'

In 1665, La Rochefoucauld published the first edition of his *Maximes*, perhaps reflecting a cynical view even of himself with the epigram: 'When vanity does not make us talk, there's not much we want to say.' Five more editions appeared before his death fifteen years later.

Also on this day
AD 180: Roman Emperor Marcus Aurelius dies of plague * c. AD 389: St Patrick, the patron saint of Ireland, is born * 1861: The Kingdom of Italy is proclaimed and Victor Emmanuel becomes its first king

18 March

Ivan the Terrible dies at last

1584 On this day death finally relieved the world of the burden of Russia's Ivan the Terrible. He had lived for 54 years, over 50 of them as ruler.

Ivan was born near Moscow on 25 August 1530. He became Prince of Moscow when his father died three years later, but he lived in fear of the *boyars* (court nobility) until he began to take an active role in state affairs at thirteen. One of his initial acts was to have the most hated boyar, Prince Andrei Shuisky, seized and torn apart by a pack of hounds.

In 1547, when he was sixteen, Ivan was proclaimed the first Tsar of all the Russias, a new title derived from the Roman 'caesar' or emperor. He greatly centralised his country and took the first steps in turning it from an Asiatic backwater into a European nation, a task finally accomplished by Peter the Great 100 years later.

Russia was at war during almost the entirety of Ivan's reign. Although he successfully defeated the Tartars and conquered Kazan, his other conflicts, especially against Poland and Sweden, were indecisive. But the losses he endured seemed to embitter him, and he increasingly shrugged off the counsel of his nobles, becoming ever more tyrannical. By the time he was 30 he was enjoying unfettered personal rule and instituted a reign of terror among Russia's nobility, justifying his despotism with the words: 'We have ascended the throne by the bidding of God.'

Prone to fits of insane rage, Ivan saw conspiracy everywhere. His answer was torture and death, and his means of execution included disembowelment, burning at the stake, impalement, drowning and burial alive, punishments that he often supervised personally. It is said that some victims were fed to wild bears.

One of Ivan's worst excesses was his massacre of the citizens of Novgorod, whom he suspected of being on the point of rebellion. Without waiting for confirmation of the charge, he led his army into the city and slaughtered 60,000 men, women and children.

In his paranoia, Ivan established a bodyguard of 6,000 men, known as the *oprichniki*, and authorised them to operate like a gang of malicious cut-throats beyond the law. He considered torture a suitable weapon of state, and once had his personal physician racked and roasted alive on a spit on suspicions of treachery.

Ivan's inhuman contempt for others reached an artistic peak on the completion of St Basil's Cathedral in Moscow. So taken was he by its splendour that he ordered blinded the group of architects who had designed it, to ensure that no other building so beautiful could ever be constructed.

One of the few people Ivan felt he could trust was his son, also named Ivan, who was heir to the throne. But when the younger Ivan was 28, one afternoon he began an argument with his father, who became so incensed that he beat him to death with an iron-tipped rod.

During his last days Ivan's body became swollen and racked with pain. When his doctors could find no cure he turned to clair-voyants and astrologers, but they helped no more than his physicians.

A few days before his death, the Tsar invited the English ambassador to his palace. Showing him some precious stones, Ivan pronounced: 'Look how they lose their colour. They proclaim my end. I have been poisoned.' When death finally came to him, he was playing a game of chess – against himself, for it was unthinkable that anyone could defeat the Tsar of Russia. He was buried in the Cathedral of St Michael in the Kremlin.

Ivan's death has been variously attributed to dysentery, syphilis and other fatal diseases, but over four centuries after his demise his tomb was opened for tests on his desiccated corpse. His body contained toxic levels of arsenic and mercury, suggesting that indeed Russia's first Tsar had died at the hands of a poisoner, proving the old adage that even a paranoid can have real enemies.

Also on this day

1455: Florentine artist Fra Angelico dies * 1745: Robert Walpole, first Prime Minister of Great Britain, dies * 1890: German Chancellor Prince Otto von Bismarck is forced to resign * 1913: King George I of Greece is shot and killed

19 March

The last Templar's last curse

1314 Today Jacques de Molay, the last Grand Master of the Templars, was burned at the stake in Paris, his eyes fixed on Notre Dame in the distance.

A French knight from Champagne named Huges de Payns founded the Order of the Temple in 1128, becoming its first Grand Master. The Templars' mission was to guard the passage of pilgrims en route to the Holy Land.

Two centuries later the Templars had grown immensely wealthy, and Jacques de Molay had the misfortune to be in charge when France's King Philip the Fair, greedy for the Templars' riches, decided on the wholesale destruction of the order.

Arrested in 1307 with all the other Templar knights in France, Molay kept a hard silence of seven long years in prison in Paris, strenuously denying any wrongdoing, even after the order was suppressed in 1312. He was determined to take his defence to the only man who could save him, the Pope. Unfortunately for Molay, however, Pope Clement V was virtually a household pet of King Philip's. (It was this same Clement, a Frenchman by birth, who moved the Papal See from Rome to Avignon.) So when the day came for Grand Master Molay to be judged, the Pope dispatched three cardinals to do the job, keeping himself well clear.

Molay was on the point of being condemned to life imprisonment, and he realised that he would have only this one chance to defend himself and the order.

The cardinals were thrown into confusion by Molay's eloquent defence, and decided to take the issue back to Pope Clement. But Philip the Fair would not wait. The same day a royal council was convoked, and the Grand Master was condemned once more, this time to the stake.

As the sun set, guards took Jacques de Molay to the place of execution, dressed only in a cloth shirt. 'God will avenge our death', he said. 'Philip, thy life is condemned. I await thee within a year at the Tribune of God.' He then asked to be turned on the stake to face the towers of Notre Dame, barely visible in the distance.

Just 31 days later Pope Clement suddenly died, and on 29 November of that same year, Philip the Fair too was dead, just as the Grand Master had foretold.

Also on this day

1452: Frederick III is crowned in Rome, to reign for 53 years, longer than any other Holy Roman Emperor * 1687: French explorer René-Robert Cavelier, sieur de La Salle is murdered by his own men

20 March

A usurper king meets his maker

1413 His face disfigured by swellings and lesions, his body weakened by a stroke, today England's usurper King Henry IV died repenting his past at the age of 46.

Grandson of Edward III, Henry was born in Bolingbroke Castle in Lincolnshire, and therefore referred to in his time (and by William Shakespeare) as Bolingbroke. As a young man he had been handsome and muscular, a fine athlete who excelled at jousting, loved music and spoke Latin, French and English. When he was eleven his cousin, who was just ten months his junior, inherited the throne as Richard II, and Henry's father, John of Gaunt, became de facto ruler during the young King's minority.

But when Richard started to rule in his own right, Bolingbroke – and most of the country's great nobles – soon lost patience with his spendthrift, feckless ways and joined a group of opposition leaders who forced the King to send his closest favourite, Robert de Vere, Earl of Oxford, into exile. Richard neither forgot nor forgave, and ten years later he exiled Bolingbroke in his turn, confiscating his property. But when Richard made the error of leaving the country for an expedition to Ireland, Bolingbroke returned at the head of an army, seized and imprisoned Richard and claimed the throne for himself as Henry IV. He then had Richard surreptitiously murdered.

Because of this usurpation, Henry faced continuous revolt during his thirteen-year reign. In 1405 he crushed an uprising at the Battle of Shipton Moor, after which he had Richard Scrope, Archbishop of York, hanged, drawn and quartered for siding with the rebels. Contemporaries report that within a few hours of this dreadful execution of a man of God, the King was screaming in pain from rashes that appeared on his face and a tumour that bulged beneath his nose. Many thought he had been stricken by leprosy. It was, his enemies insisted, celestial punishment for usurping the throne and putting the rightful King to death. (Modern science suggests that Henry's loathsome disease was actually syphilis or tubercular gangrene.)

Hoping to escape this curse, Henry made plans to go on crusade to the Holy Land, but continually postponed his departure after he heard a prophecy that he would die in Jerusalem.

On this day in 1413, Henry determined to do penance for his crimes and set out for the shrine of St Edward the Confessor in Westminster Abbey. There, as he knelt to pray, he collapsed unconscious and was carried into an adjoining room. When he came to, the stricken King asked where he was, to be told that he lay in the Jerusalem Chamber of the cathedral (so called because of tapestries depicting the history of Jerusalem hung from its walls). Remembering the terrible prophecy that he would die in Jerusalem, Henry knew his end was at hand.

The dying king blessed his son (about to become Henry V) and whispered to those around him: 'God alone knows by what right I took the crown.' In a few minutes he was dead – in Jerusalem as the prophecy had foretold.

Also on this day

43 BC: Roman poet Ovid is born * 1727: English scientist Sir Isaac Newton dies in London * 1815: Switzerland becomes permanently neutral

21 March

Thomas Cranmer perishes by fire

1556 Thomas Cranmer was the diametric opposite of his famous forerunner, Thomas Becket. Both served kings named Henry and achieved Britain's highest ecclesiastical office as Archbishop of Canterbury. Yet while Becket died a martyr defending the Church from the powers of the King, Cranmer martyred himself defending royal authority over the Church.

Cranmer sincerely believed in royal power. To Henry VIII he was the perfect minister, helping him with two divorces, promulgating the Treason Laws and generally increasing the King's authority. Henry died in 1547, but Cranmer retained his influence during the brief reign of Edward VI. When Edward died at fifteen after only six years as King, Cranmer followed the dying monarch's wish and backed Lady Jane Grey to succeed. But when Bloody Mary Tudor gained the throne instead, Cranmer was tried and convicted of treason for his support of Lady Jane Grey, and of heresy for his anti-papal acts of the past twenty years.

Sentenced to death, Cranmer at first recanted his heresy, but when asked to repeat his recantation in public, he refused, retracting it instead. For this affront to the true Church, today he paid the ultimate price, death by burning.

As the flames leapt up, Cranmer held out his right hand that had signed his recantations, saying: 'This is the hand that wrote it, therefore shall it suffer first punishment.' Then, to the horror of the onlookers, he thrust it into the fire. And so in unspeakable agony died the Archbishop who, more than any other man, built the Church of England.

Also on this day
1685: German composer Johann Sebastian Bach is born * 1804: The Napoleonic Code of laws is enacted in France * 1806: Mexican President Benito Juárez is born

22 March

'Mehr Licht!'

1832 Johann Wolfgang von Goethe was Germany's and arguably history's greatest poet, but at the age of 83 his end was upon him. Stirring on his bed, his voice steady, Goethe spoke once more. 'Mehr Licht!' he called (More light!), and then he was gone, leaving some of history's most famous dying words behind him.

What did he mean by that final cry? Was he wishing he'd had more clarity and understanding in the past? Or was he seeing ahead into the world to come?

Neither, according to today's iconoclastic historians. What Goethe actually said was: 'Open the second shutter, so that more light can come in.'

Also on this day
1599: Flemish portraitist Anthony van Dyke is born * 1646: The Battle of Stow-on-the-Wold, the last of the English Civil War, is fought * 1820: American Commodore Stephen Decatur dies in a duel

23 March

Another tsar is murdered

1801 In the 302 years that the Romanovs ruled Russia, eighteen members of the family held the throne, four women and fourteen men. Of those fourteen tsars, five were murdered. This day was the turn of Tsar Paul I.

Paul was the son of Peter III and Catherine the Great (or certainly of Catherine, who had taken at least three lovers while Peter was still alive). Paul's natural nervousness and instability were reinforced by the knowledge that his father had been assassinated, almost certainly with Catherine's connivance.

Becoming Tsar on Catherine's death at the end of 1796, Paul already showed signs of insanity, especially the megalomania so common to absolute dictators. 'In Russia, anyone to whom I speak is great', he remarked, 'but only while I speak to him'.

In order to increase his own authority, Paul downgraded the prerogatives of Russia's nobles, constantly changed officials in his government, and reduced the power of local administrations. Fatally, he instituted severe military discipline in the army, occasionally sending high-ranking officers into Siberian exile for errors on the parade ground. Even his foreign policy was disastrous: by 1800 he had broken off diplomatic relations with Austria, was on the verge of war with England and was actually at war with France.

After only four years of Paul's rule, his aristocracy had had enough. A group of high-ranking officers and nobles approached Paul's 22-year-old son Alexander (soon to be Alexander I) and persuaded him of the need for his father's overthrow, assuring him that Paul's life would be spared. Alexander believed the plotters – or wished to believe them – and gave his permission.

On 23 March 1801 the military governor of St Petersburg, Count Peter von Pahlen, and several fellow conspirators entered the Tsar's bedroom in the Mikhaylovsky Palace and cut their ruler down.

Paul was the third Romanov tsar to be murdered in 40 years. The next was his grandson Alexander II 80 years later.

Also on this day

1842: French novelist Stendhal (Marie-Henri Beyle) dies * 1887: Spanish painter Juan Gris is born * 1919: Mussolini founds his own party in Italy, the Fasci di Combattimento * 1953: French painter Raoul Dufy dies

24 March

Queen Elizabeth dies

1603 'Nature's common work is done, and he that was born to die hath paid his tribute', once wrote Elizabeth of England in a letter of condolence. Now, as the shadows of age closed in, it was her turn to pay her tribute after 45 years as Queen.

Earlier in her reign Elizabeth had told Parliament: 'As for me, I see no such great cause why I should either be fond to live or fear to die. I have had good experience of this world, and I know what it is to be subject and what to be a sovereign.' But as she grew older, doubts began to enter her mind. She was, according to Sir Walter Raleigh, 'a lady surprised by time'.

Her last years were sombre. Always vain, she wore a tawny wig to hide her grey and thinning hair, and by her decree her palace at Richmond contained not a single mirror. The friends and counsellors of her youth were gone, and she knew her time was near. It was rumoured that her gloomy ghost wandered the palace corridors, anticipating her demise.

During March 1603 for four days she refused to go to bed, remaining seated on her cushions. One day she spent all the daylight hours in silence, her finger in her mouth. Yet she was not senile, but seemingly contemplating her life and past and what was to come. Even at the end she had not lost her authority or her bite; when her closest advisor Sir Robert Cecil presumed to give her instructions, she snapped: 'Must! Is *must* a word to be addressed to princes? Little man, little man!'

On 23 March Elizabeth announced: 'I wish not to live any longer, but desire to die.' At three o'clock the following morning the greatest queen that England (and perhaps any nation) would ever know drifted away, the Archbishop of Canterbury at her side in prayer. Legend asserts that her coronation ring could be removed only by cutting off her finger, symbolising her union with her country. Elizabeth had lived for 69 years, six months and seventeen days.

Also on this day

1401: Mongol leader Tamerlane the Great captures Damascus * 1603: The crowns of England and Scotland are united when King James VI of Scotland succeeds to the English throne

25 March

Birth of the first Plantagenet king

1133 Today the town of Le Mans in north-western France is better known for its annual motor race, but in the 12th century it belonged to the counts of Anjou, whose domain centred on the fine old town of Angers on the River Loire. It was here on this day that Henry II of England was born, the first king of a dynasty that would reign longer than any other English royal house.

Henry's father was Count Geoffrey of Anjou, a handsome man with a taste for riding, hunting and women. In springtime the Anjou countryside is yellow with a type of gorse called *planta genista*, and as a young man Geoffrey took to wearing a sprig of this cheerful bloom in his hat. He enjoyed this habit so much that he soon came to be known as Geoffrey Plantagenet.

When he reached a precocious sixteen, Geoffrey married 26-year-old Matilda, daughter of Henry I of England, in a grand dynastic marriage. Four years later the future Henry II was born.

Young Henry grew into a thickset, athletic man with red-blond hair, grey eyes and boundless energy. At nineteen he arranged his own dynastic marriage, also to an older woman, the beautiful Eleanor of Aquitaine, eleven years his senior, who was the former Queen of France and the greatest landholder in the kingdom. Two years after that he inherited the throne of England.

Henry II would rule England for 35 years and sire two sons who would become among the most famous and worst kings in British history, Richard the Lion-Heart and John. In all, the Plantagenet dynasty that he founded would hold the English crown for 332 years, until the death of Richard III at Bosworth Field.

Also on this day

1347: St Catherine of Siena is born * 1436: Brunelleschi's Dome in Florence is consecrated * 1804: South American liberator Simón Bolívar leaves Spain for South America * 1821: Greece declares independence from Turkey

26 March

Beethoven bows out

1827 Opinions about Ludwig van Beethoven varied greatly, depending on whether they were about his musical ability or about the man himself. Mozart, under whom he studied, predicted when Beethoven was still only 21 that 'he will give the world something worth listening to'. On the other hand, Goethe, who met him only when he was over 40, cantankerous and almost deaf, thought he was 'an utterly untamed personality, who is not completely wrong in thinking the world detestable, but who certainly does not make it any more enjoyable for himself or for others by his attitude'.

Born in Bonn, Beethoven spent virtually all of his productive years in Vienna. He was a difficult and solitary man totally devoted to his music. Unlike Mozart, who lived and died on the edge of penury for lack of sponsors, Beethoven was recognised and supported throughout his career. Although never rich, he was comfortable. His great affliction was his increasing deafness, which started before he was 30. By the last years of his life he was completely deaf.

In December 1826, Beethoven turned 56 and was showing signs of what was thought to be dropsy but which retrospective diagnosis shows to have been cirrhosis of the liver. His condition continued to worsen until at the end of March he was on the point of death. There is no doubt that he died on the afternoon of 26 March, as a great thunderstorm raged outside, but controversy continues over his last words. One version has him histrionically murmuring the classical ending to Roman plays: 'Plaudite, amici, comoedia finita est.' (Applaud, my friends, the comedy is over.) Elsewhere he is reported to have concluded: 'I shall hear in heaven.' A third story describes him receiving a shipment of special Rhine wine which he had ordered months before. Taking a sip, he mumbled, 'Pity, pity ... Too late!'

Three days after his demise Beethoven was buried in Währing churchyard in Vienna, after a funeral attended by 20,000 people.

Beethoven remained a bachelor all his life, in spite of several attempts on his part to marry. When he died, three letters were found locked in his cabinet, all including declarations of love and addressed to his 'Immortal Beloved'. The letters are undated and had never been sent, and the identity of his 'Immortal Beloved' has never been discovered.

Also on this day

1726: Blenheim's architect, Sir John Vanbrugh, dies * 1859: English poet A.E. Housman is born * 1874: American poet Robert Frost is born * 1892: American poet Walt Whitman dies * 1902: British imperialist Cecil Rhodes dies

27 March

The passing of Eleanor of Aquitaine

1204 When she died today she had seen it, done it, lived it all: Eleanor of Aquitaine, the most remarkable woman of her time. She was raised in Poitiers in the traditions of courtly love and the troubadour. In Paris she heard the preaching of Abélard, St Bernard and later St Thomas Becket. A great beauty and sometimes a great scandal, Eleanor was a duchess, descendant of Charlemagne and the richest woman in Europe, her domain covering about a quarter of modern France. (With its own distinct language, Aquitaine was the land of the *langue d'oc*, so named because its inhabitants said 'oc' rather than 'oui'.)

Eleanor had two husbands, both kings. With her first, Louis VII of France, she went on crusade and enlivened the trip by cuckolding him with her own uncle (not an incestuous betrayal, as her uncle was her blood-aunt's husband). With her second, Henry II of England, she founded the Plantagenet dynasty that lasted over three centuries. In all she bore ten children including England's most storied king, Richard the Lion-Heart, and England's worst, King John.

One of Eleanor's granddaughters was Blanche of Castile. When Eleanor was 78 years old she personally brought Blanche from Spain to wed the King of France. At 80 she directed the defence of a town under siege from a marauding army.

Finally Eleanor slipped away at 82, an immense age for her time, carried away according to a contemporary chronicle 'as a candle in the sconce goeth out when the wind striketh it'. She lies buried where she died, in the ancient monastery of Fontevrault in the calm of the Valley of the Loire.

Also on this day

1306: Robert the Bruce is crowned King of Scotland * 1625: James I dies in his hunting lodge at Theobalds, Essex * 1770: Italian Baroque painter Giovanni Battista Tiepolo dies in Madrid * 1809: Georges Eugène, Baron Haussman, the man who redesigned Paris, is born

28 March

Constantinople becomes Istanbul

1930 For 1,599 years, ten months and seventeen days the great city had been called Constantinople. On this day the Turkish Post Office officially changed the name to Istanbul, by which it had been identified since some time in the 13th century.

There has been a town on the Istanbul site since at least the 7th century BC, when it was settled by Greeks. They called it Byzantium after the perhaps mythical Greek leader Byzas, who captured the land from wild Thracian tribes in 657 BC.

When Rome displaced Greece as the predominant power in the

area, Byzantium became a free city under Roman overlordship, and only in AD 324, almost a millennium after its founding, did it finally become Constantinople.

On 18 September 324 the Western Roman Emperor Constantine defeated his rival Licinius at Chrysopolis to take command of the entire empire. After the battle he retired for the night to nearby Byzantium, where he dreamt that he saw the guardian deity of the city, an old crone, forlorn and failing from age and infirmities. Suddenly she was transformed into a radiant young woman, and in his dream he placed a diadem on her head. When Constantine awoke he interpreted his dream as a sign from heaven, and decided to found a great city on the site.

The Emperor shortly led a group of his assistants on foot around the outskirts of Byzantium (then a smallish town), tracing the boundaries of his new city with his lance. His assistants were astonished by its size, but, according to Christian hagiographers, the Emperor insisted: 'I shall advance till He, the invisible guide who marches before me, thinks proper to stop.'

Constantine immediately undertook a huge building programme, tripling the size of the city, and on 11 May 330 dedicated it as Constantinople (Constantinopolis), replacing Rome as capital of the empire.

Constantinople became the greatest city in the civilised world, but over the centuries it had to weather many storms, including a 6th-century plague that killed most of the inhabitants. It was attacked innumerable times, but thanks to its huge 5th-century walls, it remained unconquerable.

By the 13th century, Anatolian Turks were already referring to Constantinople as Istinpolin, derived from the Greek phrase *eis ten polin* meaning 'in the city'. But even after the Turks finally conquered it in 1453 it remained Constantinople to all but some of its own inhabitants. Over the years the Turks increasingly called it Istanbul, as scarcely a reminder in the city of its Greek or Roman past remained. By the time of the official name change, no trace of Byzantium was left, and the only remnant of the Great Constantine was the eponymous burnt porphyry column that still draws the gazes of tourists in Old Istanbul.

29 March

The Rosenbergs are convicted of treason

1951 Today in New York City, a jury of eleven men and one woman unanimously convicted Julius and Ethel Rosenberg of treason under the terms of the 1917 Espionage Act for providing Communist Russia with secret information regarding the construction of the atomic bomb. One week later they were sentenced to death.

The son of a Polish immigrant garment worker from Manhattan's Lower East Side, 33-year-old Julius Rosenberg had long been a member of America's Communist Party, having joined the Young Communists' League at college when he was only sixteen. During the Second World War his wife Ethel's brother David Greenglass had become an army sergeant assigned to Los Alamos, where the development of the bomb was taking place. Soon Julius and Ethel had persuaded Greenglass to ferret out whatever secrets he could find.

Whenever new information was obtained, it was passed on to a podgy, middle-aged courier named Harry Gold, who served as the liaison with the Soviet vice consul in New York City, Anatoly Yakovlev. From there it made its way to Moscow.

Throughout the war years the Rosenbergs must have believed they would go undetected, but in February 1950 Klaus Fuchs, a British scientist and Russian spy working at Los Alamos, was arrested. Fuchs readily admitted supplying atomic data to the

Russians, and he, too, had connections with Gold. The trail soon led to David Greenglass and the Rosenbergs, who were taken into custody.

The trial was one of the most contentious in American history, as both Rosenbergs adamantly denied their guilt, and many left-wingers around the world saw the prosecution as an anti-Communist witch hunt, possibly with anti-Semitic overtones. But Julius and Ethel were convicted, mostly by the testimony of Ethel's brother, who had admitted his own guilt and turned state's evidence. The case against Julius Rosenberg was clear-cut, but the key proof against Ethel was Greenglass's wife's testimony that she had seen Ethel typing out Greenglass's handwritten notes. Greenglass was sentenced to fifteen years in prison, while Gold drew a term of 30, but the judge sentenced the Rosenbergs to death, declaring: 'I consider your crime worse than murder.'

The next two years witnessed an explosion of protest around the world, not so much against the verdict as against the sentence of death. Thousands demonstrated in America and Europe, the Pope asked for clemency, letters of protest rained on the White House, and the Rosenbergs' two sons marched carrying signs reading 'Don't Kill my Mommy and Daddy'. But neither the Supreme Court nor President Eisenhower would intervene.

Just after 8 p.m. on 19 June 1953 in Sing Sing Prison in Ossining, New York, first Julius and then Ethel was strapped into the prison's electric chair. Electrodes were applied to the calf of one leg and the shaven scalp, and dampened with a salt solution to make sure of a good contact. Then a current of some 2,000 volts crackled through the system. Unconsciousness was instantaneous, death virtually so for Julius, but Ethel required three long jolts to die. The Rosenbergs were the first American civilians ever executed during peacetime for treason (although their offences had been committed during a war).

For years after the execution, friends, family and assorted left-wingers proclaimed the Rosenbergs' innocence, and David Greenglass later wrote that the prosecution had pressured him into testifying against his sister, threatening to indict his wife if he refused. But in 1997 Alexandr Feklisov, the Rosenbergs' Russian control officer, publicly described his clandestine meetings with Julius in the 1940s, confirming his guilt. He claimed, however, that he had no first-hand knowledge that Ethel had belonged to the conspiracy.

Also on this day
1461: The Yorkists defeat the Lancastrians under Henry VI at the Battle of Towton in the Wars of the Roses * 1848: American fur and property tycoon John Jacob Astor dies in New York * 1891: French Pointillist painter Georges-Pierre Seurat dies

30 March

The bloody Sicilian Vespers

1282 Since his brother Louis IX was a crusading French king and certified saint, Charles of Anjou must have inherited the bad half of the family genes.

Master of most of Italy and Sicily, Charles's tyranny and cold-blooded cruelty soon made him detested throughout his territories, particularly in Sicily with its traditions of lawless independence.

On Easter Monday, 30 March 1282, as the citizens of Palermo flocked to vespers in the church of Santo Spirito, a French soldier grossly insulted a pretty young Sicilian woman. The girl's enraged fiancé immediately drew his dagger and stabbed the soldier to his heart. The violence was contagious, and the local populace exploded in fury against the French. Over 200 French soldiers were slain on the spot, and the killing spread to other parts of Sicily the next day. The bloody event is known in history as the Sicilian Vespers.

The overthrow of Charles of Anjou precipitated a long war for the crown of Sicily between the Angevin kings of Naples and King Peter III of Aragon, but the result for Sicily was almost a century of independence.

So inspiring to an Italian is the story of the Sicilian Vespers that Giuseppe Verdi created an opera around it in 1855.

Also on this day

1746: Spanish painter Francisco de Goya is born * 1842: Ether is first used as an anaesthetic during surgery by US doctor Crawford Long * 1853: Dutch painter Vincent van Gogh is born * 1856: The treaty ending the Crimean War is signed * 1867: Russia sells Alaska to the US for $7.2 million

31 March

Commodore Perry opens Japan

1854 After the great Japanese shogun Tokugawa Ieyasu took control of Japan in 1603, successive shoguns attempted to stabilise the country by preventing change. Social classes were frozen, and outsiders – especially Catholic missionaries – came to be seen as a disruptive and threatening influence. By the early 1630s Christianity had been effectively banned, no Japanese was allowed to travel abroad, and the country was closed to foreigners. At times the isolation was so sternly enforced that shipwrecked sailors washed ashore would be summarily executed. For over two centuries Japan lived in near total isolation, although European and North American businessmen yearned for a chance to develop what they were sure would be lucrative commerce.

In early July 1853 a fleet of four American warships anchored in the lower Tokyo Bay. Their commander was Commodore Matthew Perry, haughty, dignified, ponderous and dull, but with determination to fulfil President Millard Fillmore's orders to open Japan to American trade.

On 14 July, Perry landed at Kurihama, a tiny village at the entrance to Tokyo Bay. There he presented American demands to representatives of the shogun. Perry then sailed off to China to await a reply.

In March the following year the Commodore returned, this time with a force of ten ships and some intriguing presents for the Japanese – a telegraph instrument and a miniature locomotive. By now the Japanese had realised that they could no longer fight the inevitable. On the last day of the month the Treaty of Kanagawa was signed, guaranteeing 'a perfect, permanent and universal peace and a sincere and cordial amity' between Japan and the United States.

Perry returned home a hero, to receive $20,000 awarded by Congress. Japan was open at last. As one American observer said at the time: 'We didn't go in; they came out.'

Also on this day

1596: French philosopher René Descartes is born * 1631: The bell tolls for John Donne in London * 1732: Austro-Hungarian composer Joseph Haydn is born * 1837: English novelist Charlotte Brontë dies * 1837: English landscapist John Constable dies * 1881: The Eiffel Tower is inaugurated

1 April

Birth of the Iron Chancellor

1815 Otto von Bismarck was born today in Kniephof, Prussia, a man destined dramatically to change the history of Europe. He was one of the most contradictory leaders in history: he hated political parties, but proved a master politician; a reactionary, he instituted social security for the aged and socialised medicine; a fervent Prussian nationalist, he created a unified German state.

A giant of a man (he was six feet five inches), Bismarck came from a moderately prosperous Junker family. Early in life he showed little promise, but marriage and some sort of religious awakening converted him into the serious and determined man who became aristocratic, autocratic and so self-assured that he was accused of believing in God only because God agreed with him on all subjects. He was also a political genius who would dominate Prussia for nine years and then a united Germany for nineteen more.

An impassioned monarchist, Bismarck became Prussia's Chancellor in 1862. His foremost objective was to wrest control of the German-speaking world from the then dominant Austria and form a unified German state under the leadership of Prussia. To do this, his first task was to build up the army. Called Prussia's Iron Chancellor, his nickname derived from an address to the Chamber of Deputies in which he maintained that 'it is not by means of speeches and majority resolutions that the great issues of the day will be decided ... but by blood and iron'.

In 1864 Bismarck formed an alliance with Austria and used his expanded force to invade Denmark over the Schleswig-Holstein question, a labyrinthine issue that had been simmering since the early 1800s. (Schleswig-Holstein was a Danish province with a substantial German population. The issue was so complex that England's Lord Palmerston once remarked, 'Only three men in Europe have ever understood it, and of those the Prince Consort is dead, a Danish statesman is in an asylum, and I myself have forgotten it.') Bismarck's invasion was immediately successful, and Schleswig-Holstein became a German state.

Two years later, Bismarck launched the Seven Weeks' War against his erstwhile allies the Austrians and some smaller German states. After a major victory at Sadowa, Hanover, Hesse-Kassel, Nassau and Frankfurt, all of which had fought alongside Austria, were annexed, and virtually overnight Prussia, not Austria, had become the Germanic world's major power.

In spite of Bismarck's success (or perhaps because of it), many of Germany's smaller states continued to resist unification, which they quite correctly understood to mean dominance by Prussia. Bismarck's next move was another war – not against the recalcitrant principalities but with France, in the belief that seeing Prussia under attack would awaken pan-German nationalism and lead the way to a consolidated state. Using the ruse of a doctored diplomatic telegram, Bismarck manoeuvred the French into declaring war. Swiftly victorious, Prussia was then able to persuade the other German states to combine into a united empire, of which King Wilhelm became Kaiser Wilhelm I. (Another consequence of this war was Germany's annexation of Alsace and part of Lorraine, two French provinces with large German-speaking populations. Alsace-Lorraine became the ball in a ping-pong match, reverting to France in 1919, recaptured by Germany in the Second World War and finally reunited with France in 1945.)

Thus by 1871 the Continent was dominated by a united Germany, Germany was dominated by Prussia and Prussia was dominated by Bismarck. Confident of the new nation's power, the Iron Chancellor addressed the Reichstag with the words, 'Setzen wir Deutschland, so zu sagen, in den Sattel. Reiten wird es schon können.' (Let's put Germany, so to speak, in the saddle. You'll see that she can ride.)

On 9 March 1888 Kaiser Wilhelm I died just a few days before his 91st birthday, and then on 15 June his son Frederick III succumbed to throat cancer, bringing the intelligent but unstable Wilhelm II to the throne. Kaiser Bill, as the British came to call him, was young (29), arrogant and determined not to be overshadowed by the great chancellor. Within two years he had pressured

Bismarck into retirement, an event that sent shock waves across Europe and inspired the great political cartoon in *Punch* (29 March 1890) by John Tenniel called 'Dropping the Pilot'. It showed Bismarck descending a ladder from the German ship of state to be taken off in a pilot boat, while from the deck above the Kaiser as captain calmly surveys his departure.

Bismarck died eight years later, and within three years Kaiser Wilhelm had let Bismarck's keystone treaty with Russia lapse, leading to an alliance between Russia and France, with all its consequences for the future.

In 1914 Kaiser Wilhelm II, to use Bismarck's metaphor, put Germany into the saddle, only to find that without the Iron Chancellor, it could ride only into a brick wall.

Also on this day

1920: Germany's Workers' Party changes its name to the Nationalist Socialist German Workers' Party (Nationalsozialistische Deutsche Arbeiterpartei), or for short, Nazi * 1924: Adolf Hitler is sentenced to five years in prison for the 'Beer Hall Putsch'

2 April

Charlemagne – the greatest emperor since the Romans

742 Born this day: Charlemagne, who was to become the greatest European ruler since Roman times.

The grandson of the great Frankish leader Charles Martel, Charlemagne became joint King of the Franks along with his father and brother when he was only twelve. After the other two had died he asserted his power over all the Frankish lands, comprising present-day northern France, Belgium and western Germany. Then, over the next 30 years, he subjugated the Saxons, seized Bavaria, fought campaigns in Hungary and Spain and conquered parts of northern Italy. Backed by the Pope (and strongly supporting the Pope in a time of great conflict with the eastern empire in Constantinople), Charlemagne created one vast empire of practically all the Christian lands of western Europe except parts of Spain, southern Italy and the British Isles. He established his capital at Aachen (Aix-la-Chapelle) on the right bank of the Rhine.

One contemporary at Charlemagne's court described him thus: 'He had a broad and strong body of unusual height, but well-proportioned; for his height measured seven times his feet. His skull was round, the eyes were lively and rather large, the nose of more than average length, the hair grey but full, the face friendly and cheerful. Seated or standing, he thus made a dignified and stately impression even though he had a thick, short neck and a belly that protruded somewhat; but this was hidden by the good proportions of the rest of his figure. He strode with firm step and held himself like a man; he spoke with a higher voice than one would have expected of someone of his build. He enjoyed good health except for being repeatedly plagued by fevers four years before his death. Toward the end he dragged one foot.'

This was the man who founded the Carolingian dynasty that ruled an empire for 137 years. So much was he admired that a century after his death the Emperor Otto I emulated the great conqueror by establishing Aachen as his capital, and during the next 600 years more than 30 Holy Roman Emperors and German kings were crowned there.

Charlemagne also appears in several French *chansons de geste* (literally 'songs of deeds') of the Middle Ages, most famously in *Le Chanson de Roland* where he is portrayed leading the Christian fight against the Muslims (or Moors) of Spain.

In 1165 the then Emperor Frederick Barbarossa paid Charlemagne the ultimate compliment in badgering the Pope Paschal III to canonise him. Unfortunately for Charlemagne, Paschal was an anti-pope, claiming to be Pope but unrecognised by the Catholic Church in Rome, so the Church has never accepted his canonisation.

Also on this day

1725: Italian seducer Giovanni Giacomo Casanova is born * 1800: First performance of Beethoven's First Symphony * 1801: The British and

Danish fleets meet in the Battle of Copenhagen * 1840: Birth of Emile Zola in Paris

3 April

King John commits murder

1203 The four eaglets, as they were called, sons of King Henry II of England, were Henry, Richard, Geoffrey and John. The first died while great Henry was still alive, as did the third, Geoffrey, but not before marrying and producing a son christened Arthur.

In 1189 Henry II died, hounded by his son Richard (the Lion-Heart), who inherited the throne. But Richard's reign was brief, and just ten years later John was crowned after Richard was killed besieging an enemy castle. So John was King, but his nephew Arthur, then a boy of thirteen, was being raised in the courts of France.

By 1203 John was already hated by most of his subjects, and he could no longer ignore his dangerous nephew who had begun to sound his own claims to the throne.

By a fluke of luck, John captured Arthur in a minor battle. First, he imprisoned him at the castle of La Falaise in Normandy, then he moved him to a fortress in Rouen. But no matter where he was kept, Arthur continued to be a threat, one that John had to eliminate.

According to a contemporary source, 'On the day before Good Friday, after dinner, when he was drunk with wine and filled with the devil, he [John] killed him [Arthur] with his own hand and, tying a heavy stone to his body, threw it into the Seine. Later it was dragged up in the nets of fishermen and ... was identified and secretly buried in Notre Dame des Près ... for fear of the tyrant.' The date was 3 April 1203. John the murderer remained King, unpunished and unrepentant, until his death thirteen years later.

Also on this day
1721: Robert Walpole becomes the first Prime Minister of Great Britain
* 1882: American outlaw Jesse James is shot in the back by one of his
own gang * 1897: German composer Johannes Brahms dies in Vienna

4 April

'*A curious, odd, pedantic fellow with some genius*'

1774 Ugly to the point of caricature, with a great dome of forehead,
a protruding upper lip and very little chin, Oliver Goldsmith yet
achieved greatness writing comedy and was a much-loved friend
of Samuel Johnson, Joshua Reynolds, David Garrick and
Edmund Burke.

Goldsmith was born around 1730 and was a would-be
physician before becoming a writer. He studied 'physic' at the
University of Leiden in the Netherlands but received no degree,
then returned to London as a sometime chemist, and finally lost his
job in the medical service of the East India Company. In spite of
these setbacks, Goldsmith always insisted he was a doctor. On one
occasion he was boasting to his friend Topham Beauclerk of his
medical prowess, claiming, 'I do not practise; I make it a rule to
prescribe only for my friends.' Nonplussed by Goldsmith's
assertion, Beauclerk responded, 'Pray, dear Doctor, alter your rule
and prescribe only for your enemies.'

Although Goldsmith clearly failed as a doctor, he did not
prosper much as a writer either, for his greatest novel, *The Vicar of
Wakefield*, published in 1766, took almost a century to acquire its
reputation. His great comic play *She Stoops to Conquer* was first
performed on 15 March 1773, only thirteen months before
Goldsmith's death of kidney failure on this day in 1774. He died
without family (he had never married) and nearly broke. Yet his
friends mourned his passing, and none summed him up better than
James Boswell, who called him 'a curious, odd, pedantic fellow
with some genius'.

Also on this day
527: Byzantine Emperor Justinian is crowned * 1648: Dutch-born woodcarver and sculptor Grinling Gibbons is born

5 April

Danton goes to the guillotine

1794 Prior to the French Revolution Jacques Georges Danton had been a successful Parisian lawyer. Despite his bloated and particularly unattractive face he was a powerful speaker who could sway a mob. He became a member of the Legislative Assembly in 1791 when only 32.

From then on his actions became increasingly demagogic – and dangerous, as he practised his own preaching for 'de l'audace, encore de l'audace, toujours de l'audace'. In 1792 he instigated the September Massacres in which suspects already imprisoned were given mock trials and then turned over to the mob for slaughter.

Although Danton at first dominated the Committee for Public Safety, by 1794, led by Robespierre, it had turned on him, jealous of his power and fearful of his ambitions. He was arrested on 30 March.

His trial was a farce, the verdict predictable. On hearing his inevitable sentence, Danton grandly announced, 'My dwelling-place will soon be nothingness. My name is written in the Pantheon of history.'

On 5 April 1794 he was led to the guillotine. As he was carried to the scaffold in a horse-drawn tumbrel, he passed Robespierre's house. Shaking his fist, he called out, 'You will appear in the cart in your turn, Robespierre, and the soul of Danton will howl with joy!'

Stopping to embrace another victim at the bottom of the steps that led to the guillotine, he grandly asked, 'Why should I regret to die? I have enjoyed the Revolution. Let us go to slumber.' He then mounted the scaffold and waded through the sticky blood of previous victims, even then managing to retain his arrogance and courage. 'Show my head to the people', he commanded the executioner seconds before the drop of the blade. 'It's worth seeing.'

Also on this day
1803: Beethoven's Second Symphony is performed for the first time, in the Theater an der Wien, Vienna * 1837: English poet Algernon Charles Swinburne is born in London

6 April

Richard the Lion-Heart's last battle

1199 The tiny village of Châlus lies twenty miles south-west of Limoges. At the end of the 12th century it boasted a minor castle defended by two or three knights and their sons. Nearby a farmer had found a buried treasure of golden coins, probably Roman, and King Richard the Lion-Heart declared he would have it as his right, since he was overlord of the Limousin. Unwisely, the castle's defenders decided to resist.

Accompanied by a strong troop of mercenaries, Richard laid siege to this insignificant fortress. On the evening of 25 March he decided to inspect progress, and he carelessly neared the castle walls protected by a shield but without his armour. Suddenly through the twilight sped a crossbow bolt, striking the King in his unprotected shoulder.

Richard quickly retreated to his quarters, summoning his captain and his surgeon. The bolt had penetrated deep and was at last recovered only by the excruciating torment of laying open the flesh.

Even without Richard, the King's forces soon reduced the fortress and in the process captured the youth who had fired the shot. But by now Richard's wound showed unmistakable signs of gangrene, and the Lion-Heart knew he would soon die. Perhaps because it was the Lenten season, he performed one last chivalrous act.

Summoning the terrified youth, Richard demanded to know why he wished him injury. Emboldened, the young man replied, 'Because you killed my father and brother. Do with me as you want. I have no regrets for the vengeance I have taken.'

'Go forth in peace', said Richard. 'I forgive you my death and will exact no revenge.'

Twelve days later, on 6 April 1199, the great troubadour-knight-crusader-king was dead, at the age of 41. Ignoring Richard's forgiveness, his army captains had the young man flayed alive and hanged.

Also on this day

1528: German painter Albrecht Dürer dies * 1909: American explorer Robert Peary reaches the North Pole * 1917: The United States declares war on Germany

7 April

'The hope for an easy war and a cheap victory was gone forever'

1862 It was victory snatched from the jaws of defeat. By mid-afternoon today it became clear that the Confederate forces had been shattered by the Union counter-attack and were withdrawing. But 24 hours earlier the shoe had been on the other foot, and General Grant's Army of the Tennessee, reeling backward from the fierce rebel assault, looked on the verge of annihilation.

The Confederates named this Civil War engagement Pittsburg Landing, after a stopping place on the Tennessee River. The Union Army called it Shiloh after a small log meeting-house some four miles from the river. By either designation, it was two days of hell that 'launched the country onto the floodtide of total war'.

As early as 1 April, Confederate cavalry movements and skirmishing near the Union lines indicated an enemy advance was contemplated. Grant's headquarters ignored this evidence. 'The fact is,' Grant wrote later, 'I regarded the campaign we were engaged in as an offensive one and had no idea that the enemy would leave strong entrenchments to take the initiative ...' But Albert Sydney Johnston, the Confederate commander, had a different scenario in mind. Just before the attack, he told his senior commanders: 'Tonight we will water our horses in the Tennessee River.' They came very close in an effort that would cost Johnston his life.

At 5.00 a.m. on the 6th, as breakfast fires were being lit in the Union camp, patrols spotted Confederate skirmishers through the woods and underbrush. And suddenly, right behind them, emerged the full Confederate battle line, thousands strong, yelling and firing.

Under the shock of the attack, the Union positions disintegrated. Throughout the long day, the fighting was chaotic and relentless. At dusk, when one more Confederate attack might have destroyed what was left of Grant's army, the rebels halted, exhausted and fought out. During the night it rained and Grant brought up fresh regiments. By daylight today, the Union forces had a sizeable advantage in numbers, and the counter-attack began.

Shiloh was shocking in its carnage: a total of 20,000 men were killed or wounded, about evenly distributed to both sides. Included among the dead was Confederate general Johnston, killed on the first day of battle. That was almost twice the combined losses in all the previous engagements of the war now entering its second year. Bloody Shiloh produced a change in the war, which Bruce Catton summed up this way:

It had begun with flags and cheers and the glint of brave words on the spring wind, with the drumbeats setting a gay rhythm for the feet of young men who believed that war would beat clerking. That had been a year ago; now the war had come down to uninstructed murderous battle in a smoky woodland where men who had never been shown how to fight stayed in defiance of all logical expectation and fought for two nightmarish days. And because they had done this the hope for an easy war and a cheap victory was gone forever.

Also on this day

1300: The start date of Dante's *Divine Comedy* * 1614: Greek/Spanish painter El Greco (Domenikos Theotokopoulos) dies * 1770: English poet William Wordsworth is born

8 April

The Prince Regent makes a calamitous marriage

1795 'Her figure was very bad, short, very full-chested and jutting hips. She was stockily built, dressed dowdily, lacked moral reticence and good sense, and washed so seldom she was malodorous.' Such was the potential bride of England's future King George IV, Caroline of Brunswick, as described in the private diaries of the Earl of Malmesbury who had been sent to Braunschweig in Germany to vet the prospect.

Unfortunately for Prince George, Malmesbury equivocated in his official report, and the Prince's dynastic need for a wife was so strong that he agreed on the match, sight unseen.

Caroline of Brunswick turned out to be just as unattractive as Malmesbury's description. When George first met her he famously turned to his valet with the appeal, 'I am not very well, Harris; pray get me a glass of brandy.'

The couple were married on this day in 1795. After the official ceremony the groom resorted to the bottle to give him fortitude for the night ahead. Blind drunk, he managed to make love to his new wife that night, implanting a daughter in her womb. They never slept together again.

By 1811 when George had become regent for his mad father, George III, he banished Caroline from court, and she decamped to Montague House in Greenwich Park. Three years later she left for Italy, where she took up with an Italian named Bartolomeo Pergami, who apparently had a stronger stomach and emptier purse than Prince George. As one might throw out a mattress infested with fleas, George had Montague House demolished the moment she was gone.

When George inherited the throne in 1820 he tried to persuade Parliament to dissolve the marriage and take away Caroline's royal title on the grounds of her adultery. During a hearing, a servant testified that 'Her Royal Highness had heard of the enormous size of [Pergami's] machine and sent for him by courier.' But the House of Lords, only too aware of George's own feckless and selfish character, let the bill drop.

George's final rejection of his wife came at his coronation on 19 July 1821 when he banned her from the ceremony in Westminster Abbey, although she caused a scandal by pounding on the church door demanding to be let in.

This last denial may have finally done Caroline in, as she immediately fell ill and died nineteen days later at the age of 53.

Also on this day

563 BC: The founder of Buddhism, Gautama Buddha, is born * AD 217: Roman Emperor Caracalla is assassinated

9 April

Lorenzo de' Medici, the Renaissance's Renaissance Man

1492 Lorenzo de' Medici was the Renaissance's Renaissance Man. Italy's shrewdest balancer of power, he spent 23 years as virtual ruler of Florence, juggling the interests of Milan, Venice, Naples, the Papal States and various other powers, notably France, to the benefit of Florence. Indeed, he held the unfashionable view that war was undesirable, and while no coward, he showed little inclination for combat on the few occasions when war was thrust upon him.

But Lorenzo's greatness was not as a ruler or even a banker (the Medici bank that he controlled was Europe's most powerful), but as a man of the arts. He was an outstanding vernacular poet with a broad range from bawdy songs to celebrations of nature to laments on love and mortality:

147

Quant'è bella giovinezza	How beautiful is youth
Che si fugge tuttavia.	Which flies away soon.
Chi vuol esser lieto, sia;	Let him who would be happy, be it;
Di domani non c' è certezza.	For tomorrow is never certain.

Finally, Lorenzo was the greatest patron of Renaissance art. Andrea del Sarto painted the walls of his villa at Poggio a Caiano, while Ghirlandajo, Filipino Lippi and Botticelli decorated the one at Spedaletto. Sandro Botticelli was virtually Lorenzo's 'court painter' as well as frequent dinner companion. Other artists Lorenzo patronised included Perugino, Verrocchio and Antonio Pollaiuolo. He met and helped Leonardo da Vinci when Leonardo was only twelve, and he 'discovered' Michelangelo at the age of thirteen. Michelangelo in fact lived in the Medici palace for four years, and, according to the contemporary painter-historian Giorgio Vasari, he 'always ate at Lorenzo's table with the sons of the family'.

Ruler, diplomat, banker, lover of women and loving husband, philosopher, patron, poet: no wonder he is known as Lorenzo the Magnificent. The world had become a richer place because of him when he died at his villa in Careggi near Florence on this day at the age of 43.

Also on this day

1553: French writer and priest François Rabelais (Alcofribas Nasier) dies in Paris * 1865: The American Civil War comes to an end as General Robert E. Lee surrenders to General Ulysses S. Grant at Appomattox Courthouse * 1940: Germany invades Denmark and Norway * 1942: The Americans surrender to the Japanese at Bataan * 1945: German Admiral and head of the *Abwehr* Wilhelm Canaris is executed in the dying days of Nazi Germany

10 April

The pope who gave us our calendar

1585 Today in Rome, just two months short of his 83rd birthday, died one of the most contradictory characters of the 16th century, Pope Gregory XIII.

Gregory had been born Ugo Buoncompagni in Bologna in 1502. He had attended the city's famous university, the oldest in Europe, and then taught jurisprudence there. It was Buoncompagni's legal expertise that brought him to the attention of Pius IV, who sent him to the Council of Trent, the ecumenical assembly that brought wide reform to the Roman Church under Protestant attack. Buoncompagni continued slowly to rise in the Church hierarchy until in May 1572 he was finally elected Pope, just 37 days before he turned 70.

Despite a somewhat intemperate youth (he had fathered a child while living in Bologna), Buoncompagni devoted himself to the spiritual and particularly the temporal wellbeing of the Church. He took the name of Gregory, probably in honour of his saintly predecessor Gregory I, who had reigned a millennium before.

Gregory XIII's irresponsible spending brought the Church to financial chaos, and his reputation suffered from his complacent nepotism (he created two of his own nephews cardinals). But he is remembered most for his militant efforts to suppress emerging Protestantism. Twice he sent small armies to Ireland to bolster Irish Catholics in their revolt against England's Protestant Queen Elizabeth, and he famously celebrated the slaughter of French Huguenots during the St Bartholomew's Day Massacre by ordering a *Te Deum* sung in Rome. He then commemorated the event with a medal showing an angel holding a cross while striking down Huguenots with a sword. Gregory's own effigy decorates the back.

But Gregory also had a more productive side. In 1574 he built the monumental Quirinal Palace as a summer retreat to escape Rome's stifling heat and endemic malaria but soon turned it into the official papal residence, which it remained until 1870. Today it is the presidential palace of Italy. He also ordered the construction of beautiful fountains in the Piazza del Pantheon and the Piazza del Popolo.

But Gregory's most notable achievement is one that still affects all of us every day. In the 6th century his namesake had given the world the Gregorian chant, and in 1582 Gregory XIII gave us the Gregorian calendar and decreed that the year would always begin on 1 January.

Also on this day

1829: Founder of the Salvation Army William Booth is born * 1864: Austrian Archduke Maximilian is made Emperor of Mexico * 1919: Mexican revolutionary leader Emiliano Zapata is shot by Mexican government troops * 1925: F. Scott Fitzgerald publishes *The Great Gatsby*

11 April

A king's mistress dies for her sins

1599 Henri IV's women were many and varied, for which he earned himself the nickname 'Le Vert Galant' (the Old Playboy). But the one for whom he cared the most was the beautiful and witty Gabrielle d'Estrées, with whom he had two sons and a daughter during their nine-year relationship. Since Henri's wife, the famously promiscuous Queen Margot, had borne the King no children during 26 years of marriage, the King announced his intention to annul his marriage to Margot, wed Gabrielle (who was pregnant once again) and legitimise her sons as heirs to the French throne.

Now, as long as Henri was married to Margot, no one (least of all Margot herself) seemed to mind his love for Gabrielle. But keeping a mistress was one thing, marrying her was something else altogether. Henri tried to win the Queen's agreement to the annulment, but she was resolutely opposed. Nonetheless he petitioned Pope Clement VIII to dissolve the marriage.

All of Henri's courtiers were aghast at the King's proposed *mésalliance* with Gabrielle, and the Pope agonised over his decision regarding the annulment. (The fact that Clement was Margot's first cousin thrice removed through their mutual Medici blood may have played a role in his vacillation.)

In fact, Clement was so distraught that he prayed daily for divine guidance. On 3 April, at the end of prayer, he looked up towards heaven, apparently having seen a vision. Turning to one of his household, the Pope murmured with evident relief and apparent prescience, 'God has provided the answer.'

Six days later Gabrielle gave birth to a son – but he was stillborn. She then quickly lost first her speech, then her hearing, and finally her sight. On 11 April she died in agony, her beautiful face a tormented and hideous mask.

Gabrielle's friends said it was God's will, while her enemies credited the Devil, to whom they said she had sold herself to become mistress to a King.

Now that the scandal of Henri's marriage to Gabrielle had been avoided, Margot at last agreed to the dissolution of her own, and in December Pope Clement granted the annulment. The following October the King wed a distant cousin of both Margot and Pope Clement, the Florentine princess Marie de' Medici, a scheming but slow-witted shrew who, unlike his first wife, took strong (and fruitless) objection to his philandering. But Marie did produce the desired son and heir, and the descendants of this unhappy union ruled France without interruption for another 182 years.

Also on this day

1713: The War of the Spanish Succession ends by the Treaty of Utrecht * 1814: Emperor Napoleon abdicates at Fontainebleau * 1945: The Buchenwald concentration camp near Weimar in Germany is liberated

12 April

The South fires the first shot of the American Civil War

1861 Four months earlier, in December 1860, South Carolina had seceded from the United States, quickly followed by six other southern states. Jefferson Davis had been elected President of the Confederacy, but still no battle had been fought in the American Civil War.

Fort Sumter sits on a small island of rock opposite Charleston, the capital of South Carolina. Occupied by Union troops, it was a thorn in the flesh (and pride) of the South.

Fearing Union reinforcements to the fort, Davis ordered the Southerners to attack. At 4.30 in the early dawn of 12 April 1861 a huge mortar shell rose from the shore and exploded on Fort Sumter, followed by an intense artillery barrage from four directions. Although the fort was solid enough – walls 40 feet high and eight to twelve feet thick – the small garrison there, with supplies exhausted, was forced to surrender after 33 hours and 4,000 rounds of artillery fire.

This was the first battle of the American Civil War, which was to continue for exactly four more years, less three days. During that time over 600,000 soldiers on both sides would die and 4 million black slaves would be freed.

Also on this day

1204: Soldiers from the Fourth Crusade sack the Christian city of Constantinople * 1945: Thirty-second President of the USA Franklin Delano Roosevelt dies of a stroke

13 April

The man who wrote the American Declaration of Independence

1743 'We hold these truths to be self-evident, that all men are created equal, that they are endowed by their creator with certain unalienable rights, that among these are life, liberty, and the pursuit of happiness.' Today was born the man who wrote these famous words from the American Declaration of Independence. He was of course Thomas Jefferson.

Jefferson was born in Shadwell, Virginia, on the banks of the Rivanna River. He represented Virginia during the forming of the United States, served as the first Secretary of State, the second Vice President and the third President.

Jefferson was America's greatest political thinker, with a passion for liberty, freedom of religion, public education and the welfare of the common man. But not all of his writings were as high-minded as the Declaration of Independence. 'The tree of liberty', he wrote in 1787, 'must be refreshed from time to time with the blood of patriots and tyrants. It is the natural manure.'

Apart from being a politician/philosopher, Jefferson was also an inventor (of, among other things, the dumb waiter), architect, musician, scientist and founder of the University of Virginia. More than two centuries after his birth another American president paid tribute to his intellect. In 1962 Jack Kennedy welcomed 49 Nobel Prize winners as 'the most extraordinary collection of talent, of human knowledge, that has ever been gathered in the White House, with the possible exception of when Thomas Jefferson dined alone'.

In spite of his passionately liberal views about democracy, Jefferson had less conviction about certain subgroups. The business of women, he said, is 'to soothe and calm the mind of their husbands', and when he died at the age of 83 he still owned 250 slaves including one, Sally Hemings, who modern science has proved bore him a child.

Also on this day

Also on this day
1598: Henri IV of France issues the Edict of Nantes, giving religious freedom to the Protestants * 1605: Russian Tsar Boris Godunov dies * 1655: Louis XIV tells the French Parliament that 'L'Etat, c'est moi' * 1829: The British Parliament passes the Catholic Emancipation Act, lifting restrictions on Catholics

14 April

Abraham Lincoln is assassinated

1865 On 11 April, just two days after the South had finally surrendered in the American Civil War, President Abraham Lincoln addressed a crowd from the balcony of the White House. After promising that there would be no revenge against the defeated Confederates, he expressed hope that some blacks – 'very intelligent' men and those who had served in the Union army – would be permitted to vote.

Listening from the lawn below was a sometime actor and Southern fanatic, John Wilkes Booth. A 23 year old with dark curly hair and a droopy moustache, he had been a militia volunteer in the troop that had hanged the Abolitionist John Brown in 1859. His hatred of Lincoln and of blacks was visceral. On hearing the President, he exclaimed to a friend, 'That means nigger citizenship! Now, by God, I'll put him through!'

Three days later, on Good Friday, Lincoln and his wife Mary went to Ford's Theater in Washington to enjoy a new play called *Our American Cousin*. There the President's bodyguard, a bored Washington policeman, went into the alley behind the theatre for a drink.

During the third act Booth stepped into the President's unguarded box. Drawing a small Derringer pistol, he shot Lincoln in the back of the head, theatrically crying 'Sic semper tyrannus!' (As always to tyrants! – Brutus's words to Caesar). He then leaped to the stage, but the spur in his boot caught in a decorative flag so that as he landed he fractured his left leg. Despite his injury, he fled from the theatre.

Mortally wounded, America's greatest president was carried to a house across the street, where he died without regaining consciousness at 7.22 the following morning. He was 56 years old.

Although Booth had escaped from the theatre, two weeks later Secret Service agents and Federal troops tracked him to a barn in Virginia. They set the barn alight, and as Booth moved from corner to corner in the burning building, one of the soldiers, Boston Corbett, saw him through a crack and opened fire with his Colt revolver, hitting him in the neck. Corbett was later to claim that 'God Almighty directed me.'

Dragged from the barn, Booth lay all night on a nearby farmhouse porch, slowly bleeding to death and sucking a brandy-soaked rag given him by a charitable soldier. At dawn the next day he realised he could no longer move his hands. 'I thought I did it for the best. Useless, useless', he muttered to one of his guards just before he died. His body was whisked to a nearby federal arsenal and secretly buried under the floor.

Also on this day

978: Ethelred the Unready is crowned at Kingston upon Thames * 1471: Warwick the Kingmaker is killed at the Battle of Barnet * 1759: German composer George Handel dies in London

15 April

Mass suicide at Masada

AD 73 Masada – an unassailable fortress of rock on eighteen acres of flat, treeless mesa, baking in the Palestinian sunlight at a height of 1,400 feet. Here, near the Red Sea's south-west coast, a garrison of Jewish Zealots defied a Roman army of 15,000 men for two years before finally committing mass suicide on this day rather than surrender.

The Zealots were a fanatical group of fundamentalist Jews who were determined to establish a theocracy and destroy the hated regime of the pagan Romans in Palestine. Founded by an extremist with the historically unfortunate name of Judas, the Zealots instigated their first rebellion in the year 6, and in 66 struck again, leading a revolt in Judea during which the Roman governor was murdered and a militant regime was established in Jerusalem.

Within a year a Roman army under the command of future Emperor Vespasian had arrived in Palestine, crushing all rebel resistance. Before completion of the task, however, the then Emperor Vitellius was toppled and killed, and Vespasian left Palestine to take over the Empire, leaving his son Titus in command.

By AD 70 the Romans had recaptured Jerusalem, destroying the Second Temple in the process. But the Zealot garrison at Masada, although only 1,000 strong, thought their position could never be stormed and steadfastly refused to submit. They had not counted on the Romans' resolve and formidable siege techniques. The Roman commander Flavius Silva saw that frontal attack was impossible, and Masada's huge aqueduct-fed cisterns could keep the fortress in water almost indefinitely. His answer was to build a monumental siege ramp against the fortress's western face, which finally permitted the attackers to breach the massive defensive walls.

When the Romans at last entered the fortress, however, all they found was corpses, as the defenders, led by one Eleazar ben Jair (a descendant of the Judas who founded the Zealots), had killed themselves to a man, slaughtering even their own women and children. Only after the Romans had occupied the stronghold did two women and five children emerge from a water conduit, where they had hidden to avoid the massacre. They were the only Jewish survivors.

Also on this day

1452: Leonardo da Vinci is born * 1764: Mme de Pompadour, mistress of Louis XV, dies of lung cancer * 1891: US inventor Thomas Edison gives a public demonstration of his kinetoscope, a moving-picture machine * 1912: The British ocean liner *Titanic* sinks after hitting an iceberg

16 April

Bonnie Prince Charlie is defeated at Culloden Moor

1746 Today Bonnie Prince Charlie and his Highland troops were crushed at Culloden Moor and all hopes of a Stuart restoration to England's throne were crushed for ever with them.

Fifty-eight years earlier Charlie's grandfather, the inept and arrogant James II, had fled into exile in France, and ever since the Stuarts had been trying to regain their kingdom. In 1745, young Charlie (then only 25) determined to win back the throne for his father, the Old Pretender, who lived in exile as *de jure* James III.

Bonnie Prince Charlie's first efforts were triumphant. Having landed successfully in Scotland, he occupied Edinburgh and led his troops south as far as Derby, well into England.

Then the English army pushed him back into Scotland until this fatal day when they met a far larger English army of 9,000 men under the Duke of Cumberland at Culloden Moor.

The English opened the battle with intense and accurate cannon fire and then attacked Charlie's band of about 5,000 Scots. As the armies closed, each English soldier ignored the man directly in front of him to bayonet the vulnerable side of the man to the right. A thousand Scots were killed outright, and another thousand were hunted down and slaughtered in the following weeks. Only 50 English perished in the battle. The combat itself lasted just over half an hour.

The charismatic, charming Prince Charlie finally managed to re-cross the Channel after five and a half legendary months on the run. During the next 42 years he maintained the Stuart claim without ever being able to raise another army, and he died in France a haughty, disagreeable, dropsical old man at the age of 68.

Also on this day

1828: Spanish painter Francisco de Goya dies * 1867: American aeroplane inventor Wilbur Wright is born

17 April

Benjamin Franklin 'lies here, food for worms'

1790 'In this world, nothing can be said to be certain except death and taxes.' So had Benjamin Franklin written to a friend, just a year before his death on this day in 1790. An emphysema had burst in his left lung and Franklin passed into a coma. At about eleven o'clock that night he quietly passed away at the advanced age of 84 years and 3 months.

During his long and eventful lifetime Franklin had been many things: diplomat, writer, postmaster, militia colonel, printer, politician, inventor, philosopher. He was the most famous American of his time, and the breadth of his fame – and of his activities – can be seen in a roster of the people he had known personally.

Naturally he knew Washington, Hamilton, John Adams and Jefferson. The last of these had taken over from Franklin as ambassador to France. When asked if he 'replaced' Franklin, Jefferson replied, 'No one can replace him, sir. I am only his successor.'

Franklin's acquaintance also included: the American naval hero John Paul Jones and the British sea captain and explorer James Cook, Louis XVI and Marie Antoinette, Christian VII of Denmark, James Boswell, Edward Gibbon and Horace Walpole, Pitt the Elder, Voltaire, Edmund Burke, Joseph Priestley, Mirabeau, Danton and the French aristocrat who fought in the American Revolution, the marquis de Lafayette (before Lafayette went to America).

Many years earlier, when he was only 28, Franklin had written his own epitaph: 'The body of Benjamin Franklin, Printer (Like the cover of an old book, its contents torn out and stript of its lettering and gilding), Lies here, food for worms; But the work shall not be lost, for it will (as he believed) appear once more in a new and more elegant edition, revised and corrected by the author.'

Also on this day

1895: The Sino-Japanese War ends with the Treaty of Shimonoseki
* 1906: An earthquake destroys 28,000 buildings in San Francisco

18 April

Martin Luther defies an emperor

1521 The Diet of Worms is remembered for the clash of wills of two of history's most strong-willed men. Sitting in judgement was the young Holy Roman Emperor Charles V, only 21 but already the most powerful monarch in the long millennium between Charlemagne and Napoleon. Testifying to his faith was a German monk who defied the True Church, Martin Luther.

Luther came to Worms eager to defend himself from accusations of heresy, in spite of warnings from his friends that Worms was a town 'where his death had already been decided upon'. Begged by a supporter not to enter the city, the monk replied, 'Wenn so viel Teufel su Worms waren Siegel auf Dachern, so wollt' ich hinein.' (I am resolved to enter Worms although as many devils should set at me as there are tiles on the housetops.)

Appalled by the corruption in Rome and certain of his own principles, Luther refused to accept the absolute authority of the Church, bowing only to 'scripture and plain reason'. But Charles could not tolerate that 'a single monk, deluded by his own judgement' could presumptuously conclude 'that all Christians up till now are wrong'.

The prosecution put its case, to which the 38-year-old monk refused to agree. Finally, on this day, Luther concluded his defence with the famous words, 'Hier stehe ich. Ich kann nicht anders.' (Here I stand. I cannot do otherwise.)

Luther was condemned, but the Emperor, who had previously promised him safe conduct, refused to have him seized. Charles spent the remaining 37 years of his life unsuccessfully trying to undo what Luther had started. Luther spent the remaining 25 years of his life preaching the same 'heresy' in Protestant Germany.

Also on this day

1480: Lucrezia Borgia, illegitimate daughter of the future Pope Alexander VI, is born * 1506: The first cornerstone of a new St Peter's Cathedral in

Rome is laid * 1593: Shakespeare's poem *Venus and Adonis* is entered for publication * 1775: Paul Revere rides from Boston to Concord to warn fellow American revolutionaries that British troops are coming

19 April

Sir Francis Drake singes the King of Spain's beard

1587 Today the man Queen Elizabeth called 'my deare pyrat' sailed his fleet into the Spanish port of Cadiz and launched a pre-emptive strike against England's great enemy, King Philip II of Spain.

Flying no flags to indicate his force was anything but a friendly fleet, Sir Francis Drake, aboard his flagship the *Elizabeth Bonaventure*, led sixteen warships into an unsuspecting harbour packed with merchant shipping. Spanish galleys defending the port proved no match against English broadsides. By the next day, 24 Spanish ships laden with supplies for the Spanish armada had been looted and burned or sunk. His work done, Drake sailed out of Cadiz to continue his depredations elsewhere.

In his long career in the twin roles of bold pirate and naval commander, Drake literally covered the world. He was the first Englishman ever to sight the Pacific Ocean. He was also the first man after Magellan to sail around the world, a feat for which Elizabeth knighted him in 1580. For his repeated incursions against their treasure fleets in the Caribbean and on the Spanish Main, the Spanish called him 'El Draque' (the Dragon). They also called him 'the devil', which, not surprisingly, was the very same term the English used for King Philip.

Drake's raids against Cadiz and other enemy supply bases during the year 1587 – 'singeing the King of Spain's beard', he termed these actions – had the valuable strategic effect of disrupting Spain's preparations for the armada and delaying for a year its sailing, so gaining precious time for England to prepare for invasion. They were also a foretaste of what the armada would encounter in the way of naval combat when it ventured up the English Channel the next year.

1775: American revolutionaries defeat British troops at Lexington and Concord, the first battles of the American War of Independence * 1824: George Gordon, Lord Byron, dies of malaria in Missolonghi on his way to fight for Greek independence * 1881: British Prime Minister Benjamin Disraeli (Lord Beaconsfield) dies * 1882: British naturalist Charles Darwin dies

20 April

Adolf Hitler is born

1889 At 6.30 in the evening of this chilly, overcast Easter Saturday, in the Austrian border town of Braunau am Inn, near Linz, Adolf Hitler was born to a middle-class Catholic family living in modest but comfortable circumstances. He was the fourth child of the union but the first to survive infancy. The household, which included two older children from the father's previous marriage, would in time be enlarged by the addition of two more children (one of whom died at six), an aunt (the wife's younger sister), a maid and a cook.

The parents were second cousins, a relationship that had required dispensation from Rome before they could be married in 1885. The father, Alois, was a customs collector in the Austrian service whose hobby was bee keeping. He had been born out of wedlock with his mother's family name Shickelgruber. At the age of 39 he attempted to legitimise himself by adopting his father's name, but changing Heidler to Hitler. He was a bastard in more ways than one, being also a strict, domineering personality and, when drunk, a harsh disciplinarian inclined towards violence with family members, especially his sons.

Klara (née Polzl), Adolf's mother, was Alois Hitler's third wife. She had worked in the household as a servant during both of her husband's previous marriages. She was submissive, churchgoing, and desperately protective of her children and stepchildren, especially Adolf, who, his younger sister Paula remembered, 'challenged my father to extreme harshness and who got his sound thrashing every day'.

These events, which provide no sign of what was to come, are among the few verifiable facts of Adolf Hitler's first years. The rest is speculation or myth. Ron Rosenbaum described the record of Hitler's early life as 'a realm disguised by his own deceitfulness, camouflaged by thickets of conflicting evidence, a tangled undergrowth of unreliable memory and testimony, of misleading rumor, myth, and biographical apocrypha'.

Also on this day

1768: Italian landscape painter Canaletto (Giovanni Antonio Canal) dies in Venice * 1770: Captain James Cook discovers Australia * 1792: The French Assembly declares war on Great Britain, to last until 1815 * 1808: French Emperor Napoleon III is born

21 April

The tragic romance of Abélard and Héloïse

1142 'Sweet as cinnamon' were her embraces, wrote Pierre Abélard of his beloved mistress Héloïse, and the romance of Abélard and Héloïse still speaks to us today across almost nine centuries.

Abélard was born in Brittany near Nantes but went to study in Paris at the age of twenty. A master dialectician, his brilliant mind and impassioned oratory soon won him the mastership of Notre Dame. When he was in his early 30s he established his own school just outside the gates of Paris, drawing a large number of admiring students. For this Abélard is considered to be the founder of the University of Paris.

Shortly, however, his career was to be cut short by the most famous love affair of the Middle Ages. When Abélard was about 40, Fulbert, the canon of Notre Dame, entrusted him with the education of his beautiful niece Héloïse, then nineteen or twenty. They fell deeply in love, and she bore him a son to whom they gave the peculiar name of Astralabe. Subsequently the couple were secretly married. But Uncle Fulbert was convinced that her lover intended to abandon her. Thirsting for revenge, he had Abélard seized by hired hooligans and castrated.

Despairing for a love now irretrievably lost, Abélard then became a monk at the royal abbey of Saint-Denis and browbeat Héloïse into becoming a nun at Argenteuil. The couple exchanged some beautifully poignant love letters, most now lost. Later, when Argenteuil was dissolved, Héloïse moved into a religious community called the Paraclete, which Abélard had founded. There she became the abbess.

Abélard continued to teach but eventually found himself in opposition to Rome and so retired to the famous Benedictine abbey at Cluny in Burgundy. On this day in 1142 he died there at the age of 63. Perhaps in extremis he was not as certain of his religious principles as he had always been in the midst of life, for his final words were a plaintive 'I don't know! I don't know!'

Abélard was buried in the Paraclete church, as he had requested. Héloïse outlived him by 22 years and according to legend died with the words: 'In death, at last, let me rest with Abélard.' Initially she was buried beside her lover at the Paraclete. In the 19th century they were moved to the Père-Lachaise cemetery in Paris.

Also on this day

753 BC: Romulus and Remus found Rome * 1574: The first Medici duke, Cosimo de' Medici, dies of an apoplectic fit in the Medici Palace, Florence * 1699: French playwright Jean-Baptiste Racine dies in Paris * 1836: American political leader Sam Houston defeats Mexican general Santa Anna at the Battle of San Jacinto * 1910: American writer Mark Twain (Samuel Clemens) dies

22 April

The tale of the Potemkin villages

1787 On this day the fat and ageing Empress Catherine the Great of Russia sailed down the Dnieper from Kiev with a fleet of seven imperial galleys and over 80 other boats on one of the most astonishing royal outings in history. The Master of Ceremonies was her former lover and current Chief Minister Grigory Potemkin. Other passengers included a full entourage of courtiers and foreign envoys and her current lover, Alexander Yermolov, 24 years her junior.

The purpose of the voyage was to inspect the towns and military installations that Potemkin had established along the river and in the Crimea, recently annexed from Turkey. A secondary motive was to meet with Holy Roman Emperor Josef II to plot the destruction of Turkey and the dismemberment of Poland.

Grigory Potemkin was one of the most profligate and effective showmen the world has known. Determined to show Catherine his achievements in the best possible light, he spent millions of roubles refurbishing the towns and palaces along the route and organising fantastic military displays to impress his sovereign. It was he who had arranged the fleet with its 3,000 oarsmen and crew, including an orchestra of 120 musicians. Local peasants were rounded up to line the riverside to watch the royal procession – not difficult to arrange for serfs who had never before seen the Empress and were curious. Firework displays were frequent and stops along the way featured huge military demonstrations such as a mock attack by some 3,000 Cossack horsemen.

Eventually the procession continued by carriage into the Crimea to inspect the formidable war fleet that Potemkin had built in only two years (and that the following year the American captain John Paul Jones would command in victory over the Turkish navy). At the end of the three-month journey he brought the Empress back through Poltava, scene of Peter the Great's historic victory over the Swedes 78 years before. There he staged yet another military spectacle using 50,000 troops playing Swedes and Russians.

One reason Potemkin so desired to impress Catherine was to counter the incessant and dangerous criticism aimed at him by jealous nobles whom he had supplanted in the corridors of power. His stage management of the Empress's journey down the Dnieper was brilliant and momentarily successful, but he had reckoned without the wiles of a disgruntled Saxon diplomat named Georg von Helbig, who had not been invited on the trip. Miffed, Helbig started rumours that the towns past which the imperial fleet had sailed were in fact only pasteboard façades. He also maintained that the crowds of peasants thronging the riverbank were in fact only one group, transported each night down the river with a change of costume to deceive the onlookers. In dispatches to his masters in Germany, he coined the phrase 'Potemkinsche Dörfer' – Potemkin Villages.

Potemkin's rivals quickly took up these stories, spreading them throughout first Russia and then Europe. They were given additional substance by the testimony of Catherine's son Paul, who hated Potemkin both as his mother's lover and because of his unlimited power. Sadly for Potemkin – one of Russia's greatest ministers – today it is for the mythical Potemkin villages that he is best remembered.

Also on this day

1500: Portuguese explorer Pedro Cabral lands on the coast of Brazil, claiming it for Portugal * 1707: English writer Henry Fielding is born * 1724: Prussian philosopher Immanuel Kant is born * 1766: Swiss/ French salonière Germaine de Staël is born in Paris * 1827: English caricaturist Thomas Rowlandson dies

23 April

The coronation of Charles II

1661 It was a brilliantly sunny St George's Day when King Charles II was ferried from Whitehall Palace down the Thames to the Tower of London to start the magnificent procession to Westminster Abbey where he was to be crowned. For monarchists it was a day of rejoicing, but also one with small reminders of the Civil War and the execution of Charles's father Charles I a dozen years before.

Flanked by wildly cheering crowds, the royal cavalcade proceeded from the Tower along unpaved streets strewn with gravel towards Whitehall, where the elder Charles had been beheaded. According to the eyewitness Samuel Pepys, the procession of carriages and horses was 'so glorious ... with gold and silver that we were not able to look at it.' Reaching Whitehall at three in the afternoon, the King and his retinue dismounted to walk on a blue carpet to the Abbey, where the same Archbishop of Canterbury who had attended Charles I on the scaffold placed the crown upon the new King's head.

To mark the joyous restoration, Charles's coronation was ostentatiously splendid – it cost over £30,000, a stupendous sum in the 17th century. The ceremony at the Abbey was followed by a magnificent banquet in Westminster Hall, the same great chamber where the first Charles had been tried and condemned. But this time there was only jubilation, as the great and good of the land drank the King's health and the King's Champion rode through the hall in full armour challenging, 'If any dare deny Charles Stuart to be lawful King of England, here is a champion that calls him a liar and a false traitor and would fight with him.' Outside in the streets drunken crowds celebrated to the light of bonfires.

Charles reigned until his death almost 24 years later. His greatest achievement was the tranquillity he gave his nation after years of civil war and Cromwell's dour protectorate. He was a popular king who became known as the Merry Monarch for his carousing and whoring, supposedly fathering over twenty bastards. As one of his contemporaries recorded, 'A king is supposed to be the father of his people, and Charles certainly was father to a good many of them.'

Also on this day

1564: William Shakespeare is born * 1616: William Shakespeare and Miguel Cervantes die on the same day * 1775: British painter J.M.W. Turner is born * 1850: British poet William Wordsworth dies at Grasmere

24 April

The ill-starred marriage of Sisi and Emperor Franz Joseph

1854 Today, in Vienna's Augustinerkirche just outside the Hofburg, Austria's tall, blond 23-year-old Emperor Franz Joseph married Elisabeth Wittelsbach, his strikingly beautiful sixteen-year-old cousin known to friends and to history as Sisi. It looked to be a fairytale marriage, but the demands of empire, a domineering mother-in-law and Sisi's neurotic restlessness transformed it into a tragedy.

Franz Joseph had been meant to marry Sisi's older sister the year before but at the very first encounter – a family luncheon at Bad Ischl – his eye fell on the stunning Sisi. Two days later they became engaged. The following year she was brought down the Danube to Vienna in a great bridal ship decorated with flowers. Church bells rang and crowds cheered as her procession made its way across the city. Nearly a thousand people crammed into the church to witness the marriage ceremony, conducted by a cardinal with the assistance of 70 archbishops and bishops. At the great Coronation Ball two nights later, Johann Strauss the Younger conducted the orchestra.

So, in a setting from a Lehar operetta began a long and unhappy marriage that lasted 44 years and produced four children, among them Rudolph, the long-hoped-for male heir to the Austrian throne. But right from the beginning troubles multiplied. Franz Joseph's mother Sophie, a powerful and domineering woman, constantly interfered, virtually bringing up the first two children herself rather than letting Sisi do it. Meanwhile Franz Joseph was above all a slave to Habsburg duty and the obligations of empire, and the marriage was further weakened by his infidelities.

Sisi, an undisciplined free spirit, was unable or unwilling to adapt herself to the role of Empress, a failing suggested even before the marriage, when she told her nanny two days after Franz Joseph's proposal, 'Yes, I do love the Emperor – if only he weren't the Emperor!' She claimed she would rather marry a butcher.

Although she could be gay and vivacious, Sisi remained at heart a child, incessantly complaining and moping and bearing grudges for life. Not unlike Diana, Princess of Wales, in the next century, this dazzling woman was fixated with being thin and beautiful. Her riding became her obsession, and she became the finest horse-woman in Europe. She found court life oppressive and her husband unresponsive, and after six years of marriage she repeatedly left her family to live in seclusion on Madeira, on Corfu and in Venice. Franz Joseph's infidelities soon made her seek her own, and she entered an affair with her handsome Magyar secretary, Count Imri Hunyadi. She kept a diary in verse that reveals both her isolation and her rather jejune self-dramatisation:

Ich wandle einsam hin auf dieser Erde,	I wander lonely on this earth,
Der Lust, dem Leben längst schon abgewandt;	Enjoyment and life rejected long ago;
Es teilt mein Seelenleben kein Gefährte,	My inner soul has no companion,
Die Seele gab es nie, die mich verstand.	There was never another soul that understood me.

But neither Sisi by her travels nor Franz Joseph by his work could escape the tragedies that dogged the Habsburg family. In 1867 Franz Joseph's younger brother Maximilian, briefly Emperor of Mexico in a disastrous colonial venture, was shot to death by a

Mexican firing squad. In 1889, in one of the great scandals of the century, Crown Prince Rudolph killed his mistress and himself in the royal hunting lodge at Mayerling.

In her diary Sisi once wrote, 'Nonetheless I always go in search of my fate. I know that nothing can stop me from meeting it on the day when I must. All men must meet their fate at a given hour. Fate closes its eyes for a long time, but one day it finds us anyway.' In 1898 fate found Sisi on a trip to Switzerland.

While she was waiting on the quayside in Geneva for a steamer to take her up the lake to Montreux, a 24-year-old anarchist named Luigi Lucheni stabbed her in the side with a sharpened file. Because she was so tightly corseted she was unaware of how badly she had been hurt and walked aboard the ship. There she collapsed and died, her last words a plaintive 'What happened to me?'

Even then tragedy continued to stalk the Habsburgs. Franz Joseph's nephew Franz Ferdinand, who became Austria's heir apparent on his cousin Rudolph's suicide, was shot to death, along with his wife, at Sarajevo in 1914. With most of his family dead and the empire he was meant to preserve crumbling around him, Franz Joseph, duty-bound to the last, died at the age of 86 on 19 November 1916, having spent most of the previous night at his desk signing wartime orders.

Also on this day

1731: English novelist Daniel Defoe dies * 1770: English writer Thomas Chatterton commits suicide * 1898: Spain declares war on the US to start the Spanish–American War

25 April

Birth of a king who built a chapel and became a saint

1214 Today a baby boy was born in the town of Poissy, about 15 miles west of Paris. His father was a prince, one day to be Louis VIII of France; his mother was a redoubtable Spanish princess named Blanche of Castile. The baby, too, would be christened Louis and he also would become King of France.

Louis IX would be one of the few monarchs in history whose greatness – universally recognised by his contemporaries – would be in his character alone. He would become the great ideal of the Middle Ages, devout, charitable and just, with greater moral force than the Pope. So great was his reputation for fairness that he was often asked to adjudicate in major disputes in foreign countries.

Louis's most lasting contribution to civilisation is the magnificent Sainte-Chapelle in Paris, which he had constructed between 1243 and 1248. Sainte-Chapelle's superlative stained glass covers most of three sides of the chapel, with over 1,100 scenes in the fifteen windows.

Young Louis would reign for 44 years as Louis IX, and after his death from plague while on crusade he would be canonised a saint.

Also on this day

1599: English dictator Oliver Cromwell is born in Huntingdon * 1895: Joseph Conrad publishes his first novel, *Almayer's Folly* * 1945: American and Russian troops meet on the Elbe River during the Second World War

26 April

Guernica

1937 At 4.30 this Monday afternoon – market day – Adolf Hitler's Condor Legion, using the Spanish Civil War as a testing ground, tried out some new techniques of blitzkrieg on the residents of the historic Basque town of Guernica.

It was a success. Heinkel 111s, flying over in waves, worked for four hours dropping high-explosive and incendiary bombs on Guernica, whose normal population of 7,000 had been greatly increased by the presence of Loyalist troops and of civilians getting out of the way of the Nationalist advance. When the bombers finished, most of the town had been destroyed or was on fire. At that point Junkers took over the action and strafed civilians in the streets.

Two days later Nationalist ground forces captured Guernica. Franco's propagandists reported that Basques had set fire to Guernica as a device to whip up Loyalist resistance. But the German pilots of the Condor Legion were soon boasting of their success, and the newspapers quickly got hold of the story. There was a great deal of international outrage, but not much in the way of action. When two Basque priests, both eyewitnesses to the bombing, went to Rome hoping to inform the Pope of the atrocity, they were shunted off to Cardinal Pacelli (soon to become Pope Pius XII), whose only response was, 'The Church is persecuted in Barcelona.'

The Spanish Civil War moved on to produce more bloody events that might have obscured what happened at Guernica, except that Pablo Picasso reminded the world with his most famous painting. Guernica was a preview of what would happen in places like Warsaw, Coventry, London, Berlin, Dresden and Tokyo.

Also on this day

AD 121: Sixteenth Roman Emperor and sometime philosopher Marcus Aurelius is born * 1478: The Pazzi family fail to assassinate Lorenzo de' Medici (the Magnificent) in Florence's cathedral but kill his brother * 1765: Nelson's mistress, Emma Hamilton, is born

27 April

Magellan the great explorer is killed in the Philippines

1521 Fernão de Magalhães, better known to us as Ferdinand Magellan, was born of a noble Portuguese family in 1480 and raised in the royal household. In his late 30s, Magellan approached the Portuguese King Manuel I to finance a voyage to the Moluccas (today part of Indonesia) by a western route. Manuel had no confidence in his countryman, so Magellan turned to Spain. Luckily for him, and for us, the Spanish King was the future Holy Roman Emperor Charles V, grandson of the Catholic Monarchs Ferdinand and Isabella who had financed Columbus. A man of imagination and intelligence, Charles agreed to underwrite the voyage, and Magellan set sail across the Atlantic on 20 September 1519.

A little over a year later Magellan had crossed the Atlantic and then bore ever southward along the coast of South America to find a way through to the 'Spice Islands' for which he was searching. On 28 November 1520, having discovered the straits at the tip of South America that now bear his name, he reached the Pacific Ocean, which he then set out to cross.

As provisions dwindled, conditions aboard Magellan's ships became appalling. His men were reduced to eating putrid and worm-infested biscuit, sawdust and grilled rat. Their only good luck was the weather, which remained miraculously calm for almost four months, without a single storm. Because of this one bounty they named this new ocean the Pacific.

Continuing westward, Magellan landed on the Philippines in March and set out to explore these largely unknown islands. But on 27 April 1521 on the beach of the tiny island of Mactan, Magellan and his crew were caught up in a minor skirmish with a local tribe. Overwhelmed, Magellan tried to cover the retreat of his men and was cut down by the spears and poison arrows of the natives. He was still only 41.

Magellan's crew continued the voyage, finally returning to Spain in September of 1522, completing the first circumnavigation of the globe. This was one of the pivotal moments in history, as the voyage not only proved the world was round but also revealed that the Americas were indeed a New World, separate from Asia.

Also on this day

1737: English historian Edward Gibbon is born at Putney * 1791: Telegraph inventor Samuel Morse is born * 1822: American President and general Ulysses S. Grant is born * 1840: American writer Ralph Waldo Emerson dies

28 April

Mussolini is lynched with his mistress

1945 Caught like a rat and dispatched like one. This is the fate that befell Benito Mussolini this afternoon not far from Lake Como. He was pushed out of an automobile by Communist partisans and shot to death at the side of the road. It is ironic that the man who brought on the downfall of Italy by joining it to the Axis cause in the Second World War should die on a road named Via XXIV Maggio to honour the date in 1915 (24 May) when Italy joined the Allies in the First World War.

Gunned down by his side was his mistress Claretta Petacci. Executed nearby were fifteen members of his fascist government fleeing with their Duce to Switzerland ahead of the Allied advance and anti-fascist resistance. When the partisans stopped the column the day before, they had discovered Mussolini disguised in a Luftwaffe overcoat and helmet. After the shootings, the corpses were trucked to Milan. There in the Piazzale Loreto, the site of a fascist massacre of resistance fighters the year before, the bodies were strung up by their heels at a gas station and displayed the next day to a jeering mob. Someone tied Claretta's skirt around her legs to preserve modesty. It was a fittingly shabby end for the man whom A.J.P. Taylor described as 'a vain, blundering boaster without either ideas or aims'.

Mussolini's father named him Benito after the Mexican revolutionary Benito Juárez with whom the elder Mussolini shared an antipathy for Habsburg rule. Benito Mussolini electrified Italy and the world in 1922 with the march on Rome, a propaganda event that bluffed a timid King Victor Emmanuel III into making him Prime Minister. Mussolini was fascist dictator of Italy for the next 21 years, at one point simultaneously holding the offices of Prime Minister, Minister of Foreign Affairs, Minister of War, Minister of the Navy, Minister of Aviation and Minister of the Interior. He dazzled his countrymen with dreams of empire in Ethiopia and Albania. In foreign policy there were other courses available, but he chose the fatal alliance with Hitler. The realities of war proved his, and Italy's, undoing.

On 25 July 1943, as Sicily fell to the Allies, a majority of the Fascist Grand Council, one that included his son-in-law Galeazza Ciano the Foreign Minister, voted to deprive Mussolini of supreme military command. The King, now determined to save his country by suing for peace with the Allies, dismissed Mussolini as Prime Minister and ordered him from Rome to confinement on the island of Ponza. There he was the object of a daring rescue by SS paratroopers acting on Hitler's orders. He was flown first to safety in Germany, where news of his survival was broadcast to the world. Then Hitler returned him to Italy, to the town of Salvo on Lake Garda, where he was installed as leader of a puppet regime under German protection, intended to maintain fascist control of northern Italy. But in the spring of 1945, with defeat now inevitable, Mussolini and his followers began to pack.

Whatever else he may have been, the Duce was a family man: an Italian historian calculated that by the year 1943 over 300 relatives of Mussolini or his wife Rachele were receiving government handouts. But even family feeling could not save his son-in-law whom he sent, with others similarly guilty, before a firing squad in January 1944 for the 'treachery' of his vote the previous year.

The Duce died just two days ahead of his partner in crime Adolf Hitler, who, similarly accompanied in death by a mistress (whom he had actually married a couple of days before), committed suicide in Berlin on 30 April.

Also on this day

1758: Fifth US President James Monroe is born, whose doctrine warned European countries against interfering in the Western hemisphere * 1789: Fletcher Christian mutinies on the *Bounty*, forcing Captain Bligh into an open boat

29 April

Catherine of Siena, a saint who changed history

1380 Today died one of the few saints who truly helped change the course of history, St Catherine of Siena.

Daughter of a Siennese dyer, the mystical Catherine joined the Dominican Order at the age of sixteen at a time when the papacy was located in Avignon during the so-called 'Babylonian Captivity'. Noted for her piety and self-abnegation, she prayed that Christ would be her Heavenly Bridegroom and eventually developed stigmata on her hands and feet (although they were visible only to herself until after her death).

In 1376 the city-state of Florence rebelled against the Pope, and Catherine travelled as a sort of holy ambassador to Avignon, then the seat of the papacy. All popes had lived there since 1309 when the French King Philip the Fair, after years of conflict regarding papal versus royal authority, had persuaded the Gascon-born Pope Clement V to move there from Rome.

Now Catherine determined not only to intervene on behalf of her native Florence but also to end the papacy's stay in Avignon and bring about its return to Rome. Having no doubt that God should be on her side, she impatiently commanded the Lord, 'It is my will that you do not delay any longer.'

At least Pope Gregory XI heard her. He was so impressed with her religious fervour as well as her common sense that he not only forgave the Florentines but also agreed to come back to Rome. In January of 1377 he entered the Holy City with Catherine at his side.

Catherine died in Rome only three years later at the age of 33. Earlier she had deliberately scalded herself in the hot springs at Vigone to prepare herself for Purgatory. Evidently, however, it was wasted preparation, for she was declared a saint in 1461.

Also on this day

1429: Joan of Arc enters Orléans after relieving the English siege * 1945: US soldiers liberate Dachau concentration camp in Germany

30 April

Hitler commits suicide

1945 The huge 30-room bunker beneath the Reich Chancellery was dim and dank, the electricity faltering under the unceasing bombardment of Russian guns. The twenty or so people inside included two of the most sinister still alive in the crumbling Third Reich: the second most powerful man in Germany, the shadowy Martin Bormann, and the Nazi Minister of Propaganda, Joseph Goebbels. All waited solemnly, some with dread, others with impatience, for the death of their master Adolf Hitler. They knew that he had sworn to commit suicide with Eva Braun, the 33-year-old mistress he had married only two days before.

Outside the bunker some 100,000 Russian troops were taking Berlin street by street, vastly outnumbering the German defenders, composed of only a few seasoned soldiers leading a ragtag collection of old men and Hitler youths, boys of less than sixteen, armed for this final apocalypse. The Russian tyrant Joseph Stalin had ordered his generals to take the city no later than 1 May at all costs so that its fall could be announced in the May Day parade in Moscow.

Hitler seemed in shock, his face ashen, his left arm trembling uncontrollably as if with Parkinson's disease, his green jacket stained with spilled food. Two days earlier his friend and ally Benito Mussolini had been executed by Italian partisans and hung by his heels in a square in Milan, and Italy had capitulated yesterday. Now Hitler had learned that his most faithful lieutenant Heinrich Himmler had betrayed him by trying to negotiate surrender through neutral Sweden. The last message ever sent from the Führerbunker was an order for the arrest and execution of this traitor.

The first to die was Hitler's German Shepherd bitch Blondi, who was fed a capsule of cyanide to test the poison's efficacy. Now in the early afternoon Hitler summoned his last remaining supporters, distractedly shook their hands and bid them a listless goodbye. Just after three he led Eva to his sitting room in the lower bunker and closed the door. Two loaded pistols and two cyanide capsules were waiting for him there.

Finally at four o'clock Hitler's valet, accompanied by Goebbels, Bormann and two generals, opened the closed door to the room. Eva lay dead from the poison while Hitler slumped in his armchair, a bullet hole in his right temple. Obedient to the last, his supporters carried the bodies to the bunker courtyard, doused them with petrol and set them alight. They then honoured the burning corpses with a final Nazi salute. Shortly afterwards Goebbels and his wife Magda poisoned their six small children and committed suicide, a deluded Magda boasting, 'You see, we die an honourable death.' Bormann made his way out of the bunker but was killed not in the fighting but from having taken poison to avoid falling into Russian hands. His body was buried in the rubble.

At 10.50 that evening Russian soldiers finally seized the Reichstag, but the victorious troops were quickly shouldered aside by agents from SMERSH, a directorate of the Russian state security apparatus. Hitler's burnt skull was secreted back to Stalin in Moscow, and only years later did the Russians reveal that Hitler's body had been found.

One week later what was left of the Nazi government signed an unconditional surrender. Hitler's Thousand Year Reich was dead after thirteen years.

Also on this day

1396: The last crusade leaves from Dijon under the command of Burgundian Jean de Nevers (Jean Sans Peur) * 1803: President Thomas Jefferson makes the 833,000 square mile Louisiana Purchase from Napoleon, doubling the size of the United States * 1883: French painter Edouard Manet dies in Paris

1 May

Dante meets Beatrice

1274, 1283 From across a crowded room, love, total and imperishable, came to young Dante Alighieri today as he set eyes for the first time on the divine figure of Beatrice Portinari. 'From that time forward', he later wrote, 'love fully ruled my soul'.

Dante was not quite nine years old when he first saw Beatrice at a party given by her father Folco Portinari in his palazzo on the Corso in Florence, already a considerable walled city of about 80,000. Dressed in crimson, she was a few months younger than he. For the next nine years he worshipped her from afar, and only in 1283, also on 1 May, did she speak to him for the first time as they passed each other in the street. During the following years, Dante's love for Beatrice continued unabated, although there is no reason to think it was returned.

In 13th-century Florence, marriages among the upper classes (to which both Dante and Beatrice belonged) were invariably arranged by the families involved. In 1286 Dante married Gemma Donati, to whom he had been betrothed since the age of twelve. A year later Beatrice also married, only to die three years later, still only 24.

Despite his adventurous life and years in exile, Dante remained devoted to Beatrice (or her memory) throughout his life, writing of her in his *La Vita Nuova*, published when he was 28, and recreating her as his guide to Paradise in his *Divine Comedy*, completed when he was about 55. Spare a thought for his poor wife Gemma, who is never mentioned in any of Dante's writing.

Also on this day

1769: Arthur Wesley, later Duke of Wellington, is born in Dublin * 1707: England and Scotland form a union under the name of Great Britain * 1797: The Venetian Republic is annexed by Austria after 1,071 years of independence * 1851: The Great Exhibition opens at the Crystal Palace in London

2 May

Leonardo da Vinci dies in a king's arms

1519 In his determination to have the most splendid court in Europe, France's François I entreated Leonardo da Vinci to become his court painter, and in 1516 the ageing Leonardo at last consented. The King gave him a charming manor house in Cloux, only a few hundred yards from the royal château of Amboise on the Loire River.

Here the great painter-sculptor-architect-inventor-engineer passed his last three years until he succumbed to a stroke on 2 May 1519 at the age of 67. Tradition has it that he died in the arms of a grieving François, certain that his death was just punishment for his artistic failures. 'I have offended God and man', he said, 'because my work did not achieve the quality it should have'.

Since he was already infirm when he arrived in France, Leonardo created little of note for François, but he did bring several of his own paintings with him when he came. One of these has remained in France ever since, probably the most famous work of art on Earth, the Mona Lisa.

Also on this day

1611: The Authorised Version of the Bible (King James Version) is first published * 1660: Composer Alessandro Scarlatti is born in Palermo, Sicily * 1729: Sophia von Anhalt-Zerbst, the future Catherine the Great of Russia, is born in Stettin, Pomerania * 1808: The population of Madrid rises against Napoleon, inspiring Goya's painting *Dos de Mayo*

3 May

Death comes to the Turkish sultan who brought an end to the Byzantine Empire

1481 Today died the Ottoman Sultan Mehmed the Conqueror, so named for conquering Constantinople and bringing an end to the Byzantine Empire after 1,058 years.

At the beginning of May Mehmed had complained to his chief physician of abdominal pains, but the doctor's prescription had failed to cure, and two days later the Sultan died – probably not from natural causes, but poisoned on orders from his ambitious son Bayezid. It was perhaps a fitting ending for a man who had welcomed the news of his own father's death with public joy and whose first act afterwards was to have his infant brother drowned in his bath.

Mehmed (II) was the son of Murad II by a slave girl, but his father seemed to favour him, and when Murad abdicated after fearful losses to crusader forces, he placed Mehmed on the throne at the age of twelve. Two years later Murad returned to command the empire's armies, this time victorious, but he died in 1451 when Mehmed was nineteen, and thenceforth until his death Mehmed ruled with a hand of iron.

Mehmed's abiding obsession was the capture of Constantinople, the last stronghold of the Christian Byzantine Empire that had been born in 395, when Emperor Theodosius I had split the Roman Empire between his two sons, never to be reunited.

First Mehmed neutralised Constantinople's Christian allies, Hungary and Venice, by offering them peace treaties on very favourable terms. Then he added a fleet of 31 galleys to his army, hired a Hungarian gunsmith to cast a cannon larger than any then in existence, and, to control the Bosphorus, built the Rumeli Hisari fortress (which still stands in intimidating glory) only a few miles from Constantinople.

Not all agreed with Mehmed's determination to conquer the great city, especially the grand vizier Candarli, but Mehmed would brook no argument and besieged the city on 6 April 1453, himself as commander in the field. After a siege of 54 days Constantinople fell; one of Mehmed's first acts was to order the arrest and execution of the reluctant Candarli.

But there was more to Mehmed than pure military prowess. Immediately on capturing Constantinople he headed straight for the magnificent Hagia Sophia church and converted it into a mosque. He not only fostered the Muslim faith but also brought in an Armenian patriarch and a Jewish head rabbi and re-established the Greek Orthodox Patriarchate. Transferring his capital to the city, he imported Christian merchants and offered guarantees of safety to Greek and Italian traders. Within 75 years Constantinople (by then increasingly called Istanbul) had become the largest city in Europe.

Nor were these all of Mehmed's accomplishments. He gave the Ottoman Empire a new constitution and brought philosophers and scholars to his court while accumulating a huge library of Latin and Greek works. He summoned the Venetian painter Gentile Bellini to paint his portrait (now in London's National Gallery) and to embellish the walls of his palace. Mehmed even penned a collection of his own poems.

Throughout this cultural renaissance, Mehmed remained a merciless tyrant, meting out the harshest punishment to any who opposed his wishes, becoming the prototype for the despotic Ottoman sultans who would rule in the centuries to come. He put in place the basic structures that would sustain the empire for half a millennium, largely the same structures that would bring about its final collapse in 1922.

Also on this day

1410: Anti-pope Alexander V dies, reportedly poisoned by anti-pope John XXIII * 1469: Niccolò Machiavelli is born in Florence * 1493: Pope Alexander VI publishes the first Bull Inter Caetera dividing the New World between Spain and Portugal

4 May

Sherlock Holmes goes over the falls

1891 Mr Sherlock Holmes vanished today in Switzerland and was presumed dead, most probably at the hands of his arch-antagonist Professor James Moriarty, the 'Napoleon of crime'. The celebrated London consulting detective was on a walking trip of several miles from the village of Meiringen to the hamlet of Rosenlaui, and had taken a recommended detour to see the falls of Reichenbach. Shortly before the detour, his travelling companion on the journey, a Dr Watson, also of London, had been called back to Meiringen on a medical emergency (which proved a ruse), so that Holmes was alone when he approached the falls.

Evidence gathered at the scene – two sets of footprints going towards the gorge but none returning – suggested that Holmes and his assailant met and struggled on the narrow path, then fell, locked together, into the abyss, their bodies unrecoverable in the 'dreadful cauldron of swirling water and seething foam'. The crime-scene investigation, which was conducted by local police and Dr Watson, also found an alpenstock belonging to Holmes, his silver cigarette case, and his note to Dr Watson, evidently scribbled some minutes before the end, stating that he and Moriarty were about to have a 'final discussion of those questions that lie between us'.

Holmes's death was a serious blow – not only to crime prevention but also to literature. True to his mysterious form, however, Holmes reappeared in London almost three years later, in April 1894, to resume his career as the world's first consulting detective. It turned out that it was Moriarty, and not Holmes, who had died in the falls of Reichenbach. Holmes was brought back – from the very brink – at the insistence of millions of his devoted fans around the world left shocked and grieving over his unexpected demise. For them the three years of his absence seemed more like ten – which in fact they were. 'The Final Problem', Arthur Conan Doyle's story in which Holmes met his terrible fate, was published in the December 1893 issue of the *Strand Magazine*. But Conan

Doyle did not effect his detective's remarkable reappearance until October 1903, with the publication of 'The Empty House'.

Also on this day

1814: Napoleon arrives on the Island of Elba * 1942: The American Navy defeats a Japanese fleet during the Battle of the Coral Sea

5 May

Napoleon is murdered?

1821 Today at 5.49 in the late afternoon Napoleon Bonaparte, once emperor of half of Europe and lord to 70 million people, died on the remote island of St Helena a few months before his 52nd birthday, of what was thought to be stomach cancer. His last word was a faintly whispered 'Joséphine', a wistful final thought for his first wife who had died seven years before.

Napoleon spent the last five and a half years of his life on St Helena, an island with a population of only 2,000 but with 1,400 British troops to guard against his escape. Bored to distraction and bitter at both the enemies who had defeated him and the supporters who had betrayed him, he kept a minor court of a few French officers and their wives who had followed him into exile. His last eighteen months were passed in pain and growing weakness, characterised by extreme nausea, headaches, weakened sight, insomnia, deafness and bleeding gums. Although he faced death without flinching, on the evening of 3 May 1821 he lapsed into unconsciousness, apparently paralysed, after taking a huge dose of calomel laxative that his doctors hoped would help him. Two days later he was dead.

Napoleon was buried on the island where he died in a grave twelve feet deep, lined with stone. There he remained for nineteen years until his body was returned to Paris for entombment in Les Invalides.

In the late 20th century, scientific analysis of Napoleon's hair showed residual traces of arsenic, prompting some historians to conclude that he had not died of cancer but had been murdered, probably by one of his courtiers, Count Charles Tristan de Montholon, who had poisoned his wine. Montholon's putative motive was revenge for Napoleon's affair with his wife. Equally likely is the suggestion that the British and the restored French monarchy together persuaded Montholon to administer the fatal dosage, fearing that Napoleon might once again escape and overturn the autocratic monarchies of Europe.

Also on this day

1818: Karl Marx is born in Trier, Prussia * 1835: The first passenger railway line in continental Europe opens at Allée Verte in France, eleven years after the first British line * 1850: The Risorgimento begins, as Giuseppe Garibaldi's Red Shirts invade Sicily

6 May

The duc de Bourbon is killed sacking Rome

1527 Charles II, duc de Bourbon, was the last of France's great feudal lords. Although Constable of France, he had long been at odds with his sovereign François I and even more so with François's mother Louise, whom he had rejected with disgust when she suggested he marry her.

In 1523, Bourbon became an outlaw in France by signing an illegal alliance with Holy Roman Emperor Charles V which, if effected, would have reduced France to a state of feudal anarchy.

Abandoning his own country, Bourbon was awarded command of Charles's army in Italy. By the spring of 1527, however, the army was near mutiny, having been unpaid for months. Ever the opportunist, Bourbon joined the mutineers and on 6 May led the army to Rome to perpetrate one of the bloodiest and most violent sacks of a major Western city since crusaders had sacked Constantinople half a millennium before.

As terrified Pope Clement VII took refuge in the Castel'

Sant'Angelo, the city was assaulted with brutality and thoroughness. Nuns were raped, priests murdered, and horses were stabled in St Peter's. Some 4,000 people were slain.

Despite the army's best efforts, the Castel' Sant'Angelo resisted all attempts to storm it as the Pope cowered in one of the inside rooms. The duc de Bourbon, however, was not so lucky. While directing the assault on this day he was cut down by a harquebus bullet fired by one of the Pope's defenders, the Florentine sculptor Benvenuto Cellini.

Also on this day

1758: French revolutionary Maximilien Robespierre is born * 1856: Sigmund Freud is born in Freiberg, Austria (now Pribor, Czech Republic) * 1910: King Edward VII dies in London * 1937: The German zeppelin *Hindenburg* catches fire in New Jersey, USA, killing 36 passengers * 1954: Roger Bannister runs a mile in three minutes, 59.4 seconds, the first to break the four-minute barrier

7 May

German U-boat sinks the Lusitania

1915 The great Cunard steamship *Lusitania* was 790 feet long with four tall stacks billowing black smoke. She was carrying a crew of 702 plus 1,201 predominantly British passengers, but including 188 Americans, as she headed for Southampton from New York. Although Britain was at war, no one thought the deadly German U-boats would attack a vessel carrying only passengers, especially since so many were citizens of a neutral – and powerful – United States.

In the early afternoon of 7 May the liner was nearing the west of Ireland. Lurking unseen was the German submarine U-20.

Suddenly a torpedo rocked the ship, quickly followed by a huge second explosion. In eighteen minutes the *Lusitania* was gone – with 1,198 of its passengers and crew, including 128 Americans and 63 children.

As the German submarine commander recorded in his log: 'Clean bow-shot from 700-metre range. Shot hits starboard side behind bridge. Unusually heavy explosion follows ... Many [life] boats crowded, come down bow or stern first and immediately fill and sink ... I submerge to 24 metres and go to sea.'

The German government insisted to an appalled American public that the ship had been carrying a huge quantity of explosives intended for Britain's war effort. Not so, cried the British Admiralty. High explosives on an ocean liner, endangering hundreds of innocent civilians? An evil German fabrication. By and large the Admiralty was believed, and although the US stayed out of the war for two more years, the sinking of the *Lusitania* was a critical turning point in American opinion.

Some 67 years later a British salvage team examined the wreck – only to find that someone had beaten them to it. A large square hole had been cut in the ship's deck, and the forward hold – officially carrying only foodstuffs – had been stripped clean. Further examination revealed a gaping hole in the portside bow, which could have been caused only by a huge internal explosion. But to this day the British Admiralty sticks desperately to its story.

Also on this day

1812: English poet Robert Browning is born * 1833: German composer Johannes Brahms is born in Hamburg * 1840: Composer Pyotr Tchaikovsky is born in Kamsko-Votkinsk, Russia * 1892: Yugoslav dictator Josip Broz Tito is born in Zagreb * 1954: French forces surrender to the Viet Minh at Dien Bien Phu in French Indochina (Vietnam)

8 May

The American president who was the 'reductio ad absurdum of the common man'

1884 Harry S. Truman, 31st president of the United States, was born today in a small bedroom in his parents' house in the dusty market town of Lamar, Missouri. He was another in the line of American presidents – including Lincoln and Grant – to spring from an unremarkable background.

Truman was poorly educated and never attended college. Early in life he failed as a haberdasher and spent almost a decade barely surviving as a farmer before he entered politics as a classic 'machine politician', a creature of the corrupt Kansas City party boss, Thomas Pendergast, who controlled the city's Democratic organisation. Even his election to the US Senate was largely engineered by the Pendergast machine, and his nomination to run as Franklin Roosevelt's vice-president in 1944 was the result of more back-room politics.

But with Roosevelt's sudden death in 1945, Truman found himself President of the United States, the most powerful man in the world, in the midst of a world war.

Because of his previous association with Pendergast (who was jailed for a year in 1939 for income tax evasion), small-town lack of sophistication and innate distrust of the rich and powerful, Republicans characterised the Democrat Truman as the '*reductio ad absurdum* of the common man'. And in certain ways they were right: privately Truman was strongly prejudiced against blacks and Jews. But despite these prejudices, he was a character of uncommon sense and granite integrity who famously kept a sign on his desk with the words: 'The buck stops here.'

Truman served almost eight years as President, achieving the greatest election upset in American history in 1948. His accomplishments were decisive in the 20th century: he authorised the first use of the atomic bomb to end the war with Japan, helped create the United Nations and NATO, initiated the Marshall Plan to rebuild Europe after the Second World War, and led the free world's confrontation with Communist aggression by authorising the Berlin Air Lift and intervening in Korea.

Harry Truman died on 26 December 1972, a few months short of his 89th birthday.

Also on this day

44 BC: Julius Caesar adopts Octavian, the future Emperor Augustus * 1660: Charles II of England is proclaimed King by Parliament * 1794:

French chemist Antoine Laurent Lavoisier is guillotined * 1873: English philosopher John Stuart Mill dies * 1880: French novelist Gustave Flaubert dies * 1903: French post-impressionist painter Paul Gauguin dies in the Marquesas Islands

9 May

Birth of the last Habsburg empress

1892 She was called Zita Maria Grazia Adelgonda Michela Raffaella Gabriella Giuseppina Antonia Luisa Agnese, born this day near Viareggio in Italy. Her father was the Duke of Parma, but the family was poor, even if it did claim descent from Louis XI of France.

At nineteen Zita married Archduke Charles, the great nephew of Emperor Franz Joseph of Austria. The world was at peace and the Austro-Hungarian Empire looked as if it could survive for ever, with its tireless leader Franz Joseph on the throne.

But fate would change all that. First, the heir to the throne Franz-Ferdinand was gunned down at Sarajevo. Then the Emperor died in 1916. Suddenly Zita's husband was Emperor and she the Empress in the middle of a world war.

But not for long. Just two years later Austria-Hungary had lost the war and Charles was forced to abdicate. Twenty-nine months later he was dead. Empress Zita lived on, mostly in exile, spending 63 years in Switzerland and the United States, never relinquishing her claim to a throne that no longer existed.

Finally, at the grand age of 96, Zita died on 14 March 1989. She was buried with a massive state funeral in Vienna's St Stephen's Cathedral, her horse-drawn hearse carrying her casket past thousands of spectators through the heart of the city to the Capuchin Church, where she was to be buried in the crypt with 142 other members of the Habsburg dynasty. There the traditional ritual for Habsburg dead was performed once more.

At the door to the crypt the Master of Ceremonies knocks three times with his staff.

'Who desires entrance?', asks a simple monk from within.

'Zita, the Empress of Austria', responds the Master of Ceremonies, 'crowned Queen of Hungary, Queen of Bohemia, of Dalmatia, Croatia, Slavonia, Galicia ...', and so on and on with Zita's dozens of titles.

'I know her not', says the monk.

Once more the Master knocks; once more the monk demands, 'Who desires entrance?'

'Zita, her majesty, Empress and Queen.'

'I know her not.'

A third time the Master knocks. 'Who desires entrance?'

'Zita', he replies, 'a mortal, sinful human.' (*Ein sterblicher, sündiger Mensch.*)

'So let her come in', at last answers the monk as he opens the door.

So was buried an impoverished Italian noblewoman who was the last Habsburg to wear a crown, in a line that had worn its first in the year 1282.

Also on this day

1386: England and Portugal sign a peace treaty, the oldest in Europe still in force * 1805: German poet Friedrich von Schiller dies in Weimar * 1936: Italian troops capture Addis Ababa in Ethiopia and annexe the country * 1941: British ships capture the German submarine U-110 along with its Enigma encoding machine

10 May

Michelangelo starts work on the Sistine Chapel

1508 Today Michelangelo Buonarroti started work on what is often considered the greatest masterpiece – or collection of masterpieces – the world has yet known, on the ceiling of the Sistine Chapel.

This breathtaking fresco was painted on the orders of that

irascible pope, Julius II, who was the greatest patron of the arts who ever presided over the Vatican. At first Michelangelo was furious at the commission because he considered himself a sculptor, not a painter, and had done little painting since he was an apprentice in Ghirlandajo's studio in his teens. He suspected that the Pope had chosen him on the cunning recommendation of the architect Donato Bramante, who, jealous of Michelangelo's talents, had proposed him only because his lack of experience painting frescoes would doom him to failure. But Michelangelo knew that, if he declined the commission, he might never get another from Julius, and he undoubtedly thought his own genius would carry him through.

Julius wanted the ceiling to feature scenes from the New Testament, but the obdurate Michelangelo doggedly insisted on the Old Testament, believing it more dramatic, and proved his point with the work's centrepiece, 'The Creation of Adam'.

It took almost four and a half years to complete this great work (although Michelangelo downed brushes for almost a year in 1510–11 when no payments were forthcoming), and in all the painting covers some 10,000 square feet where more than 300 individuals are depicted. Mixed with the profound religious symbolism of the work are innumerable oak trees and oak leaves. These were the homage that Michelangelo paid to his papal patron, whose family name, della Rovere, means 'of the oaks'. Some critics have noted that Michelangelo's women are as sturdy and muscled as his men, possibly because his models for all the figures were men.

The painting of the Sistine Chapel was not only time consuming, it was also back-breaking, as Michelangelo spent hours at a time lying on his back on a scaffold as he painted. All of his work required tremendous effort. As the great painter once earthily remarked: 'Nelle mie opere caco sangue.' (In my works I shit blood.)

The chapel was officially opened on 31 October 1512 when Pope Julius II first celebrated Mass there, but even then Michelangelo's work in the chapel was not done. Julius died early in 1513, and the great painter took a twenty-year rest. But in 1534 he returned to create 'The Last Judgement' under the patronage of Pope Paul III.

Also on this day

1774: Louis XV dies of smallpox at Versailles * 1818: American revolutionary Paul Revere dies * 1857: The Sepoy revolt at Meerut triggers the Indian Mutiny * 1863: American General Stonewall Jackson dies five days after being wounded by friendly fire during the Battle of Chancellorsville * 1940: Germany begins the invasion of western Europe on the same day that Winston Churchill becomes British Prime Minister

11 May

An English PM is assassinated

1812 Had he not been assassinated, Spenser Perceval would have remained one of England's most obscure Prime Ministers, even in his own time noted primarily for his icy demeanour and religious bigotry.

At 49, Perceval had been a totally undistinguished Prime Minister for three years when, on 11 May 1812, he walked into the lobby of the Houses of Parliament just after five in the evening. As he entered, a failed English businessman named John Bellingham stepped in front of him and shot him in the chest. Bellingham had no personal grudge against Perceval, but believed that somehow the government should recompense him for a lifetime of failures in business.

Hands flying to his chest, Perceval fell to the floor crying, 'I am murdered, murdered', just before he died.

The government wasted no time with Bellingham, who had made no attempt to escape. In less than a week he had been tried and hanged.

Perceval remains the only British Prime Minister ever to have been assassinated, not a bad record compared with four American presidents and five Russian Romanov tsars.

Also on this day

AD 330: Emperor Constantine dedicates Constantinople as the capital of the Roman Empire * 1778: William Pitt the Elder (First Earl of Chatham) dies at Hayes, Kent * 1857: Indian mutineers seize Delhi * 1865: Confederate cavalry general Jeb Stewart is killed in action during the American Civil War * 1888: American balladeer Irving Berlin is born

12 May

Florence Nightingale, the Lady with the Lamp

1820 'Flit on, cheering angel!' With this whimsically appropriate anagram did Lewis Carroll of *Alice in Wonderland* fame celebrate Florence Nightingale, the dedicated, heroic, neurotic nurse who transformed the idea of military hospitals during the Crimean War.

Florence Nightingale was born today in Florence, where her wealthy parents were living. They named her after the city they loved. When her family moved back to Derbyshire, she was educated at home by her father, who taught her history and philosophy as well as Latin, Greek, French, German and Italian.

Earnest and somewhat of a mystic, at sixteen Nightingale thought she had heard God's voice telling her she had a serious mission in life, but it was only ten years later that she came to realise that the mission was to help mankind by becoming a nurse, no fit occupation at the time for a woman of her station and means.

Despite her father's strong reservations, in 1850 Nightingale went to Alexandria to study nursing, then moved on to Germany and finally, in 1853, returned to England where she became the superintendent for the Hospital for Invalid Gentlewomen in London. Then came the Crimean War. Soon grisly descriptions of the ghastly conditions of the British wounded flooded into England.

Determined to help, Nightingale offered her services to the War Office and was given authority over all nursing in British military hospitals in Turkey. In November 1854 she arrived with 38 other nurses in Scutari near Istanbul, the place to which thousands of wounded and sick British soldiers were shipped across the Black Sea from Crimean battlefields. After she saw the filthy, rat-infested conditions of the main hospital, she wrote: 'I have been well acquainted with the dwellings of the worst parts of most of the great cities in Europe but have never been in any atmosphere which I could compare with that of the Barrack Hospital at night.' At first both resented and ignored by male doctors, who thought a theatre of war no place for a woman, she quickly set about tending the sick and wounded and improving the appalling level of hygiene.

Reflecting the stern morality of the day, no nurses were allowed in the wards after eight in the evening, the only exception being Nightingale herself. Every night she made her rounds carrying a lantern, chatting with the wounded and giving encouragement. From this she earned the nickname of 'The Lady with the Lamp'. But most important, thanks to her tireless efforts and understanding of the need for cleanliness, the mortality rate among the wounded was significantly reduced.

When the war finally dragged to a close in 1856, Nightingale returned to London, a very famous, widely beloved, and almost mythic person for her heroic deeds. But she refused all honours while continuing to be involved in what she saw as her mission, advising on hospital administration and founding schools for nurses. In pressing her reforms she was dealing – as probably only a wealthy, well-connected woman could in those days – with the very highest people in the British government and society, including Queen Victoria, who gave her a diamond brooch designed by Prince Albert bearing the inscription 'Blessed are the merciful'. Among her innovations were bells for patients to summon nurses, dumb-waiters to move food up from the kitchens, and hot water piped to all floors.

But, unwilling to accept awards or be lionised, publicly Nightingale had virtually vanished, and she became a bed-ridden invalid, apparently suffering from some kind of post-traumatic stress disorder. Even then she continued to receive official visitors and to write.

In 1861 she wrote *Notes on Nursing*, in which with tart good humour she revealed: 'No man, not even a doctor, ever gives any other definition of what a nurse should be than this – "devoted and obedient". This definition might do just as well for a porter. It might even do for a horse.'

Growing older, confined to her bed, Nightingale started to lose her sight, and when she passed 80 she became completely blind. At 87 she achieved another first for a woman when Edward VII awarded her the Order of Merit.

Florence Nightingale finally died on 13 August 1910 at the age of 90. Just prior to her death she had declined the offer of burial in Westminster Abbey.

Also on this day

1812: English painter and author of the *Book of Nonsense* Edward Lear is born in London * 1949: The Russians call an end to the Berlin Blockade

13 May

The Terror begins

1793 Today began the Terror, that frenzy of republican butchery with which the rabid revolutionaries of the French Revolution cleansed the state of aristocratic blood. Later the ferocious Joseph Fouché offered this heartless justification: 'The blood of criminals fertilises the soil of liberty and establishes power on sure foundations.'

The very epicentre of the Terror was the great open square on the Seine that today we know as the place de la Concorde, now one of Paris's most spectacularly beautiful. But in 1793 its beauty was overshadowed by the sight of the guillotine, raised on a platform to give the spectators a better view, where 1,343 victims were beheaded.

The place de la Concorde was built between 1755 and 1775 and originally named for the man who ordered its construction, King

Louis XV. Initially a large equestrian statue of the King dominated it, but that was demolished during the early days of the Revolution, and the place Louis XV fittingly changed its name to the place de la Révolution.

During the Terror, thousands of people congregated here daily to see the tumbrels of the condemned arrive. Seated around the scaffold with wine and bread bought from enterprising grocers, the spectators enjoyed the sight and smell of running blood. The notorious *tricoteuses* sat knitting to the swish of the blade and the cries of terror from those waiting their turn on the scaffold.

Here the Revolution devoured its first victims and eventually itself. Not only Louis XVI, Marie Antoinette, Philippe Égalité and Charlotte Corday but also Danton, Saint-Just and Robespierre were all beheaded here.

One of the most pathetic must have been poor Madame du Barry, who on 8 December 1793 was carried to the guillotine screaming in terror, 'You are going to hurt me! Please don't hurt me!' Now a haggard 50, she had once been the ravishing, silly and frivolous mistress of Louis XV. Since Louis's death nineteen years before, she had been living in luxury outside Paris, but the mob had not forgotten her. Dragged from her château, she rent the air with pleas for her life, offering her riches to any who would spare her, as the tumbrel carried her through the city. As the poet Lamartine later remarked: 'She died a coward because she died neither for her views, her virtue nor her love, but for her vice. She dishonoured the scaffold as she had dishonoured the throne.' So, paralysed by fear, the courtesan who had once accompanied a king lost her head in the square that he had built.

Also on this day

1717: Austrian Empress Maria Theresa is born * 1787: British ships with 778 prisoners leave Portsmouth to found Sydney * 1846: The United States declares war against Mexico * 1882: French painter Georges Braque is born at Argenteuil

14 May

Henri IV is murdered

1610 On one of the blackest days in French history, today King Henri IV, France's greatest king, was stabbed to death as he rode in his carriage.

Henri was France's first Bourbon king. Inheriting the throne when the country was being torn asunder by the Religious Wars, he ended nearly 40 years of religious conflict and reunified the country. His most significant single achievement was the Edict of Nantes that gave freedom to France's Protestants, including the right to hold public office. 'Those who follow their consciences are of my religion', he declared, 'and I am of the religion of those who are brave and good'.

Once peace was restored, Henri gave the nation the kind of economic impetus it needed, with innovative programmes such as the introduction of the silk industry. He was famous for his wish to give every Frenchman *une poule au pot*, a chicken in the pot, every Sunday. He also added greatly to the beauty of Paris by building the place Royale, now the place des Vosges. On top of his many achievements for the nation, Henri also had time to indulge himself in numerous scandalous love affairs and came to be known as *le vert galant* (the old playboy).

By 1610 Henri was 56 years old and, perhaps fearing death, had premonitions of a violent end. His wife Marie de' Medici had foretold the specific method, having dreamed that Henri would be stabbed, and an astrologer even predicted the correct date. But when 14 May arrived, Henri shrugged off the warnings, determined to visit a sick friend.

When Henri's carriage stopped momentarily at the corner of the rue de la Ferronerie and the rue Saint-Honoré, a fanatical Catholic named François Ravaillac reached through the carriage window and stabbed the King. Henri tried to defend himself, only to be stabbed a second time, this time mortally, as the knife pierced his lungs.

Henri's murderer claimed he was executing a divine mission for the Church. In truth he was probably the tool of some of Henri's enemies, notably the duc d'Eperon (who was with Henri in the carriage and had singularly failed to prevent the assassination) and one of Henri's ex-mistresses, Henriette d'Entrangues. Fittingly for such a crime, Ravaillac was drawn and quartered thirteen days later in the beautiful square that Henri had created, the place des Vosges.

Also on this day

1607: John Smith and other colonists disembark at what was to become Jamestown on the Chesapeake Bay in North America * 1727: English landscape painter Thomas Gainsborough is born * 1796: English doctor Edward Jenner administers the first smallpox vaccination

15 May

The first Streltsy revolt in Russia

1682 The Streltsy (or musketeers) were Russia's only permanent armed force, acting as guardsmen, policemen and firemen, all in one. In May 1682 there was a power vacuum at the heart of Russia. Tsar Fedor had died the previous month and his only male heirs – a son and his half-brother – were both under age. This left two formidable women to struggle for power. One was Sophia, elder sister to one brother and half-sister to the other. The other was Natalya, second and surviving wife of Fedor and mother of the younger son named Peter.

Fearing her stepmother but desperate for power, Sophia secretly began to encourage the Streltsy to assert themselves and take charge of the land. On 15 May violence broke out. Thousands of Streltsy surrounded the Kremlin and then, before the eyes of ten-year-old Peter and his brother, literally tore to pieces two chief government ministers. And this was only the beginning. For the next six months the Streltsy looted and murdered, out of control, until Sophia's power was finally consolidated. By November the Streltsy revolt was over, but young Peter was never to forget it.

Peter waited sixteen long years, but by 1698 he had become Russia's sole and undisputed Tsar. Then, once again, the Streltsy staged a rebellion. But this time Peter had an army, and the revolt was quickly broken.

Not content simply at reaffirming his power, Peter wanted revenge. He ordered all 1,750 prisoners to the torture: they were flogged, roasted, burned with timbers and subject to the strappado (a torture by which the victim is tied to a rope, made to fall from a height almost to the ground and then stopped with a sudden jerk). Only to younger Streltsy did he show 'mercy'. They were branded, flogged, had their noses slit and their ears sliced off and were sent into exile. All the others were executed, some 80 by Peter himself, who had also personally conducted much of the torture.

Not surprisingly, there were no more revolts against Tsar Peter, known to history as Peter the Great.

Also on this day

1702: The War of the Spanish Succession begins * 1773: Future Austrian chancellor Klemens Metternich is born in Coblenz, Germany * 1847: In Vienna, Ignaz Semmelweiss institutes the first programme of hospital hygiene

16 May

End of a fairytale

1703 Charles Perrault thought of himself as an accomplished poet, and when he died today in Paris at the age of 75, no doubt he hoped it would be for his classic French verse that he would be remembered.

Sadly for Perrault, his poetry is now long forgotten, but happily his greatest work lives on. For Perrault was the first to write down classic fairy tales such as 'Sleeping Beauty', 'Cinderella', 'Puss in Boots' and 'Little Red Riding Hood'. (He beat the Grimm brothers to publication by 115 years.)

Perrault entitled his collection *Histoires ou contes du temps passé*. In the book's frontispiece is inscribed: 'Contes de ma mère Loye.' ('Loye' being a play on *l'oie*, goose.) Virtually every European and British child has loved Mother Goose ever since.

Also on this day

1763: James Boswell meets Dr Samuel Johnson for the first time * 1770: The future Louis XVI marries Marie Antoinette at Versailles * 1804: Napoleon is declared Emperor * 1928: The first Academy Awards ceremonies take place in Hollywood

17 May

British troops relieve Mafeking

1900 When the war in South Africa broke out in the autumn of 1899, the Boers immediately laid siege to several British-held towns. The longest and bloodiest of these sieges – and the only one to introduce a new word to the English language – took place at Mafeking, finally relieved by a British column at 7.00 this evening after 217 days of constant blockade, intermittent shelling, and occasional raids.

At first, the Boers outnumbered the Mafeking defenders by six to one, but they reckoned without the commander of the British garrison. He was a cool customer, a veteran African campaigner named Colonel Robert Baden-Powell (B-P, he was called) who offered a skilful and imaginative defence throughout the ordeal. For the British, the strategic value of holding Mafeking was simply to draw Boer forces away from the lightly defended Cape Colony until reinforcements arrived from Great Britain. B-P was the right man for the job.

With the garrison in Mafeking were several newspaper correspondents who filed their stories by telegraph, filling in their readers around the world with the events and atmosphere of the siege: tales of heroism, cowardice, raids, escapes, near misses, and the like. The public was enthralled. On 30 April, the 200th day of the siege, a cocky Boer commander sent a message into Mafeking proposing a cricket match between the two sides, to which B-P responded: 'I should like nothing better – after the match in which we are at present engaged is over. But just now we are having our innings and have so far scored 200 days, not out ... and we are having a very enjoyable game.' As it turned out, the game was just about over.

News of the relief of Mafeking produced riotous, hysterical street demonstrations around the British world, especially in London. It also produced this entry in the *Oxford English Dictionary*: 'Maffick. v.i. Celebrate uproariously, rejoice extravagantly, esp. on an occasion of national celebration (orig. the relief of the British garrison in Mafeking, South Africa, in May 1900).'

After the mafficking was over, the Boer War continued for another two years, extracting from all concerned inordinate amounts of human suffering, devastation, and money. In time, B-P went home to England, eventually retired from the Army a general, and in 1907, employing the fieldcraft he had learned and taught his troops during his days in the veldt, he founded the Boy Scouts and, a few years later, the Girl Guides.

Also on this day

1510: Italian painter Sandro Botticelli dies in Florence * 1792: The New York Stock Exchange is established at 70 Wall Street in New York * 1814: Russian anarchist Mikhail Bakunin is born in Premulkine, Russia * 1838: French diplomat Charles-Maurice, Prince de Talleyrand, dies

18 May

Eleanor of Aquitaine marries her second king

1152 Little in documented history sings with such romance as the passionate, glorious and ultimately tragic saga of King Henry II of England and his beautiful wife, Eleanor of Aquitaine.

Eleanor was unquestionably the most fascinating woman of the Middle Ages. Duchess of Aquitaine in south-west France, she was Europe's richest woman in her own right, and her capital was Bordeaux, city of troubadours. Dark haired and dark eyed, she is reputed to have been both witty and physically alluring.

First married to dull Louis VII of France, Eleanor drove him to annulment after fifteen years of marriage and not a little dalliance on her part, once complaining that she 'had married a monk, not a king'. But within two months of shedding one king she married a man shortly to be another, for on this day in 1152 she wed young Henry Plantagenet, duc d'Anjou, in her capital city. Henry was only nineteen while Eleanor was 30, but it didn't seem to matter. They may have married to combine their vast inheritances, but the attraction between the two was certainly strong; Eleanor was nearly six months pregnant.

Henry and Eleanor had eight children together, and only a year and a half after their marriage he became King of England. He would be a great king, too, and found a dynasty that would last over 300 years.

Even Henry's and Eleanor's children were from storybooks: Richard the Lion-Heart, the great warrior, and King John, England's most despicable king.

Ultimately there would be tragedy. Henry would tire of his wife and above all of her political scheming, and he would imprison her in gentle confinement for sixteen years. Eventually Henry himself would be hounded to death by his own rebellious sons.

Also on this day

1525: Flemish painter Pieter Bruegel the Elder is born * 1803: England declares war on Napoleon's France * 1846: Russian jeweller Peter Carl Fabergé is born * 1868: The last Russian tsar, Nicholas II, is born

19 May

The mysterious life of Lawrence of Arabia

1935 Today T.E. Lawrence died in self-imposed obscurity, at the age of 46, from injuries sustained in a motorcycle accident. The obscurity he maintained for thirteen years was shelter from the intense public enthusiasm and media scrutiny that greeted his exploits in the First World War as 'Lawrence of Arabia'. He had suddenly become world famous after the American journalist Lowell Thomas visited Palestine in 1917 and made films of the Arab Revolt, in which Colonel Lawrence, a British intelligence officer, had been instrumental as an advisor and leader.

As the war ended, Thomas's film and lecture presentations, seen by millions in Britain and America, showed Lawrence in Arab dress against desert landscapes, surrounded by fierce tribesmen mounted on camels and waving rifles. For audiences weary of four years' stalemate and carnage on the Western front, the scenes were irresistible: a diminutive Englishman leading Britain's Arab allies in a series of daring – and successful – guerrilla raids against the Turks, all in the promise of an independent Arab homeland in Syria when the war was over.

At war's end, however, it became known that Britain had signed a secret wartime treaty with France in which the two nations agreed to carve up between them Turkish possessions in the Middle East. Under the treaty, France was to receive Syria, which the Arabs had helped conquer during the war and fully expected to be within their homeland. Lawrence was dismayed at Britain's betrayal of its original promise to the Arabs. At a private ceremony with King George V at Buckingham Palace, where he was about to receive a DSO and the Order of the Bath, Lawrence unexpectedly refused the decorations. Surprised, the King was left, in his own words, 'holding the box in my hand'. Later, Lawrence told Winston Churchill that the refusal was the only way he knew to make the King aware of what had been done in his name.

In 1919 Lawrence, dressed once again in Arab attire, attended the Versailles Peace Conference to argue the Arab case, but the post-war settlement endorsed the Syrian mandate in France. For a while, Lawrence worked as an advisor on Middle Eastern matters to Churchill at the Colonial Office, but with the cause betrayed in which he had invested so much of himself and for which he had become a legend, he found the hero's role impossible to sustain.

Seeking anonymity and perhaps the comradeship of his war years – and no doubt as atonement for what he considered his failure – Lawrence abruptly gave up public life in 1922 and under a pseudonym enlisted as a recruit in the Royal Air Force. His cover soon blown by an attentive press, he joined the Tank Corps as a private. He returned to the Air Force as T.E. Shaw, serving for a time in Karachi where he translated *The Odyssey*. In 1926 *The Seven Pillars of Wisdom*, his account of the Arab Revolt, was published in a limited edition. In time it would be acknowledged a great classic of war writing. Lawrence left military service in 1935 to live in Dorset.

Among those who attended his funeral were Winston Churchill and the poet Siegfried Sassoon. King George V wrote to Lawrence's brother: 'Your brother's name will live in history and the King gratefully recognises his distinguished services to his country and feels that it is tragic that the end should have come in this manner to a life so full of promise.'

Also on this day

1536: English Queen Anne Boleyn is beheaded * 1890: Vietnamese leader Ho Chi Minh is born * 1898: British politician William Gladstone dies in Hawarden

20 May

Napoleon creates the Légion d'Honneur

1802 When we see a Frenchman with a red rosette or thin red ribbon in his buttonhole we know he has been recognised by his government for some significant achievement. We know he has been awarded the Légion d'Honneur or Legion of Honour.

During the French Revolution all the orders and decorations of the monarchist regime were abolished, so on 19 May 1802 (28 Floréal, Year X, according to the Revolutionary calendar) First Consul Napoleon Bonaparte proposed the Legion of Honour, insisting that, unlike most medals, it be open to all, soldiers and civilians alike, without regard to birth or religion. The following day the law setting up the new Order was passed.

In Napoleon's time about 48,000 men became part of the Legion, only 1,200 of them civilians. Even after Napoleon's fall the Legion of Honour was retained by kings and republics alike, but with ever increasing inflation of those elected. Just before the Second World War there were almost 320,000 members. Finally in 1962 the French government set the limit at 125,000. As evidence of the high regard in which this award is still held, the Legion's highest-ranking member is the President of France.

About two-thirds of those awarded with the Legion of Honour have been from the military services, the remainder being civilians. To earn it, civilians must have at least twenty years of significant achievement, while soldiers must have displayed extraordinary bravery.

For its first hundred years there were virtually no women recipients of the Legion of Honour (less than 1 per cent in 1912), but now women represent about one fifth of the new appointments.

Today, some two centuries since Napoleon first conceived the idea, the Legion of Honour remains France's highest award, civilian or military.

Also on this day

1444: Italian painter Sandro Botticelli is born * 1506: Christopher Columbus dies in Valladolid * 1688: English writer Alexander Pope is born * 1799: French novelist Honoré de Balzac is born in Tours * 1834: French democrat the marquis de Lafayette is born * 1902: The US ends the occupation of Cuba and it becomes a sovereign, independent nation

21 May

Lindbergh solos the Atlantic (followed by a woman)

1927, 1932 'I first saw the lights of Paris a little before 10 p.m., or 5 p.m., New York time, and a few minutes later I was circling the Eiffel Tower at an altitude of about four thousand feet.' Minutes later he touched down at Le Bourget Airport, where 10,000 delirious onlookers brushed aside the police cordon and rushed onto the runway to cheer his arrival. As he stepped down from his plane the police lifted him to their shoulders and carried him through the frantic crowd. Charles Lindbergh had just become the first person ever to fly non-stop from New York to Paris, covering 3,610 miles in 33½ hours.

At 7.52 the previous morning Lindbergh had trundled down the dirt runway at Roosevelt Field in Long Island in *The Spirit of St Louis*, his single-engine, high-wing monoplane only 28 feet long with a wingspan of just 46 feet. Heavily laden with fuel, he barely cleared some obstructions at the runway's end: 'I passed over a tractor by about fifteen feet and a telephone line by about twenty', he later recalled.

Lindbergh's route took him over Long Island Sound and north to Cape Cod and Nova Scotia, and then across the Atlantic as night fell. Flying through a heavy fog with no moon, he manoeuvred around threatening cloudbanks, sometimes only a few feet above the wave tops.

The following day he first knew he was approaching Europe when he sighted a small fishing boat. Soon he was flying over Ireland, then England and across the English Channel. Then 'the sun went down shortly after passing Cherbourg and soon the beacons along the Paris–London airway became visible'. Before long he was landing at Le Bourget.

The day following his flight more huge crowds cheered Lindbergh in front of the American Embassy in Paris, and President Gaston Doumerque awarded him the Legion of Honour. When Lindbergh returned to the United States (by ship this time), a convoy of warships and fighter craft accompanied him as he approached Washington, where President Coolidge presented him with the Distinguished Flying Cross.

On Lindbergh's arrival in New York the financial markets were closed for 'Lindbergh Day'. Ten thousand soldiers and sailors led the parade up Broadway through cheering throngs and ticker tape. Over 4 million people lined the route, the biggest welcome the city had ever given.

On 21 May 1932, exactly five years after Lindbergh had landed in Paris, a slender, dark-haired American named Amelia Earhart touched down in a field near Londonderry in Northern Ireland after only fourteen hours and 56 minutes in the air. 'After scaring most of the cows in the neighborhood', she later wrote, 'I pulled up in a farmer's back yard'. As she had somewhat lost her way, she asked the farmer where she was. 'In Gallagher's pasture', he replied. She had just become the first woman ever to solo across the Atlantic.

Earhart had started her historic flight from Harbor Grace, Newfoundland in a Lockheed Vega. Carrying only soup and tomato juice to sustain her, she used smelling salts to keep her awake, as she drank neither coffee nor tea. In spite of the strong winds and mechanical problems that slowed her down, her flight was faster than Lindbergh's (although the distance was also shorter).

Earhart's transatlantic solo catapulted her into enduring fame, especially with American women, for whom she became an early feminist icon. Like Lindbergh, she was feted and celebrated, receiving the National Geographic Society gold medal from President Herbert Hoover and the Distinguished Flying Cross from Congress – the first woman so honoured.

Also on this day

427 BC: Plato is born * 1471: German painter Albrecht Dürer is born in Nuremberg * 1471: Henry VI is murdered in the Wakefield Tower of the Tower of London * 1881: Clara Barton founds the American Red Cross

22 May

Constantine the Great, the emperor who legalised Christianity

AD 337 Today on Whit Sunday at Ankyrona, on the outskirts of Nicomedia in Bythnia (now Izmit in Turkey), the Roman Emperor Constantine the Great died after a reign of 31 years, the longest since Augustus three centuries before.

During his time in power Constantine transformed for ever the world he lived in. He reunited the Roman Empire for the first time since Diocletian had divided it in AD 284, he created the great city of Constantinople and moved the empire's capital there from Rome, and he made Christianity the favoured religion of Western civilisation.

Nonetheless, through the long telescope of history, Constantine remains somehow opaque, lacking human dimension. We know he was imposing in stature and strength, and in 4th-century statuary he looks like an amiable but somewhat slow-witted rugby fullback, with his cap of curly hair, his large trusting eyes, his slightly jutting ears and his thrusting full jaw. His personality is more difficult to understand.

Even the historians of his time were split about Constantine's nature. Christians portray him (as he seemed to see himself) as the thirteenth Apostle for his conversion of his Empire to Christianity, while contemporary pagans describe him as an evil tyrant who savagely crushed all opposition and squandered the empire's money for his own pleasure.

By all accounts, the laws that Constantine promulgated were repressive. Apparently a faithful husband, he seems to have been particularly disturbed by what he saw as sexual misconduct. Rapists, including men who simply ran off with their girlfriends, were burned alive, as were girls who eloped from their family's home. Any servant who aided an elopement was executed by having molten lead poured down his throat. Constantine even had his own son Crispus executed, believing him guilty of adultery. When he later discovered that his son was innocent and his second wife Fausta had falsely implicated him (or, another story goes, when she was caught in bed with a slave), she too was killed, held in a bath where the temperature was raised until she suffocated in the steam.

Constantine was 63 when he died. He had been campaigning against Persia when he fell ill and, en route back to his capital at Constantinople, he was forced to stop near Nicomedia, too sick to travel further. With the approach of death, he discarded his robes of imperial purple for the white of a Christian Neophyte and at last agreed to be baptised, this emperor who had been attempting for the past 25 years to convert an entire empire.

No sooner was Constantine dead, however, than on his instructions his corpse was brought to Constantinople where his attendants stretched him out on his golden bed in the imperial apartments. The body was reclothed in royal purple, with the imperial diadem on its head. Then, as Gibbon describes: 'The forms of the court were strictly maintained. Every day, at the appointed hours, the principal officers of the state, the army and the household, approaching the person of their sovereign with bended knees and a composed countenance, offered their respectful homage as seriously as if he had been still alive ... Constantine alone, by the peculiar indulgence of Heaven, had reigned after his death.'

Shortly, however, he was buried in the Church of the Apostles that he had built. Meanwhile, back in Rome, the capital he had visited only once in the last twenty years of his life, the Senate deified him like the pagan emperors of old.

Also on this day

1455: The Wars of the Roses begin with the Battle of St Albans * 1813: German composer Richard Wagner is born in Leipzig * 1859: British writer Sir Arthur Conan Doyle is born in Edinburgh * 1885: French novelist Victor Hugo dies in Paris * 1939: Adolf Hitler and Benito Mussolini create the Axis by signing a 'Pact of Steel'

23 May

Savonarola is burned at the stake in the Piazza della Signoria

1498 Girolamo Savonarola had the death's head of a fanatic: ascetic, hollow cheeks beneath his great beak of a nose, full, rubbery lips and piercing green eyes that were said to glow with inner zeal. Born in Ferrara in 1452, he became a Dominican friar whose principal concern was to attack pleasures of the flesh and independence of the spirit for the glory of a cleansed and purified Church.

Savonarola moved to Florence in 1489 and within two years was the most controversial figure in the city, castigating the gentry for corruption, pleasure-seeking and vanity. His aim was nothing less than the subjugation of all Florence, including the government, to his version of God's law.

Savonarola's influence grew; he had accurately predicted the deaths of Lorenzo the Magnificent and King Ferrante of Naples, and he interpreted Charles VIII of France's invasion of Tuscany in 1494 as the scourge of God he had so long foreseen.

The power vacuum left when Charles VIII left Tuscany thrust Savonarola into de facto control of Florence, and the next four years were filled with grim religiosity that often included the ritual burning of 'vanities' ranging from make-up to sumptuous clothing and jewellery. The bonfires sometimes incinerated sensual paintings even by such masters as Botticelli.

As Savonarola's power grew, so did his list of enemies. The most dangerous of these was Alexander VI, the dissolute and calculating Borgia Pope who was determined to bring the friar to heel. Alexander particularly objected to Savonarola's claim to direct communication with God, thereby putting himself above the Church and, by implication, above even the Pope himself.

After Savonarola refused to come to Rome to explain himself, Alexander tried to bribe him into silence with the offer of a cardinal's hat. 'A red hat?', Savonarola replied with scorn, 'No hat will I have but that of a martyr, reddened with my own blood.' Finally Alexander excommunicated him, but Savonarola merely advised the Pope to take immediate care of his own salvation and continued to harangue the crowds of Florence.

Savonarola's intransigence led to Alexander's final threat: unless the friar was sent to Rome, all of Florence would be placed under interdict, meaning that there could be no Mass, no taking of Communion, and no weddings, baptisms or funerals. This was the moment his enemies were waiting for. The Franciscan monks of the town, long jealous of the Dominicans' predominance, challenged his religious supremacy, and the rich and powerful families, longing for a return to more civilised days, stirred up the Florentine mob. Finally, on Palm Sunday in 1498, Savonarola was chased from his pulpit and arrested by the civil government. Torture soon led to confession and confession to conviction for heresy and promoting a schism in the True Church.

On 23 May a great scaffold was erected in Florence's Piazza della Signoria, and on it Savonarola and two of his most faithful followers were strangled just before their bodies were put to the torch. 'The culprits were burned in a few hours', wrote one eyewitness, 'and their arms and legs gradually dropped off. Then stones were thrown at the parts of the bodies still hanging, in order to make them fall, as there was a fear that the mob would get hold of them. Then the executioner and his helpers cut down the post and burned it to the ground, bringing up more wood and stirring the fire over the dead bodies so that every piece was consumed. They then brought wagons and ... took the last of the ashes to the Arno near the Ponte Vecchio so that no remains should ever be found.'

Also on this day

1335: Mongol leader Tamerlane the Great is born * 1533: Henry VIII divorces Catherine of Aragon * 1701: Scottish-born buccaneer Captain Kidd is hanged for piracy * 1706: The Duke of Marlborough defeats the French at the Battle of Ramillies * 1945: Hitler's second-in-command Heinrich Himmler commits suicide

24 May

Peter Minuit buys Manhattan for 60 guilders' worth of trinkets

1626 On this day Peter Minuit, a director of the Dutch West India Company's North American colony, made a historic barter with a local Indian tribe: in exchange for some 60 guilders' worth of pots, pans, fish hooks, tools and cloth, the Company received possession of a large island at the mouth of the Hudson River.

Peter Minuit, a ruddy, round-faced man with a goatee and large upward-sweeping moustache, was a Dutch-speaking German, born in Wesel in Germany. Two years before his appointment as director, the Dutch West India Company had established the colony of New Netherland in the lower Hudson valley and had landed its first settlers there, setting up shop in small communities on the shores of the great bay. But just as the new settlements were finding their feet, war broke out between local Indian tribes over the fur trade with the colonists. In an attempt to provide protection for the fledgling settlements, Director Minuit bought Manhattan Island – a name derived from an Algonquin Indian word meaning 'island of hills' – and moved the settlers to its southern tip. He called the new town New Amsterdam and ordered a wooden fort built at its centre. (Since American dollars did not exist in the early 17th century, the traditional tale that Minuit bought Manhattan for $24 is an anachronism, based on calculations by the 19th-century historian Edward O'Callaghan.)

In 1631 the Dutch West India Company called Minuit back to Holland and after more New World adventures, some for the Swedes, he was drowned in a hurricane in the West Indies in 1638.

Even without Minuit's leadership, however, New Amsterdam continued to prosper, but in 1664 the despotic and controversial governor Peter Stuyvesant was forced to cede it to the British during the Second Anglo-Dutch War when a powerful fleet of British warships sailed into the harbour. The British renamed the city New York in honour of the King's brother, the Duke of York (later James II).

Also on this day

1543: Polish astronomer Nicolas Copernicus dies in Frauenberg *
1685: Physicist Gabriel Fahrenheit is born in Danzig, Poland * 1743:
French revolutionary Jean-Paul Marat is born * 1819: Queen Victoria
is born in Kensington Palace * 1844: Samuel Morse sends the first
telegraph message, from Washington to Baltimore

25 May

Oscar Wilde is convicted of the love that dare not speak its name

1895 On this date a London jury found Oscar Wilde, the inter-
nationally famous author of *Dorian Gray*, *The Importance of Being
Earnest* and *Lady Windermere's Fan*, guilty of committing indecent
acts, and the trial judge immediately sentenced him to two years'
hard labour. Three months earlier, Wilde had brought a charge of
libel against the Marquess of Queensbury for calling him a
'sodomite', but the charge backfired disastrously when abundant
evidence offered by the defence showed Wilde to have indulged
with numerous young men in homosexual acts illegal under the
English law of the time. The libel action ended in acquittal for
Queensbury and arrest for Wilde.

Wilde's troubles had really started in 1892, when he had met
Lord Alfred Douglas and the two had entered into a notorious
love affair. Douglas's father, the Marquess of Queensbury, was
already enraged at his son's behaviour on several fronts. Now
seeing him bent on pursuing 'intimacy with that man Wilde', the
Marquess determined to bring his son to heel by bringing the
author to ruin. He succeeded only in the second goal. As Wilde
wrote to Douglas: 'In your war of hate with your father I was at once
shield and weapon to each of you.'

Wilde was at the top of his form at the beginning of 1895,
celebrated, hated, mocked, and cheered as an outrageous wit, a
flamboyant personality, a genius with language, an outrager of
Victorian sensibilities, and the leading spokesman for the cult of

aestheticism. Married with two sons, he had also begun to lead a dangerous and not-so-secret double life as a homosexual, meeting in hotel rooms with young men, often lower-class and paid for their services. 'Feasting with panthers' was his phrase for these encounters.

After the sensational trial and conviction, Wilde's life was completely ruined. Upon his release from prison in 1897, he fled England and his family for Europe, where he stayed for the rest of his brief life, broken if not reformed, and dependent on his remaining friends for handouts. The man who had written so many poems, novels and plays in the years before prison, and left the world so many quotable gems, wrote only one more work, *The Ballad of Reading Gaol.* He died at the age of 46 in a Paris hotel room on 30 November 1900. As he quipped in better days: 'The public is wonderfully tolerant. It forgives everything but genius.'

Also on this day

735: Anglo-Saxon historian the Venerable Bede dies * 1521: The Edict of Worms declares Martin Luther an outlaw * 1681: Spanish playwright Pedro Calderón de la Barca dies in Madrid * 1703: English diarist Samuel Pepys dies * 1803: American philosopher Ralph Waldo Emerson is born in Boston

26 May

A saint meets his bride

1234 When Marguerite of Provence met her future husband on this day in 1234, perhaps she should have paid more attention to her future mother-in-law. Her fiancé, whom she married a few days later, was Louis IX of France, whose domineering mother was the redoubtable and possessive Blanche of Castile.

During the years ahead Blanche would continually nag her son for spending too much time with his wife, once even commanding him away from her sick-bed when her death seemed imminent.

Nothing illustrates the theme of the mother-in-law from hell better than the famous tale of Marguerite and Louis at the castle of Pontoise.

The castle contained a spiral staircase, with Marguerite's bedroom at the bottom and Louis's at the top. According to a contemporary source, the royal couple were so afraid of battle-axe Blanche that 'they were wont to hold their converse on a winding stair that went from one chamber to the other, and their affair was so well planned that when ushers spied Queen Blanche coming toward her son's chamber they would knock at the door thereof with their staffs and the King, hearing it from the stair, would hastily run up into his room so that his mother might find him there'.

In spite of her possessiveness, Louis was devoted to his mother. But perhaps patience came naturally to him; eventually he was declared a saint.

Also on this day

604: St Augustine dies in Canterbury * 1650: John Churchill, the future Duke of Marlborough, is born near Axminster in Devon * 1799: Writer Alexander Pushkin is born in Moscow * 1859: English poet A.E. Housman is born * 1868: Michael Barrett is hanged at Clerkenwell for trying to free two Irish revolutionaries, the last public hanging at Newgate

27 May

Stern John Calvin goes to his rest

1564 As the author of *The Institutes of the Christian Religion*, John Calvin earned himself a place in history as the great simplifier and systematiser of Protestant thought. He also founded the merciless creed that bears his name, Calvinism, with its theories of predestination.

Born in France (and in reality named Jean Cauvin) and educated at the University of Paris, Calvin fled Catholic France for Switzerland at the age of 26 and a year later started the transformation of Geneva into a grim Protestant theocracy. The clergy were authorised to spy on men's private lives to ensure straight-forward rectitude, gambling was prohibited, restaurant diners were compelled by law to say grace before eating, and Christmas celebrations were barred. Calvin himself, with his ascetic face and long, straggling beard, ruled the community like an Old Testament prophet, strict, priggish and unforgiving.

Calvin also organised militant Protestantism throughout France, thus preparing the ground for the ferocious religious wars of half a century later.

As he grew older, Calvin suffered from a series of debilitating diseases, but still he worked on, a remote, austere figure totally devoted to his cause. In spite of his deteriorating condition, he slept little and ate only bread and water once every 36 hours. When friends saw that he was dying, they begged him to reduce his workload, but his response was typical: 'Would you that the Lord should find me idle when He comes?'

John Calvin died on this day at the age of 54, but his religion lives with us still in a much more tolerant form. No doubt it was the character of Calvin himself that inspired H.L. Mencken's famous description of Calvinism as 'the haunting fear that someone, somewhere, may be happy'.

Also on this day

1199: King John of England is crowned * 1332: Italian poet Dante Alighieri is born * 1837: American cowboy legend Wild Bill Hickok is born in Troy, Illinois * 1840: Genoese violin virtuoso and composer Niccolò Paganini dies in Nice * 1941: The British navy sinks the German battleship *Bismarck*

28 May

Jacques Bonhomme revolts against his masters

1358 France was triply devastated: the Black Death had killed a third of the population, bands of marauding mercenaries called the

Great Companies ravaged the countryside, and the English had beaten and humiliated the French nobility at war. Less than two years earlier England's Black Prince had destroyed the French at Poitiers, and the French King Jean II had been captured and hauled away to England.

Those who suffered most, of course, were the peasants, many of whom lived at a subsistence level, eating little but bread and onions, living in huts without furniture, water or heat, sleeping on straw. The peasant – or Jacques Bonhomme as the nobles contemptuously called him – lived in misery, filled with hate for the lords who repressed him.

On this day in the village of St Leu some 25 miles north of Paris, about 100 hate-filled peasants armed themselves with pitchforks, knives and clubs and attacked the nearest noble manor, burning it to the ground and killing the owner and his family. This was the first violence in what became known as the Jacquerie, the terrible peasant revolt that lasted only a month but which destroyed some 150 castles and manors. Led by Guillaume Callet, the rampaging peasants killed or tortured many nobles, and in one case a wife and her children were forced to watch a knight roasted on a spit and then to eat his flesh. As the revolt spread, peasants from the countryside teamed up with insurgents from Paris following the banner of Etienne Marcel. Perhaps as many as 100,000 peasants were on the rampage.

Even royalty was threatened. On 9 June a mob surrounded the royal family in the market-place at Meaux, but were then attacked and slaughtered by a loyalist force led by Gaston Phoebus de Foix. The following day, an army led by Charles the Bad of Navarre crushed Guillaume Callet's peasant force at Clermont-en-Beauvaisis.

By the end of June the Jacquerie was over, and an enraged and fearful nobility savaged the bands of peasants, drenching the country in blood. According to a proverb of the time: 'Oignez vilain, il vous poindra, poignez vilain, il vous oindra.' (Spare a villain, he'll cut your throat, show a villain your steel and he'll kneel.) Up to 20,000 peasants were slaughtered, and Guillaume Callet, who had styled himself their king, was crowned with a red hot iron brand

and then decapitated. Etienne Marcel was killed by one of his own men, who thought he was selling out to the enemy. Jacques Bonhomme would have to wait over 400 years for his revenge to begin in Paris.

Also on this day

1738: French doctor and inventor Joseph Guillotin is born * 1759: British statesman William Pitt the Younger is born * 1779: English furniture-maker Thomas Chippendale dies

29 May

Joan of Arc is condemned to death

1431 One of the most famous – and iniquitous – trials in history ended today with the accused found guilty and condemned to a heretic's death by fire. Five centuries later she would be declared a saint. Her name was Joan of Arc.

After leading the French army to a string of victories, on 24 May 1430 Joan was captured by the Burgundians at Compiègne. Sold to the English for 16,000 francs in one of the most sordid bargains in history, she was transferred to the English headquarters at Rouen. There, facing her English jailers with courage, she defied them while showing her knowledge of English swear words: 'You think when you have killed me you will conquer France, but that you will never do. Even if there were a hundred thousand Goddammees more in France than there are, they will never conquer that kingdom.'

Joan of Arc's trial in Rouen took far longer than most in a day when justice rarely needed more than a few hours to reach its conclusion. The judges had first been assembled in February 1431, but under the leadership of the infamous Bishop of Beauvais, Pierre Cauchon, these ecclesiastical worthies required three months to find adequate proof against this nineteen-year-old religious innocent.

Found guilty, Joan was turned over to civil justice for her punishment, as the Church itself could not or would not carry out the sentence.

Twenty-four hours later, on a Wednesday, Joan was brought to the old market-place of Rouen and burned at the stake for witchcraft, heresy and, principally, for having defeated the English army.

She remained the religious mystic until she died, claiming to the last her faith in the saintly voices that had directed her most of her life. Chained to the stake, she asked for a cross, which an English soldier made for her out of two small sticks. As she died, her last words were 'Jesus, Jesus'.

After all was over, Joan's executioner threw her ashes into the Seine so that no relic might remain. And so ended the incredible story of an illiterate peasant girl from Domrémy who led an army, restored a king and changed the course of history.

Also on this day

1415: Anti-pope John XXIII is stripped of his title * 1453: Turkish Sultan Mohammed II conquers Constantinople – the traditional 'end of the Middle Ages' * 1814: Napoleon's first wife, Joséphine de Beauharnais, dies of pneumonia at Malmaison * 1953: New Zealander Edmund Hillary and Sherpa mountaineer Tenzing Norgay become the first men to climb Mount Everest

30 May

The bons mots *of a great French writer*

1778 He corresponded with Catherine the Great, was friend and councillor to Frederick the Great and was for a while the official historian to the court of Louis XV. He was a Frenchman who lived in England, Germany and Switzerland as well as France and who amassed a great fortune through speculation.

He was also one of the greatest writers that France has produced, writing poetry, novels, philosophy and satire. Among his most famous *bons mots* are:

'Men use thought only to justify their injustices and speech only to conceal their thoughts.'

'If God did not exist, it would be necessary to invent him.'

'This body which was called and still is called the Holy Roman Empire was neither holy, nor Roman, nor an empire.'

'I disapprove of what you say, but I will defend to the death your right to say it.'

'All is for the best in the best of possible worlds.'

He was, of course, Voltaire, that Parisian son of a notary who was born plain François Marie Arouet. He died today in Paris.

Typically, Voltaire even had *bons mots* on his deathbed. When asked to renounce Satan, he declined, ruefully answering: 'This is no time to make any more enemies.' Later, on seeing the lamp next to his bed flare up, he quipped, 'What? The flames already?' Those were his last words.

Also on this day

1431: Joan of Arc is burned at the stake * 1593: Playwright Christopher Marlowe dies in London * 1640: Flemish painter Peter Paul Rubens dies

31 May

The cardinal, the queen and the diamonds

1785 Louis René Edouard, Cardinal de Rohan was perceptibly slow of wit, but he happened to head one of France's wealthiest families. Also living in Paris was a countess named Jeanne de La Motte, who carried royal blood in her veins (she descended from Henri II) but no cash in her pockets. Jeanne decided that Rohan could be bilked to her advantage.

A few years earlier, a Parisian jeweller named Böhmer had

crafted a diamond necklace of extraordinary value and vulgarity. It contained 4,647 stones weighing 2,800 carats and lay on the breast fifteen inches from top to bottom. Unhappily for Böhmer, even the extravagant Queen Marie Antoinette found the asking price of 1,600,000 livres too steep.

Here Jeanne de La Motte saw her opportunity. Pretending she was acting as go-between for the Queen, she presented to Cardinal de Rohan a series of letters purportedly from Marie Antoinette. In fact, they were forgeries prepared by Jeanne's lover. The letters asked Rohan to purchase the diamond necklace for the Queen, who, being short of ready cash, wanted to repay in three instalments. The Queen needed the Cardinal (said the letters) to act as guarantor to the jeweller for so large a sum. Jeanne de La Motte clinched the deception by having a veiled prostitute disguised as the Queen meet Rohan one evening in the gardens at Versailles.

Completely duped, the Cardinal arranged for the purchase of the diamonds and handed them over to Jeanne, ostensibly for delivery to Marie Antoinette. Jeanne immediately broke up the necklace and sold the stones.

A few months later the first instalment to the jeweller fell due. Jeanne knew the truth would have to come out, but calculated that the vain and rich Rohan would pay for the necklace himself rather than publicly admit to being so humiliatingly gulled. But she had not counted on the reaction of the jeweller. On learning of the sting, he went straight to the Queen, who promptly informed her husband, Louis XVI.

In the resulting confusion Louis and Marie Antoinette concluded that Cardinal de Rohan had used the Queen's name in order to purchase the diamonds for himself. Rohan was immediately arrested, to stand trial before the French *parlement*.

The trial was brief, Rohan admitting to his credulity rather than criminality. 'I used the full scope of my intelligence to prove that I am a fool', he said. *Parlement* believed him and, on the evening of 31 May 1785, acquitted him of all charges.

Jeanne de La Motte was not so lucky. Sentenced to prison for life, she was whipped and branded with a 'V' for *voleuse* (thief). Two years later she escaped to England, to live out her life writing scurrilous pamphlets accusing the Queen of fictitious crimes, including a passionate liaison with Rohan.

For Marie Antoinette, the whole affair was a disaster. In spite of the evidence, the French public tended to believe that somehow she had contrived to spend a fortune on diamonds, and hatred for her continued to grow.

Also on this day

1594: Italian painter Jacobo Tintoretto dies in Venice * 1672: Peter the Great of Russia is born * 1809: Austro-Hungarian composer Joseph Haydn dies * 1819: American poet Walt Whitman is born on Long Island * 1902: The Peace of Vereeniging ends the Boer War in South Africa

1 June

The brave, futile end of Napoleon IV

1879 Louis was an imperial prince, only son of France's ex-Emperor Napoleon III. At the age of 23 he found himself in England, having fled with his father into exile after the disastrous French defeat in the Franco-Prussian War. When his father died in January 1873, Louis became the head of the family, with only one goal in life: to regain power for himself and his family, in that order. In this he was ardently supported by Bonapartists everywhere, who proclaimed him Napoleon IV.

The first step in Louis's quest was to gain military glory, and Britain's war of conquest against the Zulus seemed to provide the perfect opportunity.

Britain already ruled neighbouring Natal, and in January 1879 demanded that the Zulu King disband his army and pay reparations, under the pretext that he had insulted the British. When he refused, the British invaded. Although calamitously defeated at the first battle at Isandhlwana, they soon had the Zulus on the run. It was then that young Louis used his extensive political connections to have himself attached to the British.

On 1 June Louis was on a reconnaissance patrol near Ulundi when the Zulus suddenly launched a surprise attack. Thrown from his horse during the action, while his comrades cautiously pulled back, Louis bravely but rashly moved directly towards the attackers, firing his pistol. As he made this hopeless assault he tripped and fell, and the surrounding Zulus instantly hacked him to pieces.

Louis's body was recovered and brought back to Chislehurst for burial. The Napoleonic dream of resurrection was buried with him.

Also on this day

836: Viking raiders sack London * 1794: The Battle of the First of June, or the Battle of Ushant, the first great naval engagement of the French Revolutionary Wars, takes place

2 June

Death comes to Giuseppe Garibaldi

1882 South of Corsica, north-east of Sardinia lies the tiny island of Caprera, stony and dry like its neighbours, where the weather is mild but the farmer's life is hard.

Caprera's most eminent resident was the gnarled but still hardy Giuseppe Garibaldi, the great Italian patriot, revolutionary and general. Even in old age he carried a sizeable beard, and his high, noble brow gave him a rather messianic appearance. The most famous man in Europe in the second half of the 19th century, Garibaldi had captured Europe's imagination (and indeed the fear and hatred of many European governments) with his flamboyant leadership.

'Non posso offrirgli né onori né stipendi; gli offro fame, sete, marcie forzate, battaglie e morte', he dramatically told his followers. (I can offer you neither honour nor wages; I offer you hunger, thirst, forced marches, battles and death.) And they came in their thousands, donning the famous red shirts that became their emblem (although tradition has it that Garibaldi chose the colour so that his followers would know they would be visible if they ran away in the heat of battle). Together they outfought and outfoxed the decaying monarchy of Sicily and forced the papacy to relinquish most of its territorial claims.

Garibaldi had been born on 4 July 1807. His first battles for freedom were not for Italy but for South America, where he spent twelve years fighting in one country or another, striving to throw off Spanish rule. There he learned the business of soldiering and of fighting guerrilla style. At various times he was shot, imprisoned, starved and tortured. He returned to Italy a formidable fighting man.

More than any other man, Garibaldi created the united Italy of today. He spent his last days in Caprera and here, at the age of 74, he died on this day. Here also he is buried.

Also on this day

1420: Henry V marries Catherine de Valois ('Fair Kate') * 1740: French pornographer Donatien-Alphonse-François, marquis de Sade, is born in Paris * 1840: English writer Thomas Hardy is born

3 June

Franz Kafka dies, his major works unpublished

1924 'Someone must have been telling lies about Joseph K., for without having done anything wrong he was arrested one fine morning.' The man who wrote this famous opening line died today in a sanatorium in Kierling just outside Vienna. He was Franz Kafka, a writer now considered one of the 20th century's greatest, even though almost all of his enigmatic works were published posthumously.

Kafka was born in Prague, then part of the Austro-Hungarian Empire. He came from a German-speaking assimilated Jewish family dominated by his insensitive merchant father. His early life was unremarkable. After receiving his doctorate in law at the University of Prague, he settled down into undemanding jobs at various insurance companies until, when he was 34, he was diagnosed with tuberculosis, the disease that was to kill him, and was forced to take intermittent leaves of absence. In contrast to his works of fiction, Kafka was a charming and amusing companion. Although strongly attracted to women (he never married but had several serious affairs), he seems to have suffered some anxieties about sex. At 30 he noted in his diary, 'Der Coitus als Bestrafung des Glückes des Beisammenseins.' (The sexual act is the punishment for the happiness of being together.)

But nothing about Kafka's life explains his unfathomable stories and novels or his dark vision of life. He created what one critic calls 'a baffling mixture of the normal and the fantastic'. *The Metamorphosis* opens, 'When Gregor Samsa awoke one morning from uneasy dreams he found himself transformed in his bed into a gigantic insect.' In *The Judgement* a son commits suicide at the request of his father. In Kafka's most famous work, *The Trial*, the protagonist, named simply Joseph K., endlessly queries a faceless bureaucracy but fails to discover the nature of the charges against him even though he is found guilty and eventually killed in the street 'like a dog'.

When Kafka died he left instructions for his executor Max Brod to burn all his works, but fortunately for readers everywhere, Brod disregarded his orders and prepared many of them for publication. Ever since, critics have offered endless interpretations regarding the true meaning of Kafka's works. Brod considered his novels allegories of divine grace, while others have believed the essence of his work to stem from his neurotic involvement with his father. Some credit him with anticipating the impassive and implacable totalitarianism of Nazism and Communism in novels like *The Trial* and *The Castle*. Others see his work as a metaphor for modern man's angst and alienation in an incomprehensible and indifferent world. One critic has even interpreted the men who murder the central character in *The Castle* as symbols for his testicles.

Like Dickens, Orwell, Rabelais and de Sade, Kafka is one of the very few novelists whose name has become an adjective in our everyday speech. 'Kafkaesque: impenetrably oppressive, nightmarish.' But even he would not have imagined that the nightmares he fashioned in prose would attain an even more terrible reality among those he left behind when he died; his three sisters and one of his lovers perished in Nazi concentration camps.

Also on this day

1162: Thomas Becket is consecrated as Archbishop of Canterbury * 1811: American/English writer Henry James is born * 1864: Seven thousand Union troops are killed during the first half-hour of the Battle of Cold Harbor in Virginia * 1875: French composer Georges Bizet dies * 1877: French Fauvist painter Raoul Dufy is born * 1942: American ships defeat the Japanese in the Battle of Midway

4 June

Dunkirk: 'Wars are not won by evacuations'

1940 Early this morning, as German armour pressed to within three miles of the harbour, Operation Dynamo – the evacuation of Allied forces trapped at Dunkirk – was abandoned. Left behind in the shrinking bridgehead were the remains of the rear guard, several thousand soldiers of the First French Army still defending the perimeter. But brought across the Channel to safety in Britain over the course of nine perilous days were almost 340,000 British and French troops.

On 28 May, when Operation Dynamo began, the situation of the British Expeditionary Force had seemed hopeless, its left flank suddenly exposed by the surrender of the Belgian Army. Winston Churchill, Prime Minister of Great Britain for less than three weeks, doubted whether more than 50,000 troops could be extracted. At the end, however, the rescue effort succeeded beyond all expectation – owing to good luck, German errors, and the magnificent performances of the Royal Navy and the RAF, who conducted and protected the operation.

To a British public understandably relieved at the salvation of its army, the narrow escape became 'the miracle of Dunkirk', almost a triumph in its own right, a way of disguising the magnitude of the Allies' defeat at the hands of the all-conquering Wehrmacht. But later that day, speaking to the House of Commons, Churchill chose these words to describe what had happened across the Channel: 'We must be very careful', he told the MPs, 'not to assign this deliverance the attributes of a victory. Wars are not won by evacuations.'

In spite of his caution, however, Churchill roared defiance with one of history's most stirring speeches, including the famous lines, 'We shall not flag or fail. We shall go on to the end. We shall fight in France, we shall fight on the seas and oceans, we shall fight with growing confidence and growing strength in the air, we shall defend our island, whatever the cost may be. We shall fight on the beaches, we shall fight on the landing grounds, we shall fight in the fields and in the streets, we shall fight in the hills; we shall never surrender.'

Also on this day

1783: Michel and Jacques-Etienne Montgolfier launch the first unmanned hot air balloon near Lyon * 1798: Italian seducer Giovanni Casanova dies * 1831: The Belgians elect Queen Victoria's uncle Leopold of Saxe-Coburg as King * 1941: Ex-Kaiser Wilhelm II dies in exile in the Netherlands

5 June

Kitchener goes down with the ship

1916 A great hero and symbol of his nation died this evening in the North Sea.

We remember him from the famous recruiting poster reproduced in history books: his glowering, square-jawed countenance with its bristling moustache and piercing eyes, his forefinger pointing directly at the viewer, and below it the caption, 'Your Country Needs YOU'. He was, of course, Field Marshal Herbert Horatio Kitchener, avenger of Gordon, reconqueror of the Sudan, hero of Fashoda, protector of the Northwest frontier, Commander-in-Chief in South Africa, Earl Kitchener of Khartoum, and now Secretary of State for War in the Asquith government.

When Great Britain declared war in 1914, the day after Germany's invasion of Belgium, Kitchener's name was on every lip. The Conservatives in Parliament called for him, the big newspapers demanded him, and Winston Churchill, already in the Cabinet, urged his appointment on Asquith.

'What he symbolised, I think,' wrote the Prime Minister's daughter many years later, 'was strength, decision and above all success. South Africa, Khartoum – everything that he touched "came off." There was a feeling that Kitchener could not fail. The psychological effect of his appointment, the tonic to public confidence were instantaneous and overwhelming.'

For all his immense reputation and military successes, however, he was a warrior of the 19th century facing warfare on an unprecedented industrial scale. He did foresee from the outset, when few others did, what a long war would demand in the way of manpower, and he prepared to meet the enormous expansion of Great Britain's military strength through the formation of new 'Kitchener divisions'. But he could not find a strategy to break the stalemate on the Western Front. Nor was he in favour of flanking side-shows in other theatres. He flip-flopped badly on the Dardanelles/Gallipoli campaign and ended up by opposing the only part of the operation that was a success: the final evacuation. As the war dragged on with no conclusion in sight, his influence in the Cabinet waned, and his colleagues began to challenge his decisions.

A Chief of the Imperial General Staff was appointed to handle much of the management of the war that had been Kitchener's alone. Asquith, wishing to avoid the political embarrassment of a Cabinet resignation, sent Lord Kitchener off to Russia to assess the situation on the Eastern Front. He was on the armoured cruiser *Hampshire*, sailing from Scapa Flow for Archangel, when on the evening of 5 June 1916 she hit a mine in the North Sea and quickly sank, taking with her virtually everybody on board.

David Fromkin offered this assessment of Kitchener: 'If he had died in 1914 he would have been remembered as the greatest British general since Wellington. Had he died in 1915 he would have been remembered as the prophet who foretold the nature and duration of the First World War and as the organiser of Britain's mass army. But in 1916 he had become the ageing veteran of a bygone era who could not cope with the demands placed on him in changing times.'

Also on this day

1594: French painter Nicolas Poussin is born * 1947: US Secretary of State George Marshall calls for a European Recovery Programme (the Marshall Plan)

6 June

Of two men who created Italy

1861 The two greatest builders of Italian unification were both born French. Giuseppe Garibaldi was born in Nice only ten years after Napoleon had grabbed it from Italy, and Camillo di Cavour was born in Turin, which, for a while, Napoleon had annexed to France.

The two men could not have been more different. Son of a sailor, Garibaldi proved to be a great guerrilla fighter and leader, a simple, uncomplicated man more at home on a farm than in a palace. He was tall, dark and heavily bearded, with an air of noble sincerity about him.

Cavour was the second son of a marquis, small and podgy with a fringe of beard and pig-like eyes behind rimless spectacles. He was also one of the most intelligent, resourceful and calculating politicians of the 19th century. Disraeli called him 'utterly unscrupulous'.

Cavour's life's ambition was the creation of an Italian state under the authority of the King of Sardinia, Victor Emmanuel II. Playing off the French against the Austrians, charming the British and using Garibaldi when he had to, Cavour was the great architect of the Risorgimento, the 'rising again' that eventually led to a united Italy. When the Kingdom of Italy was finally created in 1860, he was Victor Emmanuel's first Prime Minister.

Starting from about 1850, Cavour had suffered from what today we recognise as malaria, then endemic in parts of Italy. By the spring of 1861 he was almost overwhelmed by the titanic task of reunification (Tuscany, Parma and Sicily had all recognised Victor Emmanuel the year before, and the Kingdom of Italy had been proclaimed in March). Struck down by fever and weakened by repeatedly being bled, Cavour died on 6 June. According to contemporary records (and hagiographies) his last words were, 'Italy is made – all is safe.'

Also on this day

1599: Spanish painter Diego Rodríguez da Silva y Velázquez is born * 1606: French playwright Pierre Corneille is born * 1807: Napoleon's brother Joseph becomes King of Spain * 1944: The Allies land in Normandy during the Second World War

7 June

The first ship through the Panama Canal

1914 Today, after four centuries of deliberation and 32 years of intermittent construction, the Panama Canal opened for its first ship, as the concrete carrier *Cristobal* passed through the 51-mile zigzag course of dams and locks that links the Atlantic and Pacific Oceans through the Isthmus of Panama. Now, at last, ships could reach one ocean from the other without having to sail thousands of extra miles around the tip of South America.

In the 16th century Holy Roman Emperor Charles V had ordered a route surveyed for such a canal to shorten the time and reduce the risks of shipping gold from Ecuador and Peru back to Spain, but work was never started. Three hundred years later the Spanish government again studied the idea but abandoned the task after contemplating 50 inhospitable miles of jungle and mountain.

In 1882 a French company headed by the renowned Ferdinand de Lesseps, builder of the Suez Canal, began work in the isthmus, then part of Colombia. Within eight years the venture was foundering, with almost 20,000 workers dead of malaria or yellow fever, the costs of construction escalating in the difficult terrain, and the company itself engulfed in a scandal of bribery and corruption that threatened to bring down the Third Republic in France.

By the end of the century the United States government had come to realise the strategic value of a canal. In the recently concluded Spanish–American War it had taken the battleship *Oregon* two full months to sail from its home port of Seattle to reach its battle station in the Caribbean Sea. Congress therefore voted to buy out de Lesseps' moribund enterprise for $40 million and to pay Colombia another $10 million for construction rights. When Colombia dithered and then refused the offer, President Teddy Roosevelt wielded his big stick. In 1903 he sent a battleship to the isthmus to 'protect American lives', encouraged the Panamanians to declare their independence, and quickly recognised the new regime. Clearly unrepentant for fomenting an uprising, Roosevelt fumed, 'We were dealing with a government of irresponsible bandits. I was prepared to ... occupy the Isthmus.' He then added disingenuously, 'But I deemed it likely that there would be a revolution in Panama soon.'

Work on the canal began in 1904, with the President very much in charge. The first major problem was to protect the canal workers from the mosquito-borne diseases that had crippled the French effort. When the doctor in charge needed special equipment to drain the swamps, Roosevelt made sure he got it. Within two years the canal route was relatively mosquito-free. Then, when the pace of construction remained slower than hoped for, the President replaced the two civilians in charge with an Army engineer named George Goethals, who proved to be the master of all the complex challenges of the immense project.

The canal's final design followed ideas developed earlier by the French. The Chagres River was dammed to create an artificial lake (the largest in the world at the time), and electricity produced by the dam fuelled five enormous locks to raise or lower a ship 85 feet. But the biggest challenge was digging a ten-mile trench through Culebra Mountain. Almost 40,000 workers were put to the task, using 19 million pounds of dynamite to break through the rock. Four thousand wagons were needed to cart away the excavated material.

When the canal was finally opened for business in 1914, it had cost $350 million – but that was $27 million under budget. Today over 15,000 ships a year pass through it, each needing 15 to 20 hours, including waiting time. Each pays a toll dependent on her size, the most expensive ever levied coming to $141,345. The cheapest was 36 US cents, paid in 1928 by one Richard Halliburton when he swam the canal.

Also on this day

1494: By the Treaty of Tordesillas, Spain and Portugal agree to divide the New World between themselves * 1654: Louis XIV is crowned King of France * 1778: English dandy Beau Brummel is born * 1848: French painter Paul Gauguin is born

8 June

The miserable end of the Dauphin

1795 On this day died poor Louis XVII of France at the age of ten. Son of Louis XVI and Marie Antoinette, in August 1792 the young dauphin, as he was then, was imprisoned with his parents in the Temple, a 12th-century fortified monastery so named because it once housed the Templar order. In theory he became the King of France the following January when his father was executed.

Six months later Louis-Charles, as he was called, was put in the charge of a rabidly republican cobbler named Antoine Simon, who treated him with the brutality and contempt that revolution-aries reserve for royalty. Three months later it was Louis-Charles's mother's turn with the guillotine, and shortly afterwards Louis-Charles was once again imprisoned in the Temple. (The only poetic justice in the story is that Simon perished on the guillotine shortly thereafter, executed in the same group of victims as the Terror's main terrorist, Maximilien Robespierre.)

Louis-Charles was held in solitary confinement in the Temple for a year and a half, in conditions of indescribable squalor. The damp and cold and the filth of a never-cleaned cell that doubled as a toilet destroyed his health, and his mental state can only be imagined, after the loss of both parents to the guillotine. Modern scholars believe he died of tuberculosis.

As no one had access to Louis-Charles during his last months, rumours soon started to spread. Some said that he had been deliberately poisoned by his jailers, others that he was not dead at all but had somehow been rescued from the Temple. During the following years there were almost 40 pretenders who claimed to be 'the Dauphin', most famously and fictitiously in Mark Twain's great novel *Huckleberry Finn*.

Over two centuries after Louis-Charles's death, forensic scientists used DNA extracted from his preserved heart to prove conclusively that the boy who died in the Temple was indeed Louis XVII of France.

Also on this day

1290: Dante's heroine Beatrice Polinari dies at the age of 24 * 1376: English warrior Edward, the Black Prince, dies in London of dropsy * 1784: Fabled French chef Antoine Carême is born in Paris * 1804: Revolutionary pamphleteer Thomas Paine dies * 1870: Charles Dickens dies of a stroke

9 June

Nero takes his own life

AD 68 Today the notorious Roman Emperor Nero committed suicide as soldiers from his rebellious army closed in for the kill.

Only sixteen when he came to power in 54, Nero had for a time been a hard-working and generous ruler, but within five years he had become the ogre of legend, murdering at will (including his mother and two wives) and engaging in sickening sexual conduct with both sexes. (At one point he had a young slave named Sporus castrated and then married him, taking him to bed like a wife. This prompted a Roman joke that the world would have been a better place had Nero's father chosen such a wife.)

By the time Nero was in his late 20s, conspiracies were rising against him everywhere for his cruelty, extravagance and greed. The early ones were snuffed out, but in March 68 Julius Vindex, the Roman governor of Lugdunum (today's Lyon), revolted. At first Nero simply scoffed, 'I have only to appear and sing to have peace once more in Gaul.' Indeed, the Roman army easily crushed the rebels, but not before Julius Vindex had been joined by Servius Galba, the governor of Spain.

Soon other provinces joined Galba, and the Senate proclaimed him as Emperor while condemning Nero to death by flogging with rods. Then, on 8 June 68, Nero's own Praetorian commander Nymphidius Sabinus abandoned him. Knowing he could no longer cling to power, the Emperor tried to flee Rome for his eastern provinces, but his guards refused to help him, one asking derisively, 'Is it so terrible a thing to die?'

Nero then retreated to the imperial palace, only to awake at midnight to find himself alone, deserted even by his slaves. Leaving in panic, by chance he encountered one of his freedmen, Phaon, in the street. Phaon smuggled the disguised Emperor to his villa outside the city where the terrified fugitive hid in a dingy room. But soon soldiers were at the door, probably tipped off by Phaon, desperately trying to save his own skin.

Seeing no way out, Nero exclaimed at the last, 'Qualis artifex peres!' (What a great artist the world is losing!) He then stabbed himself in the throat, but, botching the job, he had to call on his private secretary Epaphroditus to finish him off. According to Suetonius, he died 'with glazed eyes bulging from their sockets'. (Epaphroditus later became the Emperor Domitian's secretary but was executed by him on the grounds that a freedman should never help in his master's suicide.) When Nero died he was still only 30.

With Nero ended the so-called Julio-Claudian dynasty of Roman rulers that had started 116 years before, when Julius Caesar defeated Pompey and assumed dictatorial powers. They all died miserably:

- Caesar was assassinated in the Senate, bequeathing money and troops to his great-nephew
- Augustus, who (some say) was poisoned by his wife Livia so that her son
- Tiberius would rule. Tiberius was smothered on orders from his nephew and successor
- Caligula, who was murdered by officers of his own guard, to be succeeded by his uncle

- Claudius, who was poisoned by his wife Agrippina to gain the title for her son
- Nero, who was driven to suicide.

On Nero's death Galba became Emperor, but he too came to a bloody end, hacked to death by his successor Otho's soldiers after only seven months of power.

Also on this day

1672: Russian Tsar Peter the Great is born * 1815: The final act of the Congress of Vienna settles Europe's boundaries until 1870 * 1866: Bismarck's Prussian troops invade Holstein

10 June

Barbarossa drowns crossing a river

1190 On this day died one of the great rulers in German history, Holy Roman Emperor Frederick I, of the Hohenstaufen dynasty, popularly known as Frederick Barbarossa because of his full red beard.

Frederick Barbarossa was Emperor for 35 years, during which he spent much of his time trying to subject Italy to his control. He invaded the country five times and had the distinction of being on the losing side at the Battle of Legnano, one of military history's watershed battles, where, for the first time, infantry defeated a mounted army of feudal knights.

Another reason Italy was a problem for Frederick was that the temporal power of the Church was greatest there. In 1159 the conclave of cardinals chose as the new pope Alexander III, who was committed to reducing Frederick's authority, but the Emperor used his influence to persuade a minority of cardinals to elect Victor IV, who was declared anti-pope by the Church. Alexander quickly excommunicated Frederick.

Emperor and Pope remained at loggerheads for eighteen years, but eventually were reconciled two years before Alexander died.

Now back in the good graces of the Church, Frederick determined to go on crusade to the Holy Land even though he had reached the advanced age (for the time) of 66. He departed in 1189, but a year later drowned while crossing the Calycadnus (now the Göksu) River in Anatolia.

But did he die? German legend has it that an enchanted Frederick Barbarossa still sleeps in a limestone cave in the Kyffhäuser mountains in Germany. He is said to sit at a stone table around which his great red beard has grown, waiting for the time to come when he will return to restore Germany to greatness.

Perhaps Frederick Barbarossa did die, but the legend did not. During the Second World War Adolf Hitler evoked the myth when he named the invasion of Russia 'Operation Barbarossa'.

Also on this day

1688: James Francis Stuart, the Old Pretender, is born * 1819: French painter Gustave Courbet is born * 1926: Spanish architect Antonio Gaudí dies in Barcelona

11 June

'Doctor Mirabilis'

1292 They called him 'Doctor Mirabilis' (Wonderful Teacher), Roger Bacon, perhaps the greatest intellect of the Middle Ages, who was laid to rest today in the university city of Oxford.

Bacon was born in Ilchester in Somerset 78 years before. He studied first in Oxford, then in Paris, where he joined the Franciscan order.

Bacon was a medieval polymath, excelling in mathematics, optics, languages and astronomy, with a particular interest in alchemy, the transformation of base metal into gold. He conceived the telescope and found that he could cause explosions by combining charcoal, sulphur and saltpetre, a mixture we call gunpowder, hundreds of years before its introduction into Europe. His greatest contribution, however, was the 'invention' of the scientific method – that is, the repetition of carefully controlled experiments until the certainties of cause and effect can be demonstrated and proved.

Because Bacon was so far ahead of his own time – and ahead of his own Church – he spent ten years imprisoned in a dark cell in his monastery, without communication with the outside world. His own Franciscan order condemned him to solitary confinement because of his heretical views about science and his virulent criticism of other scholars and theologians, while the Pope banned the reading of his works.

When Roger Bacon died two years after his release from prison, he believed his life and work to have been failures; today he is considered one of the fundamental founders of modern science.

Also on this day

1572: English dramatist Ben Jonson is born in London ＊ 1776: English painter John Constable is born ＊ 1967: The United Nations negotiates a cease-fire ending the Six-Day War between Israel and Egypt, Jordan and Syria

12 June

Stalin purges his army

1937 Today in Moscow, after the briefest of trials, Marshal Mikhail N. Tukhachevsky, one of the highest-ranking officers in the Red Army and its former Chief of Staff, was shot to death for treason, espionage and conspiracy. His execution took place in the head-quarters of the NKVD, Soviet Russia's secret police. Shot along with him on similar charges were seven other top commanders who, with the marshal, were among Soviet Russia's best and most experienced military officers.

In the 1930s Stalin began a series of purges to 'purify' Soviet

Russia of all potential opposition to his regime. By 1937 it was the Army's turn. Among the targets of scrutiny were former aristocrats, tsarist officers and anyone associated with Trotsky's command of the Red Army during the Civil War. Despite his elevation to the rank of marshal by Stalin only two years earlier, Tukhachevsky was vulnerable on all counts.

It made no difference that he was also a brilliant military reformer who had led the Soviet armed forces into much-needed innovations in combined arms, armoured formations, airborne units, tactical air support and an independent bomber force. These contributions were evidence of a capacity for 'independent thought', now the deadliest of Soviet sins.

Naturally, there was 'proof' of Tukhachevsky's involvement in a plot to seize the Kremlin and overthrow the Soviet leadership: a faked dossier of correspondence between the marshal and two German generals. Under torture the marshal confessed to all charges against him.

The purge did not stop with Tukhachevsky and his colleagues. Over the next year the 'show' trials resulted in the following losses to the Red Army through death or imprisonment: three of five marshals; fourteen of sixteen army commanders; 60 of 67 corps commanders; 136 of 199 division commanders; 221 of 397 brigade commanders; and some 35,000 lower-ranking officers – in all amounting to about half the officer corps. Their replacements were for the most part unfit or untrained as commanders.

One result of these leadership losses was the Red Army's poor showing in its 1939–40 campaign against Finland, a performance carefully noted by the German military. What followed in 1941 was worse yet: full-scale disaster at the hands of the Wehrmacht in the opening phase of Operation Barbarossa. If there was a silver lining to this defeat, it was the speedy elimination through death or capture of thousands of incompetent Soviet officers to be replaced by better material. And in the nick of time, as the German army neared Moscow late in the year, the Soviet high command reinstated many of Tukhachevsky's doctrinal innovations. It was almost too late.

Also on this day
1931: Gangster Al Capone and 68 of his henchmen are indicted for violating Prohibition laws

13 June

Alexander the Great dies in Babylon

323 BC Towards evening today in the fabled city of Babylon he died, still only 32. In his twelve years and eight months as King of Macedonia he changed for ever the Western world. He was Alexander the Great.

As always in antiquity, when a great man died young, there were stories of plots and murders. Plutarch tells us of the bad omens that foretold a coming calamity. Alexander's pet lion was kicked to death by a donkey, and ravens attacked each other over the walls of Babylon, one falling dead at the King's feet. After Alexander's death a story grew that conspirators had given him poisoned wine. Feeling as if 'an arrow had struck him in the liver', he tried to throw up the poison by forcing a feather down his throat, but the feather, too, had been poisoned, compounding the original dose.

Modern historians are sceptical, most believing that, already weakened by alcohol, the great conqueror was finally consumed by malaria.

Alexander had inherited the throne of Macedon from his assassinated father, Philip II, along with an even more valuable legacy, the finest army in the world. In addition, his mind had been trained by one of the greatest of all thinkers, Aristotle.

In late 335 BC or early 334 BC Alexander set out on his fabled conquests – first all of Greece, then Turkey, the Levant, Egypt, Syria and back through modern-day Iraq and Iran, conquering the Persian Empire. And still onwards he went, into Parthia, skirting the southern edge of the Caspian Sea into today's Afghanistan and across the Hindu Kush into Pakistan and India, where his troops finally said 'enough' and refused to go further.

Such were the conquests of the great Alexander, the man who founded at least seven Alexandrias, including the one that remains, in Egypt, where he was buried. Although Alexander's only son was born posthumously and therefore had no real chance to inherit his father's empire, Alexander did leave behind two dynasties, not in Greece but in the Middle East, and not of his own blood but through two of his generals who had been his boyhood companions. The first was Seleucus, who was about 32 at Alexander's death. After several years of in-fighting with Alexander's other generals he took control of what today is mostly Syria and Iran to form the Seleucid Empire, which lasted for 240 years.

The other was Ptolemy, who became King of Egypt. His family ruled for 293 years until his descendant Cleopatra clasped an asp to her bosom in 30 BC.

Shortly before he died Alexander ordered all Greeks to worship him as a god, which he sincerely believed he was. He had been well prepared for this role; his mother had told him that Zeus rather than King Philip was his real father, and when he conquered Egypt he became Pharaoh and thus officially the son of the greatest Egyptian deity, Amon-ra. He thus established the idea of a god-king in Europe, a concept that reached full bloom in Rome three centuries later with the Emperor Augustus and eventually transformed itself into the divine right of kings.

Also on this day

1865: Irish poet William Butler Yeats is born * 1886: Mad King Ludwig (II) of Bavaria drowns himself * 1900: The Boxer Rebellion begins in China * 1944: The first German buzz bomb (V-1) lands on London

14 June

Death of a traitor

1801 At 6.30 this Sunday morning at Gloucester Place, London, a British general died of dropsy and gout at the age of 60. In debt and out of favour, he was buried without military honours in a church crypt in unfashionable Battersea.

He had once been one of the best combat commanders on either side in the American Revolution, his name linked with such celebrated exploits as Quebec, Valcour Island and Saratoga. In those days, however, he had been an American general, not a British one. His name was Benedict Arnold.

In 1780 Arnold turned traitor and began a secret correspondence with the enemy Commander-in-Chief in New York City, Sir Henry Clinton. He proposed to give Clinton the strategic American position at West Point in return for £20,000 and a commission in the British Army. But the plot was discovered when Major John André, Sir Henry's intermediary with Arnold, was caught in disguise behind American lines, bearing papers that revealed the betrayal. André was hanged as a spy, and Arnold himself narrowly escaped to British-held New York City.

The British paid Arnold only about one third of the promised money, but they did make him a brigadier general. As the war carried on, he led British troops in operations against his former countrymen in Virginia and Connecticut. Then came the notable American victory at Yorktown.

Arnold had counted on the British continuing military operations in North America, thus providing him with a career in the Army, perhaps as commander of Loyalist forces in America. To argue that case, he took himself and his family to England in 1782, but not long after his arrival an anti-war Whig government gained office in London. He would find a home neither in English society, where he came to symbolise the now-unpopular conflict, nor in the British Army, where fellow officers considered his motives mercenary and dishonourable. Moreover, the loss to the service of the highly popular André was still mourned.

Arnold was forced to spend much of his last twenty years abroad in search of fortune in Canada and the West Indies. In contrast to Arnold's humble interment in Battersea, Major André received a monument in Westminster Abbey on which the inscription proclaimed him 'universally beloved and esteemed by the Army in which he served'.

15 June

Wat Tyler and the Peasants' Revolt

1381 In 14th-century England the villein or ordinary farmer was
close to a serf, taxed by the King, used by the nobles and bound to
the land. But as the peasants toiled in their misery, two extraordinary leaders urged them to demonstration and violence,
starting the Peasants' Revolt.

One was John Ball, an itinerant and slightly crazed preacher who
included in his anti-aristocracy sermons his revised text of a
popular ballad: 'When Adam delved and Eve span, who was then
the gentleman?' The other was an ex-soldier named Wat Tyler, the
Revolt's chief instigator.

In early June 1381 these two men led a motley army of some
20,000 villeins to London, which they shortly occupied, terrifying
the richer inhabitants, murdering many, and burning the great
Savoy palace belonging to the King's uncle, John of Gaunt. As the
flames licked higher it seemed as if the royal government could be
on the verge of being swept away.

On 15 June the beautiful blond young King, Richard II, then
only fourteen, was forced to parley with Wat Tyler outside the city
walls at Smithfield. Several nobles, including the Mayor of
London, William Walworth, accompanied him.

Separating himself from his peasant followers, Tyler approached the King and harangued him on his demands. Suddenly
there was a scuffle, and Tyler pulled out his knife but was felled by
a blow from Walworth's sword.

The peasant army reached for their weapons, but Richard rode
out to them alone, ordering them to obey him, their true King.

Miraculously, the mob obeyed, and the crowd dispersed. The Peasants' Revolt was over, Wat Tyler lying dead on the ground.

The nobles' vengeance was swift. John Ball was caught and hanged, as were other leaders. The poor peasants gained nothing. 'Villeins you are,' said the King, 'and villeins ye shall remain.'

Also on this day

1215: King John signs Magna Carta * 1330: Edward, the Black Prince, is born * 1520: Pope Leo X excommunicates Martin Luther * 1775: The Continental Congress makes George Washington Commander-in-Chief of the Continental Army

16 June

Henry VII captures Lambert Simnel

1487 Henry VII was the rarest of kings in that he sometimes exhibited both a sense of humour and a sense of mercy. An example is the tale of Lambert Simnel.

Simnel was the eleven-year-old son of an Oxford organ maker. He had been chosen by a local priest to impersonate the Earl of Warwick (who was in fact imprisoned in the Tower of London) and thus claim the throne as the rightful heir. (Warwick was the son of the dead Duke of Clarence, brother of Richard III, whom Henry had deposed.) Tutored and bedecked in fine clothes, Simnel and his mentor succeeded in this deception, and an army of dissidents and opportunists grew up around him.

Eventually King Henry took the field against Simnel and, on 16 June 1487, utterly crushed the insurgents at Stoke. Young Simnel was captured and must have expected to be executed. But the King's humour and compassion came into play, and Henry put him to work in the royal kitchens with the lowest of jobs, turning the spit. Simnel eventually rose to the job of falconer and many years later died quietly in bed.

Also on this day

1722: John Churchill, Duke of Marlborough, dies * 1846: Pius IX is elected Pope, to reign for 32 years, the longest pontificate in history * 1866: Bismarck launches a Prussian attack against Austria as the first step in the unification of Germany

17 June

Americans lose a battle but gain heart at Bunker Hill

1775 The first battle of the American Revolution had been fought only two months earlier and twelve miles away, and now rebel soldiers occupied three hills looking down on Boston Harbor, threatening British ships. The highest of the hills rose to some 110 feet. It was called Bunker Hill.

When cannon fire from the ships failed to dislodge the Americans, the British commander General Sir William Howe led his force of 2,300 men to remove the Yankees. Most of the action actually took place on neighbouring Breed's Hill. As the British advanced, American General Israel Putnam gave his famous order, 'Don't shoot until you see the whites of their eyes.' (Putnam's command was not altogether original. In destroying the Austrian army at Jagerndorf in 1745 Prince Charles of Prussia gave an almost identical order, as did Frederick the Great in 1757 at the Battle of Prague.)

The American soldiers were barricaded behind makeshift barriers of old fences packed with hay and brush. Initially the accurate colonial gunfire stopped the British attack, but eventually the Americans were forced to retreat when they began to run out of ammunition and weapons.

By nightfall the Battle of Bunker Hill was over. Some 226 British lay dead on the field, with another 826 wounded. The Americans suffered 140 killed in action with 301 more wounded. Even though they lost the battle, the Americans were jubilant. They had demonstrated that untrained militia, hastily assembled, could trade blow for blow with professional British soldiers, and American determination was strongly boosted. But the Revolution still had another six years and four months to run.

Also on this day

1292: Edward I is born at Westminster * 1600: Spanish playwright Pedro Calderón de la Barca is born * 1719: English writer Joseph Addison dies

18 June

The sayings of Waterloo

1815 Waterloo, a Flemish farming village nine miles south of Brussels. Today the 72,000-strong army of Napoleon Bonaparte lost the Emperor's last great gamble there to a mixed force of 68,000 British, Dutch, Belgian and German troops, strongly reinforced by some 45,000 Prussians led by the 72-year-old Field Marshal Prince Gebhard Leberecht von Blücher. In command of the entire Allied army was Britain's finest general since Marlborough, Arthur Wellesley, the Duke of Wellington. As subsequently pronounced by Victor Hugo, 'Wellington was the technician of war, Napoleon its Michelangelo.'

The battle started at midday with Napoleon's first attack and continued until the battered and defeated French forces started to retreat from the field at eight o'clock in the evening. In all, the French suffered over 25,000 men killed or wounded, with another 9,000 captured.

After the battle the self-assured Duke reflected on the result. 'It has been a damned serious business,' he said, 'Blücher and I have lost thirty thousand men. It has been a damned nice thing – the nearest run thing you ever saw in your life ... By God, I don't think it would have done if I had not been there.' Later he is reputed to have remarked on the steadfastness of his officers with the famous observation, 'The battle of Waterloo was won on the playing fields of Eton.'

Wellington was not the only general at Waterloo to coin a phrase. Tradition has it that the French Guard Commander Pierre de Cambronne answered a call to yield with 'La Garde meurt, mais ne se rend pas.' (The Guard dies but never surrenders.) After the battle, however, Cambronne denied the comment, claiming he made only the one-word reply 'Merde!' – the word since known to the French as 'le mot de Cambronne'.

Waterloo ended the career of the great Napoleon – he abdicated four days later. It must have galled him that his defeat came at the hands of the British, whom he had once derided as 'a nation of shopkeepers'.

Also on this day

1155: Holy Roman Emperor Fredrick Barbarossa is crowned in Rome * 1429: Joan of Arc leads the French army to victory over the English at the Battle of Patay * 1812: America declares war on Great Britain to start the War of 1812

19 June

Mexican Emperor Maximilian faces the firing squad

1867 At dawn this morning in Querétaro in central Mexico a tall, blue-eyed Austrian with a foot-long golden beard carefully donned his black frock coat in his prison cell and mounted a carriage accompanied by a priest, en route to his execution. By 6.40 a.m. he was dead, cut down by the bullets of a seven-man firing squad of Mexican soldiers. Just 34, he had been Emperor of Mexico for three years and nine days. His last words as he faced the rifles were a courageous 'Viva México'.

Maximilian von Habsburg was the younger brother of the Austrian Emperor Franz Joseph. A well-meaning lightweight, he had been persuaded by Mexican reactionaries, French Emperor Napoleon III and his own ambitious wife Charlotte to accept the imperial crown of Mexico, a country mired in a ferocious civil war between extreme reactionaries backed by the Church and anticlerical republicans.

Maximilian had thought to impose a 'liberal dictatorship' to restore order and stop the killing. Although so deeply conservative that he called his brother 'Your Majesty' even when the two were alone together, he could see that the priest-ridden society of the Mexican right, with few civil liberties, no religious freedom and a system of peonage that enslaved most of the peasants, should not continue. But he abhorred the Left's attack on aristocracy and the Church. So he accepted the poisoned imperial chalice and assumed control of a government held in power solely by a French army.

Napoleon III had invaded Mexico in 1861 for the putative reason of collecting the debts owed to France by the Mexican government, but his real ambitions were to establish French dominance in Latin America and to 'erect an insuperable barrier against the encroachments of the United States'. The timing had been ideal since the American Civil War precluded armed intervention to back up the Monroe Doctrine, which in effect banned European powers from intervening in the Western hemisphere. Napoleon saw Maximilian as little more than his puppet.

Maximilian tried to govern fairly and refused to rescind the confiscation of Church land executed by the republican government. But he was financially incompetent: Mexican debt rose from $81 million in 1861 to $202 million in 1866 and Maximilian's own imperial household expenses came to $1.5 million per year, 50 times the amount spent by his republican predecessor Benito Juárez. During his entire reign civil war continued as the republicans tried to regain lost power. In retaliation, in October of 1863 Maximilian issued the infamous Black Decree that permitted immediate execution of any captured 'rebel' soldiers, with no possibility to petition the Emperor or any other authority for mercy.

In April 1865 Maximilian's regime received a deathblow, although the Emperor was too complacent to recognise it: the American Civil War ended, and now it was only a matter of time before the Monroe Doctrine would be enforced. Within a year an army led by Philip Sheridan was massed on the Rio Grande, threatening to intervene. Napoleon III soon ordered his troops to sail for home, leaving Maximilian with a ragtag force of Austrians, Belgians and a few die-hard conservative Mexicans. He vacillated on whether to abdicate but was dissuaded by his wife, his mother and his ultra-conservative ministers who feared for themselves if the republicans should regain power. He took personal charge of the imperial army but soon was besieged, starved and finally betrayed at Querétaro, where he surrendered on 15 May 1867.

Tried within a month, Maximilian was found guilty of usurping the power of the legitimate government and using a foreign army to wage war against Mexico. Despite strong protests from Austria, France and Great Britain – and petitions from liberals like Victor Hugo and Garibaldi – Juárez refused to commute the sentence of death by firing squad.

On hearing of Maximilian's execution, Napoleon III waxed philosophical about his whole Mexican adventure: 'God did not want it; let us respect His decrees.' Republicans in Europe were jubilant. As future French Prime Minister Georges Clemenceau wrote at the time, 'Between us and these people [royalty] there is a war to the death. They have tortured to death millions of us and I bet we have not killed two dozen of them.'

Also on this day

1623: French philosopher Blaise Pascal is born * 1829: The House of Commons passes Robert Peel's law establishing a police force

20 June

Europe is saved from Attila the Hun at the Battle of Châlons

AD 451 'They all have compact, strong limbs and thick necks and are so monstrously ugly and misshapen that one might take them for two-legged beasts ... By the terror of their features they inspired great fear ... They made their foe flee in horror because their swarthy aspect was fearful and they had, if I may call it so, a

sort of shapeless lump, not a head, with pin-holes rather than eyes
... Like unreasoning beasts, they are utterly ignorant of the
difference between right and wrong.' So did a contemporary
historian describe the fearful Huns of Attila in the 5th century.

Although their origin is uncertain, the Huns were probably an
Asian people called the Hsung-nu, barbarians of such ferocity that
six centuries previously the Chinese had built the Great Wall of
China to defend against them.

Attila himself was short and stocky with a wispy beard gracing
his abnormally large head. He had become joint King of this
Mongol horde in 433, sharing the throne with his brother Bleda.
But by 445 he had murdered Bleda to take sole command.

The Western Roman Emperor at the time was Valentinian III,
who normally paid Attila an annual tribute to keep him out of his
realm. But in 450 his sister Honoria pleaded with Attila to rescue her
from a marriage that Valentinian had arranged, sending him her ring
as proof of her trust. Attila immediately declared Honoria to be his
own wife, with half of Valentinian's empire as her dowry.

In early 451 Attila led a gigantic nomad force composed primarily
of mounted archers across the Rhine and laid waste to every town
he came upon: Reims, Metz, Amiens, Beauvais, Cologne, Stras-
bourg. The devastation he wrought justified his boast that 'grass
never grows again where my horse has trod'. Even Paris was nearly
destroyed, saved only by the miraculous intervention of St
Geneviève, whose prayers inspired the defenders to hold the city
walls. In like manner Orléans escaped destruction when its bishop
Anianus (later St Aignan) restored the city's crumbling battlements
by carrying holy relics around them.

With an army mounted on horseback, Attila used speed, surprise, mobility and above all ferocity rather than military strategy.
The cruelty of the Huns and of Attila himself was extraordinary,
even in this time of cruelty, as the Western Roman Empire was
staggering towards its end.

But at last the Romans and their sometime allies the Visigoths
combined forces under the command of the Roman general
Aetius to meet this so-called Scourge of God. The two armies met
on 20 June 451 on the fields near Châlons, in what today is the

champagne country of France. Attila set the tone for the conflict by exhorting his men, 'Sunder the sinew, and the limbs collapse; hack the bones and the body falls. Huns of mine, rouse your rage and let your fury swell as of old!'

The battle lasted throughout the day, with terrible slaughter on both sides. At dusk the Visigoths finally smashed through the enemy's flank, threatening the Hun centre and almost killing their leader. Attila was forced to retreat, the first and only defeat in his marauding career.

The terrible Attila lived for only another year, spending that time laying waste to Italy. But the Battle of Châlons had turned the tide, saving much of western Europe from the ravages of the Huns. Attila's defeat also enormously boosted the prestige of the Church of Rome, which claimed much credit for resisting the heathen Huns at Paris and Orléans.

Such was the terror that Attila inspired that he appears in the legends of France, Italy and Scandinavia. He is also featured in the German *Nibelungenlied* under the name of Etzel, while he is called Atli in Icelandic sagas.

Also on this day

1756: Over 140 British subjects are imprisoned in the Black Hole of Calcutta in India * 1791: Louis XVI and Marie Antoinette flee Paris – the 'flight to Varennes' * 1923: Mexican revolutionary leader Pancho Villa is assassinated

21 June

Galileo is condemned

1633 Today Pope Urban VIII issued his verdict: Galileo Galilei was guilty of having 'believed and taught' the pernicious doctrines of Copernicus that asserted that the Earth moves around the Sun.

Ironically, Urban had originally been both a supporter and personal friend of Galileo's, and the great scientist had once dedicated a book to him. But the steady pressures of militant

Protestantism were eroding the influence of the Catholic Church, and the papacy was fighting back by reinforcing all the Church's most traditional dogmas. To make matters worse, Galileo's latest unorthodox book, *Dialogo Sopra i Due Massimi Sistemi del Mondo, Tolemaico e Copernicano* (Dialogue on the Two Great Systems of the World, Ptolemaic and Copernican), was written in Italian rather than scholarly Latin, making it accessible to a wide audience of readers.

Under pressure from the Dominicans who were in charge of the Inquisition, Urban condemned his old friend to house arrest for the remainder of his life and to public and private penance for his sins.

After hearing his sentence the 70-year-old Galileo knelt before the tribunal and devoutly recanted 'the false opinion that the Sun is the centre of the world and immobile, and that the Earth is not the centre of the world and moves'. But as he rose from his knees he muttered his celebrated denial, 'Eppur si muove.' (But it *does* move.)

Galileo spent the remaining eight years of his life under house arrest in Arcetri on the outskirts of Florence, seeing only those visitors permitted by a watching Church. Even then, however, the great scientist could not be totally silenced, as he wrote one further book (this one on the less controversial subject of mechanics) which had to be published abroad because of the papal ban on Galileo's works.

Also on this day

1377: Edward III dies of a stroke * 1652: English architect Inigo Jones dies * 1675: Sir Christopher Wren starts the reconstruction of St Paul's Cathedral after its destruction by the Great Fire of London * 1813: The Duke of Wellington routs the French at the Battle of Vitoria in Spain

22 June

Niccolò Machiavelli dies outside Florence

1527 Old, frustrated and disappointed, Niccolò Machiavelli died this day at 58 on the outskirts of Florence, the city he loved so well, the city that had elevated, enriched, imprisoned, banished and forgotten him. Machiavelli had spent the last fourteen years of his life as a gentleman farmer, living in obscurity, writing his books. Clearly he had lost none of his worldly scepticism as death approached, commenting, 'I would rather go to hell than to heaven. There I will enjoy the company of popes, kings and princes, while in the other place are only beggars, monks and apostles.'

Ironically, it was during his time in the political wilderness that Machiavelli immortalised himself as the father of power politics. His most influential work is *The Prince*, a treatise based on his observations of that ruthless, treacherous, implacable and capable soldier and nobleman, Cesare Borgia.

The Prince sets out Machiavelli's ideas on what a ruler must do to succeed. His incisive cynicism is shown by one of the book's most famous passages. In advising how leaders should treat their subjects, he wrote, 'Men should be either treated with generosity or destroyed; because they will revenge themselves for small offences but for great ones they cannot.'

He also comments on how a prince should want others to see him. 'Is it better to be loved or feared? ... It is better to be both, but it is much safer to be feared than loved, if one has to choose between them.'

Future leaders who we know were influenced by Machiavelli's writings are numerous: Richelieu, Frederick the Great, Napoleon, Bismarck, Clemenceau. Hitler kept a copy of *The Prince* on his bedside table.

Also on this day

1535: Cardinal Fisher is beheaded on the orders of Henry VIII * 1699: French painter Jean Chardin is born * 1815: Napoleon abdicates, proclaiming his son (L'Aiglon) Emperor of the French

23 June

Robert the Bruce defeats the English at Bannockburn

1314 On this day near Stirling Castle outside Edinburgh, Robert the Bruce, King of Scotland, carefully positioned his infantrymen on a hillside above a stream called Bannockburn, taking advantage of cavalry-slowing bogs on one side of his front and an infantry-concealing forest on the other. Then he waited for the vanguard of the English army.

For almost twenty years now the Scots had fought to remain independent from English domination, in a seesaw struggle with England's King Edward I, the 'Hammer of the Scots'. Edward invaded Scotland for the first time in 1296, then again in 1306, after the Earl of Carrick, as Bruce was then, was crowned the Scottish King. So, Bruce as King became an outlaw, always on the run, at one point harried clean out of Scotland, his wife, daughters and sisters imprisoned, his youngest brother beheaded.

But Edward died at the beginning of the second invasion, and Edward II proved no match for his father in matters of war. The second campaign languished, and as victories came for Bruce and his growing forces, the Scottish nobility began to favour his cause. Now, however, for a third time, an English army, 25,000 strong, had come over the border, with the intent of relieving the siege of Stirling Castle, the last English stronghold in the north of the country.

On 23 June the English delivered their main attack, the sheer weight of which, Edward was sure, must prevail. The English cavalry crowded forward over the narrow front of stable footing, but it piled up in a congested mass, unable to get past the thick clusters of Scottish pikemen. In the confusion, the English archers rained down arrows on their own cavalry as much as on the Scots.

The brutal slogging match might have ended as a bloody draw but for an ingenious ruse that decided the day. A force of Scottish camp followers – grooms, priests, cooks and porters – emerged from the forest on the English left, waving banners and shouting in simulation of a counter-attack. The English, hesitating at what appeared to be a fresh army sent against them, began to withdraw, slowly at first, but soon in panic when it became known that King Edward had decamped.

Reinvigorated, the Scots drove their enemy from the field, leaving thousands dead and wounded and capturing hundreds more. Among the English dead were 21 barons and baronets, 42 knights and 700 gentlemen-at-arms. The ransoms paid for those captured would for a time make Scotland a rich country. The most important of the prisoners taken by the Scots was the powerful Earl of Hereford, whom Bruce exchanged for his wife, his daughters and his sisters.

The great victory at Bannockburn gave substance to the Scots claim of independence and to Bruce's leadership of his nation. It did not end the war, which dragged on until 1328, when Edward III signed the Treaty of Northampton, the main clause of which read: 'Scotland shall remain to Robert, King of Scots, free and undivided from England, without any subjection, servitude, claim or demand whatsoever.'

Also on this day

AD 79: Roman Emperor Vespasian dies * 1340: Edward III's fleet defeats the French at Sluys, the first battle of the Hundred Years' War * 1611: English navigator Henry Hudson is cast adrift by his own crew in Hudson Bay, Canada

24 June

Edward III creates the Order of the Garter

1348 Today at Windsor Castle, just a few miles west of London, King Edward III held the first ceremony for what has become the most celebrated order of chivalry in the world, the Order of the Garter.

For some time the King had planned to establish a noble order of knights based on the Round Table of King Arthur. The story goes that earlier in the year the exceptionally beautiful Joan of Kent, Countess of Salisbury, inadvertently lost a blue garter during an evening's dancing at court. Gallantly, Edward picked it up and attached it to his own sleeve. Then, thinking of the lady's reputation (and perhaps of his own, for he was known to have a roving eye), he remarked to his guests, 'Honi soit qui mal y pense.' (Ashamed be he who thinks evil of it.) This was the beginning of the Order of the Garter and its motto, which have lasted to this day as England's highest honour.

Initially, the Order had twelve members, but in 1805 the number was increased to 25. Most of its recipients have come from Britain's highest aristocracy or, more recently, highest political levels. Not all, however, have been faithful to their trust, as 36 have been beheaded.

In 1790 George III offered William Pitt the Younger the Order of the Garter, then a significant financial reward as well as an honour, but Pitt refused, requesting that it might be given to his less well-off brother instead. But in 1945 Winston Churchill turned down the award on the grounds that he had just been defeated in an election. As he told a friend, 'I can hardly accept the Order of the Garter from the king after the people have given me the Order of the Boot.'

Also on this day

1509: Henry VIII is crowned at Westminster * 1812: Napoleon and the Grande Armée cross the River Nieman into Russia * 1859: Napoleon III defeats the Austrians at Solferino

25 June

Pharaoh Ramses II begins the longest reign in Egyptian history

1279 BC My name is Ozymandias, king of kings:
Look on my works ye mighty, and despair!

Today the man whose statue inspired these famous lines by Percy Shelley became sole ruler of ancient Egypt, over which he reigned in unrivalled power for 66 years. We know him as Ramses II, but like all pharaohs he had many names, one of which was Usermaatre, corrupted over the millennia to Ozymandias.

Born a commoner, Ramses was the son of one of Egypt's leading generals who as Seti I became Pharaoh on the childless demise of the previous king. When Seti died, Ramses inherited the throne.

According to the hieroglyphics on his many monuments, Ramses was a great warrior king, principally against the Hittites, but modern scholarship suggests that the conflict was more of a stand-off. But he undoubtedly was an unparalleled builder. He built a new Egyptian capital which he called Pi Ramesse Aa-nakhta or House of Ramses Great of Victories. Today only traces remain, but there are gigantic statues of Ramses throughout Egypt, particularly at Luxor and Abu Simbel, where the four enormous statues all portray the Pharaoh.

Shelley mocks the vanity of kings, but these portrait statues were not entirely for self-glorification. Egyptians of Ramses' era believed the soul could go to 'heaven' – the Kingdom of Osiris – only if the body survived, a belief that inspired the process of mummification. But some thought that the soul could also survive through an image of the body, a statue.

Ramses' long rule ended when he died in August 1213 BC at almost 100 years of age. On his death his body underwent a 70-day embalming process. Clearly the embalmers did a good job, since in June 1886 a French archaeologist opened Ramses' bandages on the recovered body to uncover the still-intact face of an old man with red hair. Today you can see the mummy in the Cairo Museum.

Apart from the many colossal statues of Ramses in Egypt, there are other reminders of him in our daily life. One of his obelisks, originally in Luxor, today adorns the place de la Concorde in Paris, brought back from Egypt by Napoleon. The Washington Monument was inspired by it.

We can also read references to him in the Old Testament, as Ramses was the pharaoh referred to in the Bible at the time of

Moses. It has been broadly established that Moses lived and worked in Egypt during Ramses' reign, and one French historian speculates that the two were actually friends. Finally, in America a leading brand of condom is called Ramses, rather inappropriately named after a ruler who fathered 46 sons and almost 50 daughters, including four whom he married.

Also on this day

1646: The surrender of Oxford to the Roundheads signifies the end of the English Civil War * 1876: American Indians annihilate General Custer's troops at Little Bighorn

26 June

The real Pied Piper

1284 Rats!
>   They fought the dogs and killed the cats,
>   And bit the babies in the cradles,
>   And ate the cheeses out of vats,
>   And licked the soup from the cooks' own ladles …

So did Robert Browning describe events in his 1842 epic 'The Pied Piper of Hamelin'. But what is the true story?

Today was the feast of St John and St Paul, a day when no one worked or went to school in the German town of Hamelin in Lower Saxony. No one knows for certain what happened that day, but records survive that show that 130 children disappeared. What is certain is that here lies the origin of the famous tale of the Pied Piper, the world's most famous ratcatcher.

Some believe the legend of the Pied Piper is purely symbolic, originating in the death of many children from the plague. In medieval times no one understood the connection between rats and the Black Death, but people must have observed the death of infected rats, followed by plague deaths of people.

Current theory concerning the substantial single-day disappearance in Hamelin, however, suggests that the children were actually led away. Their fate, however, was not Walt Disney's land of eternal youth but a German town in what is now the Czech Republic named Troppan. It seems likely that a German bishop of the period, a certain Bruno, enticed the children – who were probably teenagers – to follow him to colonise a new town. The rats were added to the tale only in the 16th century.

Also on this day

AD 363: Roman Emperor Julian the Apostate is killed in battle in Persia * 1541: Spanish conquistador Francisco Pizarro is assassinated

27 June

Jeanne Hachette saves her city

1472 Jeanne Laisné was a simple butcher's daughter, raised in the handsome walled city of Beauvais just 50 miles north of Paris. It was her misfortune to live at the time when King Louis XI and Charles the Bold, Duke of Burgundy, were warring with each other for control of France.

In the spring of 1472 Charles's Burgundian army was on the rampage. The little city of Nesle had already surrendered when, during a truce, the Duke's men had burst into the town and massacred all the men, women and children who had fled to a church for refuge. On 27 June Charles arrived beneath the walls of Beauvais.

Knowing what would be in store for them if they surrendered, the citizens of Beauvais put up a mighty resistance, and none fought so fiercely as Jeanne Laisné. Armed with her father's butcher's hatchet, she cut down the Burgundian flag bearer, seizing the standard when her battered victim fell from the walls.

Twenty-five days after the siege began Duke Charles was forced to withdraw his depleted army. Beauvais had held out, and

Jeanne became a heroine whose nickname would last for centuries – Jeanne Hachette. Her statue still stands in the city's old market-place.

Also on this day
1571: Italian painter and art historian Giorgio Vasari dies * 1722: English general and statesman John Churchill, Duke of Marlborough, dies * 1787: Edward Gibbon completes *The History of the Decline and Fall of the Roman Empire* * 1898: American Captain Joshua Slocum completes the first solo round the world voyage

28 June

Sarajevo

1914 Why the Archduke Franz Ferdinand, heir apparent to the throne of Austria, chose to visit the capital of Bosnia in this summer of Balkan discontent, we will never know for sure. 'To pay that visit', wrote Rebecca West, 'was an act so suicidal that one fumbles the pages of history books to find if there is not some explanation of his going, if he was not subject to some compulsion. But if ever a man went anywhere of his own free will, Franz Ferdinand went so to Sarajevo.'

Only eight years earlier Bosnia had been annexed by Austria-Hungary, infuriating the highly nationalist Serbs who constituted a large minority of Bosnia's population and hoped for eventual union with Serbia. Anti-Austrian feeling ran high, now exacerbated by Franz Ferdinand's decision to review military exercises in Bosnia in his role as inspector general of the Austro-Hungarian army.

When the trip was announced, the Serbian government, no friend of Austria, alerted Vienna to the strong likelihood of an assassination attempt by the secret Serbian irredentist group Crna Ruka or Black Hand, officially entitled Ujedinjenje ili Smrt, Unification or Death. This infamous organisation had become so powerful that in 1913 its leader was named head of intelligence for the Serbian General Staff.

Deaf to all advice, warnings and good sense, the ambitious and unpopular Franz Ferdinand determined to carry out the military inspection, perhaps viewing the visit as a rehearsal for his own emperorship. Whatever his motive, off he went, more arch-fool than archduke.

After attending two days of Austrian army manoeuvres, provocatively conducted near the Serbian border, Franz Ferdinand, now joined by his wife Sophie, started a processional drive through Sarajevo at 10.00 a.m. this Sunday morning – an offensive choice of date since it was Vidovdan, Serbia's national day.

You might have guessed that in such circumstances Austrian troops would have been posted along the route. But there were none, only local police. And surely the tour would have been cancelled after someone flung a bomb that glanced off the royal automobile and exploded under the next car, wounding an aide-de-camp. But the tour proceeded as scheduled to the Town Hall.

There the welcoming festivities were cut short and a route change agreed, but somehow no one informed the chauffeurs. At 11.15 a.m. the tour resumed. When the lead car with the deputy mayor of Sarajevo turned to follow the old route, there was confusion among the security detail. The second car, carrying the royal couple, came to a stop while things were sorted out. At this point, Gavrilo Princip, a nineteen-year-old Bosnian student and member of the Black Hand, stepped from the crowd of on-lookers, drew a revolver and fired, one bullet hitting the archduke, another his wife who had thrown herself across the car to shield him. Both died within minutes. It was their fourteenth wedding anniversary.

Princip was instantly captured, tried within four months and sentenced to twenty years in prison, the maximum allowable for criminals under twenty. In less than four years he was dead of tuberculosis.

But one month to the day after the assassination, even before Princip was brought to trial, Austria declared war on Serbia, precipitating the First World War.

29 June

The Globe Theatre burns down

1613 The actual shape of London's Globe Theatre, where most of Shakespeare's plays were first performed, is still largely a matter of educated guesswork. It was probably a twenty-sided building cylindrical in shape, with a diameter of 100 feet. What is certain is that it had a thatched roof, which on this day was set on fire by a stage cannon, fired during a scene from *Henry VIII*. In less than an hour this seminal theatre of English drama was gone, burned to the ground.

The Globe was built in 1599 by two brothers, Richard and Cuthbert Burbage, of whom the former was a leading actor, the first to play Richard III, Romeo, Henry V, Hamlet, Macbeth, Othello and King Lear. The company of players who acted there was called the Chamberlain's Men, of which Shakespeare was a member. It is thought that Shakespeare and several other of the players owned shares in the Globe along with the Burbages.

Only eighteen months after its incineration the Globe had been rebuilt, this time with a tile roof. Although Shakespeare died just two years later, it continued as London's leading playhouse until 1642, when high-minded Puritans pulled it down, along with all of London's other theatres, in order to make room for housing for the poor.

For over three centuries what was left of the Globe was covered over and built over, but in 1970 an American actor named Sam

Wanamaker established a project to recreate it. In 1987 the first work on the new Globe started some 200 yards from the original site, and two years later the foundations of the original Globe were discovered, although they could not be fully excavated since they lay beneath another building.

Even before the new Globe was completed, plays were held there, and on Thursday 12 June 1997 Queen Elizabeth II officially inaugurated the building, a close replica of the original where Shakespeare's plays are still performed in the round.

Also on this day

1577: Dutch painter Peter Paul Rubens is born ∗ 1855: Trade unions are legalised in the United Kingdom ∗ 1861: English poet Elizabeth Barrett Browning dies in Florence

30 June

The greatest cosmic explosion in the history of civilisation

1908 It was already full daylight at 7.40 this morning when an enormous pale blue fireball trailed by a 500-mile tail of bright, shimmering, multicoloured bands hurtled across the Siberian sky and consumed itself in the greatest cosmic explosion in the history of civilisation.

This cataclysmic detonation occurred four miles above the Earth's surface over a huge, inaccessible and almost uninhabited pine forest near the Podkamennaya Tunguska River in central Siberia. Equal to 1,000 Hiroshima bombs, the blinding flash could be seen from 500 miles away.

This colossal blast produced no crater because it occurred so high above the Earth, but its shock wave flattened half a million acres of forest, and more than twenty miles from the epicentre scorched and splintered trees lay pointing radially outward in a vast circle of destruction. Almost 60 miles away at the trading post of Vanavara people were knocked to the ground by the force of the blast, and an hour later the seismic wave was picked up at the South Kensington Meteorological Office in London almost 4,000 miles away.

The debate still rages about the true nature of this titanic explosion. Most agree that some sort of extraterrestrial body, travelling at perhaps 60,000 miles an hour, detonated when it collided with the Earth's atmosphere. Some maintain that it was a 100,000-ton asteroid, others believe that it was a football-field-sized meteorite, and some insist it was a wayward comet fragment composed mainly of ice and dust. A more abstruse theory holds that the cataclysm was caused by a chunk of anti-matter, but a few assert that it was the explosion of the main drive reactor in a UFO manned by aliens bent on invading the Earth.

Also on this day

1520: Spanish conquistadors murder Aztec Emperor Moctezuma * 1934: Adolf Hitler orders the purge of his own party in the 'Night of the Long Knives' * 1936: Margaret Mitchell's *Gone with the Wind* is published

1 July

Teddy Roosevelt's Rough Riders storm San Juan Hill

1898 In the midday Cuban sun, thousands of American soldiers lay along the trough of the San Juan River, waiting for orders, sweltering in the riverbed, low on food, water and ammunition. Ahead of them, past the jungle fringe, they could see open ground leading to their objective, the strong defensive positions atop San Juan Hill and neighbouring Kettle Hill, from which Spanish rifle fire was having effect.

On the far right of the line was First US Volunteer Cavalry Regiment, a picturesque contingent of cowboys and college men who like thousands of their peers had joined the crusade to free Cuba from Spanish tyranny. An appreciative press had dubbed the regiment variously 'Teddy's Terrors', 'Rocky Mountain Rustlers', and finally, still alliteratively and most pleasing to its lieutenant colonel, 'Roosevelt's Rough Riders'.

Not too many weeks earlier, Theodore Roosevelt had been the Assistant Secretary of the United States Navy. But Roosevelt knew an absolutely bully opportunity when he saw one, and with war declared against Spain he resigned his office to raise a regiment of volunteers.

Around 2.00 p.m., Gatling guns were brought forward and went into action, clearing the Spanish soldiers from the top of San Juan Hill. Now, commanders shouted out orders to advance, and from the jungle beyond the riverbed a long line of blue-shirted figures emerged and started across the meadows. The Rough Riders were in reserve, but when Roosevelt got the message, 'Move forward and support the regulars', he decided it called for an all-out charge. Gesticulating with his hat, he led the way, mounted on his horse Texas, followed by a crowd of Rough Riders and black troopers from the Ninth and Tenth Cavalry. In a rush, they took Kettle Hill.

To his left, he could see the main advance stalled on San Juan Hill some 700 yards away, as American artillery, two miles to the rear and so far largely inactive, suddenly opened up on the summit. Frantic waving of hats and flags called off the firing, but the delay allowed Roosevelt time to join the attack for its final drive. In a few glorious minutes it was over, and all along the ridgeline American soldiers stood, firing at the backs of the retreating enemy and gazing down at the city of Santiago.

It was 4.00 p.m. Roosevelt brought order to the happy confusion of victory, formed up the soldiers on the summit, and prepared to meet the press. One historian wrote of the occasion: '... as the newspaper dispatches went off describing the heroism of the Rough Riders and their lieutenant-colonel, another military genius had been given to American history'.

Hostilities were over by August, and Secretary of State John Hay pronounced the outing 'a splendid little war'. And so it was for the United States, which in acquiring Puerto Rico, Guam and the Philippine Islands became a world power; for Cuba, which gained its independence after 400 years of Spanish rule; and for Colonel Roosevelt, his nation's newest hero, who went on to become governor of New York, vice president for President William McKinley, and on McKinley's death on 14 September 1901, President of the United States.

Also on this day

1646: German mathematician and philosopher Gottfried Leibniz is born in Leipzig * 1863: The Battle of Gettysburg, the bloodiest battle of the American Civil War, begins * 1916: British troops attack German positions to begin the Battle of the Somme, suffering 60,000 killed, wounded or captured on the first day

2 July

Amelia Earhart, America's first and foremost aviatrix, vanishes in flight

1937 'KHAQQ calling *Itasca*. We must be on you but cannot see you but gas is running low ... unable to reach you by radio, we are flying at 1,000 feet ... one-half hour fuel and no landfall.'

At 7.42 this morning the US coastguard cutter *Itasca* received this short message from Amelia Earhart's Lockheed Electra as the great aviatrix tried to negotiate the last 2,556 miles from Lae in Papua New Guinea to the tiny coral atoll of Howland Island in the remote Pacific. Just over an hour later she briefly radioed her plane's position. She was never heard from again.

By 1937 Amelia Earhart was nearing 40, already the most celebrated woman pilot on Earth. She had been the first woman to solo across the Atlantic, the first to solo non-stop across the United States, the first to solo from Hawaii to California. She was determined to take up what she considered the ultimate challenge – flying 29,000 miles around the world.

On the first day of June she and her navigator Fred Noonan took off from Miami on the first leg of the trip headed for San Juan in Puerto Rico. From there she followed the north-east rim of South America, then headed north-east again to cross Africa at its widest point. Skirting the Persian Gulf, she proceeded on to Karachi and Calcutta and then to Rangoon, Bangkok, Singapore, Java, Port Darwin in northern Australia and finally Papua New Guinea. She now had covered over 22,000 miles.

Earhart knew the next leg flying eastward from New Guinea would be the most difficult one. Even with all inessentials removed from the plane to accommodate extra aviation fuel, she calculated that she had a safety margin of only about 10 per cent. But finding Howland Island would be challenging under the best of circumstances, a tiny dot in the wide Pacific just above the Equator, only a mile and a half long and half a mile wide.

The *Itasca* and three other ships were positioned as markers along her route. When they received her fuel shortage warning the *Itasca* changed its fuel mix to send heavy black smoke billowing upwards in the hope of providing the flyers with some sort of visual landmark, but the sky remained empty. As the hours ticked by it became certain that the plane had been lost.

President Franklin Roosevelt immediately dispatched nine ships and 66 aircraft to search 250,000 square miles of ocean, but no trace of the plane or its passengers was ever found.

Americans love conspiracies, and there were plenty put forward to explain Amelia Earhart's disappearance. Some claimed she had deliberately crashed into the ocean, while others maintained that she had been on a secret mission from President Roosevelt and had been captured by the Japanese. One bizarre notion was that she had been captured and then turned traitor, becoming the radio voice of Tokyo Rose during the war. For years there was 'hope' that she would be found on some isolated Pacific island, living with the natives.

Serious historians, however, are unanimous in their view that Earhart simply lost her way and crashed into the ocean when her fuel ran out. She had been well aware of the dangers she faced, writing to her husband shortly before her departure, 'Please know I am quite aware of the hazards ... Women must try to do things as men have tried. When they fail, their failure must be but a challenge to others.'

Also on this day

1566: Fortune-teller Nostradamus dies * 1644: The Roundheads defeat Prince Rupert and the Cavaliers at Marston Moor in the English Civil War * 1778: French philosopher Jean-Jacques Rousseau dies * 1850: British Prime Minister Robert Peel dies after being thrown from a horse * 1870: Italian King Victor Emmanuel II enters Rome on the unification of Italy * 1881: American President James Garfield is shot and fatally wounded by religious fanatic Charles Guiteau

3 July

Birth of the Universal Spider

1423 Today in the city of Bourges the future Louis XI of France was born, a king remembered in history as 'the universal spider' for the plots he spun and the enemies he entrapped as he broke the feudal power of France's medieval barons.

Although fat and ugly, Louis was shrewd, intelligent, witty, devious and ruthless. He was informal at a time when pomp and ceremony were universally admired, and he had little respect for title or family. (He infuriated the nobility by sending his barber, the famous Olivier le Daim, as an ambassador.) Suspicious and superstitious, he suffered agonies from haemorrhoids and thought that lack of sex made them worse. Although devoutly religious, he still locked up the traitorous Cardinal Balue in an iron cage for over ten years.

During his reign of 22 years, Louis fought almost every powerful noble within reach. The list includes Holy Roman Emperor Frederick III, the Dukes of Bourbon, Armagnac and Brittany, Jean II of Aragon and his own brother, Charles of France. His most renowned enemy was Charles the Bold of Burgundy, who once held Louis prisoner but whom Louis eventually destroyed.

But the crafty Louis did not always have to do battle in order to best his foes. When England's Edward IV invaded France in 1475, Louis called for a parley and then arranged three days of sumptuous banquets and celebration with Edward and his captains before proposing a peace treaty. Then the cunning king offered Edward a pension in exchange for agreeing to recognise Louis's claim to all of France. Most pleased with this arrangement, Louis remarked to one of his courtiers, 'I have chased the English out of France more easily than even my father [Charles VII] did, for my father drove them out by force of arms, while I have driven them out with venison pies and good wine.'

Louis made the French monarchy more powerful than it had been since the time of Philip the Fair a century and a half before. He felt strongly about his rights and power as King of France and set the precedent for arrogance by French heads of state by telling his barons, 'I am France.' (In 1655 Louis XIV echoed this grand sentiment with his celebrated 'L'Etat, c'est moi', and three centuries after that Charles de Gaulle proclaimed 'Je suis la France!' He subsequently maintained that 'When I want to know what France thinks, I ask myself.')

Also on this day

1853: Russia invades Moldavia to start the Crimean War * 1866: Venice becomes part of a united Kingdom of Italy * 1940: British warships destroy the French fleet anchored at Mers-el-Kebir

4 July

Thomas Jefferson and John Adams die on Independence Day

1826 Today the United States reached its 50th birthday, firm in democracy, independence and progress. Instead of the thirteen original states, now there were 24, including two west of the Mississippi. The population had quintupled to 12 million, the country was at peace and one of its great selfless servants, John Quincy Adams, was President.

It had been hoped that celebrations in Washington would be embellished by two of the nation's surviving founders, John Adams, second president, signer of the Declaration of Independence and father of the current president, and Thomas Jefferson, America's greatest political thinker, author and signer of the Declaration of Independence and third president. But Adams was 90, living quietly in Quincy, Massachusetts, while Jefferson at 83 had long since retired to his beloved Monticello in Virginia.

So Washington had to celebrate without these two great men. It was only two days later that the news finally arrived: Jefferson had died quietly at one o'clock in the afternoon on 4 July, and John Adams followed him shortly before six. A poignant aside, among Adams's last words were 'Jefferson survives'.

John Quincy Adams interpreted this strange and solemn marking of America's 50th birthday as a 'visible and palpable' indication of divine favour to the two departed founders and to the nation they had helped to create.

Also on this day

1187: Saracen leader Saladin annihilates the Christian army of the King of Jerusalem at Hattin * 1190: English King Richard the Lion-Heart and French King Philip Augustus leave together on crusade * 1776: The US Declaration of Independence is signed * 1807: Italian revolutionary Giuseppe Garibaldi is born

5 July

Napoleon's last victory

1809 A map of Paris is virtually a monument to the Emperor Napoleon. Almost 30 streets are named after his generals, the Avenue de la Grand Armée honours his army, the sixth arrondisement boasts a rue Bonaparte, a street where he lived was re-christened rue de la Victoire, and all Napoleon's military glory is commemorated together in the Arc de Triomphe. On top of that, twelve of his great victories are commemorated in place names: there are streets called Castiglione, Arcole, Rivoli, Pyramides (as well as a square), Aboukir, Marengo and Ulm. His most famous triumph, Austerlitz, has a street, a bridge, a port, a quay and even a railway station. Then comes Iéna with a walk, a square and a bridge and finally there are the avenues – Eylau (which is also a villa), Friedland and Wagram.

The last of these, Wagram, was fought today outside Vienna, and it was indeed the last, for Napoleon never won another major victory.

Wagram was a bloody, two-day battle fought by huge armies in terrible midsummer heat. It was especially notable for the massed artillery fire with which Napoleon buttressed the uncertain performance of his Saxon and Italian units; and for the extraordinary feats his engineers performed in bridging the Danube, which allowed the 188,000 soldiers and 488 guns of the Grande Armée to make a timely night crossing to the battlefield. The Austrian army, 155,000 soldiers under the command of Archduke Charles, was decisively defeated but withdrew intact. Six days later Austria asked for an armistice, which Napoleon granted.

Battle losses were extensive: over 32,000 killed, wounded or captured for the Grande Armée, almost 40,000 for the Austrian army. Among the Austrian casualties of war might be counted the great composer Joseph Haydn, aged 77, who died of shock and humiliation at the French occupation of his beloved Vienna.

In the peace treaty that followed the end of hostilities, the

Austrian Emperor Franz I was forced to pay a heavy war indemnity and to cede huge tracts of territory – including Salzburg, part of Galicia, Trieste and the Dalmatian coast – to France and her allies.

Eager to celebrate his victory, Napoleon sent for his Polish mistress Marie Walewska, installed her in the Schönbrunn Palace outside Vienna, and to his delight – and relief – quickly impregnated her, thus demonstrating that he was not sterile. The happy news prompted him to consider the prospect of a new marriage, one that would produce an heir to his empire. The news was less happy for Marie and the Empress Joséphine, both of whom would be cast aside for a new empress. She turned out to be a daughter of the Austrian Emperor, the Archduchess Marie Louise, whom Napoleon married the following April.

Finally, the Russian Tsar Alexander I, on hearing of Wagram and its aftermath, drew the prescient conclusion that the Austrians had been too quick to capitulate. 'People don't know how to suffer', the Tsar remarked to an aide-de-camp. 'If the fighting went against me, I should retire to Kamchatka rather than cede provinces and sign, in my capital, treaties that were really only truces. Your Frenchman is brave; but long privations and a bad climate will wear him down and discourage him. Our climate, our winter, will fight on our side.' Paris boasts no rue de la Russie.

Also on this day

1810: American showman P.T. Barnum is born * 1853: British empire builder Cecil Rhodes is born * 1950: American forces engage the North Koreans for the first time at Osan, South Korea

6 July

Sir Thomas More is beheaded

1535 On this day Sir Thomas More, writer, humanist philosopher and one-time Lord Chancellor to Henry VIII, met his end under the axe in the Tower of London. His crime had been double: he refused to support Henry's claim to supremacy over the Pope, and he refused to attend the King's marriage to Anne Boleyn, with the implication that Henry was still married to Catherine of Aragon.

Brought to trial for treason, More's conviction was never in doubt; three of the judges were Anne Boleyn's father, uncle and brother. For good measure, the prosecution used perjured testimony. Nothing better expresses the tyranny and callous injustice of Henry's reign than Sir Richard Riche's accusation condemning More's refusal to speak: 'Even though we should have no word or deed to charge against you, yet we have your silence, and that is a sign of your evil intention and a sure proof of malice.' But the ultimate cause of the conviction was the simple fact that Henry wanted it.

More kept his equanimity to the very end. As he walked to the scaffold on Tower Hill he said to his guard, 'See me safe up, and for my coming down let me shift for myself.' He then tied his own blindfold.

As he knelt to put his head on the block, More pushed aside his long beard, saying, 'it has never committed treason'. Then, turning to the executioner, he spoke for the last time. 'Pluck up thy spirits, man, and be not afraid to do thine office; my neck is very short; take heed therefore thou strike not awry, for saving of thine honesty.' And then the axe fell and one of the 16th century's noblest men was dead at the age of 57.

Four hundred years later, More, the man whom Erasmus had dubbed 'a man for all seasons', was declared a saint.

Also on this day

1189: Henry II of England dies at Chinon * 1415: Czech religious reformer Jan Hus is burned at the stake * 1685: The army of James II defeats the rebel Duke of Monmouth at Sedgemoor in the last land battle ever fought on British soil * 1762: Tsar Peter III is assassinated in prison, with the collusion of his wife Catherine the Great

7 July

The shot that started the Second World War

1937 The First World War began one morning in Sarajevo with the killing of an archduke. The Second World War began one night at a railway junction in China with the killing of a common soldier.

Twelve miles west of Peking, there is a place called Lukouchaio, where the railway line from Tientsin joins the Peking–Hankow line. It is in an area of northern China that had been ceded for commercial exploitation to Japan under a 1933 treaty. On the night of 7 July a brigade of the Japanese Kwantung Army was conducting night exercises in the area. At some point, a shot rang out, and not long afterwards Japanese troops discovered the dead body of one of their comrades lying near the ancient Marco Polo Bridge.

It has never been established who killed the soldier, but the Japanese government chose to make the China Incident, as it referred to the event, a *casus belli*. It presented China with an ultimatum: agree by 18 July to hand over the two northern provinces of Hopei and Chahar or Japan would act.

The only question now was what Chiang Kai-shek, the leader of Nationalist China, would do. Over the past decade the Generalissimo had shown reluctance to tangle with the Japanese over their numerous grabs of Chinese territory, preferring to pursue civil war against the Communists while waiting for the Western powers to help him defeat both of his foes.

Some seven months earlier, however, Chiang had experienced something rarely encountered by heads of state: he had been kidnapped by one of his own generals who wanted to force Chiang to abandon the civil war and form a united front against Japan. To preserve face, it was important for Chiang to avoid giving the impression of having secured his release by making a political bargain with his kidnapper. But there was no doubt that he had.

In the face of the Japanese ultimatum, there was initial silence from Nanking, the Nationalist capital. When at last Chiang responded, it was no ringing declaration, no call to arms for his people. He did nothing beyond stating that no more Chinese territory would be surrendered to Japan, but the implication of his words seemed clear: armed resistance would meet another incursion. At least that is how the residents of Peking interpreted the broadcast of Chiang's message, for they ran into the streets cheering and beating gongs.

A few days later Japan began the invasion of China, for which she had long planned, needing only a China Incident to begin it. Ten thousand of her troops crossed over the Great Wall and advanced into Hopei province. At first, the conflict was known as the Second Sino-Japanese War, but in a few years the world would come to see it as the first act of the Second World War.

Also on this day

1860: Austrian composer Gustav Mahler is born in Kaliste, Czechoslovakia * 1887: Russian painter Marc Chagall is born

8 July

Ernest Hemingway's wound inspires a great novel

1918 Shortly after midnight at Fossalta on the Piave front in northern Italy, an Austrian mortar shell exploded near a lonely farmhouse that was serving as a canteen for Italian soldiers. Among the casualties was an American Red Cross driver named Ernest Hemingway, severely wounded by shrapnel. An ambulance took him to a field hospital in Treviso, where he was transferred by train to Milan and the Ospedale Croce Rossa Americana. Here young Hemingway, just nineteen years old, underwent two operations, and then did what all wounded men at war are supposed to do: he fell in love with his nurse.

She was 26-year-old Agnes Korowsky, of Washington, DC. Their affair, such as it was, was enjoyable, but rather one-sided (his), and brief. Ernest went home to Oak Park, Illinois, in January 1919, and began the process of transforming himself into a war hero. Agnes stayed on in Italy as a nurse, and in March wrote him a 'Dear John' letter. For the world at large, however, it may have been the best way for things to turn out, because eventually Hemingway would write about his experiences – in Italy, being wounded, falling in love – and put them in a book that has one of the most memorable openings of any modern novel:

'In the late summer of that year we lived in a house in the village that looked across the river and the plain to the mountains. In the bed of the river there were pebbles and boulders, dry and white in the sun, and the water was clear and swiftly moving and blue in the channels. Troops went by the house and down the road and the dust they raised powdered the leaves of the trees. The trunks of trees too were dusty and the leaves fell early that year and we saw the troops marching along the road and the dust rising and leaves, stirred by the breeze, falling and the soldiers marching and afterward the road bare and white except for the leaves.'

It is the beginning of *A Farewell to Arms*.

Also on this day

1521: Ferdinand von Habsburg marries Anne of Hungary, leading to the incorporation of Hungary into the Austrian Empire * 1709: Peter the Great defeats Charles XII of Sweden at the Battle of Poltava * 1822: English poet Percy Bysshe Shelley drowns off Leghorn, Italy * 1839: American oil tycoon John D. Rockefeller is born

9 July

The end of the Medici

1737 For thirteen years Gian Gastone de' Medici had ruled as Grand Duke of Tuscany, but his few well-intentioned efforts to rebuild his state were washed away by his laziness, his alcoholism and his taste for bright young boys. Florence was now a bankrupt backwater, with only the jewels of its buildings and art treasures to remind the world of its vanished greatness, and Gian Gastone himself was the only reminder of the great Medici family that had been so vital in creating that greatness.

Since Cosimo the Elder had first dominated Florence in 1434, the Medici had produced a vast array of illustrious and prominent people. The most famous undoubtedly was Lorenzo the Magnificent, Cosimo's grandson, the greatest art patron the world has known. Lorenzo's son Giovanni became Pope Leo X, the first of the Medici popes. Later came Clement VII, the illegitimate grandson of Lorenzo's father, and finally Leo XI, Lorenzo's great-grandson.

Other illustrious Medici include Alessandro, Duke of Florence (the illegitimate son of the illegitimate Pope Clement VII), and two queens of France, first Catherine de' Medici (Lorenzo's great-granddaughter) and then Marie, a distant cousin.

By 1569 the Medici were so powerful that another Cosimo, descended from Cosimo the Elder's brother, became the Duke of Tuscany. He was followed by five more Grand Dukes, of which the last was Gian Gastone.

In 1737 Gian Gastone was a tired 65. Given his predilection for boys, it is not surprising that he was childless. He spent most of his days in bed, beard straggling and body unwashed. Thus it was almost expected when death came to him on 9 July. And so the great Medici family came to an end after 303 years of pre-eminence.

Also on this day

1497: Portuguese navigator Vasco da Gama leaves the River Tagus on a historic voyage to India via the Cape of Good Hope * 1553: Lady Jane Grey is proclaimed Queen

10 July

El Cid's last great (posthumous) victory

1099 Greatest of Spanish folk heroes, knight and conqueror, scourge of the Moors, faithful defender of Christian Spain. Such is the legend of Roderigo Díaz de Bivar, known to history as El Cid.

El Cid was in fact a mercenary warlord who fought for the Moors as well as against them. Even his popular name is revealing: El Cid comes from *Cid-y*, meaning 'my lord' in Arabic. But whoever's side he was on, El Cid was one of the most powerful figures in 11th-century Spain and undoubtedly its greatest general. He played an important role in saving his country from complete Moorish domination.

Although myth makes El Cid a noble knight on a par with King Arthur, the truth is less glorious. When he conquered Valencia from the Moors, he promised the Moorish commander Ibn Jahhaf that he would be spared. But as soon as he had fully taken over the town he had Ibn Jahhaf burned alive.

Many legends surround El Cid but none greater than that of his death on this day in Valencia, which he ruled.

Ailing and middle-aged (he was 56), El Cid died while the city was under siege from King Bucar and a vast Moorish army. But, following his deathbed instructions, El Cid's generals waited twelve days and then strapped his armoured body upright on his faithful horse Bavieca. At midnight, with El Cid in the lead, the entire army rode out through the city gates. Then, as the noble corpse moved forward with the baggage train, the Spanish knights turned and attacked the sleeping Moors from behind.

According to the *Chronica del Cid*, an almost contemporary account, 'it seemed to King Bucar that before them came a knight of great stature upon a white horse with a bloody cross, who bore in one hand a white banner and in the other a sword which seemed of fire and he made great mortality among the Moors ... And King Bucar and the other kings were so dismayed they never checked the reins until they had ridden into the sea.'

After the Moors had fled, El Cid's body was taken to the monastery of San Pedro de Cardeña, near Burgos, where for ten years it remained seated on an ivory chair before receiving proper burial. Not surprisingly, a superstitious cult soon grew up around the tomb.

El Cid's posthumous triumph in Valencia was not to last. The Moors reoccupied the city less than three years later and controlled it until 1238.

El Cid lives on in Spanish legend, and he is celebrated in the most famous Spanish epic poem, *El Cantar de mío Cid* (The Song of the Cid). Over 500 years later Pierre Corneille commemorated him again in his great drama *Le Cid*.

Also on this day

AD 138: Roman Emperor Hadrian dies at Baiae * 1509: Founder of Calvinism John Calvin is born * 1830: French painter Camille Pissarro is born * 1871: French novelist Marcel Proust is born * 1940: The Battle of Britain begins

11 July

The most famous duel in American history

1804 Alexander Hamilton may have been the most influential American politician who never attained the presidency. His vision of America as a powerful and prosperous industrial nation governed by a strong central government formed the basis for the economic and political system that still exists.

But during his career, Hamilton made a bitter enemy of Aaron Burr, another New York politician who favoured a more pastoral, decentralised America.

In 1799 Hamilton's influence helped gain the presidency for Thomas Jefferson, and Burr had to settle for the vice-presidency. Four years later Hamilton helped thwart Burr's hopes of becoming governor of New York.

Hating Hamilton for his influence – and for his attacks on his honesty – Burr challenged him to America's most famous duel.

At dawn on 11 July, the two adversaries and their seconds were rowed across the Hudson River to Weehawken in New Jersey – duels were illegal in New York. By morbid coincidence, it was the same spot where Hamilton's son had been killed in a duel three years before. Grimly they measured their positions, pistols in hand. The time was just 7.30.

Two shots broke the morning calm. Hamilton's was wide, but Burr's aim was true, and Hamilton fell, clutching his stomach, blood seeping through his fingers.

Although constantly attended by a surgeon, Hamilton died 28 hours later, at the age of only 49. Burr lived on another 32 years, the only American vice-president to fight a duel (although one president, Andrew Jackson, killed a man in a duel before he became president). The dead Hamilton had more influence over his nation than the man who shot him and survived.

Also on this day

1274: Scottish King Robert the Bruce is born * 1754: Language bowdleriser Thomas Bowdler is born

12 July

The birth of Julius Caesar

100 BC Born today was Gaius Julius Caesar, the greatest man of ancient times, perhaps of all time. He came from an aristocratic Roman family that fancied it could trace its lineage back through Aeneas to his mother, the goddess Venus. For all that, the Julian family was not particularly rich, and Caesar achieved what he did through a combination of outstanding intelligence, brilliant generalship, hard calculation and the ability to make men, especially his soldiers, love him. He was an outstanding swordsman and horseman and totally fearless in battle, always leading from the front, wearing a scarlet cape so that his men could see him. The great Roman statesman Cicero called him 'an instrument of wrath, terrifying in his vigilance, swiftness and energy'.

Caesar was tall, fair and well-built with brown eyes. His only physical defects seem to have been that he suffered from epileptic fits and in later life started to go bald.

Caesar demonstrated his cool courage and colder determination early in life. Still in his teens, he was en route to Rhodes to study when he was captured by pirates. He charmed the pirates and scolded them for setting his ransom too low, telling them that he was worth far more than they imagined. In apparent jest, he also promised that he would crucify them all when he was released, a threat he carried out by raising a naval force at his own expense and hunting them down. His only show of mercy was to have their throats cut before crucifixion.

Although Caesar was an unparalleled womaniser, there were rumours that he bedded men as well. These stemmed from time spent in his youth in Bithynia in the company of the effeminate King Nicomedes. Later in life, when Caesar had become a power in Rome, one of his political enemies jibed that he was 'the Queen of Bithynia, who once wanted to sleep with a king and now wants to be one'.

Caesar changed the course of history twice, once by conquering Gaul, where for nine years he was the governor, thereby turning France into a Latin nation, and once by assuming the dictatorship of Rome, ending for ever the Roman Republic. Although he was never a Roman emperor, to this day derivations of his name mean emperor, as in 'kaiser' in German and 'tsar' in Russian.

In 45 BC Caesar instituted the Julian calendar, which was in universal use until 1582. (At the time Cicero joked, 'Even the stars now obey Caesar in his commands.') Although the calendar itself has been superseded, we still have the month of July, named after the great man who was born on the twelfth day of it. Contrary to common belief, however, Caesar was not delivered by Caesarean. Two thousand years ago such an operation was invariably fatal to the mother, and we know that Caesar's mother lived until he was an adult.

Also on this day
1536: Dutch humanist Desiderius Erasmus dies * 1730: American
writer Henry David Thoreau is born * 1884: Italian painter Amadeo
Modigliani is born

13 July

Charlotte Corday stabs Marat in his bath

1793 Although born in Switzerland to a Swiss mother and Sardinian
father, Jean Paul Marat eventually became one of France's most
fanatical and implacable revolutionaries.

Marat's early history suggested a more conventional life. In his
30s he moved to London, becoming an eminent physician as well
as the author of a number of scientific books. At 34 he returned to
Paris to become doctor to the personal guards of Louis XVI's
brother, the future Charles X. He continued to conduct scientific
experiments and publish learned tracts while attracting patients
from the upper classes. He even corresponded with Benjamin
Franklin.

Marat had an exaggerated view of his own achievements, considering himself superior to Sir Isaac Newton. But few shared this
exalted opinion, and he was rejected by the Académie des
Sciences. Over the years he came to feel not only unappreciated but
betrayed by the world in which he lived and blamed it on the
French aristocracy that set the standards. The more he considered
the injustices done to him, the more he related them to social
injustices done to the people. He became a revolutionary.

In the 1780s he turned to publishing, becoming the editor of the
incendiary newspaper *L'Ami du Peuple*. By 1790 he was telling the
public, 'Five or six hundred heads cut off would assure your
repose, freedom, and happiness.'

Forty-nine years old in the summer of 1793, Marat was a dark,
intense man who suffered terribly from open sores on his face and
body, the result of prurigo contracted while hiding in the Paris

sewers earlier in the Revolution. This affliction caused him great pain, and the only relief available to him was through soaking in the bath.

On this day in 1793 Marat was taking just such a therapeutic bath at his house at 30 rue des Cordeliers when a servant handed him a note. 'Have the goodness to receive me,' it read, 'I can help you to render a great service to France.' Intrigued, he agreed to see the visitor, a young aristocrat from Caen named Charlotte Corday.

Although of noble family, Charlotte Corday was a strong believer in democracy, but she thought Marat was leading France into radicalism and anarchy. Entering the room where he was bathing, she at first pretended to reveal secret information, naming putative royalists in Caen. Marat smiled and unknowingly guaranteed his own death with the response, 'They shall all go to the guillotine.'

Pulling a dinner knife from her bodice, Corday stabbed Marat to the heart, killing him instantly. Four days later she went calmly to the guillotine for her deed.

Jacques Louis David immortalised the murder in one of his greatest paintings. Like Marat, David was a radical member of the National Convention, and thus the painting is perhaps the only one of a murder painted by a great artist who actually knew the victim he portrayed.

In death Marat became a national hero, with 21 towns named in his honour (of which only one remains). In recognition of his revolutionary fervour, the Soviet Navy named one of its first battleships after him.

Also on this day

1643: Lord Wilmot leads royalist troops to victory over the Roundheads in the Battle of Roundway Down in the English Civil War * 1870: Chancellor Otto von Bismarck sends the doctored 'Ems Telegram' to incite the French into declaring the Franco-Prussian War

14 July

The fall of the Bastille

1789 Over the centuries we have come to imagine the Bastille as a grim, grey fortress of cold stone in which innocents withered away and died, chained to the wall in bleak cells on the order of reactionary and contemptuous French kings. And when we think of 14 July – Bastille Day – we envision the heroics of a downtrodden people overcoming the King's heavily armed guards to free the hundreds of innocent prisoners inside.

The 'real' Bastille in Paris was indeed a massive medieval fortress. Built in the 14th century, it consisted of eight round towers connected by walls 100 feet high. In the summer of 1789 it was manned by 114 guards under the command of Bernard de Launay.

On Tuesday 14 July, a mob of some 800 revolutionary Parisians decided to assault the Bastille, a symbol of royal repression. Gathering outside the walls, they attacked with muskets and cannon captured in the Invalides earlier in the day. But it soon became apparent that the defenders could hold out indefinitely; some 100 of the mob had already been killed.

Although in no immediate danger, de Launay wished to avoid more bloodshed and offered to open the gates if his soldiers were spared. The attackers gave assurances of safety, and the drawbridge was lowered. Immediately the rioters rushed in and massacred the garrison, including its commander.

And so trickery rather than force of arms took the Bastille. Inside there were a mere seven prisoners.

The start of the French Revolution is generally dated to the fall of the Bastille, but it was another three years before the abolition of the monarchy. Even then it took a further 88 years before Bastille Day was established as a national holiday in France.

Also on this day

1835: American painter James Abbott McNeil Whistler is born * 1881: American outlaw Billy the Kid is shot dead by Sheriff Pat Garrett * 1933:

Germany passes the Law for the Protection of Hereditary Health, the beginning of the Nazi euthanasia programme

15 July

The Crusaders conquer Jerusalem

1099 Today, with the aid of assault towers and scaling ladders, 15,000 crusaders stormed the walls of the holy city of Jerusalem crying, 'Help us, God!' The First Crusade had triumphed.

'Jerusalem is the navel of the world', had cried Pope Urban II at the Council of Clermont four years earlier. His call for a holy war might seem a trifle tardy – Jerusalem had been a Muslim city for over 400 years – but it was only in 1071 when the Seljuk Turks swept down from central Asia that the city was cut off from Christian travellers. So Urban called out, and the First Crusade was launched.

Perhaps as many as 50,000 knights, soldiers and camp followers started on this great adventure, including minor nobles seeking their fortunes and peasants seeking their freedom from the feudal ties that bound them at home. For three years the weary crusaders trudged across Europe and Asia Minor, attacked by hunger, thirst, disease, bandits and Turkish guerrillas. Finally reaching Palestine, they were roasted in their armour by the terrible heat, but still they came on. By the time they reached the Holy City in June 1099, more than half had died, deserted or simply wandered off.

When the inspired crusaders finally breached Jerusalem's walls, the Saracen defenders fled to the Temple of Solomon, but soon the attackers had smashed through its gates. There, according to an eyewitness, 'in this temple almost ten thousand were decapitated. If you had been there, you would have seen our feet splattered with the blood of the dead ... Not a single life was spared, not even women or children. You would have seen a wondrous sight, when our poorest soldiers, learning of the Saracens' cleverness, cut open the stomachs of the slain to take from their bowels the jewels they had swallowed while still alive. A few days later the bodies were piled up in a great heap and burned in order to find coins more easily in the burnt ashes.'

When at last the crusaders ran out of Muslims, they herded resident Jews into their main synagogue and burnt it to the ground.

Thus 15 July is the day of Christianity's greatest military victory. It resulted in the establishment of the Latin Kingdom of Jerusalem, of which the first ruler was Godefroi de Bouillon, the first Christian knight to stand on the conquered city's walls. He rejected the title of king, preferring Defender and Baron of the Holy Sepulchre, saying, 'I will not wear a crown of gold where my Saviour wore one of thorns.'

The Christian kingdom lasted for almost two centuries, although Jerusalem itself fell to the great Saracen leader Saladin in 1187. Ironically, the day the Christians took Jerusalem from its Muslim defenders was the exact anniversary of the Hegira, the day in 622 when Mohammed fled to Medina and which is considered the traditional beginning of the Muslim Era.

Also on this day

622: Mohammed flees from Mecca to Medina – the Hegira – the beginning of the Muslim era * 1606: Dutch painter Rembrandt van Rijn is born * 1834: The Decree of Suppression brings an end to the Spanish Inquisition * 1904: Russian playwright Anton Chekhov dies at Badenweiler, Germany

16 July

The threat of Muslim domination in Spain is extinguished at Las Navas de Tolosa

1212 Almost exactly half a millennium before – in 711 – a bold Arab chief named Tarik led some 12,000 warriors across the eight-mile channel that separates Morocco from Spain, to land at a point that still bears his name, Jebel-al-Tarik (meaning mount of Tarik), corrupted over the centuries to Gibraltar. For the next 500 years the Arabs (or Moors) continually advanced northward in Spain until they ruled most of it, in spite of Christian efforts to halt them.

In 1158 three-year-old Alfonso VIII inherited the throne of Castile and León. During his long years as King, Alfonso became increasingly determined to rid the peninsula of Moorish, that is to say Muslim, domination, and in 1212 he finally acted decisively.

First the King called on that redoubtable pope, Innocent III, to lend his spiritual (and political) support. Innocent was the instigator of two crusades to the Holy Land and another against the Albigensian heretics, so Alfonso felt confident that he would enthusiastically join any effort to attack the Muslims in Spain.

Innocent responded as anticipated; he proclaimed a crusade and urged the rulers of Aragon, Navarre and Portugal to join the Castilian army under Alfonso's leadership.

On 16 July Alfonso's formidable army met the Moors at the Battle of Las Navas de Tolosa (40 miles north of modern Jaén in Andalucía). Alfonso personally led the Christian forces into battle, and their victory was total. (Pope Innocent's fervent support for the campaign may have been noticed on high, for he was called to heaven precisely four years to the day after the battle.)

Las Navas de Tolosa was one of the decisive battles of European history. Although it took more than two centuries fully to defeat the Moors, from this day forward the Christians were predominant, the Moors in retreat. The threat of a Muslim Spain – or Europe – was over, until more than 300 years later, when the Muslim danger came from another direction, with the Turkish armies of Suleiman the Magnificent.

Also on this day

1796: French painter Camille Corot is born * 1918: Communist insurgents shoot Tsar Nicholas II, Alexandra and their four children in a cellar at Ekaterinburg * 1945: The first atom bomb explodes at Alamogordo, New Mexico, at 5.24 a.m.

17 July

The end of the Hundred Years' War

1453 Today, as French cannon ceased firing on a vanquished English army at Castillon on the lower Dordogne, the Hundred Years' War – which actually lasted for 116 years – at last came to an end.

It had all started in 1337 when Edward III of England laid claim to the crown of France through the blood of his mother, Isabelle de Valois, daughter of King Philip the Fair of France. At first the English must have thought the war an enormous success with the great English victories at Crécy, Poitiers and Agincourt, but then the French had their turn with the stirring triumphs of Joan of Arc.

The defeat at Castillon left the kings of England no more of France than Edward III had controlled 100 years before.

But Britain did gain one lasting heritage from the war. During the century of fighting England's triumphs were primarily thanks to the longbow, the powerful weapon that could fire armour-piercing arrows two and a half feet long.

So formidable were the English longbows that the French cut off the first two fingers of any captured bowmen so they could no longer fire their bows. The bowmen's reaction to the French threat was to lift two fingers in contempt at the enemy, thus giving birth to the derisive two-fingered signal that the English use to this day to mock their opponents.

Also on this day

1674: The bones of two boys are found in the Tower of London, presumed to be the children of Edward IV * 1793: French patriot Charlotte Corday is guillotined * 1872: Mexican President Benito Juárez dies at his desk of a heart attack

18 July

Nero burns Rome

AD 64 On this night soldiers acting on the orders of their emperor touched off one of the great fires of history.

Among Rome's degenerate emperors, Nero grew to be one of the worst. Becoming Emperor at the age of sixteen, at first he modelled himself on his great-great-grandfather, the Emperor Augustus. During his first four years in power he reduced taxes, banned circus performances in which people were killed or injured and eliminated capital punishment. He even forgave writers of scurrilous criticism of himself and failed to put a single senator to death, a revolution in moderation for the time.

But as Nero became increasingly aware of his unlimited power, he began to change. He took to carousing in the streets at night and acting totally without restraint when it came to his own pleasure. He also fancied himself a great actor and scandalised the Roman nobility by appearing on stage, sometimes even taking the part of a woman. He wrote second-rate poetry and forced audiences to hear him recite it. As the historian Suetonius writes, 'No one was permitted to leave the theatre during his performances. We read of women in the audience giving birth ... and of men who were so bored they pretended they had died in order to be carried away for burial.'

Many of Nero's acts were those of insane egotism. He had one wife executed so he could marry someone else and kicked another wife to death while she was pregnant because she complained when he came home late from the chariot races. His most revolting deeds involved his revolting mother, Agrippina. (Agrippina was an interesting role model for Nero. She murdered her second husband so she could incestuously marry her own uncle, the emperor-to-be Claudius, having already contrived to murder Claudius's previous wife. Five years later she poisoned Claudius so that Nero could inherit supreme power, and four months after that poisoned Claudius's son by his first wife to eliminate a potential rival.)

Nero is reputed to have carried on an incestuous relationship with Agrippina, but when she interfered too much with his imperial powers he tried to drown her by putting her to sea in the Bay of Naples in a boat designed to sink. When she saved herself by swimming ashore, Nero gave orders for her execution, which was duly carried out in her own house. Before she died she cried out to her executioners, 'Strike my womb first!'

But of all Nero's acts of criminal insanity, the most famous is the burning of Rome, then a mighty city of some 900,000 inhabitants. Historians debate whether Nero really was responsible for the fire, but Suetonius claims that on 18 July 64, Nero had his troops wantonly fire the city.

The great conflagration lasted six days and seven nights, destroying huge parts of Rome and killing hundreds. Contrary to popular legend, however, Nero did not fiddle while Rome burned. Mostly he watched the blaze from the Tower of Maecenas, enchanted by what he called 'the beauty of the flames'. He then put on his actor's costume and sang his own composition, *The Sack of Ilium*.

Nero was only 27 at the time of the great fire. Four years later he was overthrown and driven to suicide, to the relief and joy of his people.

Also on this day

1610: Italian painter Caravaggio (Michelangelo Merisi) dies at Porto Ercole * 1811: English novelist William Makepeace Thackeray is born in Calcutta * 1817: English novelist Jane Austen dies * 1869: Pope Pius IX proclaims the doctrine of papal infallibility * 1936: General Francisco Franco orders his troops to rise against the Spanish government, starting the Spanish Civil War

19 July

The first feminist convention in America

1848 Today in the scenic Finger Lakes district of west-central New York State a crowd of about 250 women and 40 men met at Seneca Falls 'to discuss the social, civil, and religious rights of women'. Led by Elizabeth Cady Stanton and Lucretia Mott, who eight years earlier had been barred from the World Anti-Slavery Convention in London on the grounds of their gender, this was the first formal meeting in America of dedicated feminists. After two days of discussion they drew up a list of women's grievances and demands, including the contentious (some said preposterous) notion that women be allowed to vote.

Although American women had been permitted to stand for election since 1788, like their sisters in Great Britain they were long denied equality with men in the election booth.

In Great Britain women's suffrage had been an important cause since at least 1792 when Mary Wollstonecraft made a case for it in her *Vindication of the Rights of Woman*, but the first women's suffrage committee was formed in Manchester only in 1865, seventeen years after the American Seneca Falls Convention. Progress was slow, as even the backing of John Stuart Mill, whose wife was a strong 'suffragette', failed to get Parliament to enact favourable legislation due to the implacable opposition of Queen Victoria.

In 1903, two years after Victoria's death, a strident feminist named Emmeline Pankhurst and her two daughters founded the Women's Social and Political Union. Initially in favour of non-violent protest, in frustration the group turned increasingly militant, smashing Regent Street windows, burning postboxes and cutting telegraph wires. When suffragettes (a term coined by the newspapers) were sent to prison they responded with hunger strikes, and the authorities resorted to force-feeding.

In 1918 the British government finally caved in, but only women over 30 were enfranchised. Ten years later, in a society changed for ever by the war, women were at last given equal rights to men.

Back in the United States women had to wait until 1920 when on 26 August Congress passed the Nineteenth Amendment to the Constitution which stated: 'The right of citizens of the United States to vote shall not be denied or abridged by the United States or by any State on account of sex.'

Both the US and Great Britain were well behind several other nations. As early as 1893 the women of New Zealand had been enfranchised, and other countries that beat them in extending voting rights to women include Australia, Finland, Norway, Russia and Canada. Even Germany allowed women to vote before the United States, in spite of a Prussian law of 1851 that forbade women, along with mentally ill schoolchildren, even from attending meetings where political subjects were discussed.

Not all European countries were so hasty. In France women gained voting rights only in 1944 when the Free French leader in exile Charles de Gaulle issued a wartime decree, and in Italy Mussolini actually rescinded all women's voting rights, restored only after the end of the Second World War.

Also on this day

1374: Italian poet Petrarch dies near Padua * 1799: The Rosetta Stone is found in Egypt * 1834: French painter and sculptor Edgar Degas is born * 1870: Napoleon III declares war to start the Franco-Prussian War * 1903: Maurice Garin wins the first Tour de France cycle race

20 July

The plot to murder Hitler

1944 'I must go and telephone. Keep an eye on my briefcase. It has secret papers in it', whispered Colonel Claus von Stauffenberg to Colonel Brandt sitting next to him. Then he quietly rose from the crowded table and slipped from the conference room while Germany's top brass made their gloomy reports to their supreme leader in his fortified bunker at the Wolfsschanze (Wolf's Lair) headquarters in Rastenburg, in what is now north-eastern Poland. Three minutes later, at 12.42, the bomb that had been concealed in a shirt in von Stauffenberg's briefcase exploded, killing four people including Colonel Brandt but doing little damage to its target, Adolf Hitler. Needing more leg room, the unfortunate Brandt had shoved the briefcase to the far side of a heavy table support, miraculously shielding Hitler from the worst effects of the blast.

The 36-year-old von Stauffenberg was a career army officer born to the Prussian nobility. An early supporter of Hitler, he had participated in all the Führer's major campaigns and had been severely wounded while serving with the 10th Panzer Division of Rommel's Afrika Corps in Tunisia. There in early 1943 Allied fighters had strafed his convoy, and von Stauffenberg had lost his left eye, his right hand, and the last two fingers of his left hand.

It was probably in Russia, after witnessing atrocities committed by the SS, that von Stauffenberg began to lose his faith in Hitler, and by mid-1944 it was clear to all but the most fanatical Nazis that Germany would lose the war. Von Stauffenberg became a key member of a conspiracy code-named Walküre (Valkyrie) whose aim was to seize control of the government and seek favourable peace terms from the Allies to save the country from total destruction.

The plotters searched for a way to get at Hitler, and on 1 June 1944 fortune smiled on them when von Stauffenberg was made chief of staff of the Reserve Army, giving him access to the Führer's most important military meetings. Then he was summoned to the Wolfsschanze conference on 20 July. By this time his earlier belief in Hitler had turned to loathing. 'Fate has offered us this opportunity,' he said, 'and I would not refuse it for anything in the world. I have examined myself before God and my conscience. It must be done because this man is evil personified.' Flying to Rastenburg in the early morning, he set the bomb's ten-minute timer just before entering the meeting. Immediately after the explosion he bluffed his way through three SS checkpoints and, believing his mission accomplished, flew back to Berlin to help take over the government.

Sadly, *Walküre*'s conspirators showed an incomprehensible lack of both planning and resolve, and the plot started to disintegrate the moment it became clear that Hitler, whose legs were burned, eardrums punctured and hair singed, was not dead after all. In fact, that same afternoon he conducted his final meeting with Mussolini and bragged that God had saved him to lead Germany's revenge on the world.

Hitler's vengeance was swift and savage. When von Stauffenberg arrived in Berlin late in the day, an SS countercoup was already rounding up most of the conspirators. At about midnight von Stauffenberg and three others were taken to a courtyard at the War Ministry and shot, the colonel shouting at the last, 'Long live our sacred Germany.' The bodies were buried nearby, but on Himmler's orders the corpses were dug up and burned, their ashes scattered to the winds.

Plotters all over Germany were arrested, tortured and executed. Eight were strangled with piano wire attached to meat hooks, their death agony filmed for Hitler's enjoyment. Some officers committed suicide, at least one by walking into no man's land at the front to be shot by the enemy, and Germany's most illustrious field marshal Erwin Rommel was forced to take poison to save his family. An estimated 4,980 people were executed while another 15,000, mostly relatives of conspirators, were sent to concentration camps. The killings continued into April 1945, even as Russians were in the streets of Berlin.

After the assassination attempt Hitler became even more morbidly suspicious and reclusive. He gulped pills offered by his doctors, his right hand suffered from severe tremors, and he rarely agreed to be photographed. Nonetheless, his determination remained undiminished. All hope of negotiation vanished. In December Hitler told his Luftwaffe aide, 'We'll not capitulate. Never. We can go down. But we'll take the world with us.'

Also on this day

1881: Sioux chief Sitting Bull surrenders to the US Army * 1917: Alexander Kerensky becomes the premier of Russia

21 July

Hotspur dies in battle

1403 Two stars keep not their motion in one sphere,
Nor can one England brook a double reign,
Of Harry Percy and the Prince of Wales.

So did Shakespeare comment on the bitter conflict between two of England's most celebrated medieval heroes, Henry Percy, called Harry by his friends and known to us by the picturesque name of Hotspur, and Prince Henry of Lancaster, the future Henry V, son of the usurper king Henry IV.

Hotspur came from the powerful and aristocratic Percy family that had come to England with William the Conqueror. By the 14th century the Percys were rulers of Northumberland, which formed a buffer against armed raids from Scotland. It was the Scots who gave Hotspur his nickname for his indefatigable patrolling of the Scottish/English border.

Hotspur and his father (also called Henry) initially backed Henry IV and battered the Scots while the King was trying to subdue the Welsh. The problem was, the Welsh resisted successfully and Henry IV refused to give the Percys his promised rewards. It was only then that the Percys, capable and honourable knights, rebelled against their king. But once the rebellion had started, the Percys determined to go all the way and take the throne of England for themselves.

It was on this day that the conflict reached its denouement, when Henry IV and his son decisively defeated the Percys at Shrewsbury. According to Shakespeare, Hotspur was struck down by the sixteen-year-old Prince of Wales, but historians believe he died from a blow from an unknown hand when he lifted his visor to wipe sweat from his face.

Ill-weaved ambition, how much art thou shrunk!
When that this body did contain a spirit,

A kingdom for it was too small a bound,
But now two paces of the vilest earth
Is room enough.

Hotspur's head was set on the gate of York to discourage further rebellion, while his brother Thomas Percy was decapitated after the battle so that his could decorate London Bridge. The Percys of the time seemed to have a knack for dying in battle. Hotspur's father Henry, who escaped from the field of battle at Shrewsbury, was eventually slain at Bramham Moor in 1408. His son died on the field at the first Battle of St Albans (1455), and his grandson was killed six years later at Towton.

The Battle of Shrewsbury greatly strengthened the Lancastrian hold on the throne of England and also proved an invaluable training ground for young Prince Henry, who only ever fought in one more full-scale pitched battle, against the French at Agincourt.

Also on this day

1667: The Peace of Breda ends the Second Anglo-Dutch War ∗ 1798: Napoleon defeats the Egyptians at the Battle of the Pyramids ∗ 1831: Leopold of Saxe-Coburg becomes the first King of Belgium ∗ 1861: The South trounces the Union at the Battle of Bull Run in the American Civil War ∗ 1899: American novelist Ernest Hemingway is born

22 July

'Kill them all'

1208 Pope Innocent III had launched the Albigensian Crusade less than six months before, but already a sizeable army was marauding its way through southern France. Its aim was to extirpate the dangerous heresy known as Catharism, which not only denied the divinity of Christ, but also, in its non-authoritarian asceticism, stood in marked contrast to the corruption, worldliness and hypocrisy of the Church of Rome.

On this day the army reached the walls of Béziers in the very south of France, west of Marseille. Leading this band of opportunists, criminals seeking absolution, adventurers and religious fanatics were Simon de Montfort and his spiritual advisor, the papal legate Arnald-Amaury. At the city gates de Montfort handed the Bishop of Béziers a list of 222 Cathars to be handed over for execution. But the city leaders, not themselves Cathars, refused to provide the victims, saying, 'We had rather be drowned in the salt sea than surrender our fellow citizens.'

Now de Montfort ordered an assault, and the rampaging army began a brutal sack. There was to be no mercy for the heretics, but how, Arnald-Amaury was asked, can one tell a Cathar from the numerous devout Catholics in the population? 'Kill them all', said the Pope's representative. 'God will know his own.'

Except for those few who managed to flee, the entire population of Béziers – 15,000 men, women and children – were put to the sword, 7,000 alone in the vast Romanesque Church of Sainte-Madeleine where they had sought sanctuary.

Also on this day

1208: Troops of Simon de Montfort kill 15,000 men, women and children during the sack of Béziers during the Albigensian Crusade * 1461: Charles VII of France dies * 1812: The Duke of Wellington defeats the French at Salamanca in the Peninsular War * 1832: Napoleon's son the Duke of Reichstadt (L'Aiglon) dies of TB at Schönbrunn Palace in Vienna

23 July

Ulysses S. Grant: great general, terrible president

1885 Tortured by throat cancer and nearly broke, America's great Civil War general and eighteenth president Ulysses S. Grant died today in his cottage at Mount McGregor in the Adirondacks at the age of 63.

Grant had shown scant promise of greatness as a young man,

graduating 21st in a class of 39 at West Point Military Academy. After fighting in the Mexican War, he left the army and was working in his father's leather goods store when recalled to service during the Civil War. Due to his strategic understanding, willingness to innovate and sheer tenacity in combat, he became the North's commanding general, eventually bringing the South to its knees.

In 1868 Grant at 46 became at the time the youngest man ever elected President. At first a popular success, he earned a second term in 1872, but his trusting and perhaps naïve attitude towards his subordinates allowed corruption to mushroom in the government, and he worsened the situation by accepting presents from admirers. Scandals in railroads, whiskey and gold and a Secretary of War who was impeached for accepting bribes all but destroyed Grant's reputation, although he was entirely honest himself.

Grant's last years were as full of failure as his middle ones had been of success. He joined his son in a brokerage firm that went bankrupt owing the colossal sum of almost $17,000,000 due to the fraudulent activities of one of the partners. By this time he was already suffering from the throat cancer that would kill him, no doubt the result of his lifetime habit of smoking 50 cigars a day. But despite his illness, he was determined to recoup at least some of his family's fortune by writing his memoirs.

Grant began writing in the autumn of 1884, with his oldest son Fred and another researcher checking facts, securing documents and reviewing the manuscript. In October his cancer was diagnosed as fatal, and the work became a race to the finish. As his health worsened and the pain increased, cocaine and morphine were prescribed. The manuscript of the first of two volumes of memoirs was sent to the compositor in April. In May he began dictating his narrative to a stenographer, but when he developed difficulty speaking, he huddled under a blanket in his library and laboriously wrote out his story by hand. So painful was the condition of his throat that to communicate he was reduced to writing notes.

In June Grant left his home in New York City on doctor's orders in the hope of being able to complete his memoirs before he died. (He had earlier signed a publishing contract with his friend Mark Twain, and the memoirs earned nearly $450,000, but by the time they were published he was dead.) A special train took him north, crowds gathering at stations along the route to wave. At Saratoga Springs, where he changed trains, veterans greeted him with cheers. Twenty years after the end of the Civil War, Grant remained a popular hero.

Settling into his cottage at Mount McGregor, he wrote his doctor a series of notes describing his deteriorating condition and the effects of the medicines he was taking. His very last note, written just a couple of days before his death, read: 'I do not sleep though I sometimes doze off a little. If up I am talked to and in my efforts to answer cause pain. The fact is I think I am a verb instead of a personal pronoun. A verb is anything that signifies to be; to do; or to suffer. I signify all three.'

Grant's funeral bore testimony to the respect in which he was held not only by comrades in arms but also by former enemies. Marching as pallbearers beside the Union generals William Sherman and Philip Sheridan were two Confederate generals, Joe Johnston and Simon Buckner. In his life Grant had defeated the South; in his death he helped to reconcile it with its Union conqueror.

Also on this day

1745: Bonnie Prince Charlie lands in Scotland in an abortive attempt to gain the throne of Great Britain * 1757: Italian composer Domenico Scarlatti dies * 1865: British revivalist preacher William Booth founds the Salvation Army * 1951: French marshal, traitor and head of the Vichy government Philippe Pétain dies in prison

24 July

England snatches Gibraltar

1704 A narrow peninsula of only two square miles, with neither springs nor rivers, consisting mainly of a great barren rock that rises

1,400 feet: such is the tiny territory of Gibraltar one mile off the south coast of Spain that has been fought over for centuries.

In ancient times Gibraltar was thought of as one of the Pillars of Hercules (the other being Mount Hacho, across the Mediterranean on the African coast). In 711 the Moors crossed over from North Africa and took it, and in 1501, after the Spanish defeat of the Moors, Spain annexed it.

At the very beginning of the 18th century Spain found herself without a king. Then Louis XIV of France decided his grandson would do nicely and installed him as King Philip V. This decision was instantly challenged by the Holy Roman Empire, quickly joined by Holland and England, in what became known as the War of the Spanish Succession.

The war itself achieved very little, as Louis's grandson remained King of Spain, but during the conflict England made one enduring conquest. On 24 July 1704 a British force led by Sir George Rooke attacked and seized Gibraltar.

The Rock, as it is popularly known, has remained British ever since, but not without controversy.

Spain besieged Gibraltar from 1779 to 1783 but failed to oust its British occupiers. In the 1960s Spain again demanded its return, denouncing British colonialism as an anachronism from a bygone era. But the British organised a referendum in which Gibraltarians were asked to choose between a highly subsidised and tax-free existence under democratic Great Britain or absorption into the impoverished dictatorship of Francisco Franco. The result was no surprise: 12,138 voted to remain British versus 44 who wished to become part of Spain. Later Spain closed its borders with Gibraltar, depriving the community of Spanish workers and trade as well as access to Spanish beaches, but finally lifted the blockade in 1985.

Gibraltar today remains one of the last colonies in a post-colonial world.

Also on this day

1783: South American liberator Simón Bolívar is born in Caracas, Venezuela * 1797: Admiral Horatio Nelson loses his right arm while attacking the Spanish at Tenerife * 1802: French writer Alexandre

Dumas, author of *The Count of Monte Cristo* and *The Three Musketeers*, is born

25 July

'Paris vaut bien une messe'

1593 Technically Henri de Navarre had been King of France since 1589, when Henri III had died from stab wounds administered by a frenzied monk. But Henri was a Protestant in a country populated largely by Catholics, and he thus spent the first four years of his reign trying without success to conquer his own country. Ranged against him were the forces of the Catholic League, largely supported by that fanatical Catholic, Philip II of Spain, and much of the French population, particularly in Paris, which Henri had been unable to capture or control.

But Henri IV was a wise and tolerant man who put his people and his country above his sect, and he finally decided to turn Catholic to gain his kingdom.

On the morning of this day, Henri remarked to his beautiful mistress Gabrielle d'Estrées, 'It is today, my dear, that I take a perilous leap.' He then rode off to the gothic cathedral of St Denis just north of Paris, where France's kings are buried, where he abjured his Calvinism to join the Church of Rome. His real objective, however, was political rather than religious, as witnessed by his famous comment just before he entered the cathedral, 'Paris vaut bien une messe.' (Paris is well worth a Mass.)

By becoming Catholic Henri IV did indeed become King of France in fact as well as in name, and by his act he finally brought to a close more than 30 years of religious wars that had come close to destroying France.

Also on this day

1394: Charles VI of France expels all Jews from the country * 1554: Mary I of England (Bloody Mary) marries Philip II of Spain * 1587: Chief

Imperial Minister Hideyoshi bans Christianity and orders all Christians to leave Japan * 1603: James I is crowned at Westminster, uniting the crowns of England and Scotland * 1848: British Prime Minister Arthur James Balfour is born * 1934: Nazis shoot and kill the Austrian chancellor Engelbert Dollfuss

26 July

The last execution of the Spanish Inquisition

1826 When he was hanged today in the town of Rizaffa, Cayetano Ripoll became the very last victim of the Spanish Inquisition, that holy office that had been hanging, burning and torturing heretics in Spain since its institution under Isabella of Castile in 1478.

Ripoll was a schoolteacher who was imprisoned for two years and then executed for the grievous crime of insisting that the only necessary religious teaching was the keeping of the Ten Commandments.

The original Inquisition was created by Pope Gregory IX in 1231. Initially the accused had ample opportunity to repent, and punishment (carried out not by the Church but by secular authority) ranged from simple prayer to life imprisonment. Only the secular arm could condemn to death.

The Inquisition came to Spain in the wake of the Spanish conquest of the Muslim Moors and reached its peak under the tender ministrations of the first Grand Inquisitor, the Dominican Tomás de Torquemada. Torquemada probably condemned about 2,000 people to the stake, that gruesome process called by the remarkable euphemism *auto da fé* or 'act of faith'.

The Spanish Inquisition executed no more victims after Ripoll, and the institution itself was finally suppressed in 1834. The Spanish Inquisition's offspring, the Inquisition in Mexico, lived on, however, with the last *auto da fé* taking place in 1850.

Also on this day

1529: Holy Roman Emperor Charles V issues a royal warrant authorising Francisco Pizarro to explore and conquer Peru * 1847: Liberia becomes independent, the first African colony to do so * 1856: Irish playwright George Bernard Shaw is born in Dublin

27 July

A cannonball kills a great soldier

1675 Today the man Napoleon considered the greatest military leader in history was killed by a stray cannonball as he reconnoitred his army's position.

Henri de la Tour d'Auvergne, vicomte de Turenne, had been born to the highest French aristocracy in 1611 and had already been entrusted with the command of an infantry regiment by the age of nineteen. For the next 45 years he was almost continuously on the battlefield, particularly during the Thirty Years' War.

Turenne successfully served Louis XIII and Louis XIV in turn. The first Louis's widow, Anne of Austria, was regent of France during her son's infancy, and it was she who made Turenne a marshal at the age of 31.

In 1675 Louis XIV was fighting yet another of his interminable wars, this one against the Austrians. Yet again Marshal Turenne was expected to save the day. On 27 July the French and Austrian armies clashed at Sasbach, and it was here that the fatal cannonball found its mark, prompting from a dying Turenne the plaintive remark, 'I did not mean to be killed today.'

As soon as the news was known in Paris, the court went into deep mourning, Louis declaring that the French had 'lost the father of the country'. Turenne's finest epitaph, however, comes from his contemporary Voltaire, who wrote, 'The virtues and abilities that he alone had made people forget the faults and weaknesses he shared with so many others.'

Turenne's final honour was to be buried among France's kings at St Denis, but during the Revolution the cathedral there was desecrated by the republican mob and his remains were transferred to the Musée des Monuments. Finally in 1800 an admiring Napoleon had the great general re-interred in the Invalides in Paris.

Also on this day

1694: The British Parliament founds the Bank of England * 1809: The Duke of Wellington defeats the French at the Battle of Talavera in the Peninsular War * 1946: American writer Gertrude Stein dies * 1953: The Korean War comes to an end

28 July

Robespierre gets poetic justice

1794 Maximilien Robespierre was born of good bourgeois stock in the town of Arras, where he once served as a choirboy in the local cathedral. Compulsively neat, righteous, ascetic (he was indifferent to both fine food and women), he later became the most feared man in France as head of the Committee for Public Safety, which initiated the Reign of Terror during the French Revolution.

The public called Robespierre 'the Incorruptible' for his apparently selfless revolutionary zeal, and he termed himself 'a slave of freedom, a living martyr to the Republic'. But in fact Robespierre was a mean and vindictive tyrant, who sent his political enemies to the guillotine more often than enemies of the state.

Eventually the bloody Reign of Terror Robespierre had done so much to create devoured him in its turn. In the early hours of 28 July 1794 he was seized by French troops at the Hôtel de Ville, and in the scuffle was painfully shot in the lower jaw. Later the same day he was arraigned before the Revolutionary Tribunal and sentenced to death, along with 22 of his supporters, including his brother. About eight o'clock that evening he was taken to what today is called the place de la Concorde, where the great guillotine waited. His face was wrapped in a bloodstained bandage, but he made no sound. Just before the final act the executioner ripped off the bandage and Robespierre's lower jaw fell open and blood poured from the gaping wound.

A witness reports that he 'let out a groan like a dying tiger, which could be heard across the square'. And then the blade whistled down, severing his head from his body in one of history's greatest cases of poetic justice. He was only 36 years old.

Also on this day

1540: Henry VIII marries Catherine Howard on the same day that Henry's principal advisor Thomas Cromwell is beheaded * 1741: Antonio Vivaldi dies * 1750: Johann Sebastian Bach dies * 1914: Austria declares war on Serbia, starting the First World War * 1920: Mexican outlaw and revolutionary Pancho Villa surrenders

29 July

The Armada

1588 To Philip II of Spain the situation had finally become intolerable. The heretic English were supporting Dutch rebels against Spanish rule, and that famous admiral-buccaneer Sir Francis Drake was raiding Spanish ports in the Caribbean, severely damaging the Spanish economy. Even worse, England's Queen, the bastard Elizabeth, persisted in allowing Protestant heresies rather than continuing her sister Mary's return to the true Catholic faith. The only answer was invasion.

For two years King Philip assembled his attacking force: over 130 ships, 19,000 soldiers, 8,000 sailors, 2,000 galley slaves, 1,000 noblemen and some 600 priests and monks. In July this enormous Armada set sail for England.

On 29 July the English first sighted the Armada off the coast of Cornwall. Sir Francis Drake was enjoying a leisurely game of bowls at his home near Plymouth Hoe when Thomas Fleming, captain of his flagship *Golden Hind*, came galloping to report the Spanish approach. On hearing the news, Drake refused to be hurried, replying, 'We have time enough to finish the game and beat the Spaniards, too.'

Battle was soon joined. The English had faster and more manoeuvrable ships and superior cannon, allowing them to bombard the Spanish at long range, but the Spaniards had superior numbers. The battle seemed stalemated, and for a week the opposing fleets drifted up the Channel, neither side gaining a decisive victory. Then the Spanish anchored off Calais with the intent of picking up more troops coming from the Spanish Netherlands. At midnight on 7 August Drake changed the whole course of battle when he cut loose eight blazing fire ships to drift down upon the Spanish fleet. In panic the Spaniards cut their cables to flee, at the very moment the English fleet launched its attack.

What followed was the decisive moment in the English defence against the Armada. The Spanish fleet was completely disorganised, its formation destroyed. The English cannon started to take a heavy toll, largely without response since many of the Spanish heavy guns had been dismounted during the night. By the end of the day the Spaniards knew they were beaten, and the dispersed fleet sailed north, the only way to avoid the English warships and to return to Spain.

Up around Scotland and finally off the Irish coast sailed the Spaniards but the north Atlantic gales (what Protestant Drake called 'the Winds of God') further dispersed the fleet, causing many ships to founder.

Eventually only 66 ships returned to Spain, and some 15,000 Spanish soldiers and sailors had perished, including the Prince of Ascoli, Philip II's illegitimate son. England was safe for ever from the threat of Spanish invasion.

To celebrate the victory Queen Elizabeth ordered struck a commemorative medal bearing the inscription *Deus flavit, et dissipati sunt* (God blew, and they were scattered).

Also on this day

1830: The 'Citizen King' Louis-Philippe usurps the French throne * 1885: Italian Fascist dictator Benito Mussolini is born * 1890: Vincent van Gogh shoots himself * 1900: King Humbert of Italy is assassinated by anarchists at Monza

30 July

Bismarck the Iron Chancellor dies

1898 On this day died Prince Otto von Bismarck, a resentful and bitter old man of 83.

Bismarck had indelibly changed the face of Europe during his 28 years as Prime Minister of Prussia and nineteen as Chancellor of a united Germany. What once had been a hodgepodge of mini-kingdoms was now the single greatest power, industrial and military, in Europe. The theoretical Germanic hegemony once based in Vienna was now true domination controlled from Berlin.

Autocratic but brilliant, Bismarck had once famously said that 'die Politik ist die Lehre vom Möglichen' (politics is the art of the possible). But later he had told the Prussian House of Deputies that the great issues of the day could be settled only 'durch Blut und Eisen' (through blood and iron).

In domestic policy the mighty chancellor was an extreme reactionary who had fought for years to eradicate all forms of social democracy, especially the Socialist Party. In his mind he grouped together all liberals, from socialists to anarchists, terming them 'this country's rats [who] should be exterminated'. But in 1890 a group of leftist parties gained control of the Reichstag, and the 21-year-old Kaiser Wilhelm II felt compelled to ease the ageing, inflexible chancellor from office.

Although out of office and bitter towards the Kaiser and the government, Bismarck retained his acute political insight to the end. One of his last predictions was that, 'If there is ever another war in Europe, it will come out of some damned silly thing in the Balkans.'

Also on this day
1818: British novelist Emily Brontë is born * 1857: American economist Thorstein Veblen is born * 1865: American automobile tycoon Henry Ford is born * 1898: British sculptor Henry Moore is born

31 July

Jean Jaurès is shot

1914 On this day a shocking event occurred in Paris. While lunching at his favourite restaurant, the Café du Croissant in the rue Montmartre, the revered French Socialist leader Jean Jaurès was shot to death by a crazed young patriot-extremist. The assassin evidently hoped to prevent a general strike by French workers that would disrupt France's imminent mobilisation for war against Germany. Ironically, Jaurès was a patriot in his own right who had just two days earlier called for his followers to join their regiments should France be attacked.

It was a moment of crisis for the French nation, divided as it was on the eve of war by political feuds and rivalries. There was no time for deliberation, for Germany had already ordered her mobilisation in response to that of France's ally, Russia. The war was expected to be a quick, decisive affair, surely to be lost by any country that failed to call up its reserves in time.

With their most trusted leader dead, would the working classes answer the mobilisation order, set for the next day? Or, feeling they had nothing to lose but their chains, would they go on strike and refuse France's call to arms?

President Poincaré's government had no idea what to do, how seriously to take the pacifist rhetoric spouted so noisily by the leaders of the anti-militarist left. As to the leaders, Clemenceau's advice to the government was 'Crack down!' But for the workers themselves, the prediction of the chief of the Sûreté proved accurate: 'They will follow the regimental bands.'

And so they did, Jaurès's death notwithstanding. The mobilisation went calmly, the army was deployed, and the Great War began two days later on 3 August. The expectation that the war would be quick and decisive turned out to be quite wrong: it lasted four years, three months and eight days.

Also on this day

1556: Jesuit founder St Ignatius of Loyola dies in Rome * 1886: Hungarian composer and piano virtuoso Franz Liszt dies

1 August

Nelson wins the Battle of the Nile

1798 Napoleon Bonaparte had left his fleet of seventeen ships in Abu Qir Bay near the mouth of the Nile, while he stormed through Alexandria and Cairo. He was not to know that Rear Admiral Horatio Nelson was closing in. Today the British would score a crushing victory at the Battle of the Nile.

Nelson was determined to make his mark. The day before the battle he affirmed: 'Before this time tomorrow I shall have gained a peerage, or Westminster Abbey.'

A few hours before nightfall Nelson attacked. In a brilliant tactical thrust he sent five British men-o'-war between the French ships and their shore batteries, opening fire from both sides of his ships at once. When the French fired back they were in danger of overshooting the British fleet and hitting each other.

At about ten at night the battle reached its climax when the French admiral's 120-gun flagship *Orient* exploded, killing most of its crew and the admiral himself. The British continued to attack the remains of the French fleet, finally capturing or sinking all but two of the enemy's ships of the line.

The Battle of the Nile was exceptionally bloody; French losses approached 10,000, while the victorious British sustained almost 1,000 casualties, including Nelson, who suffered a minor head wound. But later that year Nelson gained his peerage as he had predicted.

This was Nelson's first great triumph against Napoleon, but oddly enough the battle was most famously commemorated by a contemporary bit of English doggerel that celebrates the French, not the English. The English poetess Felicia Hemans immortalised the heroism of the son of the captain of the French flagship, who tried to halt the flames of his father's foundering ship:

The boy stood on the burning deck
Whence all but he had fled;

The flame that lit the battle's wreck
Shone round him o'er the dead.

Sadly, the boy failed and went down with the ship.

Also on this day

10 BC: Roman Emperor Claudius is born * 1498: Christopher
Columbus discovers South America * 1714: Queen Anne dies,
bringing George I and the Hanoverian dynasty to the English
throne * 1798: Horatio Nelson destroys Napoleon's fleet at the Battle
of   the   Nile
* 1934: German President Paul van Hindenburg dies, clearing the path
for Adolf Hitler

2 August

Hannibal destroys the Romans at Cannae

216 BC Today the great Carthaginian general Hannibal Barca
totally annihilated a huge Roman army at the Battle of Cannae.

Six hundred years earlier, in 814 BC, Phoenician traders from
Tyre had founded a new city on the north coast of Africa (where
today's Tunis stands), calling it simply 'Kart-Hadasht', or 'new
town'.

Over the centuries Carthage developed into a powerful and
prosperous Mediterranean power, a rival of Rome, with colonies in
Spain, Sicily and Sardinia, but in 264 BC a minor encounter in Sicily
grew into the First Punic War with Rome, a conflict that gained its
name from the Roman word for Carthaginians, *Punici*, which itself
comes from Phoenician, the language of ancient Carthage.

Hannibal was born in Carthage of noble parents during this war
in 247 BC. When the conflict ended six years later, victorious
Rome stripped Carthage of much of its wealth and territory.
Brought up in Carthage-controlled Spain, he learned to hate the
Romans for the humiliation and impoverishment of his country, and

vowed revenge.

Hannibal was an arresting man. Tall, clean-shaven, handsome and athletic, he was an outstanding swordsman and a fearless rider. His appearance revealed his Phoenician (Semitic) bloodlines, with a slightly hooked nose, curly hair and dark eyes (one of which he later lost during his fight against Rome). By 26 he was already a general.

At 29 Hannibal embarked on one of the most daring military exploits in all of history to achieve his goal of a decisive victory on Roman soil. To avoid having to challenge Rome's naval dominance of the Mediterranean, he marched his huge force – Carthaginian and Iberian foot soldiers, Numidian cavalry and 37 elephants – north from Carthago Nova ('New Carthage', today's Cartagena in Spain) and across southern Gaul. It was nearing winter when he reached the Alps, but, despite severe losses of men and pack animals, in only fifteen days he led his army through the mountains and down into Italy. Somehow all the elephants survived.

Even in his first battles against the Romans Hannibal displayed his military genius in a series of devastating victories. He was a master of deception, one night tying lighted faggots to the horns of cattle to convince his enemies that his army was on the move when in fact they were waiting in ambush. Within two years he had covered much of Italy, leaving Rome terrified but not beaten.

In the spring of 216 BC, Hannibal moved south to capture a Roman supply depot at Cannae, a small village on the Achilles Heel of the Italian boot. Determined to rid Italy of the Carthaginian invader, the Roman consuls Lucius Aemilius Paulus and Gaius Terentius Varro advanced with a huge army of about 80,000 men to do battle with an enemy force of only half their size. Hoping to break the Carthaginian line with a heavy attack in the centre, the Romans massed their infantry and charged. Hannibal ordered his line to bow backward under the weight of the Roman assault, encouraging Varro to pile more infantry into the centre. Then the Carthaginian sent his two wings to envelop the concentrated Roman infantry on both sides, and his cavalry, which had already bested the Roman horse, completed the encirclement by attacking from the flanks and rear. The battlefield became a killing ground.

Up to 50,000 Romans perished in the slaughter (the near-contemporary historian Polybius says 70,000). Whatever the true number, it represented the greatest one-day loss in all of Rome's history, a massacre that was unsurpassed in any battle anywhere until the 20th century.

So great was the terror inspired by Hannibal's triumph that for centuries Roman parents would frighten mischievous children with the words 'Hannibal ad portas!' (Hannibal at the gates!).

Also on this day

1100: King William II (Rufus) of England is killed, perhaps murdered, in the New Forest * 1589: Friar Jacques Clément stabs King Henri III of France to death * 1788: British portrait and landscape painter Thomas Gainsborough dies of cancer * 1876: Wild Bill Hickok is shot dead in the Number Ten Saloon, Deadwood, South Dakota

3 August

Columbus sets sail with three good ships

1492 Ever since he was 23 (in 1474), Christopher Columbus had been trying to persuade someone to finance a voyage to the West, to seek a route to the Indies. Son of a wealthy weaver from Genoa, his first appeals had been to the Florentine geographer Paolo Toscanelli, and by 1483 he was seeking help from King John II of Portugal, but all to no avail.

Finally in 1486 Columbus approached the Catholic Majesties, Ferdinand and Isabella of Spain. At first he was rejected, but in 1492 he was called back to the Spanish court and the project was agreed.

So, on the fateful morning of 3 August 1492 Christopher Columbus sailed from Palos de la Frontera in Andalucía with a crew of 88 on his three good ships, the *Niña*, the *Pinta* and the *Santa María*, on history's greatest voyage of discovery.

Two months and nine days later the little convoy first sighted land in the New World. Two months after that the *Santa María* ran aground and was lost on the coast of present day Haiti. Today there exist neither pictures nor descriptions of any of Columbus's ships, so the myriad depictions and reconstructions to be found may represent typical 15th-century ships but cannot show us the way the originals really looked.

Also on this day

1876: British Prime Minister Stanley Baldwin is born * 1914: Germany declares war on France * 1936: To the fury of Adolf Hitler, Black American athlete Jesse Owens wins the first of four gold medals in the Berlin Olympics

4 August

Queen Philippa saves the burghers of Calais

1347 In his endless quest to claim the crown of France, England's Edward III needed a deep-water port to ensure transport of supplies from England, and the logical choice was Calais, a strongly fortified town that Edward claimed by right in his role as Count of Ponthieu. Encircling the city with his army on 3 September 1346, he determined to starve it into submission.

For month after month the good citizens of Calais resisted, devouring first their horses, then their dogs and finally their cats and rats. But still no French army came to the rescue, and although their defences held firm against the English attack, at length starvation forced them to surrender on this day after eleven months of siege.

Furious at Calais's long resistance, Edward demanded that the six most important men of the town come to him barefoot, clothed only in their shirts, with ropes around their necks. Six of the richest burghers appeared as ordered, sweating from the heat and shivering in their fear of the King's wrath.

But just as Edward was about to signal their execution, his beautiful wife Queen Philippa, who had accompanied her husband throughout the siege, knelt before the King. 'Gentle Sire', she begged, 'I humbly beseech you in the name of the son of Holy Mary and for your own love of me to show mercy to these men'.

Impressed by the goodness of his noble wife, Edward relented and let the burghers go free. Such is the touching story of the burghers of Calais, a tale so moving that over half a millennium later the great sculptor Auguste Rodin created one of his most famous statues based on the event.

Calais remained English until the reign of Mary Tudor, when France seized it back permanently.

Also on this day

1792: British poet Percy Shelley is born at Horsham, Sussex * 1914: German cavalry cross into Belgium for the first attack of the First World War

5 August

Farragut damns the torpedoes at Mobile Bay

1864 Today American Admiral David Farragut earned his place in naval history, as well as in all future books of quotations.

Farragut commanded a Union fleet of eighteen ships during the American Civil War. As the mists evaporated on this hot August morning, the admiral led his fleet past Fort Morgan, a Confederate stronghold that guarded Mobile Bay on the Alabama coast of the Gulf of Mexico. Immediately the enemy opened fire, and the intrepid Farragut had a sailor lash him to the mast so he could use both hands to hold his telescope and see above the swirling smoke.

In addition to firing their cannon, the Confederates had laced the channel with mines (then called torpedoes), and the leading Yankee warship, the *Tecumseh*, blew up and sank with all hands.

Near panic, the *Brooklyn* hove to, and Farragut's whole line hesitated, uncertain whether to attack or retreat, as the guns of Fort Morgan continued their deadly cannonade.

Refusing to be intimidated, Farragut cried, 'Damn the torpedoes! Full speed ahead', and led his fleet safely through the minefield to destroy the Southern fleet waiting within the bay and forcing the surrender of Fort Morgan.

This famous victory effectively closed the last Confederate port still successfully defying the Union naval blockade, and made a major contribution to the North's march to victory.

Also on this day

1850: French writer Guy de Maupassant is born * 1858: Queen Victoria exchanges greetings with US President James Buchanan when the first transatlantic cable is opened * 1861: The first US income tax is introduced * 1864: American Admiral David Farragut damns the torpedoes and goes full speed ahead in defeating the British at Mobile Bay

6 August

The last Holy Roman Emperor resigns his title

1806 According to Voltaire, it was neither holy nor Roman nor an empire, yet that amorphous political entity known as the Holy Roman Empire influenced and often dominated European affairs after Charlemagne revived the idea of Augustan Rome in the year 800. But Charlemagne had constructed a very different empire from that of the Romans. It included most of modern Germany, France, Belgium, Switzerland and Holland, extending from the Elbe River in the east to the Atlantic Ocean and including most of Europe south of Denmark to central Italy. His capital was at Aachen rather than in Rome.

Charlemagne's successors soon let his empire disintegrate into chaos, but in 962 it was restored with the coronation of Otto I, the first of an unbroken line of emperors to stretch over eight centuries.

The Holy Roman Empire is of course much associated with the house of Habsburg. The first Habsburg emperor was Rudolf I, known as Rudolf the Founder, who assumed the title in 1273. Once or twice after that a non-Habsburg wore the crown, but from 1438 onwards every Holy Roman Emperor was a Habsburg.

In 1806 another Habsburg, Franz II, was Emperor, but he lived in a Europe dominated by Napoleon, who controlled much of the Empire's theoretical territorial sphere of influence. Believing the imperial title an unrealistic anachronism (and willing to keep a lesser title rather than lose a grander one), Franz renounced it on this day, henceforth styling himself the Emperor of Austria.

Thus came to an end the Holy Roman Empire, an idea whose time had gone after 844 years and 67 emperors.

Also on this day

1623: Shakespeare's wife Anne Hathaway dies * 1637: English dramatist Ben Jonson dies in London * 1680: Spanish painter Diego Velázquez dies in Madrid * 1809: English poet Alfred, Lord Tennyson is born * 1945: The US drops an atomic bomb on Hiroshima, killing 70,000

7 August

The Marines storm ashore at Guadalcanal

1942 'Now hear this! Now hear this! Stand by to disembark! ...' This was the sound you would have heard aboard US Navy transports lying in Ironbottom Bay at 0600 hours on this calm, clear, tropical morning. It was the sound of the First Marine Division going to war. Over the side, down the cargo nets, into the Higgins boats they went, company by company, battalion by battalion, as the division landed on the beaches of Guadalcanal Island. For American forces, it was the first offensive ground operation of the Second World War.

The Marines took the beaches unopposed, but that was a condition that did not last for long. Guadalcanal would prove to be the longest battle of the entire Pacific war. It was a laboratory of warfare for the Marine Corps and Army troops who fought there – and for the naval and air forces that provided crucial support – where they learned the techniques of joint combat operations required to defeat the Japanese in the excruciating jungle terrain. And learn they did, for despite the blunders and losses of the ensuing months, they survived, prevailed, and finally forced the remaining 16,000 Japanese off the island in February 1943.

Historian Robert Leckie, who was a machine-gunner and scout with the First Marine Division on Guadalcanal, estimated that as many as 28,000 Japanese soldiers may have died in the battle, while American losses in the ground combat were about 1,600 deaths and some 4,200 wounded. Combined naval and air losses may have reached a similar total. Next to the Japanese, the toughest foe the Americans faced was the female of the anopheles mosquito: over 5,000 troops were incapacitated with malaria.

In the Marine cemetery on Guadalcanal someone scratched the following epitaph on a mess kit left by one of the graves:

And when he gets to heaven
To St Peter he will tell:
'One more marine reporting, sir —
I've served my time in hell.'

Also on this day

1485: Henry Tudor (the future Henry VII) lands at Milford Haven to challenge Richard III * 1815: Napoleon is exiled to St Helena * 1819: The Spanish surrender to revolutionary Simón Bolívar at Boyaca, Colombia

8 August

Hadrian, Rome's great builder emperor, rises to power

AD 117 Late tonight Hadrian, Rome's most peripatetic emperor, assumed imperial power when his adoptive father Trajan was felled by a stroke in Selinus (in modern Turkey) at the age of 63.

Trajan had ruled nineteen years, six months and fifteen days, during which time he enlarged the empire to its greatest extent with his conquests in Parthia and Dacia and directed a massive construction programme in Italy and Spain. Today, however, he is most kindly remembered for his tolerance to Christians, a policy that earned him a place in Dante's *Paradiso*, the sole pre-Christian emperor so honoured. According to the 2nd-century Roman historian Cassius Dio, his only flaw was his excessive fondness for wine and young boys.

The new emperor Hadrian preferred improving his empire to expanding it and spent the next 21 years roving across his vast territories, building as he went. He left us four of the most renowned Roman monuments that we can still visit today.

Although the Pantheon in Rome was initially constructed in 27 BC by Augustus' great general Agrippa, Hadrian completely rebuilt it, adding the mammoth dome 141 feet in diameter that was the largest ever built until the 20th century. Today the Pantheon is a church where Italy's first two kings and many great artists such as Raphael are buried, but the massive building with its heavy bronze doors remains much as it was when Hadrian ordered its construction almost two millennia ago.

Also in Rome on the banks of the Tiber is a huge brick drum over 60 feet high crouched on a square base that today we call the Castel' Sant'Angelo but which originally was built as Hadrian's tomb, started about two years before the Emperor's death in AD 138. Hadrian's Tomb received its current name in 590 when, during a procession to pray for the end of an outburst of plague, Pope Gregory the Great saw a vision of St Michael hovering over the building, sheathing his sword. The plague instantly abated, and the Pope renamed the tomb Castel' Sant'Angelo (Castle of the Holy Angel). In 1752 a bronze statue of St Michael was placed on top. Over the centuries Hadrian's Tomb has served as a place of sanctuary for popes under siege and later, until 1901, as a prison. (In Puccini's *Tosca*, set in 1800, Angelotti is locked up there and Tosca leaps from its battlements.) It is now a military history museum.

Another of Hadrian's monuments was his fabulous villa at Tivoli, eighteen miles east of Rome. The Emperor spent about ten years constructing this vast 750-acre complex of gardens, pavilions, dining halls, baths, libraries and theatres to create the most magnificent villa of Roman times.

The fourth great Hadrianic monument is his huge wall in northern England, started in 122. Designed to keep barbarous Picts and Scots from invading Roman Britain, the wall originally stretched 73 miles from coast to coast with forts every five miles. Up to ten feet wide and fifteen feet high, it continued to serve as a defensive barrier until the Romans pulled out of Britain in the early 5th century. It is the largest construction project in the history of Great Britain and today, even after having been used as a quarry for centuries, it remains formidable testimony to Roman power and construction skills.

Hadrian's ceaseless travel ended at Baiae on the Bay of Naples at his seaside villa that had been built by Julius Caesar. He had been ill and suffering for some weeks, and had begged to be put out of his misery, but his adopted son Antoninus Pius forbade such an impious act. 'How miserable a thing it is to seek death and not to find it', complained the Emperor. On 10 July 138 he finally expired at the age of 62, probably of dropsy.

Also on this day

1827: George Canning dies after only four months as Prime Minister * 1883: Mexican revolutionary leader Emiliano Zapata is born * 1925: The first national congress of the Ku Klux Klan opens

9 August

Caesar defeats Pompey at Pharsalus

48 BC On the hot, arid plain of Pharsalus in central Greece the direction and fate of the Roman Empire was determined today when Julius Caesar annihilated the army of his long-standing rival, Pompey the Great. The battle guaranteed his dominance of the Roman state but hastened the end of the Roman Republic that had been established almost five centuries before, in 509 BC.

Caesar and Pompey had once been firm allies, both opposed to the clique of knights who dominated the Roman Senate and obstructed all progress to reform a creaking Roman government. But Caesar's alarming military success in Gaul made Pompey fear that he would lose his position as the first man in Rome, and he was persuaded to side with the knights when in 49 BC Caesar and his battle-hardened legions crossed the Rubicon and entered Roman Italy.

Pompey fled the capital, accompanied by consuls, conservative senators and some of his army. Caesar now faced a two-front war, as two of Pompey's lieutenants commanded legions in Spain, while Pompey himself had holed up in Greece. Caesar showed his scorn for his adversaries with the comment: 'I am going to Spain to fight an army without a general, and then to the East to fight a general without an army.'

In Spain, Caesar persuaded the enemy legions to join him rather than fight him and then pursued Pompey to Greece, repeatedly offering compromise rather than battle. Perhaps because he had defeated Caesar at Dyrrhachium, Pompey underestimated his opponent's military genius. When Pompey failed to capture him during that battle, Caesar dismissively concluded that Pompey 'has no idea of how to win a war'.

When the armies faced each other at Pharsalus, Pompey initiated the battle, confident of victory with some 50,000 troops compared to 30,000 under Caesar's command. He planned to roll up Caesar's right wing with his cavalry and then crush the enemy with his superior numbers. But Caesar had hidden 2,000 of his most experienced legionnaires behind his front lines. When the Caesarean wing fell back under Pompey's onslaught (as Caesar had planned that it should), Caesar's legionnaires suddenly attacked the cavalry, using their javelins as spears to stab the enemy horses. Confounded by the attack, the cavalry fled from the field, enabling Caesar to outflank Pompey and start a general massacre. Knowing victory to be his, Caesar attempted to diminish the killing, calling out to his troops: 'Spare your fellow Romans!' He allowed his men to save one enemy soldier apiece.

At the close of the battle Caesar had lost just 200 men killed, but 15,000 of Pompey's troops were dead or missing, with another 23,000 captured. Surveying the enemy dead after the battle, Caesar remarked bitterly, 'Hoc voluerunt' (This is what they wanted), referring to the knights' and Pompey's refusal to compromise.

Pompey escaped, but not for long. Caesar pursued him to Egypt, where an officer of King Ptolemy murdered him. When Caesar reached Egypt he was presented with Pompey's preserved head.

After Caesar's dictatorship and the civil wars that followed his assassination, Rome became an empire under Caesar's protégé Octavian (Augustus) and remained under the command of Roman emperors for 500 years in Europe and 600 in the east, from Constantinople.

Also on this day

AD 378: The Visigoths defeat and kill Roman Emperor Valens at Adrianople * 1595: Izaak Walton, author of *The Compleat Angler*, is born * 1974: Richard Nixon becomes the first and only US president to resign

10 August

A victory on the Feast of St Lawrence inspires the building of a palace

1557 Of the thousands of battles fought throughout history, most are now forgotten, but the one fought this day at St Quentin in Picardy left a memorial over 600 miles away that stands in gloomy splendour to this day.

At the Battle of St Quentin, Spain's new king, Philip II, utterly routed a French army, killing over half its number. Being of a grave religious bent, Philip was aware that 10 August is the Feast of St Lawrence, that unfortunate Roman deacon who was roasted on a gridiron for his Christian beliefs. Hence, in commemoration of the great victory on St Lawrence's Day, King Philip sent orders to Spain that a great palace in the shape of a gridiron should be built in the Guadarrama mountains north-west of Madrid.

Philip intended the building to serve as a monastery for Hieronymite monks, a palace for himself and a grand burial place for the kings of Spain. To symbolise its royal and religious importance, it was constructed entirely of blue-grey granite and would be one of the largest religious buildings in the world. Its ground plan covers almost 377,000 square feet. This sombre memorial has 86 stairways, 1,200 doors and 2,710 windows.

Twenty-seven years after Philip's victory at St Quentin the palace-monastery was finally completed. It is called El Escorial. Philip died there in his spartan bedroom in 1598.

Also on this day

1810: Italian patriot and unifier Camillo Benso, Count Cavour, is born * 1874: US President Herbert Hoover is born

11 *August*

The story of the most beautiful chapel in France

1239 Louis IX of France was not only a king but also a saint, so not surprisingly he was an avid collector of religious relics. In the year 1239 he learned that Christ's Crown of Thorns could be had from Venetian traders, and he instantly dispatched his agents to buy it.

On 11 August of that year the Crown was brought into France, and King Louis determined to build for it a shrine worthy of housing such a holy treasure. He conceived of a church designed as a reliquary, with stone in place of metal and stained glass instead of gems and enamel.

Work on the chapel-reliquary was started immediately and completed in a mere 33 months. What became of the Crown is uncertain, but fortunately that gem of a building with all its deep-toned glass is still with us today, every bit as beautiful as Saint Louis intended. It is located on the Ile de la Cité in Paris and is fittingly called the Sainte-Chapelle.

Also on this day

AD 117: Hadrian is acclaimed Roman Emperor by his troops * 1492: Roderigo Borgia is elected Pope Alexander VI * 1495: Flemish painter Hans Memling dies

12 *August*

Castlereagh commits suicide

1822 At 53 he was exhausted, despondent and so paranoid that he imagined his long-time friend and political ally the Duke of Wellington was intriguing against him. On this day Robert Stewart, Lord Castlereagh, Great Britain's Foreign Secretary and one of his nation's greatest diplomats, slit his own throat at Cray Farm, his country retreat in Kent.

Son of an Anglo-Irish peer, Castlereagh had been educated at Cambridge and at 21 elected to the Irish Parliament, soon rising to the position of Lord Lieutenant of Ireland. An early supporter of Pitt the Younger, he resigned his office with Pitt when Parliament refused to grant Catholic emancipation in Ireland, but on Pitt's return to power was appointed as Secretary of State for War in 1805. One of his most perceptive acts was to use his influence to have Sir Arthur Wellesley – later the Duke of Wellington – given the command of the British expeditionary force sent to Spain to fight the Peninsular War against Napoleon.

In spite of his apparent success, Castlereagh found an implacable enemy in the then Foreign Secretary George Canning. Discovering that Canning was conniving to have him dismissed from his post, he challenged him to a duel during which Canning was slightly wounded, and both men were forced to resign from government.

But by 1812 Castlereagh was back as Secretary for Foreign Affairs, and after the assassination of Prime Minister Spenser Perceval he became leader of the House of Commons as well. And here he performed with brilliance. His astute diplomacy created the coalition that finally defeated Napoleon and he, along with Metternich, became the driving force at the Congress of Vienna after Napoleon's downfall, where he successfully established the principle of 'balance of power', resisting the territorial ambitions of Russia and Prussia.

But peace brought Castlereagh more problems than war ever had, as England fell into depression and rebellion was in the air. When soldiers killed eleven protesters and injured more than 500 at the Peterloo Massacre in Manchester in 1819, Castlereagh was widely condemned by English liberals for his known repressive beliefs. In his famous poem *The Mask of Anarchy*, inspired by the massacre, Shelley wrote:

I met murder on the way —
He had a face like Castlereagh —
Very smooth he looked, yet grim;
Seven bloodhounds followed him.

After an abortive plot to assassinate the Cabinet in 1820, Castlereagh always carried a pistol in case he was attacked. Held in contempt by England's liberals and hated by the lower orders, he began to develop the paranoia that would destroy him.

During the summer of 1822, Castlereagh revealed to an astonished Duke of Wellington that he was being blackmailed both for entering a brothel three years earlier and for an unspecified homosexual act. (It remains unclear whether Castlereagh was actually being blackmailed or whether he in reality committed either of these acts. He had been supposedly devotedly married to the beautiful Emily Hobart for 28 years, but the couple had no children.)

In August Castlereagh was residing at his Kent estate, so edgy, depressed and suspicious that his wife clandestinely removed his razor and pistols. On Monday 12 August in an explosion of distrust, he wildly accused his wife of joining a conspiracy against him, then, apparently realising that he was unbalanced, called for his doctor named Bankhead.

When Bankhead arrived he found that Castlereagh had retreated to his dressing room, where he stood with his back to the door facing the window, looking upwards as if to inspect the ceiling. 'My dear lord, why do you stand so?' asked the doctor. Turning, Castlereagh cried in anguish: 'Bankhead, let me fall upon your arm; it is all over.' As the doctor caught the collapsing man he saw blood spurting from his throat, a small pearl-handled knife gripped in his right hand. Castlereagh fell forward, slipped from Bankhead's grasp and crumpled face downwards on the floor. In moments he was dead.

Earlier, another of Castlereagh's liberal foes, Lord Byron, had penned this dreadful epitaph:

Posterity will ne'er survey
a nobler grave than this.
Here lie the bones of Castlereagh:
Stop, traveller, and piss.

1827: English poet and painter William Blake dies * 1896: Gold is discovered near Dawson City, Yukon Territory, Canada * 1898: Hawaii is formally annexed by the United States

13 August

How Blenheim Palace got its name

1704 A few miles north-west of Oxford in the rolling Cotswold hills stands the great palace of Blenheim, a gift by the grateful English nation to John Churchill, first Duke of Marlborough.

The bloody battle after which Blenheim is named took place on this day near the small Bavarian town of Blindheim, anglicised in English history to Blenheim. The battle was part of the War of the Spanish Succession, a struggle by a coalition of European nations to prevent Louis XIV's grandson from becoming King of Spain, thus setting the stage, they feared, for France and Spain to come together under the rule of a single king.

Blenheim was the first decisive battle of Marlborough's career, although he was already 53 at the time. It was also his first collaboration with that other celebrated general, Prince Eugene of Savoy.

During the course of this long day 56,000 French soldiers were overwhelmed by combined forces of 52,000 Austrians, Prussians, Dutch, Hessians, Danish mercenaries and English. Although Marlborough was in overall command, only 12,000 troops were from his own country.

When the battle finally ended at nightfall, 12,000 of the victors lay dead or wounded. But Marlborough and Eugene between them had killed or wounded 20,000 of the enemy while taking 14,000 prisoners, 5,400 supply wagons, 40 cannon and 34 coaches filled with French officers' women.

Although a glorious triumph, the Battle of Blenheim hardly settled the war, which dragged on for another ten years. And at the end Louis XIV's grandson was still King of Spain, although France and Spain were never united under a single monarch. Almost a century later the English poet Robert Southey penned his famous satirical lines:

> Now tell us about the war,
> And what they fought each other for ...
> 'And everybody praised the Duke,
> Who this great fight did win.'
> 'But what good came of it at last?'
> Quoth little Peterkin.
> 'Why that I cannot tell', said he,
> 'But 'twas a famous victory.'

Also on this day

1521: Spanish conquistador Hernán Cortés recaptures Tenochtitlán (Mexico City), and overthrows the Aztec empire * 1598: Henri IV signs the Edict of Nantes, giving freedom of worship to France's Protestants * 1624: Louis XIII appoints Cardinal Richelieu as chief minister * 1704: The Duke of Marlborough and Prince Eugene of Savoy defeat the French at the Battle of Blenheim * 1863: French painter Eugène Delacroix dies * 1923: Kemal Atatürk is elected the first President of Turkey

14 August

Portugal fights to keep its independence

1385 João o Bastardo he was called, John the Bastard, not for his personality but because of his illegitimate birth as son of Portugal's King Pedro I. In his early years he kept a low political profile befitting his station, especially after his half-brother inherited the throne. But then the half-brother died, and his widow Queen Leonor was manoeuvred into recognising John I of the neighbouring kingdom of Castile (in north central Spain) as Portugal's new king.

Even in the 14th century Portuguese patriotism was strong, and soon a group of fervent Portuguese nationalists, led by a 25-year-old soldier named Pereira Nuno Alvares, persuaded João to assassinate Leonor's chief minister and seize power for himself. Fearing for her own life, Queen Leonor fled from Lisbon, imploring John of Castile to put down João's coup.

Soon John of Castile was on the march with a large army. They succeeded in entering Portugal, but on this day João and Pereira, reinforced by a small contingent of English archers, met them on the road to Lisbon at Aljubarrota and inflicted a devastating defeat. So thankful was João for the English support that the following May he signed the Treaty of Windsor with England, pledging 'an inviolable, eternal, solid, perpetual and true league of friendship'. The alliance is still in force today, the oldest in European history.

Two years after the battle, João married the English duke John of Gaunt's daughter Philippa, with glittering results. Philippa not only created a court of high culture in Portugal but also produced highly talented children, one of whom was the famous explorer Henry the Navigator.

Thus the Battle of Aljubarrota ensured independence for the Portuguese and a throne and glorious reign for João. Pereira's rewards were even greater, although it took a little longer for him to collect them all. Because of his military achievements, João made him constable of the kingdom, and Pereira became rich enough to found a Carmelite monastery in Lisbon, where he became a friar in 1423. Five hundred years later he was declared a saint.

Also on this day

1900: A British-led international military force captures Peking to put down the Boxer Rebellion * 1945: Japan announces its unconditional surrender in the Second World War

15 August

Napoleone is born

1769 Ajaccio was a small, dusty port on the island of Corsica, only recently part of France, having been purchased by Louis XV from the Republic of Genoa. But now, fifteen months later, the people still followed Italian customs, including the celebration of *ferragosto* or the feast of the Assumption on 15 August. So young and beautiful Letizia Buonaparte, still not yet twenty, insisted on going to Mass although she was heavily pregnant.

Returning home immediately after the service, she lay down on the living room sofa and, just before midday, gave birth to a black-haired son. There was joy in the household as Letizia and her husband Carlo celebrated the birth of a living child. Their six years of marriage had produced three previous births, but only one baby, a boy they named Giuseppe, had survived.

The proud parents named their new child Napoleone, a good Italian name in a family that had originally come from Tuscany two centuries before. In spite of his name and language (his native tongue was Italian), Napoleone was born a French citizen thanks to Louis XV's timely purchase of Corsica. But it was only when he was 27 and already firmly established as a French general that he frenchified the spelling of his name to Napoléon Bonaparte, eventually persuading his elder brother to convert from Giuseppe to Joseph.

During the next half-century Napoleon would win 60 of the 70 battles he fought, conquer most of Europe, and honour his family in an orgy of nepotism, sprinkling glorious titles among his brothers and sisters. Joseph became King of Spain, Louis King of Holland, Jerome King of Westphalia, and Lucien Prince of Canino. Sister Caroline became Queen of Naples by virtue of her marriage to Napoleon's cavalry commander, 'King Joachim' Murat, and even Napoleon's stepson by his first marriage was made Viceroy of Italy. Napoleon himself, of course, famously crowned himself

Emperor, lost all that he had won, and arguably became the most famous man in history.

Also on this day

778: Charlemagne loses the Battle of Roncesvalles, inspiring the legend of the *Song of Roland* * 1057: Macbeth, King of Scotland, dies * 1534: Ignatius Loyola and Francis Xavier make apostolic vows from which the Society of Jesus (Jesuits) is born * 1771: Scottish writer Walter Scott is born

16 August

Eugene of Savoy's greatest victory

1717 The Turks had controlled most of the Balkans since the 16th century, and Suleiman the Magnificent once reached the gates of Vienna. It was only in the late 17th and early 18th centuries that Austria (or, more properly, the Holy Roman Empire) wrested the territory away, and much of this success was due to one man, Prince Eugene of Savoy, who inflicted one defeat after another on the Turks.

Eugene's first great victory was at Zenta in 1697, and on this day twenty years later he achieved his last and greatest triumph at Belgrade.

Eugene had been besieging the city when a massive Turkish army came to its relief, trapping the Prince's forces between the city walls and the Turkish host. Eugene commanded some 60,000 men, many weak from disease, and the Turks had four times that number. Some of his commanders begged him to withdraw to save the army, but Eugene held his position and waited for nightfall. Then, under cover of darkness and a thick fog, he launched his attack.

The battle was fierce and brutal, but when the fog lifted at daylight, the Prince's forces annihilated the Turkish army, which broke and fled. The Austrians gave no quarter, killing all the stragglers unable to escape.

Today the battle is largely forgotten, except in the famous German song 'Das Prinz Eugen Lied'. Probably written by a Bavarian trooper who fought at Belgrade, the song is still sung by German soldiers.

Also on this day

1819: Police in Manchester fire on a crowd demanding suffrage at the so-called Peterloo Massacre * 1948: American baseball icon Babe Ruth dies * 1977: Rock and roller Elvis Presley dies at Graceland, his mansion in Memphis

17 August

The passing of Frederick the Great

1786 Frederick the Great of Prussia died today in the early morning, sitting up in an armchair. He had lived for 74 years, five months and 24 days, and was 46 years a king.

Frederick was one of history's most extraordinary rulers. He was highly cultured, an accomplished musician and poet. He neither smoked nor drank and paid no attention to women, including his wife, whom he totally neglected. He may have been homosexual, but essentially this mocking, detached man had little affection for people. 'He has no heart whatever', said a contemporary. Although a German, he almost invariably spoke French.

Frederick's greatness was in his supreme military ability. In reference to the Seven Years' War, when Prussia was attacked by Austria, France and Russia together, no less an authority than Napoleon said of him: 'It is not the Prussian army that for seven years defended Prussia against the three most powerful nations in Europe, but Frederick the Great.'

Frederick not only established Prussia as a major European power but also ensured the dominance of his family – the Hohenzollerns – who ruled Germany until defeat in the First World War.

Frederick died at Sans Souci, the exquisite palace he built in Potsdam, just outside Berlin. Knowing death was imminent, he spoke to his valet Strutzki for the last time: 'La montagne est passé, nous irons mieux.' (We're over the hill, we'll be better now.) He had planned to be buried in his beloved palace and had ordered an inscription carved on the base of a statue there: 'Quand je serai là, je serai sans souci.' (When I shall be there, I shall be without care.) But his heirs had him buried in the Garrison Church nearby. Almost two centuries later an admiring Adolf Hitler kept a portrait of him on the wall of his bunker in Berlin.

Also on this day

1786: Legendary American frontiersman Davy Crockett is born * 1850: French novelist Honoré de Balzac dies * 1876: The first performance of Wagner's *Götterdämmerung* is given in Bayreuth * 1896: Gold is first discovered near the Klondike River in the Yukon Territory of Canada, igniting the Klondike Gold Rush

18 August

The last of Genghis Khan

1227 When Genghis Khan died on this day at about 65, he had created the greatest land empire in history through his great generalship and utter, barbaric ruthlessness.

Genghis Khan's given name was Temujin. He was born holding a clot of blood in his hand, a sure sign of great military prowess.

The main weapon with which Genghis Khan defeated and united the numerous Mongol tribes was his formidable cavalry. According to legend, its pungent stench signalled the approach of death even before you could see the dust or hear the drumming of hooves. These fearsome warriors could fire an arrow with deadly accuracy from a distance of 200 yards. One Persian account claims that Genghis Khan's soldiers were so filthy that lice covered them 'like sesame growing on bad soil'.

In victory Genghis Khan was totally merciless, once ordering the massacre of all those taller than the height of a cart axle. In 1206 the conquered Mongol tribes awarded him the title of Genghis Khan, which probably means universal leader.

When Genghis Khan conquered an enemy city he either annihilated the population entirely or sold it into slavery. At Herat in Afghanistan after a full week of carnage his army is said to have slaughtered 1,600,000 people. He told his chiefs to 'show no clemency to my enemies without a direct order from me. Rigour alone keeps such spirits dutiful.' People were not the Great Khan's only victims; he sacked major cities and razed important cultural centres such as Samarkand and Bukhara.

But no one could deny the effectiveness of his draconian methods: by the time of his death he had destroyed the Chin dynasty of China and his empire extended from Peking to the Caspian Sea.

Also on this day

1503: The notorious Borgia pope, Alexander VI, dies in Rome of malaria – or poison * 1587: Virginia Dare, the first English child born in what would become the United States, is born in the Roanoke Island colony * 1830: Austrian Emperor Franz Joseph I is born

19 August

Caesar Augustus, Rome's first and greatest emperor – was he murdered?

AD 14 Today died Rome's first and greatest Emperor, Caesar Augustus, who had ruled the civilised world for 44 years, greatly enlarging and enriching his empire while creating such firm underpinnings that it would last, in one form or another, for another 462 years in the west and 1,439 years in the east.

Augustus died in Nola, just north-east of Naples, only a month short of his 76th birthday, after several days of severe stomach aches and strong diarrhoea. Suetonius tells us his last words were addressed to Livia, his wife of 52 years: 'Livia, do not forget our marriage. Farewell!' But was this the natural passing of an ageing man or was it murder?

According to Tacitus, tongues wagged that Livia did him in. She had married Augustus under duress – she was already married and pregnant when he forced her to divorce her first husband and marry him. Although all reports suggest they lived contentedly together, he is known to have been flagrantly unfaithful, perhaps including young men among his conquests. And Livia was desperate for one of her sons by her first marriage (she had none by Augustus) to inherit the empire. Rumours insinuated that she had already arranged the deaths of three of Augustus's grandsons from his earlier marriages, and she had managed to persuade him to name her own son Tiberius as joint inheritor along with his sole surviving grandson, Agrippa Postumus. But as the great man aged she was tormented by the fear that at the last he would drop Tiberius in favour of Agrippa Postumus, because he was linked to Augustus by blood.

The story relates that a few days before his death Livia offered Augustus some grapes that she had poisoned, carefully leaving several clean ones for herself to avert suspicion.

Whatever the truth, Augustus's corpse was taken to Rome and cremated on the Campus Martius. And his stepson Tiberius duly became Emperor. Livia lived on for another fifteen years and died at the glorious age of 87. Her grandson, the Emperor Claudius, later deified her.

Also on this day

1631: English poet John Dryden is born * 1662: French mathematician, philosopher and writer Blaise Pascal dies in Paris * 1692: Six 'witches' are executed during the Salem witch trials in Massachusetts * 1871: Aviation pioneer Orville Wright is born in Dayton, Ohio * 1942: The Allies launch a disastrous raid against German-held Dieppe in which three-quarters of the attackers are killed or captured

20 August

The Spartans defy the Persians at Thermopylae

480 BC Mighty Xerxes, King of Persia, the greatest empire the world had known, had resolved to conquer the stubborn Greeks, who had defeated his father Darius at Marathon ten years before. So great was his army that it took them seven days and seven nights to cross the Hellespont. (Herodotus tells us that the Persians numbered two and a half million men, but modern estimates suggest a more reasonable 200,000.) Knowing that all Greece was in mortal danger, a force of 7,000 hoplites (infantry) from several Greek city-states was rushed to meet the invaders under the leadership of the Spartan king, Leonidas. Indifferent to the odds against him, Leonidas declared: 'If you reckon by number, all Greece cannot oppose even a part of that army, but if by courage, the number I have with me is enough.' The armies clashed at Thermopylae in one of history's most heroic defences.

Thermopylae means 'hot gates', named for the hot sulphur springs nearby. It is a narrow mountain pass only 50 feet across at its widest, accommodating just a single wagon track. On one side tower high cliffs while on the other is a precipitous drop to the sea. It was through this restricted defile that the Persian army had to pass to enter central Greece. Even before the battle the location had dramatic connotations for every Greek, for it was on nearby Mount Oeta that Heracles had died, poisoned by the blood of a dead centaur.

Upon seeing the tiny Greek force, Xerxes demanded that Leonidas lay down his arms, to which the Spartan king tersely challenged, 'Come and take them'. As the defenders waited for the onslaught, one fearful soldier speculated that the Persian archers were so many that their arrows would hide the sun. 'Good', answered the Spartan Dieneces, 'then we shall fight them in the shade'.

To open the battle the Persian king ordered his Medes and Cissians to lead the charge. But the Greeks, armed with long spears and protected by large round shields, crested helmets and lower-leg greaves, were more than a match for the invaders, who had shorter spears and weaker armour, better suited to warfare on the open plains than to the narrow defile of Thermopylae. Soon Xerxes was forced to call on his élite infantry, the Immortals, but even they could make no progress against the ferocious defenders, who slew thousands of the enemy during the first two days of battle. So many Persians were killed that the front ranks had to be driven into battle with whips.

But then came treachery. A Greek traitor, Ephialtes, hoping for a rich reward, told Xerxes of a mountain path through which the Persians could send an encircling force. On the night following the second day of battle the Immortals started working their way behind the Greek position.

Once Leonidas learned that the Persians were closing in from behind, he sent all the Greek warriors except his own 300 Spartans home to defend their cities. Then he settled down with his men for a last meal, bleakly ordering, 'Breakfast well, for we shall have dinner in Hades'. He was determined to fight to the last.

At nine o'clock on this third day of battle, the resolute Spartans marched out for the final confrontation to the sound of their flutes. Although fighting with ferocity, they were soon overwhelmed, Leonidas among the first to fall. Finally the last defenders were surrounded on a small hill. Herodotus relates that 'they fought in a frenzy, without concern for their lives ... Most had already lost their spears, and they cut down Persians with their swords ... [they] defended themselves with daggers ... and with their hands and teeth ... while those [Persians] who had come round the mountain completed the circle.' But, despite their fanatical struggle, soon all 300 Spartans lay dead. In his anger at the stubborn Spartan resistance, Xerxes had Leonidas's lifeless body crucified, his severed head stuck on a pole.

Herodotus says that the Spartans killed 20,000 Persians at Thermopylae, no doubt an exaggeration but in any case not enough to prevent Persian invasion of the Greek mainland and the capture of Athens. Greece was saved not by Thermopylae but by the naval victory of Salamis the next month.

On the small hill where the Spartans made their last stand the Greeks erected a monument, now long vanished, with the inscription from Simonides of Ceos:

Go, stranger, and to listening Spartans tell
That here, obedient to their laws, we fell.

Also on this day

1625: French playwright Pierre Corneille is born * 1940: Russian Bolshevik Leon Trotsky is assassinated in Mexico on orders from Stalin

21 August

Napoleon's marshal Bernadotte becomes Crown Prince of Sweden

1810 Two years earlier, Napoleon had made his favourite cavalry commander, Joaquim Murat, King of Naples. Today Jean-Baptiste Bernadotte became the second of the Emperor's marshals to take a royal title when he became Sweden's Crown Prince, taking the name of Charles John.

Born in the foothills of the Pyrenees and son of a lawyer, Bernadotte joined France's republican army at the age of seventeen, displaying his zeal by having 'Death to tyrants!' tattooed on his arm. He first met Napoleon in Italy in 1797, after he had already become a brigadier general. The two generals impressed each other, and in 1798 Bernadotte even married one of Napoleon's former sweethearts, Désirée Clary, who was also a sister-in-law of Napoleon's brother Joseph.

A strong republican, Bernadotte condemned Napoleon's rise to absolute power, but he finally offered his support when Bonaparte declared himself Emperor in 1804. A few months later Bernadotte's loyalty, military skill, and family connections were fully rewarded when the Emperor made him a marshal, and a year later he received the title of Prince of Ponte-Corvo for his heroic participation in the great French victory at Austerlitz.

Although not a brilliant commander, Bernadotte always scrupulously obeyed the rules of war, treating both his troops and his enemies with generosity and good sense. Thus, when Sweden found itself ruled by the ageing, childless King Charles XIII in 1809, the Riksdag invited Bernadotte to become Charles's successor.

Much to Napoleon's chagrin, the new Prince's loyalties were now to Sweden rather than France, and he joined the allied forces at the Emperor's bloody defeat at Leipzig in 1813.

On 5 February 1818 old King Charles finally died, and the once staunchly republican general became a conservative and autocratic king who restricted the press and put a stop to liberal reforms. Unlike Napoleon's other marshal-king – Murat was deposed and shot after seven years as King of Naples – Bernadotte ruled for 26 years until he died in bed at the worthy age of 81. Shortly before his death he smugly but accurately murmured, 'No one living has made a career like mine'. To this day his descendants still wear the crown of Sweden.

Also on this day

1745: Sophia von Anhalt-Zerbst (Catherine the Great) marries Grand Duke Peter, heir to the throne of Russia * 1872: English illustrator Aubrey Beardsley is born

22 August

Richard III dies at Bosworth Field

1485 This is one of the most significant dates in all of English history. In defeating Richard III today in the Battle of Bosworth Field, Henry Tudor accomplished more than he knew. His victory ended the Wars of the Roses, that periodic and bloody rivalry for the English crown that had afflicted the country since 1455. Moreover, Bosworth Field, resulting as it did in the death of King Richard, brought to an end the great Plantagenet dynasty which had supplied every English king for the past 332 years, starting with Henry II in 1154. Finally, when Henry Tudor took the crown as Henry VII he began his own dynasty that lasted for 118 years and sent to the throne such notables as Henry VIII, Bloody Mary and Elizabeth I.

At the time of the battle, Richard III had been King for only two years and two months, having usurped the throne from his twelve-year-old nephew Edward V, whose murder in the Tower of London he had ordered. His opponent Henry Tudor also had only the flimsiest of claims to the English crown. Through his mother he could trace his blood back five generations to King Edward III, and his entitlement to royalty on his father's side was even thinner. His paternal grandfather had (perhaps) been married to Catherine de Valois, the widow of Henry V.

But Henry Tudor was the only living male member of the House of Lancaster and so became its champion in the Wars of the Roses. Gathering an army in France, he landed at Milford Haven in Wales on 7 August and headed north until he met Richard's forces at Bosworth Field, twelve miles west of Leicester.

Richard might have defeated Henry had not some of his most important barons defected at the last moment, guaranteeing a Tudor victory. But even when defeat was certain, Richard challenged his fate. 'I will not budge a foot', he swore to his lieutenants, 'I will die king of England'. A few minutes later he was unhorsed and killed.

Richard was only 32 when he fell at Bosworth Field, the last English king to die in battle.

Also on this day

1642: The English Civil War begins when Charles I raises his standard at Nottingham * 1806: French painter Jean-Honoré Fragonard dies in Paris * 1864: The International Red Cross is founded by the Geneva Convention

23 August

Stalin and Hitler celebrate a pact

1939 Reflecting the celebratory mood of the occasion, Joseph Stalin rose and offered an extraordinary toast: 'I know how much the German nation loves its Führer. I should therefore like to drink his health.' Around the Kremlin conference table, all glasses were drained in an instant. Stalin's gesture honoured one of the unholiest alliances ever created, for earlier that day a non-aggression pact had been signed between Nazi Germany and Soviet Russia.

In their treaty, the two signatories – so recently adversaries in the Spanish Civil War – promised to refrain from aggressive action against one another, but also, in a secret side agreement signed at the same time, they agreed on the imminent carving up between them of the nations of Eastern Europe, from the Baltic to the Black Sea. For Germany, with its eyes on the west, the treaty was insurance against a two-front war. For Russia, it bought time.

Churchill described the treaty as 'an unnatural act'. Its spirit, however, was best caught by the great English political cartoonist David Low, who drew the two dictators standing over the corpse of Poland bowing to each other elaborately, and offering fulsome greetings: 'Scum of the earth, I believe?' says Hitler. 'Bloody assassin of the workers, I presume?' replies a cordial Stalin.

Just nine days later, Nazi Germany invaded Poland. On 15 September, Soviet Russia advanced from the east to take her share.

The non-aggression treaty was stipulated to last ten years. In fact, it lasted just 22 months, until 22 June 1941, when the German army launched Operation Barbarossa, the invasion of Russia, thus lending strength to the old adage that there is no honour among thieves.

Also on this day

1244: Jerusalem falls to the Muslims and the armies of the Sultan of Egypt seize Damascus * 1305: Scottish rebel William Wallace is hanged, drawn and quartered * 1839: The British capture Hong Kong * 1944: Free French and American troops enter Paris during the Second World War

24 August

The Massacre of St Bartholomew

1572 At dawn today, the feast of St Bartholomew, the great bell of Paris's Saint-Germain-l'Auxerrois church began to toll, signalling the start of the greatest religious massacre in European history. Fired by holy fanaticism, Catholic bands roamed the streets, killing Huguenots and putting their houses to the torch. Over 3,000 were slaughtered, men, women and children.

The real spark-plug for the massacre had come nine years earlier when, in an attempt to bolster the power of the Huguenots, Admiral Gaspard de Coligny had ordered the assassination of the arch-Catholic leader, François de Guise. Guise's murder had produced the desired results, for within a decade Coligny had become the most trusted advisor of France's neurotic King Charles IX, and Protestant power was at its zenith. But Coligny had made two miscalculations. He had neglected Guise's son Henri, who swore to avenge his father's death, and, worse, his influence with King Charles had appeared threatening to Charles's devious and power-mad mother Catherine de' Medici, who feared losing her control over the King.

Henri de Guise bided his time until both he and Coligny were in Paris during the steamy days of August 1572 for the wedding of the King's sister. Then he struck.

Guise's first attempt to murder the Admiral failed when, on

341

22 August, his hired marksman merely wounded the Huguenot leader. The following day a bandaged Coligny was again closeted with the King, but here he made his last, fatal blunder. He warned King Charles not to trust his mother, saying that she lusted only for power. Later that day poor weak Charles repeated this to Catherine, and Coligny's fate was sealed.

Summoning the King, his brother and several Italian courtiers, Catherine soon persuaded them that Coligny had to die. 'Kill the Admiral if you want', screamed Charles hysterically. 'But you also have to kill *all* the Huguenots, so that not one is left to reproach me. Kill them all! Kill them all! Kill them all!' Quickly the Queen Mother authorised Guise to try again.

The final attempt began at 2.30 the next morning, on the feast of St Bartholomew. Guise and a band of followers stormed Coligny's house (located where today stands number 144 rue de Rivoli) and cornered the Admiral in his bedroom. Coligny seemed resigned to death. He addressed one young assailant with the words: 'Young man, you should respect my grey hairs, although you can shorten my life but little.'

Attacked with daggers, the Admiral quickly fell dead, and his corpse was thrown from the window for the waiting crowd of Catholics to dismember and hang for all to see. Then the general massacre began, first in Paris and then spreading throughout the rest of France, leaving in its wake over 8,000 dead Protestants. Fanatical Catholics everywhere applauded, and in Rome Pope Gregory XIII ordered a *Te Deum* to celebrate the slaughter.

In the end, the great loser was France itself as religious war continued for the next seventeen years and many Huguenots, among France's most successful merchants, left the country for England and Holland. King Charles spent his remaining two years on Earth racked with guilt, and Henri de Guise was assassinated in his turn by Charles's brother sixteen year later. The only winner was the sinister Catherine de' Medici, who continued to dominate her sons for another seventeen years.

AD 79: Pliny the Elder, Roman naturalist and writer, dies during the eruption of Vesuvius * AD 410: Alaric leads the Visigoths in the sack of Rome * 1724: English horse painter George Stubbs is born in Liverpool * 1812: The British burn Washington during the War of 1812

25 August

The last days of Pompeii

AD 79 'Although it was daybreak, the light was still pale and weak. Around us the buildings were trembling ... Our carriages ... rolled about first in one direction, then in another, even though the ground was completely flat, and would not stop even when blocked with stones. We saw the sea sucked away ... by the earthquake, ebbing from the beach so that great numbers of sea creatures were left on the dry sand. Inland great bursts of forked and tremulous flame burst through a forbidding black cloud, which opened to reveal great tongues of fire, like enormous flashes of lightning.'

So reported Pliny the Younger, an eyewitness from the nearby port of Misenum to today's colossal eruption of Mount Vesuvius, during which his uncle, the admiral, naturalist and writer Pliny the Elder, perished from the fumes.

The eruption had started about noon on the previous day when the volcano started spewing out an enormous black cloud which, according to Pliny, rose to a great height like a massive umbrella pine, probably not dissimilar to the mushroom cloud of a nuclear explosion. Below, at the south-eastern base of the mountain, the city of Pompeii was buried in pumice and ash to a depth of nine feet. But worse was yet to come.

The following morning, surges of pyroclastic material accompanied by toxic gases rolled over Pompeii's walls and asphyxiated most of the city's remaining inhabitants who had survived the ash and volcanic debris of the day before. By the time the eruption was over, the city and some 20,000 of its citizens were covered with over twenty feet of pumice and the nearby town of Herculaneum had been overwhelmed by a gigantic mud-flow.

Vesuvius has erupted many times since the year 79 and is still active today. Its crater now measures 2,000 feet across and 1,000 feet deep, and on its slopes is grown a sweet fizzy wine known as Lacrima Christi, the Tears of Christ.

Also on this day

1270: Louis IX of France (St Louis) dies of plague in Tunis * 1530: Ivan IV ('the Terrible') is born * 1688: Welsh buccaneer Sir Henry Morgan dies in Jamaica * 1830: The Belgian revolution starts, resulting in modern Belgium * 1944: Free French units under General Jacques Leclerc enter Paris during the Second World War

26 August

The Battle of Crécy

1346 If you drive north from Paris to Calais, just beyond Abbéville you pass by the small town of Crécy. There on this day over six centuries ago the age of knightly chivalry received a mortal wound from which eventually it would die.

Here on this showery Saturday afternoon England's King Edward III took on the might of France during the Hundred Years' War with a force of some 11,000 men, including 7,000 longbowmen.

The French army was nominally under the command of King Philip VI, but in fact it was composed of too many undisciplined knights who thought of themselves as allies rather than subjects and were determined to win glory (and ransom from noble English prisoners). The number of the French force is reckoned somewhere between 35,000 and 60,000, but by any estimate far larger than the English. Among the French were 8,000 Genoese crossbowmen.

The difference in bows and bowmen was critical to the battle. The crossbow had first been used in Europe in the 10th century. It fired a heavy, armour-piercing bolt, but the rate of fire was no more than two per minute. The longbow, first developed in Wales, fired a metal-tipped armour-piercing arrow three feet long that required a strong bowman, as the longbows of the time required a 100-pound force to draw. But the English longbowmen could fire five arrows a minute and more.

The French sent their crossbowmen to open the attack, but before the Genoese came within effective range the English longbowmen responded with a murderous shower of arrows, overwhelming their enemy in a matter of minutes and sending them into full retreat. Seeing the slaughter, the French mounted knights rode down their own bowmen in their haste to attack the English, but once again a deadly shower of arrows brought down men and horses in thousands. Once the knights had been unhorsed, the English men-at-arms quickly finished them off with swords and maces. It has been estimated that in all the English bowmen fired some 500,000 arrows at the French.

The battle had its pathetic moments of 'honour'. Blind King John of Bohemia asked his captains: 'Gentlemen, as I am blind, I request you to lead me so far into the engagement that I may strike one stroke with my sword.' He then charged into battle with a French knight guiding him on each side – and was almost immediately slaughtered. (His crest of three ostrich feathers with the motto 'Ich dien' was taken by Edward's son, the Black Prince, and is still used today by English Princes of Wales.) But each new charge was met by another lethal flight of arrows, and the cavalry could not attack the longbowmen whose positions were protected by rows of sharpened stakes. Eventually darkness brought the grisly slaughter to a close.

The following day the English counted the casualties. Fewer than 100 English had lost their lives but 15,000 French and Genoese soldiers lay dead on the field and a further 1,500 French knights had been captured or killed.

With the introduction of the longbow, a new type of warfare had been invented. Never again was the charge of knights in armour to determine the course of victory. The Battle of Crécy did not, however, have much effect on the Hundred Years' War, which continued spasmodically for another 107 years.

Also on this day

55 BC: Julius Caesar lands in Britain * 1666: Dutch painter Frans Hals dies * 1676: First English Prime Minister Robert Walpole is born * 1819: Prince Albert, Consort to Queen Victoria, is born in Coburg, Germany * 1920: In the United States, the 19th Amendment is proclaimed by the Secretary of State, enfranchising women on an equal basis with men

27 August

Krakatoa erupts

1883 The volcano on the uninhabited island of Krakatoa had been rumbling ominously since May, telling the natives of Java that Orang Aljeh, the mountain devil, had been disturbed. About midday today, a Sunday, the volcano started its titanic eruption.

All that day rock, steam and smoke were spewed high into the air, blotting out the sun. The ocean churned wrathfully and winds blew at hurricane force. Through the night it continued, and at ten o'clock the next morning suddenly the great cone-shaped mountain literally exploded, producing the loudest noise in history, clearly heard over 3,000 miles away. The eruption discharged nearly five cubic miles of rock fragments.

The island of Krakatoa vanished completely, leaving in its place a submarine cavity 1,000 feet deep. The gigantic explosion created a tsunami or giant tidal wave 120 feet high, moving at 300 miles per hour, which crashed into the coast of Java, completely obliterating the town of Anger and travelling some fifteen miles inland. In all, about 36,000 people were killed, and for days afterwards the straits around Java and Sumatra were jammed with hideous debris – the corpses of humans, cattle, fish, snakes, tigers and pigs floating together.

Although the cataclysm of 1883 is the most famous of Krakatoa's eruptions, one over a millennium earlier, in 535, probably killed even more people, as scientists believe it triggered an onslaught of the bubonic plague in 542, which killed over 250,000 inhabitants of Constantinople and subsequently millions more in the rest of Europe.

The bubonic plague originated in Africa, and is carried by fleas. When Krakatoa erupted, the enormous cloud of debris covered much of Africa, shielding the land from the sun and causing temperatures to drop. But at lower temperatures the flea's gut becomes blocked, dooming the flea to starve to death for lack of blood in its own intestines. This drives the flea to seek new sources of blood at a voracious rate, thereby spreading the plague at exponentially increased speed.

During the 6th century Constantinople enjoyed a thriving ivory trade with Africa. Ivory traders and vermin hosting infected and hungry fleas were carried by ship from Africa to the Gulf of Suez, crossed the isthmus and then sailed across the Mediterranean to Constantinople, igniting the epidemic there. Once Constantinople was struck, its fleeing citizens spread the plague all over Europe.

In sheer explosive force, however, the eruption of Krakatoa in 535 was far smaller than that of 1883, which was long considered the greatest explosion, natural or otherwise, in the recorded history of man. Recent scientific research, however, suggests that the eruption of the Greek island of Thera (today's Santorini) in about 1470 BC might have been two to four times more powerful, destroying the Minoan civilisation on Crete with its gigantic tsunami.

Also on this day

551 BC: Chinese philosopher Confucius is born * 1576: Italian painter Titian dies * 1635: Spanish playwright Lope de Vega dies in Madrid * 1770: German philosopher Georg Wilhelm Hegel is born in Stuttgart

28 August

Goethe – the greatest Renaissance Man since the Renaissance

1749 Born this day in Frankfurt am Main was arguably the greatest Renaissance Man since the Renaissance. Although trained as a lawyer, he became an accomplished scientist, an expert in biological morphology; he conducted orchestras as well as opera performances; a gifted painter, he was chief minister to his German state of Weimar and was an occasional journalist; he spoke German, French, English, Italian, Latin, Greek and Hebrew, and translated Cellini, Voltaire and Byron into German. He appreciated all forms of art, and once defined architecture as 'eine erstarrte Musik' (frozen music). He was also a talented and successful womaniser, but above all he was a great poet and dramatist, who practically created the literary movement known as *Sturm und Drang* (storm and stress). His name was Johann Wolfgang von Goethe.

Goethe's talent and fame was so great in his own day that even heads of state clamoured to be introduced to him. When Napoleon met him at Erfurt in 1808, he remarked: 'Voilà un homme!' (What a man!)

Goethe lived to a grand old 82. Strangely enough, today he is best known for his great poetic drama, *Faust*, but the second half of *Faust* was published only after his death.

Also on this day

1640: The Indian War in New England ends with the surrender of the Indians * 1808: Russian novelist Leo Tolstoy is born * 1850: Richard Wagner's *Lohengrin* is performed for the first time at Weimar

29 August

Great Britain takes Hong Kong

1842 On this day the Chinese and British signed the Treaty of Nanking, which not only ended a war but also ceded Hong Kong Island to Great Britain.

During the century and a half since the Treaty was signed, Hong Kong has represented the ultimate in unfettered trade and tax-free wheeling and dealing that made its businessmen rich and eventually financed the spectacular Hong Kong skyline. The foundation of Hong Kong's thriving economy and frenetic business life was opium.

In the early 19th century, freewheeling British traders realised there was a fortune to be made in selling opium to the Chinese. And these men were just in the right position to grasp the opportunity, since opium was grown in abundance in British-controlled India. The Chinese objected (not so much to the sale of opium but to foreign traders garnering all the profits), but the British continued illegally to import the drug.

In 1839 the Chinese government decided to act, and launched an anti-opium campaign in Canton that culminated in the military take-over of a British factory and the confiscation of some 20,000 chests of opium. While the British were angrily demanding a return of their property, some inebriated British sailors killed a local Chinese, and the British government refused to hand over the culprits to the Chinese authorities. Deemed an insult to national sovereignty, the killing sparked the first Opium War, principally a naval conflict in the sea around Hong Kong.

The war lasted three years, and the British were easily victorious. But they could see that they now needed a safe and insulated base from which to trade. The result was the Treaty of Nanking.

This should have ended the problem of opium trading, but it did not. In 1856 the British, this time joined by the French, fought a second Opium War, won it, and as a result took over Kowloon, across the bay from Hong Kong. Finally, in 1898 Britain leased the New Territories (partly mainland, plus over 200 islands) for 99 years.

Britain built Hong Kong into one of the great trading and commercial cities of the world, but was forced to return it to China on 1 July 1997 when the lease on the New Territories expired and the Communist Chinese made it clear that they intended to take back all of Hong Kong, not just the part under lease.

Also on this day

1789: French painter Jean-Auguste Ingres is born in Montauban * 1833: The British Parliament passes the Factory Act, the first legislation protecting workers * 1835: The city of Melbourne is founded in Australia

30 August

Cleopatra clasps an asp to her bosom

30 BC Today amid the delicacies of a royal feast the last pharaoh of Egypt died by her own hand. She was the fabulous Cleopatra, the original femme fatale, lover of Julius Caesar and Mark Antony and extolled by Shakespeare for her 'infinite variety':

... other women cloy
The appetites they feed, but she makes hungry
Where most she satisfied.

Ever since Menes 3,000 years before, Egypt had been ruled by pharaohs, and since 323 BC by the dynasty established by Alexander the Great's general Ptolemy. Cleopatra was the last in Ptolemy's line. Her first language was Greek, but she spoke eight other languages as well, her voice 'an instrument of many strings', according to Plutarch.

Cleopatra had first beguiled Mark Antony at Tarsus, sailing up the Cydnus River in her opulent barge that 'like a burnished throne, burned on the water'. During eleven years they produced three children and hoped to rule the world together, Mark Antony as the new Caesar, Cleopatra as his partner and Queen of Egypt. But ever since Julius Caesar's death, his heir Octavian (the future Emperor Augustus) had laid claim to imperial power and resolved that Egypt should be just another Roman province rather than an independent kingdom.

In 31 BC Octavian crushingly defeated Mark Antony's and Cleopatra's fleets at Actium, and within a year his legions were marching towards Alexandria. Mark Antony led his army out of the city to do battle, but first his fleet defected and then his cavalry followed suit. His infantry was soon overwhelmed, and Mark Antony fled back into the city.

Dreading the fate awaiting her, Cleopatra secreted herself in her new mausoleum and had the rumour spread that she was dead. On hearing this direful news, Mark Antony attempted suicide but succeeded only in stabbing himself in the stomach, fainting on his couch. When he came to, one of Cleopatra's servants informed him that she was not dead after all, and summoned him to her presence. Carried by litter to her mausoleum, he was hoisted through a high window by Cleopatra's serving women, too frightened of Octavian's imminent arrival to open the gates. There, stretched out on his lover's couch, Mark Antony died of his wounds.

A few days later Octavian arrived at the head of his army. When Cleopatra refused him entry into the mausoleum, he sent soldiers in through the windows to disarm her before she could stab herself.

Octavian allowed her to arrange a splendid funeral for Mark Antony, who was interred in her mausoleum. But all the while he kept her surrounded with guards. In a desperate attempt to use her seductive charms one more time, she dressed in her most transparent garments and threw herself at her conqueror's feet, but he was immune to her allure. Now realising that her fate was to be paraded in chains through the streets of Rome, a prized captive, Cleopatra determined on suicide. Legend has it that she ordered condemned prisoners to be executed with various poisons to establish which would cause the least painful death.

On 30 August she returned to her mausoleum on the pretext of visiting Mark Antony's tomb. There she bathed and ordered a sumptuous feast. Among the delicacies delivered was a basket of figs in which was secreted an asp, an Egyptian symbol of divine royalty but more importantly for Cleopatra, deadly poisonous.

Her banquet completed, the Queen wrote to Octavian, pleading to be buried with her lover. The Roman instantly sent soldiers to prevent her suicide, but when they arrived they found her lying dead on her golden bed, two of her servant girls expiring at her feet. According to tradition, she had pressed the asp to her breast, but other reports suggest that two puncture wounds from the snake's fangs were found on her arm. She was still just 39 and had been pharaoh for 22 years.

On his return to Rome Octavian proudly announced to the Senate: 'I have added Egypt to the Empire of the Roman people.' His achievement lasted over six centuries, until the Arab conquests in 639, but through the magnificent drama of her life and death Cleopatra had become immortal, the most famous of all the queens of history.

Also on this day

1748: French painter Jacques-Louis David is born * 1797: *Frankenstein* writer Mary Wollstonecraft Shelley is born * 1823: Simón Bolívar becomes the dictator of Peru

31 August

Caligula – the story of a monster

AD 12 Born today at Antium, near modern Anzio on the Mediterranean coast of Italy, was history's prototype monster of despotic cruelty, the future third Roman emperor, Gaius Caesar Germanicus, commonly known as Caligula.

Caligula was related to the most powerful figures of the Roman Empire. Augustus was his great-grandfather (as was Mark Antony), and Tiberius, who became Emperor when Caligula was two, his great-uncle. His father Germanicus was a great military leader who took his young son on campaign with him, dressing him as a miniature soldier. From this he acquired the nickname of Caligula, or Little Boots, from his father's adoring soldiers.

When Caligula was seven, Germanicus died in Syria, many believed poisoned on orders from Tiberius, who was jealous of his reputation for bravery, generosity and military leadership. Ten years later the half-mad emperor exiled Caligula's mother Agrippina (the Elder) to the island of Pandateria, supposedly for plotting against him, and summoned Caligula, then eighteen, to live in the royal palace on Capri.

It was on Capri that Caligula first displayed his love of torture, eagerly attending executions. By that time he had also (according to that old gossip, Suetonius) enjoyed incestuous relations with all three of his sisters. A year after his arrival on the island, the paranoid Tiberius had Caligula's two elder brothers executed on flimsy charges of treason, and two years later Agrippina was forced to starve herself to death. This brought to four the number of immediate family members who died at Tiberius's hands, but Caligula continued to play the sycophant at court. It seems, however, that the Emperor was not fooled, once boasting that he was 'rearing a viper for the Roman people'.

When Caligula was 25, Tiberius died at the age of 78, some say smothered on the orders of his impatient great-nephew intent on inheriting the throne. For the first seven months of his rule Caligula was both just and generous, but he then fell severely ill, emerging from the sickness as the ogre of legend.

A huge spendthrift, he soon went through the three billion sesterces left by Tiberius, and started wholesale executions in order to confiscate rich men's property. He even initiated a tax on prostitutes, opening a brothel in a wing of the imperial palace to collect more fees.

Caligula's love of inflicting pain was notorious. He often witnessed the killings he ordered, telling the executioner to kill his victim slowly in order to 'make him feel that he is dying'. When one man cried out that he was innocent of the charges against him,

Caligula halted the execution to have his tongue cut out, then proceeded to put him to death. He even had convicted criminals slaughtered to feed his collection of wild animals. When the prisoners were lined up before him, Caligula ignored the charge sheet specifying their crimes, simply commanding the executioner to 'kill every man between that bald head and that one', indicating two bald criminals on either end of the line.

Tall and ungainly with only a fringe of hair around the ears, Caligula was so sensitive about his baldness that he made it a capital offence for anyone to look down on him. Even his family was not safe from his vindictive cruelty, as he forced his father-in-law to cut his own throat with a razor and probably poisoned his grandmother Antonia.

Caligula eventually concluded that he was a god, and ordered the Senate to treat him as one. On moonlit nights he would invite the moon goddess to join him in bed, and he talked openly to Jupiter, once threatening: 'If you do not raise me up to heaven I will cast you down to hell.' He even built a temple for himself on the Palatine Hill.

The most famous story about Caligula concerns his favourite horse Incitatus, which he housed in an ivory stall in a marble stable and adorned with a collar of precious stones and blankets of royal purple. He suggested, perhaps in jest, that he would make Incitatus consul, but never actually did so.

At the age of only 28, after less than four years as Emperor, Caligula was assassinated by two of his imperial guards on 24 January 41.

Also on this day

1422: English King Henry V dies at Vincennes outside Paris * 1688: English preacher and writer John Bunyan dies in London * 1867: French writer Charles Baudelaire dies in Paris * 1888: The first victim of Jack the Ripper, 'Polly' Nichols, is found dead and mutilated in Buck's Row, London

1 September

Kublai Khan and the Divine Wind

1281 The Mongol Empire of Kublai Khan was the greatest the world had known, extending from Hungary in the west to Korea in the east. But one country not yet conquered was Japan, and the great emperor, grandson of the fearsome Genghis Khan, was determined to add it to his territories.

In August 1281 Kublai Khan assembled a huge invading force of 140,000 battle-hardened soldiers aboard a vast fleet. The Mongols landed on the coast of Japan at Hakata Bay but were fought to a standstill by Japanese samurai, who denied them a beachhead. Withdrawing to their ships, the invaders planned another attack.

But while the Mongols planned a second D-Day, unknown to them an ominous date arrived, 1 September, the 210th day of the Japanese lunar calendar, famous for storms. And so it was, before the Mongols could mount their next assault, a massive typhoon struck, wreaking havoc with the Mongol fleet, destroying hundreds of ships and drowning thousands – some say over 100,000 – of the invaders.

The remaining Mongols sailed away or were captured and butchered. Ever since that day the Japanese have referred to the great enemy-destroying typhoon as the divine wind, or Kamikaze.

Also on this day

AD 70: Roman Emperor Titus orders the destruction of Jerusalem * 1339: England's King Edward III declares war on France to start the Hundred Years' War * 1715: Louis XIV of France dies * 1870: Prussia defeats the French at the Battle of Sedan, capturing Emperor Napoleon III * 1939: Germany invades Poland and captures Danzig, starting the Second World War

2 September

Octavian crushes Mark Antony at Actium

31 BC Today at the Battle of Actium, Octavian became master of the civilised world through his decisive victory over Mark Antony. The Augustan age had begun.

First there were three who controlled the Roman Empire: Octavian, Mark Antony and Lepidus. Together they avenged the murder of Julius Caesar, crushing the army of Marcus Junius Brutus at Philippi in 42 BC, a victory that left Brutus no way out but suicide. Then slowly Marcus Lepidus was moved aside until, in desperation, he raised an army in Sicily in an attempt to regain his authority. But even Lepidus's soldiers knew he was a lost cause and deserted, and Octavian sent him into forced retirement. Now there were only two, Mark Antony controlling the East, Octavian the West of the empire.

At first Mark Antony and Octavian maintained an uncomfortable alliance, cemented by Mark Antony's marriage to Octavian's sister, Octavia. But soon Mark Antony was openly living with Egypt's Queen Cleopatra, comporting himself in the style of an Oriental potentate. He then repudiated Octavia and married Cleopatra, an act contrary to all Roman laws under which no Roman could marry a foreigner. Together he and Cleopatra followed a licentious lifestyle in ostentatious luxury, proclaiming themselves incarnations of Dionysus and Aphrodite.

Meanwhile Octavian had been winning the propaganda war, inciting fury in Rome when he read to the Senate what he claimed to be Mark Antony's will in which he left all to his children by Cleopatra, stated his wish to be buried in Egypt and revealed his intent to relocate the capital from Rome to Alexandria. This gave Octavian all the justification he needed to declare war on Cleopatra, although his real target was Mark Antony.

The two armies came together near the bay of Actium (modern Punta), on the west coast of Greece. Both Octavian and Mark Antony commanded about 75,000 troops, and each had 400–500 ships. On the advice of Cleopatra, Mark Antony decided to launch a naval attack instead of an assault by his army.

Mark Antony drew up his fleet facing west, with Cleopatra's 60 galleys behind in reserve. At first the battle was furious, with neither side able to take a decisive advantage, but then some of Octavian's ships struck through the centre of Mark Antony's line. Fearful of capture, Cleopatra ordered her squadron to turn and row for safety, although she might have saved the day had she committed her reserve. Seeing the Queen in full retreat, Mark Antony turned and followed with a few of his galleys, leaving the rest of his fleet and his land army to surrender to Octavian.

Within fourteen months both Mark Antony and Cleopatra had committed suicide, while Octavian soon received the title Augustus and ruled the Roman Empire for another 45 years.

Also on this day

1666: The Great Fire of London starts in a baker's shop in Pudding Lane * 1752: Britain and its colonies change from the Julian to the Gregorian calendar; the following day becomes 14 September * 1898: Lord Kitchener leads British troops to defeat the Sudanese at the Battle of Omdurman, with the last cavalry charge in British history * 1910: French painter Henri Rousseau dies

3 September

Geronimo surrenders

1886 Today at Skeleton Canyon, cornered and outnumbered, the last great war chief of the Apaches agreed to surrender himself and his desperate band to the United States Army. Some 5,000 soldiers and 500 Indian auxiliaries and trackers had been pursuing Geronimo's tiny group of only 35 warriors for the past five months. Here, in this remote corner of the Arizona Territory near the Mexican border, the squat, broad-shouldered Geronimo conversed briefly with the tall soldierly figure of General Nelson A.

Miles before returning to his encampment to collect his people for the march north to Fort Bowie and captivity.

For almost a century, Apache tribes had fiercely resisted the intrusion of European settlers into their territory. The chiefs who led them in this long guerrilla struggle of raids and retreats became legendary: Mangus Colorado, Cochise, Victorio, Nana – and finally Geronimo. But the cavalry, employing mobile columns, Indian trackers and the heliograph, proved relentless and ultimately successful. Over the years, band by band, the Apaches were hunted down, killed when they resisted, and sent away to reservations. Now it was the turn of Geronimo and his Chiricahua Apaches, whose elusiveness General Miles declared had 'never been matched since the days of Robin Hood'.

Arriving at Fort Bowie four days after their surrender in the canyon, the Apaches were herded into railroad cars for their journey to Florida and exile. They were never again to see their homeland. A thoughtful farewell touch was provided by the 4th Cavalry band, which played 'Auld Lang Syne' as the train pulled away. So at last the Apache war – the 'Geronimo war', the cavalry had begun to call it – was over; there was peace in the desert.

Still, a residual bit of resistance occurred many years later, as reported in this wire-service story filed from Tucson on 22 April 1930: 'Riding out of their wilderness hideout, high in the Sierra Madre Mountains, a band of wild Apache Indians scalped three persons, April 10, in a settlement near Nacori Chico, Sonora, Mexico, it was reported by V.M. White, a mining engineer. ... Armed parties immediately set out to trail the painted savages and attempt to engage them in battle before they reached their impregnable and historic cliffs. The Apaches are believed to have been led, White said, by Geronimo III, the grandson of the Geronimo who was chased by the U.S. Army for three years during the '80's in Arizona.'

Also on this day

1189: Richard I (the Lion-Heart) is crowned at Westminster Abbey
* 1650: Oliver Cromwell defeats the Scots at the second Battle of Dunbar
* 1651: Oliver Cromwell defeats Royalist troops under Charles I at

Worcester, ending the English Civil War * 1658: Oliver Cromwell dies * 1939: Britain declares war on Germany

4 September

The last Roman emperor

AD 476 History – or at least tradition – tells us that Romulus and Remus founded Rome on 21 April, 753 BC, from which small beginning it came to dominate the known world.

On this day, 1,229 years, four months and fourteen days later, the last Roman emperor, a sixteen-year-old also named Romulus – Romulus Augustulus – abdicated his imperial office, bringing to an end the Roman Empire (although its eastern half continued as the Byzantine Empire for another 977 years).

Romulus Augustulus was forced to resign by his own German mercenaries, who had revolted in August, killing his father. Eleven days later young Romulus Augustulus too was gone. He was replaced by Odoacer, the chief of the mercenaries and son of one of Attila the Hun's lieutenants, who took the title of King of Italy. In the words of Edward Gibbon: 'Odoacer was the first barbarian who reigned in Italy, over a people who had once asserted their just superiority above the rest of mankind.'

In the beginning Rome had been a kingdom, but in 509 BC the city's nobility revolted against the tyrannical Tarquinius Superbus and established the Roman Republic. Initially dominated by the Etruscans, Rome gradually grew in power and dominion with its conquests of neighbouring kingdoms in the early 5th century BC.

For the next four centuries Rome was an empire without an emperor, ruled by the Roman Senate, which annually elected two consuls to serve for a single year. In times of crisis the Senate appointed dictators to rule for six months, although later ones, notably Sulla and Julius Caesar, forced the Senate to accept them on a more or less permanent basis. The first leader of Rome to be called Emperor – *imperator* – was Augustus, who awarded himself the title in January of 42 BC.

In all there were 90 Roman emperors, most of whom came to unpleasant ends. Five committed suicide, six were killed in battle, three more were executed after having been captured in war, and 35 were murdered. One, Petronius Maximus, was lynched by a Roman mob, but perhaps the unluckiest was Carus, who was struck by lightning.

Also on this day

1260: Tuscan Ghibellines supporting Holy Roman Emperor Rudolf I defeat the Florentine Guelphs, who support Pope Alexander IV, at the Battle of Montaperto * 1870: Léon Gambetta, Jules Favre and Jules Ferry proclaim the Third Republic from the Hôtel de Ville in Paris * 1907: Norwegian composer Edvard Grieg dies

5 September

The lucky conception of Louis XIV

1638 This story really starts nine months earlier, in December 1637, when King Louis XIII of France was caught in a driving thunderstorm after visiting a convent near Paris. Louis had already ordered his household to a château some distance away, but the cold, wet weather made it impossible for him to reach it that night. Where then to sleep?

Louis's quick-thinking captain of the guard urged him to go to the nearby Louvre, where his wife Anne of Austria lived. They had been married for 23 years but estranged for fifteen.

Louis hesitated. No doubt he remembered his wife's affair with the Duke of Buckingham and the famous diamonds (on which Dumas later built his tale of musketeers). But at last he grudgingly agreed. Even his wife's hospitality would be better than camping out in the storm.

It seems his wife's hospitality proved exemplary, as on 5

September 1638, exactly nine months later to the day, she gave birth to a son at the royal château at Germain-en-Laye. Like his father, the son would be called Louis, the fourteenth of that name, and he would reign for 72 years, longer than any other monarch in European history.

Also on this day

1566: Turkish sultan Suleiman the Magnificent dies * 1569: Flemish painter Pieter Bruegel the Elder dies * 1857: French philosopher and founder of sociology Auguste Comte dies in Paris * 1877: American Indian chief Crazy Horse is killed in a scuffle with his prison guards

6 September

Barbara Frietchie defies General Robert E. Lee

1862 Today we remember the importance of winning hearts and minds.

When, on the heels of the great Confederate victory at the second battle of Bull Run, Robert E. Lee brought his Army of Northern Virginia splashing across the Potomac fords into Maryland – Union territory – he had a strategy in mind. First, he expected his forces to be greeted as liberators by a Southern-sympathising population that would eagerly rebel against the Union and join the Confederate cause. He also counted on resupplying his forces from the rich harvest of a grateful countryside. Then the army would proceed into Pennsylvania, well ahead of any pursuit, and for the first time bring the experience of war to Northern states. Finally, in Lee's grand strategic vision, these moves might offer the opportunity for some dazzling military triumph – before Philadelphia, perhaps, or near New York City – which would induce a demoralised Federal government to sue for peace.

The first sign that things might go wrong occurred today as the Confederate army wound its way through the streets of Frederick.

There, in a very public act of defiance, a woman displayed a United States flag from the attic window of her house and then loudly disputed the right of the Confederate troops to shoot it down. According to John Greenleaf Whittier's war ballad, it was 95-year-old Barbara Frietchie who showed the Stars and Stripes that day and uttered the words: 'Shoot if you must this old grey head, but spare your country's flag.' Whittier's famous account is, however, poetic licence based on a real incident: a Mrs Quantrill, another resident of Frederick, did stand with her daughter before their gate that day and insultingly wave a Union flag at the Southern soldiers in the street.

At this time, the Army of Northern Virginia, 55,000 strong, was starving, exhausted, shoeless, and inclined towards pillage – 'a most ragged, lean, and hungry set of wolves', one observer called them. Despite the heavy posting of provost guards along the route of march, a third of the troops would disappear over the next few days. Nor were the army's invading presence and the prospect of its resupply welcomed by the citizens of Maryland. Farmers left their crops unharvested in the fields and drove their cattle to safety in the mountains; merchants and tavern keepers locked their doors. The army remained famished; Maryland stayed in the Union.

None of the other goals of Lee's invasion was realised. Surprised by the alacrity of the Union pursuit, the Army of Northern Virginia never got as far as Pennsylvania, never found its dazzling war-ending victory. Instead, reduced to fewer than 40,000 through straggling and desertion, it went to ground at Sharpsburg, Maryland, fought a sanguinary draw with 75,000 Federals, and retired to war-ravaged Virginia and another two and a half years of conflict.

Given the way the Civil War divided families, it is not perhaps so surprising that Mrs Quantrill, the staunch Union patriot who became Whittier's 'Barbara Frietchie', turns out to have been a relative of William Quantrill, the bloodiest of the Confederate guerrillas.

Also on this day

1522: Ferdinand Magellan's seventeen surviving crew members reach Spain for completion of the first round-the-world voyage * 1620: The

British ship *Mayflower* sails from Plymouth to North America * 1664: The British take over New Amsterdam (New York) from the Dutch * 1901: Leon Czolgosz shoots and fatally wounds American President William McKinley * 1944: The Germans fire the first V-2 missile at Paris

7 September

'Voilà le soleil d'Austerlitz!' 'Voilà le commencement de la fin'

1812 Today the meteoric career of Napoleon Bonaparte reached its apogee and started its precipitous descent towards catastrophe as the Emperor fought the Russians in one of the bloodiest battles of the 19th century.

At the end of June Napoleon had marched into Russia with an army of 530,000, the greatest concentration of troops in Europe since the Persian king Xerxes had invaded Greece in 480 BC. With this vast array came over 1,000 guns, 30,000 supply wagons and 28 million bottles of wine.

For weeks the army marched through the vast emptiness that was Russia, as the Tsar's army refused to be drawn into a major battle. Slowly Napoleon's front-line force was reduced, mostly to guard his ever-lengthening lines of communications but also owing to sickness, accident and the occasional guerrilla ambush. By early September the Emperor's forces ready for battle were only about 130,000.

On 6 September the French army (which in fact was only one-third French, the rest being conscripts from Napoleon's empire) arrived at the town of Borodino, a little over 60 miles west of Moscow. There at last the Russians turned to fight, 120,000 strong under the command of 67-year-old General Prince Mikhail Kutuzov, a fat and heavy-drinking noble who had lost an eye fighting the Turks but who possessed the cunning, determination and ruthlessness to match his adversary.

On the morning of 7 September Napoleon rose early and,

remembering the brilliant weather at his most famous victory seven years before, he welcomed a glorious sunrise with the optimistic exclamation: 'Voilà le soleil d'Austerlitz!' (Look, the sun of Austerlitz!) At six he ordered his cannon to open fire to start a day of frightful carnage.

By nightfall the stubborn Russians had lost some 45,000 men killed or wounded, but these could be replaced. Napoleon had suffered 30,000 casualties of irreplaceable troops 1,500 miles from home. (For a compelling if slightly fictionalised narrative of the battle, try Tolstoy's *War and Peace*.)

The following morning Kutuzov ordered a retreat, enabling the French to claim a victory and to begin the march on Moscow. But the Battle of Borodino was in fact Napoleon's greatest defeat. During the next three months his soldiers occupied a deserted Moscow which burnt to the ground around them, and then struggled back to the Polish border in the dead of Russian winter, attacked by Cossacks, guerrillas, the bitter cold and starvation. Only about 10,000 of the original force of over half a million survived the campaign. As Tsar Nicholas I later remarked: 'God punished the foolish; the bones of the audacious foreigners were scattered from Moscow to the Nieman.'

After the Battle of Borodino Napoleon's sun had passed its zenith and the Emperor's days in power were numbered. As the crafty old Talleyrand said on hearing of the battle: 'Voilà le commencement de la fin.' (There is the beginning of the end.)

Also on this day

1191: Richard the Lion-Heart's heavy cavalry routs Saladin and his army at the Battle of Arsuf * 1533: Queen Elizabeth I is born in Greenwich Palace * 1901: The Boxer Rebellion in China ends with the signing of the Peace of Peking

8 September

Huey Long is assassinated

1935 On this warm Sunday evening in Baton Rouge, a man stepped out from behind a pillar in the state capitol building and fired a revolver. What he hit – and destroyed – was a true force of nature on the American political scene: Huey Pierce Long, Jr, United States Senator from the state of Louisiana, the great Kingfish himself.

Flamboyant in dress and personality, with a face ready-made for cartoonists – and dubbed 'Kingfish' by his cronies after a character in a popular radio show of the era – Long was often called a demagogue, a breed he resembled in his campaign oratory but departed from by actually keeping the promises he made to get elected. In 1927, at the age of 34, he won the governorship of Louisiana and proceeded to finance his extensive public works programme – free schoolbooks, bridge and road construction, and a state hospital offering free medical care to all – by raising taxes on the wealthy and on the corporations doing business in the state. In so doing, he won the support of the state's rural population but the undying enmity of Standard Oil and the planter class.

Long had an intuitive genius for political leadership. For all his country-bumpkin manner, he was shrewder and tougher than any of his rivals. On his way to unsurpassed power in the state, he smashed all opposition.

With his Louisiana base secure, Long charged onto the national scene, taking up a seat in the US Senate in 1932. Now he encountered a rival of a very different sort: President Franklin Delano Roosevelt, whom he initially supported, then hoped to dominate, and finally came to distrust. In a nation gripped by economic depression, Long's 1934 Share Our Wealth programme – his Louisiana programme writ large, with its captivating slogan 'Every Man a King' – proved so attractive to voters around the country that it appeared Long might hold the balance of political power in the 1936 presidential election. He determined to run for President as a third-party candidate and deny Roosevelt a second term.

Long was now at the top of his form. He even wrote a book, published in 1935, called *My First Days in the White House* – 'a mixture of nonsense and wisdom, frivolity and gravity', one historian called it – recounting the early actions of 'President Long', including his Cabinet selections, among which was FDR as Secretary of the Navy.

But if Long's supporters around the nation were numerous, his enemies – 'polecats', he called them – were legion. For those on the right he was a radical socialist; for those on the left an American Hitler or Mussolini; and for many in between an unclassifiable but diverting political phenomenon. Visiting America, H.G. Wells admired Long as a 'Winston Churchill who had never been at Harrow'. Rebecca West took a dimmer view and found him 'the most formidable kind of brer fox'.

If others were puzzled by Huey Long, one man in Baton Rouge, Dr Carl Austin Weiss, a respected ear–nose–throat specialist and son-in-law of one of Long's Louisiana adversaries, seemed to have made up his mind. For motives that are still unclear, Dr Weiss took matters into his own hands and fired the shot from which Long died two days later. The Kingfish's last words were: 'God, don't let me die. I have so much to do.'

Also on this day

1157: Richard the Lion-Heart is born * 1886: After gold is discovered nearby, the city of Johannesburg is founded

9 September

William the Conqueror dies in France

1087 Today died the last man successfully to invade England, William the Conqueror, at the age of 59.

For the past twenty years William's main concern had been his subjugated kingdom in England, but he had in no way forgotten his original patrimony, the Duchy of Normandy. Thus when a

French army started to pillage his duchy in the summer of 1087 he quickly crossed the English Channel with his own troops.

William soon routed the enemy near the town of Mantes, but during the fight his horse stumbled and he fell forward onto the hard iron pommel of his saddle, receiving severe internal injuries.

Five weeks later the injured king was moved by litter to the outskirts of his Norman capital of Rouen. On Thursday morning, 9 September, the tolling of the bells of Rouen Cathedral awakened him. Construing this as a divine signal, he commended himself to God and died instantly.

During his 21 years as King of England this illegitimate issue of a Norman duke and a tanner's daughter had ruled his conquest with a hand of steel. Indeed, one Norman monk's account says that on his deathbed he bitterly repented the brutal repression he had visited upon the conquered land.

William left much that is still with us today. He built the White Tower in the Tower of London and he created a vast deer preserve in what is still called the New Forest in Hampshire. But most of all he introduced into Saxon England the values of Norman France, along with its triumphalist Gothic cathedral architecture.

William is buried at the monastery he founded of St Stephen at Caen.

Also on this day

1585: French 'Eminence Rouge' Cardinal Richelieu is born * 1828: Russian novelist Leo Tolstoy is born * 1901: French painter Henri de Toulouse-Lautrec dies

10 September

The English enter France through the hole in the Duke of Burgundy's head

1419 Today the treacherous murder of the Duke of Burgundy plunged France into chaos, leaving the country defenceless against the invading forces of Henry V of England.

France was being torn apart by the bitter rivalry between Burgundians and Armagnacs, two great feudal houses each struggling to grasp power from the mad French king, Charles VI. The Burgundians were led by their formidable duke, known as Jean Sans Peur for his valour. Their trump was insane King Charles whom they virtually held captive.

But the Armagnacs held the King's sixteen-year-old son, Dauphin Charles. And already leading a marauding army across northern France was England's Henry V, who claimed the French throne as part of his inheritance.

Recognising the danger from the English, the Burgundians and Armagnacs finally agreed to meet in the hope of reaching some sort of power-sharing agreement. On 10 September Jean Sans Peur and the young Dauphin met at Montereau, where a bridge spans the Seine about 40 miles from Paris.

Dauphin Charles, surrounded by his bodyguards, was already at the bridge when Duke Jean arrived. The Duke knelt to show his obeisance, but as he rose his hand accidentally brushed his sword handle in a movement that one of the guards found threatening. 'Would you put your hand on your sword in the presence of My Lord the Dauphin?' he cried. Instantly another Armagnac noble, Tanneguy du Châtel, struck Jean full in the face with a small axe, and the Duke fell dead on the bridge.

His Armagnac bodyguards quickly led the frightened Dauphin away, paralysed with shock. The most powerful man in France had been murdered, and chaos was certain. Fearful for their lives and hungry for revenge, the Burgundians quickly signed an alliance with the English king, and eight months later the French were forced to sign the Treaty of Troyes by which Henry would marry mad King Charles's daughter and become heir to the French throne. As a French prior from Dijon later famously said: 'The English entered France through the hole in the Duke of Burgundy's head.'

Also on this day

1813: American Commandant Oliver Hazard Perry defeats the British at the Battle of Lake Erie * 1823: South American revolutionary Simón Bolívar is named President of Peru * 1898: On a quay in Geneva an

Italian anarchist stabs to death Elisabeth of Bavaria (Sisi), the estranged wife of Austrian Emperor Franz Joseph

11 September

Eugene of Savoy's greatest victories

1697, 1709 On this date twelve years apart Prince Eugene of Savoy, one of Europe's greatest generals, gained two of his most momentous victories. By far the more important was the first one at Zenta, when Eugene was 34 and had only recently received his command in the Imperial (Austrian) army.

Ever since the mid-16th century the Turks had been threatening Austria, and more than once had come to the very walls of Vienna. Thanks to a great Austrian victory there in 1683 the Turks had retreated into the Balkans, but the threat of their return was always there.

In 1697 the Austrian Emperor Leopold I ordered Eugene vigorously to attack the Turks in an attempt to end the constant menace. On this day Eugene caught up with the army of Sultan Mustafa II near Zenta (in present-day Yugoslavia) where the Danube meets the Tisza. Discovering that Mustafa had already crossed the smaller river with his artillery – but had left his infantry for the moment on the other side – Eugene ordered an immediate attack, even though his force was far smaller than the Turk's.

Without cannon the Turkish soldiers were helpless. Many ran in panic, and mutinous Janissaries (élite soldiers who were kidnapped as boys from Christian families and converted to Islam) murdered the Turkish general on the field of battle. When the rout finally ended at ten o'clock that night, 20,000 Turks lay dead with 10,000 more drowned in the river trying to escape. Austrian losses amounted to only 300 killed.

The victory was enormous, and the resulting peace treaty ceded all of Hungary and Transylvania to the Austrian Emperor. Zenta was Eugene's first major victory.

Twelve years later to the day Eugene and the Duke of Marlborough celebrated another major triumph, this against the French at Malplaquet. Although undoubtedly a victory for the Austrians and English (in the end the French retreated), it was hardly as glorious, as the allies suffered 22,000 casualties against only 12,000 for the French. After the battle the beaten French commander, the duc de Villars, wrote to his king, Louis XIV: 'If God should grant us another such defeat, our enemies would be destroyed.' And the War of the Spanish Succession in which the battle was fought continued for another five years.

Also on this day

1297: Scottish rebel William Wallace defeats the English at the Battle of Stirling Bridge * 1855: During the Crimean War the Russian city of Sevastopol falls to British, French and Piedmontese forces after a siege of almost a year * 1885: English writer D.H. Lawrence is born

12 September

Vienna is saved from the Turk as croissants and cappuccino are invented

1683 Today we celebrate a famous victory that saved Vienna for ever from the threat of Turkish conquest and gave the rest of the world two recipes for the perfect Continental breakfast.

Ever since the reign of Suleiman the Magnificent a century before, the Turks had lusted for the great capital of Vienna, and now a vast Ottoman army a quarter of a million strong was camped around the city. Every day for two long months the guns of Grand Vizier Kara Mustafa crashed against the walls; the outer fortifications had been captured and the Turks were tunnelling through to the inner walls. It was only a matter of time before the Austrian defences would collapse, the barbarously cruel Turkish brand of murder and rapine would begin and the nation's Christianity would be extirpated for the glory of Islam.

So confident was the Grand Vizier that he complacently ignored the camp fires twinkling down from the Kahlenburg Heights only a few miles north of the city. But there the Polish King John Sobieski, who had come to Vienna's rescue in return for a huge subsidy from Pope Alexander VIII, joined the Austrian army under the command of Charles of Lorraine. Acting as the Pope's emissary was the Capuchin monk Marco d'Aviano, whose job it was to ensure co-operation among the various Christian commanders.

At first light on 12 September some 80,000 Christian soldiers thundered down into the mass of Turks. The battle lasted for fifteen hours, but in the evening a devastating charge by the Polish horse completely routed the invaders, who left their guns, vast stores of food, Kara Mustafa's fabulous jewels and tens of thousands of corpses on the field. In his dispatch to the Pope, the Polish king modestly paraphrased Caesar, reporting: 'I came, I saw, God conquered.'

What remained of the Vizier's army fled through Hungary towards Turkey, but Kara Mustafa reached only as far as Belgrade, where he was ceremoniously strangled with a silken cord, sent on orders from the Sultan at first news of the defeat.

Vienna was saved, Christianity remained triumphant and Ottoman rule in the Balkans was badly shaken. Among the victorious troops who celebrated that evening was a nineteen-year-old prince named Eugene of Savoy who would utterly crush the Turk fourteen years later at Zenta and who would become the greatest general ever to serve the Holy Roman Empire.

This tale of Vienna's salvation also has two remarkable culinary addenda. The first comes from Vienna's bakers, who commemorated the Austrian victory by creating a new roll in the shape of the crescent moon from the Turkish flag and christened it a *Kipfel*, German for crescent. The Kipfel gained immediate popularity in Vienna, and in 1770 Marie Antoinette (daughter of Empress Maria Theresa of Austria) introduced it to France when she married the future Louis XVI. Today we usually call it by the French word for crescent, *croissant*.

The second gastronomic creation of the battle perfectly complements the first. Among the supplies abandoned by the

Turks as they fled the field was a vast store of coffee. Finding it too bitter for their tastes, the Christian soldiers sweetened it with milk and honey, some say at the suggestion of the friar Marco d'Aviano. In any case, the tasty drink, whose colour resembled the friar's habit, was named Cappuccino in honour of the Capuchin order to which he belonged. For this, and other holy deeds, Marco was beatified in 2003.

Also on this day

1494: François I of France is born ＊ 1852: British Prime Minister Henry Herbert Asquith is born ＊ 1943: Italian dictator Benito Mussolini is rescued by German troops

13 September

General James Wolfe dies while winning Quebec

1759 Early this morning, after nearly three months of frustration, British Major General James Wolfe finally outwitted the French defenders of Quebec and under cover of darkness snuck an advance party up the steep heights above the St Lawrence River and onto the Plains of Abraham. He had finally discovered the unlocked back door to the great bastion. By first light his seven battalions – 4,800 men – were deployed in a battle line stretching across the mile-wide tract of open land. Now he awaited the French response.

Since his expedition had arrived by ship in front of Quebec in late June, Wolfe had probed up river and down but found no way to crack the stout defences behind which lay the marquis de Montcalm and a force of 12,000. Now time was running out: with winter in the offing, the British fleet would soon retire down river, and with it all chance of taking the city this year. But at last he spotted a route up the cliffs.

When the French emerged onto the Plains at 9.00 a.m., the British held their fire until the enemy was within 60 yards, then unloosed volley after volley, halting the attackers and routing them back inside their fortifications. That evening the French regulars left Quebec and retreated up river. The fortress surrendered on the 18th. Thus, the glorious deed was done. But in the doing, Wolfe was shot three times and bled to death. His adversary, Montcalm, also severely wounded, died the next day.

The battle of Quebec was decisive. The French retreated to Montreal, which fell the next year. Canada was now British.

The battle on the Plains of Abraham became a celebrated event for many in that and later times. It inspired Benjamin West's 1776 painting, *The Death of Wolfe*. It may have added to the popularity of Thomas Gray's 'Elegy in a Country Churchyard', known to be Wolfe's favourite poem, whose famous line seemed to capture both his exploit and his fate: 'The paths of glory lead but to the grave.'

Finally, we know that in the dire military situation of Korea in the summer of 1950, General Douglas MacArthur drew inspiration from Wolfe's surprise manoeuvre at Quebec to plan his brilliantly successful backdoor landings at Inchon.

Also on this day

1506: Italian painter Andrea Mantegna dies * 1592: French essayist Michel de Montaigne dies in Bordeaux * 1598: Philip II of Spain dies at El Escorial * 1814: American defence at the Battle of Fort McHenry inspires the writing of the 'Star Spangled Banner'

14 September

'Onorate l'altissimo poeta'

1321 Today, during the black hours of pre-dawn, the first great modern poet, Dante Alighieri, died in exile in Ravenna at the age of 56.

In some ways Dante was the precursor of the versatile Renaissance Men who were to spring forth from his native Florence a century and more after his death. Philosopher, dashing cavalryman (he had fought for Florence against Arrezo at the battle of Campaldino), councilman, servant of princes, ambassador – Dante was all of these as well as the creator of arguably the greatest single poem ever penned.

Dante spent the last nineteen years of his life in exile from Florence, banished by the pro-pope faction, the Black Guelphs, whose views Dante opposed. During that time he composed his masterpiece, *The Divine Comedy*, an epic of 100 cantos written in *terza rima*, with a rhyming pattern of aba bcb cdc, etc. Originally he called it simply *La Commedia* (The Comedy) because of the happy ending with Dante being guided through Paradise. Only two centuries after his death did the epic have the word 'divine' added to its title.

In the centuries since Dante's death, *The Divine Comedy* has inspired many other great artists. Botticelli, Michelangelo, Blake and Doré all produced illustrations for it, and Rossini, Schumann and Liszt used it as a basis for their compositions. Longfellow translated it into English, and because of it T.S. Eliot placed Dante on a par with Shakespeare as one of the two greatest of all poets.

Dante himself was also an admirer of previous poets, most notably the Roman Virgil, whom he selected to be the guide in his voyage through the Inferno. Most would consider the words Dante used to describe Virgil as equally suitable for Dante himself: 'Onorate l'altissimo poeta.' (Honour the greatest poet.)

Also on this day

1516: French King François I wins the Battle of Marignano * 1812: Napoleon enters Moscow * 1852: The Duke of Wellington dies at Walmer Castle in Kent * 1901: Theodore Roosevelt becomes the 26th President of the United States on the death of the assassinated President McKinley * 1950: American Marines land at Inchon during the Korean War

15 September

The first day of the Congress of Vienna

1814 Vienna. In Roman times it was a frontier outpost called Vindabona, but it must have had some importance, for the Emperor Marcus Aurelius chose it as his military headquarters in his fight against barbarian German tribes, and he died there in AD 180. Centuries later it became the Habsburg capital of the Holy Roman Empire and three times withstood the siege of the Turks. Later Napoleon crushed the Austrian army at Wagram, 110 miles west of the city, entered Vienna in triumph and forced the Austrian Emperor to offer him his daughter in marriage.

But in all its varied history, never had Vienna, that magical and beautiful city on the Danube, been as much at the centre of history as it was on this day in 1814, which marked the formal opening of the Congress of Vienna.

Organised to restore peace and the balance of power in Europe after the Napoleonic wars, the Congress was possibly the greatest gathering of political power in history. It was hosted by Emperor Franz II of Austria (whose daughter Napoleon had married) at a cost in today's terms of $50,000,000. A tsar, three kings, eleven princes and over 90 ambassadors and plenipotentiaries attended it. In the cast were Castlereagh from Great Britain, as well as the illustrious Duke of Wellington, the famous Russian Foreign Minister Nesselrode and the two greatest masters of diplomacy and intrigue of the century, Talleyrand, representing the restored French monarchy, and Metternich, Austria's arrogant Foreign Minister. (This wily and aristocratic pair had much in common. Both became princes, and Talleyrand's most recent mistress was Dorothea, Duchess of Dino, while Metternich had formerly been the lover of her elder sister, Wilhelmina, Duchess of Sagan. Not surprisingly, the two men worked well together.)

The Congress lasted six months, marked by a brilliant succession of entertainments, including a concert of Beethoven's Seventh Symphony conducted by Beethoven himself. But most of all it is remembered for its endless series of balls. Indeed, some questioned that any progress was being made. As the Belgian Prince de Ligne famously punned: 'Le congrès ne marche pas, il danse.' (The Congress doesn't walk [i.e. work], it dances.)

Distracted by waltzes as it may have been, the Congress of Vienna accomplished its stated task of carving up Europe and establishing a peace that lasted for nearly 40 years until the Crimean War. Most of the boundaries established in 1815 remained for almost a century, until the First World War.

Also on this day

1613: French aphorist François, duc de La Rochefoucauld is born in Paris * 1916: Britain uses tanks against German positions, the first time tanks are used in battle * 1917: Russia is proclaimed a republic with Alexander Kerensky as Prime Minister

16 September

The death of Torquemada, the implacable fanatic of the Spanish Inquisition

1498 Today in the quiet of the Monasterio de Santo Tomás in Avila died a frail 78-year-old Dominican monk, weary from a life dedicated to God. No one has ever less deserved a peaceful death; he was the first and worst Grand Inquisitor of the Spanish Inquisition, Tomás de Torquemada, whose name appropriately means 'burnt tower'.

In 1483 Pope Sixtus IV had chosen Torquemada to head the Spanish Inquisition, but even the Pope had no inkling of the demented zeal with which his appointee would perform his task of cleansing Spain of heretics. Torquemada's special target was the so-called Marranos, Jews who claimed to have converted to Christianity but who secretly still followed the Jewish faith. Using unspeakable torture to extract confessions and punishing the guilty with execution at the stake, this fanatical monk used a network of spies to ferret out suspects and crossed the country attended by 50 armed knights and 200 foot soldiers to enforce his will.

Historians still debate how many 'heretics' Torquemada burned in the name of God, but the minimum suggested is 2,000, with another 25,000 convicted and punished less harshly.

In his persecution of the Jews, Torquemada was a chilling forerunner of the Nazis half a millennium later. His ultimate goal was to establish nothing less than *sangre limpia* (pure blood) in Spain – that is, Christian blood. He made the Marranos forfeit their property, forced them to wear the *sambenito*, a yellow shirt sewn with crosses, and had them flogged in public at the entrance to a church. He even issued a set of tell-tale signs by which good Christians could detect secret Jews, e.g. 'If on Saturday your neighbours wear clean clothes, they are Jews.'

After ten years of religious cleansing of the secret Jews, Torquemada stepped up his efforts to persuade King Ferdinand and Queen Isabella to expel all Jews. But then some wealthy Jews offered 30,000 ducats if the Jews could remain, and the King and Queen were sorely tempted.

On hearing of the offer, Torquemada hurried to the palace and, holding his crucifix before him, confronted the royal pair. 'Judas sold Jesus Christ for thirty pieces of silver', he admonished. 'You would sell Him for thirty thousand. Here, take Him and sell Him, and I will leave my office and you will explain your agreement to God.' He then turned and left the room. Not surprisingly, in the face of such holy intransigence, on 31 March 1492 the King and Queen ordered all Jews to leave the country no later than 1 July or face execution. More than 160,000 fled.

Many have wondered over the centuries what drives a man like Torquemada to such extremes of relentless persecution. Some believe that, like Hitler's notorious SS officer Reinhard Heydrich, Torquemada was subconsciously compelled by the knowledge of his own tainted bloodline: his grandmother had been a converted Jew.

Also on this day

1387: Henry of Monmouth (Henry V of England) is born at Monmouth Castle, Wales * 1620: The British ship *Mayflower* leaves Portsmouth to found the first permanent colony in North America * 1701: British King James II dies in exile at Saint-Germain in France

17 September

A bridge too far – the largest airborne operation ever

1944 With Paris liberated, Antwerp captured, and the Germans everywhere on the run in north-west Europe, an intoxicating optimism ran through the Allied camp. Imbibing this spirit, the normally cautious Field Marshal Montgomery advanced a bold strategic plan that gave promise of ending the war by Christmas.

It called for a great thrust northward through Holland to get past the Siegfried Line, Germany's formidable frontier defences, and then a swing eastward towards Berlin and final victory. Not everyone among the Allied brass agreed, but General Eisenhower, the Supreme Commander, was willing to give Monty's plan a try, at least the first part, a combined ground and airborne operation to get forces across the Lower Rhine River, the last great water barrier before Germany itself. The operation bore the deceptively pastoral codename Market Garden.

Accordingly, on this sunny late summer morning, from airfields across southern England, a great armada of transport planes and gliders took off for Holland carrying 20,000 paratroopers from three Allied divisions. The mission was to 'lay an airborne carpet' behind German lines along a 65-mile corridor running north from the Allied front line to the town of Arnhem on the far side of the Rhine. The paratroopers would seize key bridges along the corridor, then hold them until the ground forces of XXX Corps came through on their way to Arnhem.

Allied planners viewed the retreating enemy as demoralised and incapable of strong resistance. They discounted intelligence indicating a formidable concentration of German units in the very area through which Market Garden would pass. At a top-level briefing for Market Garden commanders, the general commanding the British 1st Airborne Division asked how long his men would have to hold Arnhem before XXX Corps got through to them. 'Two days', Monty told him confidently. 'They'll be up with you by then.'

On the ground it was very different. The Germans met 1st Airborne's drop near Arnhem with unanticipated quickness and ferocity. Only one battalion of British paratroopers managed to reach the town. The rest came under heavy fire and by nightfall went to ground west of town. At the southern end, as the Guards Armoured Division leading XXX Corps got under way its lead units were ambushed by heavy fire from anti-tank guns. The column halted while infantry was brought up to flank the ambushers and bulldozers cleared away the wreckage of vehicles. The tanks resumed their advance, but the pattern was set for a painfully slow, stop-and-go advance. When the Guards reached Eindhoven, just eleven miles from the start line, they were already 24 hours behind schedule.

In seizing their assigned bridges, the paratroopers of the 101st and 82nd US Airborne Divisions had done a remarkable job; but so had the German defenders in attacking the Allied columns that jammed the single roadway north. At the town of Nijmegen it took XXX Corps two days of heavy fighting, including an amphibious assault by the 82nd, to clear the bridge across the River Waal.

The advance continued, but time was running out. With one isolated battalion desperately holding the north end of the Arnhem bridge against 9th SS Panzer Division, the rest of 1st Airborne was pinned in a shrinking pocket, backs to the Rhine. An attempt to fly in reinforcements went disastrously awry when anti-aircraft fire forced Polish paratroopers to jump early, putting them on the wrong bank of the river.

Reduced to 2,200 from the 10,000 paratroopers who had landed eight days earlier, the division was almost out of food, ammo and medical supplies, and could no longer care for its growing number of wounded. Montgomery, finally realising that XXX Corps, close as it was, would not reach Arnhem in time, gave 1st Airborne the order to withdraw. During the night and under intense fire, the survivors were ferried or swam to safety across the Rhine.

Market Garden failed utterly. In the gallant effort, 17,000 Allied troops had been killed, wounded or captured. Arnhem proved to be, in a phrase that would become famous, 'a bridge too far'. Critics of the operation compared it to Dunkirk and the Dardanelles. The Allies would need to find a different strategy from Monty's single thrust. There would be one more Christmas at war.

Also on this day

1630: John Winthrop founds the town of Boston * 1631: Protestant Swedes and Saxons under King Gustavus Adolphus defeat forces of the Holy Roman Empire at Breitenfeld * 1787: The Constitution of the United States of America is signed * 1796: President George Washington delivers his 'Farewell Address' to Congress * 1862: The Battle of Antietam is fought in the American Civil War, the bloodiest single day in US history

18 September

Another Roman emperor is done in by his wife

AD 96 Today one of Rome's more loathsome emperors met his death at the hands of his own wife and servants, to the contentment of the Senate and the joy of dozens of his subjects who feared for their lives.

Domitian was the son of a great emperor, Vespasian, and the brother of a good one, Titus, against whom Domitian ceaselessly plotted during the two years that Titus ruled. When Domitian was 29, Titus fell seriously ill, and Domitian ordered his attendants to leave him for dead even while he was still alive, thus accomplishing passive fratricide.

On inheriting his brother's imperial rank, Domitian was at first a competent ruler, but he soon showed his inherent sadism by frequently sequestering himself in his office to catch flies and stab them to death with his pen. As he grew older, despite his athletic frame, he grew paunchy and bald, for he took no exercise except sex, which he jocularly referred to as 'bed wrestling'. One of his mistresses was his own niece (Titus's daughter) Julia. He also became increasingly autocratic, insisting on being addressed as *dominus et deus* (master and god).

According to the historian Suetonius (who was 30 when Domitian was murdered), the Emperor's 'lack of funds made him greedy, and fear of assassination made him cruel'. Whatever the cause, as time went by Domitian increasingly condemned people to death on the flimsiest of pretences, convinced that all were plotting against him and eager to appropriate their wealth.

Domitian could also be maniacally vindictive. Before becoming Emperor, he had forcibly taken and married Domitia Longina, who was the wife of another man, one Aelius Lamia. Shortly afterwards Aelius had been joking with Domitian's brother Titus, who encouraged him to remarry. 'What?' asked Aelius, 'Are you looking for a wife too?' For this idle repartee, years later Domitian had Aelius executed.

Domitian's irrational malevolence was also demonstrated when his wife entered an affair with an actor named Paris. The Emperor first banned her but later took her back ('recalled her to my divine bed', was how he described it). But subsequently he had one of Paris's student actors executed purely on the grounds that he was Paris's pupil and apparently much resembled him physically.

According to Suetonius, a number of augurs foretold that Domitian would be assassinated, one even predicting the exact date. Terrified by the threat, the Emperor proscribed or executed so many people that even those with no guilty secrets lived in mortal terror of the imperial summons.

Among those living in dread were his wife Domitia Longina, who feared further imperial retribution, and Stephanus, the steward of the Emperor's niece Domitilla, whom the Emperor had sent into exile. Stephanus had been accused of embezzlement and, afraid for his life, sought out several equally panicky members of Domitian's household staff. Together they hatched a murderous plot.

For several days Stephanus went everywhere with his arm in a bandage, beneath which he concealed a dagger. Then, on the morning of 18 September, Domitian's attendants announced that the steward had arrived to warn the Emperor of an assassination plot. When Stephanus entered the royal bedchamber he handed Domitian a scroll supposedly containing the details of the scheme, but when the Emperor reached for it, the steward stabbed him in the groin. Suetonius relates that 'Domitian wrestled Stephanus to the ground, where the two men fought long and hard, Domitian trying to grab the dagger and to claw out his attacker's eyes with his torn and bleeding fingers'. Before either man could subdue the other, four of Stephanus's confederates joined the fray and stabbed the Emperor seven more times, leaving him dead on the floor. It was just four days after he had celebrated his fifteenth anniversary as Roman Emperor, the most powerful man in the world.

Also on this day

AD 324: Roman Emperor Constantine defeats Licinius at Chrysopolis, becoming the sole emperor of the whole Roman Empire, east and west * 1709: Samuel Johnson is born in Lichfield, Staffordshire * 1851: The first issue of *The New York Times* appears

19 September

The Black Prince captures a French king

1356 The Hundred Years' War had already been running for nineteen years when the English routed their French foes today at the Battle of Poitiers.

In early September the English heir to the throne, Edward, the Black Prince, led a raiding party of only 7,000 men out of English-held Bordeaux, but he soon found himself pursued by King Jean II of France with a vastly superior force. The armies fought briefly on 17 September but arranged a truce for the following day, a Sunday. This day of rest gave the Black Prince the time he needed to organise his army in a damp marshland where the Clain and Miosson Rivers come together near the town of Poitiers.

Ten years earlier, at Crécy, the French had found themselves in a very similar situation – outnumbering the enemy but stymied by bogs that gave their war-horses no footing. Lack of discipline plus the accuracy of English longbows had destroyed the French then, just as happened today at Poitiers.

The French charged repeatedly, each time losing dozens of knights to England's lethal arrows, and when they pushed their advance further their horses bogged down in the marsh and English foot soldiers quickly dispatched their riders, helpless on the ground.

Poitiers was a particular disaster for the French because King Jean, who had quixotically led the final charge against the English, was captured and carried off to London for four years of luxurious captivity.

The battle may have seemed decisive at the time, but it was in truth just another blip in this seemingly endless conflict that dragged on for another 97 years.

Also on this day

1777: Americans win the Battle of Saratoga in the American Revolution * 1812: Mayer Amschel Rothschild, founder of the House of Rothschild, dies in Frankfurt

20 September

How the Great Papal Schism began

1378 Pope Gregory XI had died shortly after bringing the papacy back to Rome, ending the so-called Babylonian Captivity, that period of almost 70 years when popes lived in Avignon under the thumb of French kings. Now the Neapolitan Bartolomeo Prignano sat on St Peter's throne, having taken the name of Urban VI. He was stubborn, dictatorial and difficult, wildly accusing his cardinals of lasciviousness and simony, seeing vice in every corner. But to a large group of French cardinals, his greatest crime was his refusal to return the papacy to Avignon after having gained their votes by his promise to do so.

At first the furious cardinals tried to depose Urban, calling him 'anti-Christ, devil, apostate, tyrant, deceiver' and other mild condemnations. But Urban stubbornly clung to power.

Moving to Fondi, near Naples, the cardinals held their own conclave and on 20 September 1378 elected another Frenchman, Robert of Geneva, as their new pope and whisked him back to Avignon. Robert styled himself Pope Clement VII, but the problem was, Urban VI remained Pope in Rome.

Popes and anti-popes were nothing new in the Church. A certain Hippolytus was the first anti-pope way back in the year AD 218. Clement VII was rather a late-comer to the trade, the 34th anti-pope since St Peter founded the Church.

But the split (called the Great Schism) that started with Clement and Urban was much the most serious disruption in the Church's history. During the next four decades there were five 'legitimate' popes and four anti-popes, with at least two and sometimes three enthroned simultaneously, one in Rome, one in Avignon and occasionally one in Bologna.

Eventually, on 26 July 1417 Martin V became the sole Pope when the Council of Constance deposed one of the pretenders, Benedict XIII. The Great Schism had lasted 38 years and 309 days.

Unfortunately, the papacy's papal problems were far from over at the end of the Great Schism, as there were still two more anti-popes to come. But the last of these, Felix V, abandoned his claim in 1449.

Also on this day

356 BC: Alexander the Great is born * 1519: Ferdinand Magellan starts his round-the-world voyage with five ships and 280 men * 1857: The siege of Delhi ends, leading to the collapse of the Indian Mutiny * 1870: The reunification of Italy is completed as Garibaldi enters Rome

21 September

The Greeks annihilate the Persians at Marathon

490 BC The mighty Persian empire stretched from the edge of India to the Aegean, and King Darius the Great had set his sights on the still independent city-states of Greece.

Two years earlier Darius's first attempt had ended in failure when his fleet was storm-wrecked off Mount Athos, but now he was armed with a secret weapon, what amounted to a fifth column, in the Alcemaeonidae family in Athens who secretly favoured a Persian victory, hoping it would restore their political power. If the Athenian army could be drawn away from the city, perhaps Athens would fall by insurrection rather than costly invasion.

In September of 490 BC Darius landed an army of 15,000 men on the Bay of Marathon, which lies about 26 miles north-east of Athens. Frantic, the Athenians immediately sent a messenger, Pheidippides, to plead for reinforcements from the Spartans. Although Pheidippides covered 150 miles in less than two days, his mission was fruitless, for the Spartans announced they could not march before the completion of certain religious festivals, still ten days away. The Athenians would have to face the Persians alone.

In mid-September 10,000 Greeks, including the poet Aeschylus, reached Marathon, and there for eight days uncertainly faced the invading Persians, the Athenians fearful of Persian military might, the Persians hoping to hear that, with the Greek army out of Athens, the Alcemaeonidae were overthrowing the government.

On 21 September the Greek commander Miltiades saw that the Persian cavalry had re-embarked, probably to mount a direct attack on Athens. He also learned that Persian reinforcements were on their way. He chose this moment to strike.

The Athenian infantry charged forward and were immediately counter-attacked by the Persian front line. The Greek centre bowed backwards under the assault, as the Persians hurled themselves forward, thinking the Greeks were in retreat. Then Miltiades brought his two reinforced wings around in a double envelopment, smashing into the Persian flanks.

The result was massacre. The Greeks lost only 192 men, but 6,400 Persians died on the Plain of Marathon. What was left of the Persian army fled to their ships and headed for home.

Now the Persian threat had been stymied, what of the threat of revolt in the city? Knowing that the Alcemaeonidae could not act without Persian military support, the Greeks immediately dispatched a messenger (some say Pheidippides again) to herald the great victory. Without pause for rest or water, he ran the 26 miles between Marathon and Athens, announced the Athenian triumph ('Nike' in Greek, meaning victory) and then fell dead from exhaustion.

Almost two and a half millennia later, the Greeks commemorated this famous run by instituting the first 26-mile 'marathon' race in the 1896 Olympics, held in Athens. Appropriately, it was won in two hours, 58 minutes and 50 seconds by Spyridon Louis, a Greek.

Also on this day

19 BC: Roman poet Virgil dies * 1452: Fanatical preacher Girolamo Savonarola is born in Ferrara * 1558: Holy Roman Emperor Charles V dies of malaria at Yuste * 1792: The French monarchy is abolished and France is declared a republic * 1832: British writer Sir Walter Scott dies

22 September

The most barbarous royal murder in history

1327 Today three henchmen of the Queen of England and her lover committed the most barbarous royal murder in history. The victim was the Queen's husband, King Edward II.

Handsome, silly, weak and dominated by male favourites, Edward II had been overthrown by Queen Isabella and her paramour Roger de Mortimer. He was now a prisoner and had been moved from London to the more remote Berkeley Castle in

Gloucestershire under the guard of Sir Thomas Gurney, Sir John Maltravers and William Ogle. But no matter how securely the King was imprisoned, he still represented an intolerable threat to the usurpers of power.

Perhaps hoping Edward would succumb to natural causes, his jailers locked him in a small, cold room and fed him with scraps, but his constitution was rugged, and he showed no signs of sickness or deterioration. Something had to be done.

During the night of 21 September the three henchmen entered Edward's cell while he slept and pinned him to the bed with a table. Then one of them thrust a red-hot spit up through his anus, burning out his internal organs. This indescribably agonising method of execution both served as an evil parody of the King's homosexuality and left his body outwardly unmarked, so that it could later be laid out in state for inspection.

Edward's death – publicly explained as due to sudden illness – permitted Queen Isabella to control the state as regent for her fourteen-year-old son, now Edward III, with her lover Mortimer acting as unofficial co-ruler. Neither the Queen nor Mortimer understood young Edward's hatred for their usurpation or his steely determination as he grew older. When he reached his majority three years later he sent his mother to forced retirement while ordering a traitor's execution for Mortimer, to be hanged, drawn and quartered.

Although Edward II had accomplished little during his lifetime, his horrible death produced one of England's great buildings. The monks at Gloucester treated him as a martyr, and soon his tomb became a focus for pilgrimage. The enormous offerings left behind by pious visitors enabled the monks to rebuild the cathedral in Perpendicular style, the first and greatest example in England.

Also on this day

1692: Six women and one man are hanged during the Salem witch trials in America * 1776: American patriot and spy Nathan Hale is hanged in New York * 1862: US President Abraham Lincoln issues the Emancipation Proclamation, freeing America's slaves, which comes into force the following 1 January

23 September

The Greeks save the Western world at Salamis

480 BC Persia's mighty King Xerxes had sent his heralds throughout Greece demanding earth and water, symbols of submission, but the Athenian general Themistocles responded with a brutal symbol of his own: he had the messenger put to death for daring to make his barbarian demands in the Greek language. Enraged, Xerxes resolved to conquer those foolish enough to resist him.

Soon Xerxes had assembled a huge army, estimated by Herodotus at 2,641,610 men, but assumed by modern historians to be a more modest 200,000. To cross from Asia Minor into Greece he constructed two boat bridges across the Hellespont, and when waves destroyed them during a storm, he ordered the sea scourged with 300 lashes. He then threw a pair of shackles into the water, grandly pronouncing: 'Ungracious water, your master condemns you to punishment for having injured him without cause. Xerxes the king will pass over you, whether you consent or not!' By then the storm had abated, and his army easily crossed over on a new bridge.

In spite of the defensive league formed by the Greek city-states, the Persians rolled irresistibly forward. In August of 480 they defeated the heroic Spartans at Thermopylae, opening the route to Athens, which the Athenians then abandoned, leaving only a heavily fortified Acropolis. Soon that too had fallen, with all defenders slain.

The assembled Greek generals as ever bickered interminably over tactics. Some wanted to withdraw to Corinth, while Themistocles argued vehemently for a naval engagement. At length it seemed that the Athenian had won the dispute, but only by threatening to withdraw his ships and men. But on 22 September yet another debate erupted, and this time Themistocles took an even greater gamble. He sent a slave with a secret message to Xerxes: Themistocles is on your side, and the rest of the Greeks are ready to run away. Attack now while they are still arguing what to do and you shall have a great victory.

Having heard from his own spies about dissension in the Greek camp, Xerxes believed Themistocles' message and launched his attack. The Greeks suddenly had no choice but to stay and fight.

Themistocles' brilliant plan was to lure the Persian fleet into the narrow straits between the port of Piraeus and the island of Salamis, where the enemy would have no room for manoeuvre. Outnumbering the Greeks more than two to one, on this day some 1,000 of Xerxes's galleys fell into the Greek trap. According to Herodotus, Themistocles delayed the final action 'until the time when there is regularly a strong breeze from the open sea that brings a high swell into the straits, which presented no difficulty to the low-built Greek ships but was harmful to the slow and cumbersome Persians, with high sterns and decks, as it made them vulnerable to the quick attacks of the Greeks'.

For seven long hours the Greeks harried the Persians. Greek triremes ran up alongside the enemy galleys, shearing off their oars, and then returned to ram or board. When day became evening, some 300 Persian galleys lay shattered on the seabed, against losses of only 40 for the Greeks.

Xerxes had remained on dry land, sitting in his golden throne high upon a promontory to watch his inevitable victory. As more and more of his ships went down, his ally Artemisia, Queen of Helicarnassus, rammed and sank an enemy trireme, at which the King lamented: 'My men have become women, my women, men.'

Defeated and fearful of being cut off in Greece, Xerxes scuttled back to Persia, leaving behind an army to achieve on land what he had so conspicuously failed to do by sea. But in August the following year that army was destroyed at the Battle of Plataea.

The Battle of Salamis was much more than the first great naval battle in history. With the victory at Plataea, it ended the Persian threat for a century and a half, until Alexander the Great finally conquered the Persian Empire in 331 BC. More than that, it prevented Greece from being crushed by Oriental despotism, leaving it free to develop its systems of democracy and the philosophical ideals that have pervaded Western civilisation ever since. In the words of historian Will Durant: 'It made Europe possible.'

Also on this day

63 BC: Roman Emperor Augustus is born * 1779: Just before sinking, American Captain John Paul Jones's ship *Bon Homme Richard* captures the British ship *Serapis* * 1938: British premier Neville Chamberlain flies to Munich to meet Hitler * 1939: Austrian founder of psychoanalysis Sigmund Freud dies

24 September

Isabeau of Bavaria – France's worst queen?

1435 France has had its share of dreadful queens – Catherine de' Medici comes to mind. Today died a lesser known one, Isabeau of Bavaria, who harmed her nation as much as any invader.

She was born Elizabeth, daughter of the Duke of Bavaria. But when she married Charles VI of France her name was gallicised to Isabeau, a distinctive name for a distinctively depraved and selfish woman.

Beautiful and intelligent as well as exceptionally sensual, she was married to Charles at the age of fourteen, but after seven years of marriage it became clear that the King was going mad. During the next 30 years he suffered 45 fits of insanity, some lasting several months, when often he could not recognise her. Although Isabeau bore the King six children, she also took a series of lovers, including both the King's brother and his cousin. In between titled paramours she entertained strapping soldiers of the palace guard. According to legend, she would also have her soldiers bring handsome men in off the streets, make love to them, then have them tied up in sacks and thrown into the Seine.

All of this could have been just good fun, but Isabeau also wielded power. Her most disastrous act was to sign the Treaty of Troyes by which King Henry V of England became heir to the French crown in place of Isabeau's own son Charles, who was to be sent in exile from France.

As she grew older Isabeau's beauty vanished and she grew

increasingly fat, until she finally had to be carried everywhere in a litter. During her last years she witnessed the heroic deeds of Joan of Arc and the recognition of her son Charles (VII) as the rightful King of France. She died at the age of 64, held in contempt equally by the English she had helped and the French she had betrayed.

Also on this day

1541: Swiss physician and alchemist Paracelsus dies * 1789: President George Washington signs the Judiciary Act of 1789 to establish the United States Supreme Court * 1896: American novelist F. Scott Fitzgerald is born

25 September

Another calamitous crusade

1396 A mission to save the Christian world from Muslim domination had first been proposed in 1095 with Pope Urban II's impassioned call for the forces of Christendom to join the First Crusade. During the next two centuries Europeans launched seven more great campaigns, gradually ceding dominance of the Middle East to the Turks. Today another crusade, even more futile than its predecessors, reached its unhappy denouement at the Battle of Nicopolis in Bulgaria.

By the late 14th century the Ottoman Turks had reduced the once mighty Byzantine Empire to little more than the city of Constantinople itself. And now the Turkish Sultan was the fearsome Bayezid, called the Thunderbolt for his sudden and devastating attacks. Determined to widen his rule yet further, in 1395 he marched west, to the alarm of Christian Europe. By the beginning of July he had reached Nicopolis, a Bulgarian fortress on the banks of the Danube. There, after a brief siege, he shattered the defenders, killing the Bulgarian Tsar Ivan Shishman in the process.

Now Christian Europe was in panic. This time Pope Boniface IX led the call for a crusade to halt the Muslim threat. In July 1396 the Duke of Burgundy's son Jean de Nevers set out with a motley army of 10,000 Frenchmen, 2,000 Germans, 1,000 Englishmen and assorted soldiers from Poland, Austria, Lombardy and Croatia, as well as a contingent of Knights Hospitallers. As they marched east they were joined at Buda by a huge army of 30,000 Hungarians under the command of their king Sigismund. The crusaders' aim was nothing less than to turn the Turks out of the Balkans and then to march through Anatolia and Syria to Jerusalem to recapture the Holy City. Their first major target would be the recently conquered Nicopolis, now occupied by the Turks.

Throughout the centuries, crusader courage and determination had been far stronger than their planning and preparation. The crusade of 1396 was no exception, for the European armies had brought no siege equipment and so were forced to surround and isolate Nicopolis rather than overpower it. This error gave the defending Turks several weeks to hold the fort and wait for help.

Reinforcements were not long in coming. Resolved to save Nicopolis, Bayezid the Thunderbolt marched out from Turkey at the head of a large army, including the feared Janissaries, infantry composed of Christian boys kidnapped from their families, forced to convert to Islam and (perhaps worse) to remain celibate. Joined by loyal Serbian allies, Bayezid soon arrived at Nicopolis and took up defensive positions on the city road with his flanks protected by deep gullies.

Lusting for blood, the impatient French knights immediately launched an attack, in spite of pleas for caution from King Sigismund. At first they met with success, routing the Turkish infantry and light cavalry and launching themselves at the Janissaries. Then suddenly the French cavalry were forced to halt; they had charged into a field of sharpened stakes planted in the ground and had to dismount or disembowel their horses. But even on foot they were formidable fighters, breaking the Janissary line while killing thousands.

Now the French and their allies charged up a small hill in the hope of looting the Sultan's quarters, only to find the Ottoman heavy cavalry massed there. Cut off from the rest of the Christian army, they were surrounded and slaughtered or captured.

Meanwhile the crusaders' Hungarian infantry initially fared

better, routing the Turkish force before them until Bayezid's Serbian soldiers emerged from ambush to stampede the whole crusader army into panicky retreat.

Only a few of the crusaders escaped. Sigismund fled to the Danube and got away by ship, and Jean de Nevers was captured and later ransomed. But the day after the battle, Bayezid, incensed by his heavy losses, massacred most of his prisoners. The few survivors were given to his soldiers as slaves.

Once again, Islam was triumphant. For five centuries the Bulgarians were plunged into the Dark Ages under oppressive Islamic domination, what they refer to as the 'Turkish yoke'. The Bulgarian nobility was destroyed – aristocrats were coerced either to accept Islam and 'Turkicisation' or face execution. The peasants were turned into serfs while the Turks instituted what Bulgarians call 'the blood tax', as thousands of young boys were compelled to convert and pressed into the Janissary Corps. Only in 1878 did the Bulgarians at last regain their freedom.

Also on this day

1066: English King Harold II defeats Harald Hardrada of Norway at the Battle of Stamford Bridge * 1534: Medici Pope Clement VII dies * 1897: American novelist William Faulkner is born

26 September

A conquistador discovers the Pacific

1513 Today a Spanish conquistador discovered a gigantic new ocean, the Pacific. Three centuries later John Keats celebrated the event with his stirring lines:

> Or like stout Cortez when with eagle eyes
> He stared at the Pacific – and all his men
> Looked at each other with a wild surmise –
> Silent, upon a peak in Darien.

Fortunately Keats was a better poet than historian, since the man who sighted the Pacific was not Cortés but Vasco Núñez de Balboa.

Balboa was born and raised in the Extremadura of western Spain, that flat, arid province whose very name means 'extremely hard'. He was the first of the tough and uncompromising conquistadors from that area, a list that includes Cortés and Pizarro.

At 25 Balboa first came to the New World on a voyage of exploration to Colombia. Later he tried to settle down in Hispaniola (current Haiti), but by the time he was 35 he was mired in debt and fled the island as a stowaway, landing at Darién on the north coast of the Isthmus of Panama where it joins South America. There at last he began to prosper, and had soon taken command of the Spanish settlement.

Balboa was shortly leading expeditions into the interior in search of gold and slaves. Although he never resorted to the wholesale slaughter of the Indians as some of his Spanish contemporaries did, he used bribes, force where necessary, and occasionally terror, once having 40 Indians torn to pieces by Spanish war dogs.

In 1513 Balboa heard rumours of vast hoards of gold somewhere in the interior and determined to find it. Selecting 190 men and several hundred Indian guides and bearers, on 1 September he set out to cross the stifling rain forests of the Isthmus of Panama, jungle so thick that for days he and his men could never see the sky.

For 25 days the rugged and indefatigable Spaniards slogged their way through virtually impenetrable jungle and foetid swamp, finally emerging on the south coast of the isthmus to see a mountain peak looming before them. Ordering his men to halt, Balboa climbed to the top and in the distance saw the ocean.

According to Balboa's own account, he immediately dropped to his knees to give thanks to God and the saints and then called his men to join him at the summit, where they carved the name of the Spanish king (Ferdinand) on tree trunks to establish possession.

Four days later Balboa reached the ocean itself. Plunging into the water in full armour, he brandished his sword and claimed it for Spain.

Discovering the Pacific was Balboa's crowning achievement. Only six years later he became embroiled in a terminal conflict with Pedrarias Davila, who was both his father-in-law and technically his superior, in charge of the Spanish colony. Davila was jealous of Balboa's achievements and hated him for his reports to Spain condemning Davila's performance. When news arrived in the colony that Davila was being replaced, he summoned Balboa and had him tried on trumped up charges of treason. The great explorer and three of his comrades were beheaded in the main square of Darién, their corpses fed to vultures.

Also on this day

1791: French painter Théodore Géricault is born in Rouen * 1820: American frontiersman Daniel Boone dies * 1888: American (later British) poet T.S. Eliot is born * 1898: American composer George Gershwin is born in Brooklyn

27 September

Cosimo de' Medici is born

1389 Today marks the birth of one of Florence's great patricians and bankers, Cosimo de' Medici, whose family claimed descent from a stalwart knight named Averado who served the Emperor Charlemagne in the 9th century. They maintained that their coat of arms proved it.

According to the Medici tradition, one day Averado was riding north of Florence when he met a cruel giant who was terrorising the local peasantry. Taking up arms for the victims, Averado slew the giant and in the fight received three dents on his shield from the giant's mace. Hearing of his courageous victory, Charlemagne allowed him to add to his escutcheon a gold field bearing three red balls symbolising the dents. From that time forth the Medici used this insignia. (Historians have a more prosaic explanation, that the balls represent three Byzantine coins, symbols for money-changing.)

Historical evidence suggests that the Medici origins were somewhat more humble. The family were originally Tuscan peasants from Cafaggiolo, 16 miles north of Florence. In the 12th century they moved into Florence itself and within a hundred years had become one of the city's great banking families.

Cosimo de' Medici was born in Careggi just outside Florence, the son of Giovanni di Bicci de' Medici. Giovanni had come from moderate wealth, made much more and married well. A supporter of the arts for his city, he had been one of the backers for Ghiberti's magnificent doors for the Baptistery, although they were not finished until well after his death.

Cosimo was 40 and rich when his father died. But his path to real dominance over Florence was sometimes difficult. The city's ruling Albizzi family feared him and coveted his wealth in equal measure, and had him arrested on the capital charge 'of having tried to raise himself up higher than others'. Cosimo bought first his life and then his freedom with Medici cash and went into exile for a year, only to return and become the de facto ruler of the city, banning the Albizzi for ever. He was so powerful that Pope Pius II described him as 'a king in everything but name'.

As well as Europe's richest and most influential banker, Cosimo was also a scholar, an early humanist and one of history's most eminent art patrons, supporting many of the great artists of his day, including Fra Angelico, Donatello, Ghiberti, Filippo Lippi and Gozzoli. He encouraged Brunelleschi to complete his great dome for Florence's cathedral, and ordered the construction of the Medici Chapel at Santa Croce and the convent of San Marco. He built the Palazzo Medici and established the ascendancy of the Medici family that was to last for 200 years.

Cosimo had a sceptical mind and a mordant sense of humour. As he grew older, he was aware that death was closing in on him. Once, when his wife asked him why he sat so long with his eyes shut, he answered simply, 'To get them used to it'.

His foreboding was accurate. Feverish, frail, sorely afflicted by the family disease of gout, he died on 1 August 1464 at the age of 75. The sad but grateful citizens of Florence named him *Pater Patriae* (father of his country) after his death.

1826: The world's first passenger railway opens from Stockton to Darlington * 1917: French painter Edgar Degas dies * 1944: French sculptor Aristide Maillol dies

28 September

The real King Wenceslas is murdered

929 Good King Wenceslas looked out
On the Feast of Stephen,
When the snow lay round about
Deep and crisp and even.
Brightly shone the moon that night,
Though the frost was cruel,
When a poor man came in sight
Gathering winter fuel.

This merrie carol was written in 1853 by an English preacher named Neale to a 16th-century Swedish tune. Even today we still sing about that good king of Bohemia (who was actually a duke), who was assassinated today on the way to church.

Wenceslas's father died young, but the boy was raised a good Christian by his saintly grandmother Ludmila. Unhappily, Wenceslas's mother Drahomira remained a pagan and soon had her mother-in-law murdered so that she could hold power as regent for young Wenceslas.

When Wenceslas came of age he took over the reins of government, instantly showing he had all the right instincts during the wrong time in history. He took vows to remain a virgin, encouraged the spread of Christianity in Bohemia and, much to his soldiers' disgust, made peace with the German Emperor, Henry the Fowler. He infuriated his nobles by his Christian rectitude, particularly his desire to help the poor.

In the year 929 the 22-year-old duke left his capital of Prague to visit his brother Boleslav. After an evening of magnificent entertainment, Wenceslas rose early to attend matins. But as he was about to enter the church, henchmen sent by his brother brutally struck him down.

Boleslav got what he wanted: to become Duke. But Wenceslas got to be the patron saint first of Bohemia and then of Czechoslovakia.

Also on this day

48 BC: Roman general Pompey the Great is assassinated * 1215: Mongol Emperor of China Kublai Khan is born * 1573: Italian painter Caravaggio (Michelangelo Merisi) is born * 1841: French Prime Minister Georges Clemenceau is born * 1864: Karl Marx founds the First International in London * 1895: French scientist Louis Pasteur dies

29 September

The first Habsburg emperor

1273 Today Herzog (Duke) Rudolf von Habsburg was elected Holy Roman Emperor by his fellow German princes, the first Habsburg to hold that office. With the election, his family was well on the way to becoming the most powerful in Europe for most of the next 600 years.

The Habsburg family took its name from their fortress perched high among the crags in what today is Switzerland – the Habichtburg or Hawk Castle. Over the centuries the name was shortened to Habsburg. In the second half of the 13th century Rudolf inherited his father's dukedom. He was an intelligent and enterprising warrior whose family was too weak to be a threat to other German princes. In fact, Rudolf's weakness became his cardinal strength, as his fellow nobles elected him Emperor largely on the grounds that he represented no danger.

Although Rudolf proved to be a fine emperor (he defeated both the powerful Bohemians and the French), he was unable to persuade the electors to grant the imperial throne to his son. But the fact that he had become Emperor set a precedent that helped Habsburgs to gain the crown intermittently until 1438, when they pretty well gained it for good, until Napoleon finally forced Emperor Franz II to resign his title in 1804, bringing the Holy Roman Empire to an end.

Also on this day

1582: St Teresa dies in Alba * 1758: British admiral Horatio Nelson is born * 1910: American painter Winslow Homer dies

30 September

Richard II becomes the first English king to abdicate

1399 Today before Parliament in Westminster Hall, hard by the cathedral where he had been crowned 22 years earlier, Richard II, King of England, calmly declared his abdication to the benefit of his first cousin Henry Bolingbroke, whose land Richard had previously confiscated. Bolingbroke was now King Henry IV.

At the age of ten Richard had inherited the throne from his grandfather, Edward III, and for the next seven years was content to let his uncle John of Gaunt rule the kingdom while he grew into a tall, blond and handsome young man with a strong interest in culture but little in the normal kingly pursuits of jousting and war.

In the years after he started to rule in his own right, Richard became increasingly selfish and extravagant, while entertaining a number of favourites, first Robert de Vere and later Edmund, Earl of Rutland. As his liaisons became more open, Richard grew increasingly authoritarian, paying scant regard to Parliament, first packing it with his supporters, then dismissing it altogether. In his megalomania he even tried (unsuccessfully) to be elected Holy Roman Emperor.

Among the nobles who resented Richard's spendthrift ways and court favouritism was his cousin Henry Bolingbroke, son of

John of Gaunt. At one point Bolingbroke and four confederates forced the King to banish de Vere and thus earned Richard's undying enmity. The King's revenge was not long in coming. In 1398 he exiled Bolingbroke and subsequently seized his property to distribute to his friends.

A year later Richard made the misjudgement of going on an expedition to Ireland, giving Bolingbroke (now, after John of Gaunt's death, the Duke of Lancaster) the opening to invade England as champion of all the dispossessed nobles. On 4 July 1399 Bolingbroke landed at Ravenspur in Yorkshire and soon took control of most of England. Hurrying back from Ireland, Richard found every hand turned against him and was forced to surrender to Bolingbroke's supporters, who incarcerated him in the Tower of London. There he was threatened and demoralised until, fearing for his life, he finally agreed to renounce his throne. On 30 September he abdicated before Parliament, and on 13 October Bolingbroke was crowned King Henry IV.

King Henry imprisoned Richard in Pontefract Castle in Yorkshire, and four months later he was dead, possibly a suicide from starvation but more probably murdered on the orders of the new king.

Richard II was one of four English kings to abdicate; the others were Edward II, James II and Edward VIII.

Also on this day

1520: The rule of Suleiman the Magnificent in the Ottoman Empire begins * 1791: The first performance of Mozart's *The Magic Flute* takes place in Vienna

1 October

Alexander the Great conquers the Persians at Gaugamela

331 BC Today the man who was perhaps history's greatest general destroyed the Persian Empire in his greatest victory at Gaugamela, in what is now northern Iraq.

Alexander the Great had been taught by his father Philip of Macedon and his tutor Aristotle to hate the Persians, who had been invading and harrying Greece since the time of Xerxes a century and a half before. But Alexander had also developed revolutionary ideas of his own. He was a fervent believer in the superiority of Greek civilisation and thought he had a mission to spread it to the barbarian world.

When Alexander succeeded to the Macedonian throne on his father's assassination, he inherited a kingdom, a superb army and a fledgling plan to invade the great Persian Empire that ruled from Anatolia to the plains of India. In the spring of 334 BC he crossed the Dardanelles with an army of about 50,000 men, including some 7,000 cavalry, determined to conquer. 'Heaven cannot support two suns, nor the earth two masters', he portentously announced.

Within three years Alexander had defeated many of the Persian Emperor Darius III's satraps (governors of his provinces), and Darius attempted to buy him off, promising to cede substantial territory and pay 10,000 talents in gold if Alexander would return to Greece.

When told of the offer, Alexander's most senior general Parminio advised, 'I would accept it were I Alexander', to which the haughty Alexander replied, 'And so truly would I if I were Parminio.'

Forced at last to fight, Darius now massed near the town of Arbela a vast army of perhaps 200,000 that included vicious scythe-chariots and at least fifteen elephants.

Darius picked his ground carefully. Nearby lay the Plain of

Gaugamela, perfect terrain for cavalry and chariots. To ensure his victory, the Emperor ordered trees felled and the ground roughly flattened in order to give his superior force a better chance of surrounding the invading Greeks.

When Alexander arrived on the high ground before Gaugamela his generals urged immediate action, but instead he ordered his troops to rest for the night while giving the impression that attack was imminent, thus fooling Darius into keeping his men up all night awaiting the assault. By the next morning the Persians were already exhausted when they went into battle.

Once the battle began, the Persian cavalrymen moved forward to charge, leaving a gap in their line into which Alexander led his own horsemen and drove them directly at Darius. When the Emperor fled, Alexander wheeled to attack the enemy's flank, starting the general disintegration of the Persian army.

There are various estimates of battle casualties, none reliable, but what is certain is that the Persians suffered grievous losses, perhaps 40,000 killed, while only a few hundred of Alexander's Greeks died on the field.

Following the battle Alexander pursued Darius, but before he could catch up with him the Emperor was murdered by one of his own generals. Alexander's victory at Gaugamela gave him control of what to that time was the greatest empire the world had known, but perhaps an even more important result was the spread of Greek values and Alexander's own concept, unique in his era, that the good men of the world, Greek or barbarian, should unite to rule the world for the benefit of mankind.

Also on this day

1066: William the Conqueror lands at Pevensey in Sussex * 1684: French playwright Pierre Corneille dies * 1936: Francisco Franco becomes Head of State in Spain

2 October

Saladin retakes Jerusalem

1187 Today the holy city of Jerusalem fell to the forces of Islam after less than a century of Christian rule.

When European Christians had first captured the city from the infidel during the First Crusade, they had established there a kingdom, but by the close of the 12th century the royal house was in steep decline. When King Baldwin IV died of leprosy, the throne should have passed to his young nephew, but Baldwin's sister Sibylla had other ideas. With her husband Guy de Lusignan she seized the crown for herself and had Guy declared King.

But Guy had neither the intelligence nor the ruthlessness of former Christian rulers, and their Saracen adversary was the formidable and experienced Sultan Saladin, who had already been Commander-in-Chief of the Saracen army for sixteen years.

Born in Mesopotamia (modern Iraq), Saladin was a devout Muslim, totally committed to the idea of jihad against the Christians and the recapture of Jerusalem. In July 1187 he completely routed the Crusader army at Hattin and then marched on the holy city. After only a short siege, it fell to the Muslim host. To the delighted astonishment of the conquered Christians, Saladin and his men treated them with kindness and courtesy rather than the indiscriminate slaughter that followed the Crusaders' capture of the city.

Nonetheless, for Christians in Jerusalem and all over Europe, the fall of the holy city was considered a major catastrophe. To the Saracens, however, the date itself must have confirmed their belief in the divine righteousness of their cause, for it was also on 2 October over half a millennium before that Mohammed had ascended to heaven from that self-same place, Jerusalem.

Jerusalem had been Christian for exactly 88 years, two months and seventeen days.

Also on this day

632: The Prophet Mohammed ascends to heaven from Jerusalem * 1869: Indian leader Mohandas Gandhi is born * 1968: French artist Marcel Duchamp dies

3 October

St Francis dies at Assisi

1226 Among the rolling hills of Umbria lies a medieval jewel called Assisi, now damaged by earthquake and tacky souvenir shops but nonetheless much as it was three-quarters of a millennium ago when its most famous citizen expired nearby at the monastery of Porziuncola.

When St Francis of Assisi died today at the age of 44, he was already widely recognised as a saint for his personal piety, various miraculous healings he brought about and his founding of the Franciscan order for men and the Poor Clares for women. In spite of his total dedication to God and the Church, he was one of history's more likeable saints, with his love for animals, which he referred to as 'brothers' and 'sisters'.

When Francis was 42 he experienced a dramatic vision. St Bonaventure, leader of the Franciscan order later in the 13th century, describes it: 'As it stood above him, he [Francis] saw that it was a man and yet a Seraph with six wings; his arms were extended and his feet conjoined, and his body was fixed to a cross.' When the seraph vanished, Francis found the wounds of the stigmata on his body. Later he became almost completely blind, probably from an infection he had picked up on an earlier trip to the Middle East.

Francis was a mystic who loved life but hated property, so much so that during his last hours he requested his fellow Franciscans to lay him on the bare ground to die. Knowing that he was *in extremis*, he murmured, 'Welcome, sister death.'

So venerated was he that only two years later he was named a saint, and only 27 years after his death the majestic cathedral in Assisi that was built to honour him was consecrated.

Also on this day

1656: Myles Standish, leader of the Plymouth Colony (the first permanent settlement in North America), dies * 1867: French painter Pierre Bonnard is born in Fontenay-aux-Roses * 1896: English artist William Morris dies * 1910: Leading republican Miguel Bombarda is murdered by a maniac, igniting the Portuguese revolution

4 October

The Crimean War begins

1853 Russia's Tsar Nicholas I had contemptuously called Turkey 'the sick man of Europe' and in May had marched into the Danubian principalities (now Romania) that in theory were under joint Russian and Turkish 'protection'.

France, Austria and Great Britain protested loudly, and by September crowds were rioting in Constantinople against the Russian incursion. The tension was palpable, as two corrupt and dying empires, Ottoman Turk and Romanov Russian, eyed each other for the main chance.

Knowing that they had the principal European powers behind them, the Turks enthusiastically declared war on this day in 1853 to begin the Crimean War.

By March of the following year France and Britain had thrown their lot in with the Turks, and eventually even the Kingdom of Sardinia would send a regiment.

The Crimean War dragged on in appalling conditions for almost two and a half years, men dying of war wounds, of cold and most of all from diseases that ravaged all sides. In the end Russia conceded a few trifling border changes and fighting ground to a halt. The war witnessed some legendary if futile heroics such as the Charge of the Light Brigade, and Florence Nightingale became a British heroine for ministering to the wounded during the conflict. But in total some 250,000 men died in the Crimea, one of the most purposeless wars in history.

Tsar Nicholas, the man who had started the war, did not survive to see the end of it, dying on 2 March 1855, some eleven months before the finish. Some historians maintain that he committed suicide in despair over Russia's mounting losses, but it seems more likely that he succumbed to pneumonia, his exhausted body too weak to resist.

Perhaps the sole beneficial result of the Crimean War was the enrichment of the English language regarding apparel. From it came the balaclava helmet, invented to combat the murderous cold and named after the 1854 Battle of Balaclava, the raglan sleeve, originally designed to be worn by the one-armed British commander Field Marshal Raglan, and the cardigan sweater, named for its inventor, British General Sir James Cardigan.

Also on this day

1582: Pope Gregory XIII establishes the Gregorian Calendar, specifying 1 January as the first day of the year * 1669: Dutch painter Rembrandt van Rijn dies in Amsterdam * 1720: Italian artist Giambattista Piranesi is born * 1814: French painter Jean François Millet is born * 1830: Belgium declares independence from the Kingdom of the Netherlands

5 October

Napoleon gives the rabble a whiff of grape

1795 It was 13 Vendémiaire, An IV, according to the French republican calendar. Both Louis XVI and Robespierre had already been fed to the guillotine, but hard-eyed monarchists and fanatical revolutionaries still roamed the streets of Paris. Now royalist agitators, bizarrely backed by their former enemies on the hard left, were marching at the head of a mob of 30,000 armed and excited protesters. Their goal: the Tuileries, where the Convention was meeting. The government must fall, no matter who was there to pick up the pieces.

In charge of security was vicomte Paul Barras, a brawny provincial nobleman who had helped bring about the executions of both Louis XVI and Robespierre. As commander of the Army of the Interior and the police, he was one of the most powerful men in the country. He had recently begun a new affair with a tempting 32-year-old widow from Martinique named Joséphine de Beauharnais.

Realising that only military force could quell the mob, Barras called on a young unemployed brigadier general named Napoleon Bonaparte and put him in charge of the Convention's defences. Bonaparte instantly recognised the need for artillery and ordered Major Joachim Murat, whom he now met for the first time, to commandeer 40 cannon and place them at key points around the Tuileries.

In mid-afternoon the excited rabble approached. Bonaparte held fire until the crowd reached point-blank range, then commented contemptuously, 'We'll give them a whiff of grape.' The cannon spat out murderous grapeshot, instantly cutting down over 200 and wounding twice as many more. The mob fled in panic, and the government was saved.

In an uncanny way, the lives of many of the principal players from 13 Vendémiaire would be intertwined in the years to come. A year later Bonaparte married Joséphine de Beauharnais, whom he had met at Barras's house. Barras went on to even greater power in the government but was precipitously driven from office and eventually exiled from France by Bonaparte, the general he had drafted. Murat became one of Bonaparte's most successful marshals, ultimately becoming the King of Naples. And of course in his *coup d'état* of November 1799 Bonaparte also destroyed the republican government that he had so well protected.

Also on this day

1791: Russian army officer, statesman and lover of Catherine the Great Grigory Potemkin dies * 1889: The Moulin Rouge opens in Paris * 1910: Portugal is proclaimed a republic as King Manuel II is driven from the country

6 October

The execution of the man who wrote the English Bible

1536 William Tyndale was the sort of religious fanatic whom religious fanatics hate. Ordained a Catholic priest, he joined the faculty at Cambridge University and there was converted to the idea that the Bible rather than the Church hierarchy should be the authority for religious doctrine. He also became committed to providing a Bible that was accessible to all worshippers. His life's work became the translation of the Bible into English.

Tyndale completed his version of the New Testament in 1525, and a decade later 50,000 copies had been printed, the first English text of the New Testament to be published.

But Tyndale's views were too hot for England to hold. Another fanatic, Sir Thomas More, condemned his religious beliefs, his criticism of divorce drew the wrath of King Henry VIII, and Henry's Chief Minister Thomas Wolsey tried to have him arrested even after he had fled England for Germany.

Tyndale eventually made the tragic error of trying to hide in Antwerp, then part of the Spanish Netherlands. There the greatest fanatics of them all, the administrators of the Spanish Inquisition, condemned him to a heretic's death.

On this day Tyndale was brought forth from his cell and led to the *quemadero*, the burning place. As he was roped to the stake he is reported to have prayed, 'Lord, open the eyes of the King of England.' Then he was strangled by the hooded executioner and his body burned.

It is nice to think that William Tyndale may be looking down on us, for if he is, he has seen the triumph of his efforts. The men who persecuted him and the Inquisition have long since vanished, but his translation still forms the basis for the King James Version of the Bible.

Also on this day

AD 105: At Arausio (now Orange in Provence) the German Cimbri and Teutoni tribes rout the Roman armies of Caepio and Mallius, killing

80,000 * 1887: Swiss architect Charles-Edouard Le Corbusier is born, La Chaux-de-Fonds * 1891: Irish nationalist Charles Stewart Parnell dies at Brighton * 1892: Alfred, Lord Tennyson dies

7 October

Christian Europe defeats the Turk at Lepanto

1571 It is fitting that this day was a Sunday, the Lord's Day, when the Christian forces of Spain, Venice and the papacy combined to destroy the Turkish fleet at the Battle of Lepanto, ending for ever the danger of Islamic conquest of Europe.

The two fleets met at dawn off the west coast of Greece. The huge European armada with 316 vessels outnumbered the Turks, who had only 245 ships. But in the 16th century naval battles were won primarily using heavily manned rowing galleys carrying soldiers who fired on enemy ships and then boarded them, and the Turks had a critical advantage in number of galleys.

In command of the Christian flotilla was Don Juan of Austria, the dashing illegitimate son of retired Holy Roman Emperor Charles V and thus half-brother to Spain's King Philip II. Although only 24, he had already proved himself against Barbary pirates. As the fleets approached each other he ordered the attack. His captains urged caution, to which Don Juan replied, 'Gentlemen, it is no longer the hour for advising, but for fighting.'

The battle lasted four hours and was decided not by the galleys and soldiers but by the Christians' sailing ships – galleons, frigates and galleasses heavily armed with cannon. The Europeans' superior firepower proved decisive, slaughtering enemy troops and sinking their galleys before they could bring their soldiers into play. When his galley was overrun, the Turkish commander dropped to his knees, offering a huge ransom in return for his life. Disdainfully a Spanish soldier lopped off his head as he knelt, then displayed it on the end of his pike.

This was the first engagement in naval history where sailing ships supplanted galleys as the primary weapon. When the battle ended, over 8,000 Christians had perished, but almost 30,000 Turks had been cut down or drowned. In addition, about 15,000 Christian galley slaves had been set free from the Turkish vessels.

The Battle of Lepanto marked the end of Turkish domination of the seas and destroyed the myth of Turkish invincibility that had been created earlier in the century during the reign of Suleiman the Magnificent. It was also a decisive experience for a 24-year-old Spanish soldier wounded in the left hand by a Turkish bullet. He abandoned his military career, perhaps believing that a pen in his good right hand would prove mightier than the sword. His name was Miguel de Cervantes.

Also on this day

1769: Captain Cook discovers New Zealand * 1777: American revolutionaries defeat the British at the Second Battle of Saratoga * 1849: American writer Edgar Allan Poe dies of drink * 1900: Heinrich Himmler, head of the Nazi SS and organiser of extermination camps in Eastern Europe, is born

8 October

Backwoods hero – Corporal Alvin York

1918 Of all the American heroics of the First World War, none are more celebrated than those of Corporal Alvin York, a backwoodsman from the Tennessee mountains who single-handedly put 35 German machine guns out of action, killed over twenty machine gunners and captured 132 enemy soldiers in a single morning.

York's platoon was part of a 328th Infantry Battalion attack against heavily fortified enemy positions in the Argonne forest. At dawn on 8 October the assault began, but the Americans were almost immediately riddled with machine gun fire, pinned down and seemingly helpless. German machine guns continuously raked their position, and American casualties were heavy. In desperation, seventeen men including York's squad determined to work around behind the enemy through a concealed gully.

Miraculously they succeeded in getting behind the Germans, only to have the enemy machine gunners turn around to face them, immediately killing six of them.

By now York was the most senior man left. Here is his own account of what happened next. 'As soon as the machine guns opened fire on me, I began to exchange shots with them. There were over thirty of them in continuous action, and all I could do was touch the Germans off as fast as I could. I was sharpshooting. I don't think I missed a shot ... In order to sight me or to swing their guns on me, the Germans had to show their heads above the trench, and every time I saw a head I just touched it off ... Suddenly a German officer and five men jumped out of the trench and charged me with fixed bayonets. I changed to the old automatic and just touched them off too. I touched off the sixth man first, then the fifth, then the fourth, then the third, and so on. I wanted them to keep coming. I didn't want the rear ones to see me touching off the front ones, I was afraid they would drop down and pump a volley into me.'

Terrorised and bewildered by this American killing machine, the remainder of the Germans surrendered to York, who marched them to the rear holding a pistol to the senior German officer's head.

For his spectacular heroism York was promoted to sergeant and received the Medal of Honor directly from General Pershing, the commander of all American forces in Europe.

Also on this day

1085: St Mark's Cathedral in Venice is consecrated * 1754: British novelist Henry Fielding dies in Lisbon * 1871: The Great Chicago Fire starts in Patrick O'Leary's cowshed, killing over 250 people and making 95,000 homeless

9 October

The man who wrote Don Quixote

1547 Today is the first trace we find of Miguel de Cervantes – the day of his baptism in the small town of Alcalá de Henares about 20 miles from Madrid. We do not know the day of his birth, but a good bet is 29 September, the feast day of San Miguel. We think we know the date he died (23 April 1616), although it is disputed. We do not know where he was buried. That, like the details of much of his life, has vanished in the haze of passing centuries.

No portrait of Cervantes exists, but we have one verbal description, written by Cervantes himself when he was in his mid-60s: 'of aquiline countenance, with dark brown hair, smooth clear brow, merry eyes and hooked but well-proportioned nose; his beard is silver though it was gold not 20 years ago; large moustache, small mouth with teeth neither big nor little, since he has only six of them and they are in bad condition and worse positioned, for they do not correspond to each other; the body between two extremes, neither tall nor short; a bright complexion, more pale than dark, somewhat heavy in the shoulder and not very light of foot'.

Cervantes led an unexpectedly exciting life for a man most of us know only as the author of the world's first novel, *Don Quixote*.

He was probably raised in Madrid, the son of an itinerant barber who doubled as an apothecary-surgeon. Before he took up writing he was a courageous soldier, at 24 fighting against the Turks at the great naval battle of Lepanto, where he received three gunshot wounds, the last of which crippled his left hand for life. Four years later he was captured by Barbary pirates, who held him as a slave in Algiers for five years, waiting for his family to produce 500 gold escudos for his ransom.

At 40 he was living in Seville where he was temporarily excommunicated for having stolen supplies from the cathedral, and he was later twice imprisoned for shady dealings at his job as ship's purveyor for the Spanish crown.

Cervantes almost certainly wrote *Don Quixote* for money. Part I was published when he was already 58, and Part II did not appear until nine years later, just two years before his death. Today, almost 400 years later, the world still considers *Don Quixote* the greatest novel ever written in Spanish, and the Spanish of course think it the greatest novel in any language.

Also on this day

1000: Scandinavian explorer Leif Erikson lands in North America * 1779: The first Luddite riots, against the introduction of machinery for spinning cotton, begin in Manchester * 1835: French composer Charles Camille Saint-Saëns is born in Paris

10 October

Charles the Hammer earns his name

732 Charles Martel – Charles the Hammer – earned his nickname today.

In the 8th century the most aggressive and successful military power in the world was militant Islam, intent on endless conquest for the glory of Allah. In 711 the Moors crossed from North Africa into Spain to begin an occupation of almost eight centuries. Twenty years later they were again on the march, this time into France.

Abd ar-Rahman, the Moorish governor of Spain, led his invading cavalry into Aquitaine in south-west France. There he easily defeated Aquitaine's Duke Eudes and headed towards Tours in search of the city's reputed vast wealth.

Desperate, Eudes fled to Paris to beg for support from his one-time enemy, Charles, the de facto ruler of the Franks. Charles welcomed him with caution and agreed to help only on the condition that Eudes swear fealty to him, something that the distraught duke was only too happy to do.

Assembling an army perhaps 30,000 strong, Charles and Eudes headed for Tours. Somewhere between Tours and Poitiers they met the forces of Abd ar-Rahman, numbering about 80,000 mounted men.

For seven long days the two armies nervously watched each other. The Moors trotted on their horses, magnificent with lances and scimitars but without body armour, depending on the will of Allah and their own ferocious courage to defeat their enemy. The Franks were primarily on foot but lightly armoured and equipped with axes, swords and javelins.

At last Abd ar-Rahman gave the order to charge, and several thousand horsemen swept down on the waiting Franks. But Charles had formed his men into impenetrable squares that, in charge after charge, the Muslim cavalry could not break. The Moors knew no other battle tactic than the wild cavalry charge, and their casualties began to mount under the rain of javelins and thrown axes.

Suddenly a cry went up among the Moors. Their treasure – all they had plundered since leaving Spain – was under attack. They would lose it all. Several squadrons of cavalry turned to protect their goods. They soon discovered that the cry was false, but by then it was too late. The Franks had cut down Abd ar-Rahman, and other Muslim troops were turning from the field. The battle was effectively over.

The remaining Moorish horsemen fled back towards Spain, and the Muslim threat to western Europe was over until Suleiman the Magnificent marched into Austria in the 16th century.

Ever after this battle Charles was known as Charles Martel for his hammering defence that broke the Moorish onslaught. Two years later Eudes died, allowing Charles to march into Bordeaux to take direct control. By 739 he had also taken possession of Burgundy, substantially enlarging his Frankish domain. Charles died in 741 at the age of 53, leaving behind a virtual kingdom that was to be enlarged into an empire 50 years later by his grandson, Charlemagne.

Also on this day

1469: Italian painter Fra Filippo Lippi dies in Spoleto, possibly poisoned by the parents of a girl he had seduced * 1684: French painter Jean-Antoine Watteau is born in Valenciennes * 1813: Italian opera composer Giuseppe Verdi is born in Le Roncole * 1911: China's Imperial Dynasty abdicates, and Sun Yat-Sen proclaims a republic

11 October

A militant Protestant falls in battle

1531 When one thinks of militant Christians, the first name that comes to mind may be John Calvin, that unforgiving founder of Puritanism, or perhaps even more readily that of Ignatius Loyola, a former soldier who structured his Jesuit order on military lines. But perhaps the most militant of all was Huldrych Zwingli, a 16th-century military chaplain and Church reformer who largely established the basis for Protestantism in Switzerland.

Born in St Gall, Zwingli became a priest at the age of twenty, and before he was 30 was acting as chaplain to a group of Swiss mercenary soldiers. He fought on the losing side at the Battle of Marignano when the Swiss were hired to defend Milan against the troops of France's François I.

In between wars Zwingli fought for 'protestantisation' of the Catholic Church. He had images removed from churches and destroyed organs. Among his most important teachings were that Christ alone, not the Pope, was at the head of the Church, that there is no biblical foundation for the idea of purgatory, and that dead saints cannot intercede for the living. He also strongly disputed the idea of transubstantiation and made an enemy of Martin Luther by his stand. When he was 36 Zwingli's preaching helped incite revolts against religious fasting and priestly celibacy, and two years later in 1524 he set the style for clerical marriage by contracting his own.

In 1531, when he was 47, Zwingli once more marched out as chaplain with his Swiss soldiers, this time defending the Protestant community of Zurich from five Catholic Swiss cantons that wanted to stop the spread of Protestantism, if necessary by force of arms. On the border between the cantons of Zurich and Zug, at the monastery of Kappel, the two armies clashed, and Zwingli was seriously wounded during the mêlée. On the point of death, he professed his faith with the stoic remark, 'What does it matter? They can kill the body but they cannot kill the soul.' A few minutes later he was dead. Today an engraved boulder sits on the spot where he was cut down.

Also on this day

1689: Russian Tsar Peter the Great takes personal control of the government, to which he will dictate for the next 35 years * 1899: The Boer War begins

12 October

Edith Cavell before the firing squad

1915 At 7.00 this morning, in the city of Brussels, an English nurse was marched before a German firing squad. Before stepping to the execution post she pinned her skirt tightly around her legs to prevent it from flaring up on the impact of the bullets. Moments later four shots were fired, and she died instantly.

When the German army entered Brussels in August 1914, Edith Cavell, 49 years old, was working as a matron at a Red Cross hospital. The Germans offered her and other nurses safe conduct to Holland, but she chose instead to remain tending the Allied soldiers wounded in the opening days of the First World War. She was arrested in August 1915 and taken before a German military court, where she admitted the charges brought against her: that she had helped some 200 British and French POWs and Belgian civilians to escape to neutral Holland.

The night before her execution, she told a British chaplain that 'Patriotism is not enough. I must have no hatred or bitterness towards anyone.' Her words became famous, but public reaction in Great Britain and the United States was not so Christian in attitude. A celebrated war poster soon appeared showing a nurse's corpse on the ground and standing above it a German officer wearing a spiked helmet, a smoking pistol in his hand. The poster's legend was 'Gott Mit Uns' (God with us).

At war's end her body was brought home to England. In May 1919 her memorial service at Westminster Cathedral was thronged, the streets around lined with mourners. A statue was erected just north of Trafalgar Square.

There was also a memorial to Cavell in Paris, but on 23 July 1940, after an early morning's tour of the vanquished capital, Adolf Hitler, with a veteran's bitter memories of the last war, ordered the monument torn down, along with other offensive reminders of French victory.

Also on this day

1492: Columbus sights his first land in discovering the New World, calling it San Salvador * 1809: American explorer Meriwether Lewis, of the Lewis and Clark expedition, commits suicide * 1822: Brazil gains independence from Portugal * 1870: Confederate general Robert E. Lee dies in Lexington, Virginia

13 October

Emperor Claudius is poisoned by his wife

AD 54 The Roman Emperor Claudius was murdered today by his wife Agrippina. Some men never learn.

Claudius had become Emperor almost by accident when he was 40. His nephew, the schizophrenic Caligula, had been assassinated by his own officers, and a member of the guard had found Claudius cowering behind a curtain in the imperial palace. Taken by force to the army barracks, he was proclaimed Emperor, a decision the Roman Senate was in no position to dispute.

Tall and white haired, Claudius was considered little more than a clumsy clown by his family. He stammered, dribbled and occasionally suffered fits of uncontrollable laughter. (Modern science suggests that he had cerebral palsy.) He spent his early years writing history under the tutelage of the great Roman historian Livy. And he married.

Claudius divorced his first wife Plautia Urgulanilla on the grounds of scandalous behaviour and suspicion of murder. He divorced his second wife for what the historian Suetonius calls 'minor offences'. Then he married wife number three, the infamous Messalina, whose adulteries ranged from minor actors to prominent senators. Worse, to destroy her enemies and rivals, she persuaded her husband that they were plotting against him. Between her enemies and Claudius's own, some 35 senators, over 300 knights and Claudius's own niece were put to death. Another victim was Appius Silanus, who had recently married Messalina's mother but unwisely rejected the advances of his lascivious new stepdaughter. Finally, however, Messalina went too far; although already wed to the Emperor, she openly married one of her lovers. Claudius had both of them killed. Messalina was still only 26.

But hope sprang eternal within Claudius's breast. Within a year of disposing of Messalina, he married for the fourth time. His new wife was his niece Agrippina, who had been accused of poisoning her husband only a few months before. She persuaded the Emperor to give her son (the future Emperor Nero) preference over his own son Britannicus, but she soon became apprehensive, on hearing Claudius's claim that it was 'his destiny to suffer and finally to punish the infamy of his wives'.

Claudius unwisely kept an official poisoner named Locusta on the palace payroll. On the evening of 12 October, Agrippina bribed Locusta to spice some fresh mushrooms with a delicate poison and then enlisted the aid of Halotus, the official taster, to offer them up to the Emperor. When Claudius was seized with diarrhoea but showed no signs of dying, Agrippina brought on Xenophon, the court doctor. Most sources agree that Xenophon administered the fatal dose, but there are different versions of his method. One historian says that, on the pretence of making Claudius vomit, he put a feather that he had poisoned down the Emperor's throat. Another version says the good doctor added poison to an enema.

In the small hours of the following morning Claudius died in agony at the age of 63, after fourteen years as the most powerful man in the world.

Agrippina succeeded in her aim of securing the throne for her son Nero, who deified the dead Claudius, whimsically claiming that mushrooms must be the food of the gods, since Claudius had become a god by eating them. A year later Agrippina struck again, this time poisoning Claudius's son Britannicus, leaving Nero without a rival. Four years after that, Nero rewarded his loving mother by having her put to death.

Also on this day

1775: The United States Navy is founded * 1792: President George Washington lays the cornerstone of the White House * 1815: King and Marshal Joachim Murat is executed trying to regain his Kingdom of Naples

14 October

Rommel the Desert Fox is forced to commit suicide

1944 In the old photographs we see him in a weathered leather field coat, sporting goggles on the brim of his battered officer's cap. Nazi Germany's most coveted medal, the Iron Cross, hangs from a ribbon around his neck. He is Field Marshal Erwin Rommel, who today was forced to take his own life.

Rommel was born in 1891, son of a schoolmaster. He chose a military career, and at the age of twenty, fresh out of Cadet School, he joined an infantry regiment. After war broke out in 1914 his regiment fought in France, Romania and Italy. He won his first Iron Cross in September 1914 when he was wounded in France, and another in 1915, but his highest medal of the war was for action in Italy, where he won the Pour le Mérite, then the highest award for gallantry in action given by the Imperial German Army.

After the First World War Rommel remained in the military, just another infantry officer in a defeated army. It was only in 1933 with the rise of Adolf Hitler that his star began to rise. In 1937 he published *Infanterie greift an* (*The Infantry Attacks*), a military textbook based on his combat experiences, and came to be considered a superior military thinker. Hitler was impressed and made him commander of his bodyguard.

At the outbreak of the Second World War Rommel, by this time a major general, was commander of Hitler's field headquarters during the invasion of Poland. From this special vantage point in the fast-moving campaign, where he accompanied Hitler both in the field and at conferences, he grasped the potential that tanks offered to the determined attacker. Even though his experience was in infantry, he now asked for an armoured division, and, with Hitler's intervention smoothing the way, received command of the 7th Panzer Division in time for the invasion of the Low Countries and France.

Once France had been subdued, Rommel was sent to North Africa as commander of the Afrika Korps. There he gained fame for his brilliant tank attacks across wide expanses of open desert, earning the nickname used by both Germans and the Allies, the Desert Fox.

Rommel used speed and surprise to outwit the British, driving them 600 miles back into Libya. He was also a master of deception, once having brooms and rags tied to the back of his tanks to raise clouds of desert dust, making the enemy believe he had superior numbers. In June 1942 he reached his greatest success with the capture of Tobruk.

In October of 1942, however, superior British numbers and firepower – plus the careful planning of the British Field Marshal Montgomery – defeated the German force at El Alamein. On learning of the Afrika Korps' imminent defeat, Hitler ordered its commander to hold to the last man, but, knowing the cause was hopeless, Rommel ignored the order. The British captured 230,000 Germans and Italians.

Returning to Germany, Rommel was still a national hero. His next assignment was to defend Normandy against Allied invasion. He wanted a mobile defence with 1,500 tanks positioned behind the beaches, but he was overruled in this disposition, and the result was just what he feared: the landings weren't met with sufficient German strength to stop the attackers on the shore and drive them back into the sea.

On 4 June 1944 he left on leave to celebrate his wife Lucie's 50th birthday. Two days later the Allies landed in Normandy. Hurrying back to the front, he was wounded when an RAF fighter strafed his staff car. The injured field marshal was sent home to convalesce.

The following month Colonel Claus von Stauffenberg led a group of senior army officers in an attempt to assassinate Hitler, but the bomb he placed in Hitler's headquarters succeeded only in wounding the dictator. Hitler's vengeance was swift, terrible and all-encompassing.

The Gestapo suspected that Rommel might have been involved in the plot, but although he had been approached, he had refused to participate. But any connection to the bungled assassination was enough for Hitler, who ordered Rommel's death.

The only obstacle to a quick trial and execution was Rommel's stature as one of Germany's most heroic field marshals. Therefore two army generals were dispatched to call on him at his home, there to offer him a grim choice: either to commit suicide or to be disgraced in a public trial and executed, leaving his family at the mercy of the Gestapo.

On this day the generals arrived at his home in Herrlingen, near Ulm. To save his wife and son Rommel left with the generals and took poison in the staff car. The public was told he had died of war wounds, and the government arranged a solemn state funeral, which Hitler refused to attend. Goebbels, Göring and other top Nazi leaders, all of whom knew that Rommel had in effect been executed, sent odious notes of condolence to his widow. Hitler's, dated 16 October 1944, read: 'Accept my sincerest sympathy for the heavy loss you have suffered with the death of your husband. The name of Field Marshal Rommel will be forever linked with the heroic battles in North Africa.'

Also on this day

1066: William the Conqueror defeats Harold at Hastings * 1806:

Napoleon defeats the Prussians at the Battle of Jena * 1890: American President Dwight D. Eisenhower is born * 1947: American pilot Chuck Yeager becomes the first man to break the sound barrier

15 October

Scipio overwhelms Hannibal at Zama

202 BC Today was fought one of history's pivotal battles, when two of antiquity's greatest generals faced each other at Zama to determine hegemony of the Mediterranean world.

After the calamitous annihilation of the Romans at the Battle of Cannae in 216 BC, it looked as if the formidable Carthaginian general Hannibal would force Rome to sue for terms, restoring Carthage to the pre-eminence lost in the First Punic War 39 years before. But the obdurate Romans simply refused to be defeated. As Livy wrote two centuries later, 'No other nation could have suffered such a tremendous disaster and not been destroyed.'

This was Hannibal's problem. In spite of his victories, he could not force his enemies to submit. He continued to roam Italy for another thirteen years, once coming within three miles of Rome, but with no siege machinery, he could not attack the great city.

Then Hannibal's problems got worse. A young Roman patrician named Publius Cornelius Scipio had escaped the slaughter at Cannae. Now he had become a general, and, in a series of brilliant tactical engagements, he reconquered virtually all of Carthage's vast territories in Spain. Then, in 204 BC, he embarked for North Africa with an army of 35,000 to strike at Carthage itself.

Scipio brilliantly defeated the Carthaginian forces at Bagbrades, reportedly killing 40,000 men, while destroying enemy towns and cutting off Carthage's food supply. As Scipio knew it must, the Carthaginian government ordered Hannibal to return from Italy to protect the home front.

Two years later these two illustrious generals met on this day at

Zama (five miles south of today's Tunis) to determine the fate of the Western world.

Hannibal's army of 45,000 infantry and 80 elephants looked stronger than Scipio's force of only 34,000. But the Carthaginian troops were largely raw and untrained, and Roman and allied Numidian cavalry came to 9,000 horse, three times the mounted strength Hannibal could put in the field.

In the early stages of the battle the Romans managed to panic the Carthaginian elephants with the deafening blare of trumpets and horns. Then the Roman horse put the Carthaginian cavalry to flight, apparently leaving the battle to be settled by the lines of infantry. At first it appeared that the larger Carthaginian force would prevail, but while the Roman soldiers held, their cavalry came charging back into the conflict, taking the enemy from the rear. Some 20,000 Carthaginians died on the field. The defeat of Carthage opened the way for complete Roman domination of southern Europe and North Africa for over half a millennium.

A magnanimous victor, Scipio permitted Hannibal to remain in Carthage, where he was elected the country's ruler. When the two generals met shortly afterwards, Scipio, perhaps fishing for compliments, asked Hannibal who he thought were the three greatest generals in history. The Carthaginian named Alexander the Great, Pyrrhus and himself. 'And what if you rather than I had won the Battle of Zama?' asked the Roman. 'Then I would be the greatest of all', answered the confident Hannibal.

In gratitude, the Roman Senate awarded Scipio the title of Africanus. In 25 years of warfare this remarkable commander never lost a battle.

Hannibal was not so fortunate. A few years after Zama the Roman Senate decided it wanted revenge, forcing him to flee for a secret life in exile. Finally, when he reached the age of 64, his enemies found him in Bythnia. As Roman soldiers surrounded his house to capture him for return to Rome and execution, the great general escaped their clutches in the only way possible, by taking poison. 'Let us relieve the Romans of their continual dread and care,' he said, 'who think it long and tedious to wait for the death of a hated old man.'

Also on this day

70 BC: Roman poet Virgil is born * 1764: Edward Gibbon, in Rome, first gets the idea of writing his monumental history of the Roman Empire * 1839: Queen Victoria proposes marriage to Prince Albert * 1917: Mata Hari is executed by the French after being convicted of passing military secrets to the Germans

16 October

Marie Antoinette's last ride

1793 Marie Antoinette, raised in the court of her mother Empress Maria Theresa of Austria and now Queen of France, rose early this morning and dressed in a white piqué gown, a white bonnet, a muslin shawl and plum-coloured high-heeled shoes. Then she drank a cup of morning chocolate.

Shortly after eleven she found herself en route for what today is called the place de la Concorde. Her arms were tied as she sat in the tumbrel. She was headed for her own execution.

Marie Antoinette's husband, fat Louis XVI, had already faced the guillotine with dignity nine months before. Her children had been taken from her and she was imprisoned first in the Temple, then in the Conciergerie in an eleven-foot-square cell. The cell was damp and dark, and it contained three beds, one for the Queen, another for her female attendant and a third for the two gendarmes who never left, even when the women had to satisfy the needs of nature. As Marie Antoinette said to her daughter the last time she saw her, 'God Himself has forsaken me – I no longer dare to pray.'

Now the tumbrel clanked through the Parisian streets, crowds jeering from every side. When it pulled up at the scaffold, the Queen was trembling so badly that she had to be helped from the cart. At the top of the steps she tripped and stepped on the executioner's foot. 'Monsieur', she apologised. 'Excuse me, I didn't do it on purpose.' She never spoke again, and a few minutes later the blade swept down, neatly severing her head from her body. She was still only 37.

17 October

The start of the Spanish Inquisition

1483 On this day Pope Sixtus IV established the most brutal, feared and loathsome institution in European history prior to the creation of the Third Reich – the Spanish Inquisition.

Sixtus was a classic Renaissance pope. A scion of the ducal house of Urbino, he meddled incessantly but ineffectively in politics, was notorious for his nepotism and contributed significantly to the culture of his and our times. It was Sixtus who built the Sistine Chapel with its delicate frescoes by Botticelli, Perugino, Pintoricchio and Ghirlandajo. (Michelangelo's great work was commissioned in a later pontificate, under Sixtus's nephew, Julius II.) Unfortunately, his solutions for the spiritual ills of the time were as disastrous as his culture was refined.

At this time Spain was the only European country with a substantial population of *conversos*, Jews and Muslims who had converted to Christianity. Spain's Catholic Monarchs King Ferdinand and Queen Isabella feared that many *conversos* were really only feigning their belief in Christ while secretly following their old faith. To help root out these dangerous heretics, on this day Pope Sixtus issued a Bull establishing the Consejo de la Suprema y General Inquisición or Supreme Council of the Inquisition in Spain, appointing a 63-year-old Dominican monk named Tomás de Torquemada as the first Grand Inquisitor.

Torquemada had been a prior in a monastery in Segovia for 22 years when he took up his new post, but he already had the confidence of Ferdinand and Isabella. He had known the Queen since her childhood and was the confessor and sometimes advisor to both.

Torquemada served as Grand Inquisitor for fifteen terrifying years, during which time he encouraged the use of torture to extract confessions, including such Spanish delicacies as the *toca*, in which water is forced down your throat, the *garrucha*, in which your hands are tied behind your back and you are then lifted by the wrists and let fall to dislocate your joints, and the *potro*, a form of the rack.

Torquemada was also active in widening the scope of crime for which the unhappy victims could be accused. Although the Inquisition was established to combat heresy, only a year after taking office he extended its range to include sodomy, blasphemy, usury and sorcery.

Torquemada did not introduce Spain to the *auto da fé* – a technique of persuasion first employed in Granada in February 1481 – but he brought it to new heights of glory, ordering about 2,000 souls to be burnt at the stake during his tenure.

Pope Sixtus was shaken when he learned of the Inquisition's excesses and issued a Bull deploring the rigged trials, torture and horrors of the *auto da fé*, but it had no effect on the fanatical monk, who continued diligently at his task. Finally, on 16 September 1498, Torquemada died in the Monasterio de Santo Tomás in Avila at the age of 78. But the Spanish Inquisition lived on, finally suppressed only on 15 July 1834 after 351 years.

Also on this day

1651: England's Charles II flees to France * 1777: The British under General John Burgoyne surrender to American forces at the Battle of Saratoga, causing France to recognise the new nation and openly give military aid * 1849: Polish-French composer Frédéric François Chopin dies of consumption at 12 Place Vendôme in Paris

18 October

Napoleon retreats from Russia

1812 Today the 90,000 men remaining from Napoleon's Grande Armée trooped out of Moscow to begin the most famous retreat in military history.

Thirty-five days before, Napoleon and his army had at last reached the Russian capital after twelve long weeks of plodding across 500 miles of empty and desolate Russian countryside, laid waste by Russian peasants before they abandoned it.

Yet Moscow, too, was ominously quiet and empty. Indeed, only 15,000 of its quarter of a million inhabitants remained, mostly foreigners, vagabonds and criminals. The rest had deserted the city on orders from its governor.

Then came the fires, deliberately set by the Russians, which razed four-fifths of Moscow. No word came from the Tsar, no surrender, no discussion of terms. Each day food became scarcer; each day there was less left to burn to fight the murderous cold.

Recognising that his plight was desperate, Napoleon appealed to Alexander I for a truce, but the Tsar refused even to answer the Emperor's letter. Later he wrote to an ally, 'We would rather be buried beneath the ruins of the empire than make terms with the modern Attila.'

Finally Napoleon understood that his only hope was withdrawal, and he gave the order to abandon the city.

Now the army tramped 500 miles in retreat, numbed with fatigue, frozen by the terrible Russian winter, with regular frosts of −25° centigrade. As described by future American President John Quincy Adams, who was in Moscow at the time as his country's ambassador, 'The invader himself was a wretched fugitive and his numberless host was perishing by frosts, famine, and the sword.'

Badgered by guerrillas and marauding Cossacks, tracked by the main Russian armies, Napoleon's men and horses fell and died, left equally for the howling wolves. For seven weeks the army struggled on, at last reaching sanctuary in Vilna (now Vilnius in

Lithuania). By then perhaps 20,000 were left, and Napoleon could only repeat his now famous observation, 'Du sublime au ridicule il n'y a qu'un pas.' (From the sublime to the ridiculous is only a step.) The days of the Empire were numbered.

Also on this day

1520: Portuguese explorer Ferdinand Magellan finds a strait to the Pacific – now the Straits of Magellan * 1663: Eugene of Savoy is born in Paris * 1685: Louis XIV revokes the Edict of Nantes, effectively banning Protestantism in France * 1697: Italian topographical painter Canaletto (Giovanni Antonio Canal) is born in Venice * 1859: French Nobel-Prize-winning philosopher Henri Bergson is born * 1865: British Prime Minister Henry Temple, Lord Palmerston dies * 1931: American inventor Thomas Edison dies

19 October

The American Revolution ends with a victory at Yorktown

1781 With no way out by land or sea, and no prospect of timely relief, General Cornwallis today surrendered his 8,000 British troops to General Washington and an allied army at Yorktown, Virginia, bringing to an end major military operations in the War of the American Revolution. The victory was the result of a combined American–French land–sea campaign that remains a model of timing and co-operation.

Throughout six years of war in America, the British had always enjoyed the considerable advantage of command of the sea. But suddenly – and only briefly – a window of naval opportunity opened for the rebels. With his army around New York City, Washington received word in August that Admiral de Grasse and his French fleet in the West Indies were sailing north for Chesapeake Bay, where he could be available for operations until mid-October. The presence of a French fleet in such a position would cut communications between the British armies in Virginia and New York, leaving the southern army especially vulnerable to blockade and attack.

Washington set his army moving southward from New York in forced marches, accompanied by a French army under the command of General Rochambeau. Arriving in Virginia in mid-September, the joint force was joined by another American army under General Lafayette. The French fleet, with 3,000 more troops and siege artillery, had already arrived off Chesapeake Bay and driven off a British fleet. On 28 September, with 17,000 allied troops on hand, half of whom were French, Washington began siege operations at Yorktown. Cornwallis soon recognised his position as hopeless and on 17 October requested a truce.

And so, the Americans, with crucial help from their French allies, beat the mightiest military power in the world. It seemed an amazing turn of events, at least as amazing as the examples offered in the old tune to which (legend has it) the British soldiers marched out from Yorktown this morning to lay down their arms:

If ponies rode men, and if grass ate the cows,
And cats should be chased into holes by the mouse ...
If summer were spring, and the other way 'round,
Then all the world would be upside down.

Also on this day

1216: King John of England dies of dysentery at the Abbey of Swineshead * 1469: Ferdinand of Aragon marries Isabella of Castile * 1745: Irish satirical writer Jonathan Swift dies in Dublin * 1872: The Holtermann nugget, weighing 630 pounds, is mined at Hill End, Australia, the largest gold-bearing nugget ever found

20 October

The Long March that changed Chinese history

1935 Today some 8,000 bedraggled survivors of Mao Tse-tung's Communist army reached safe haven in Communist-controlled

Shensi Province in north-western China after one year and four days of retreat from the repeated attacks of Chiang Kai-shek's Kuomintang troops. The Long March was over, and over 90 per cent of the Communist army had perished, but Mao had survived, achieving in the process de facto leadership of China's Communist Party.

The previous October Mao, his pregnant wife and 100,000 soldiers of the Red Army had abandoned their capital of Juichin in Kiangsi province to start a trek of over 6,000 miles from one side of China to the other. During the next twelve months they covered some of the world's most inhospitable terrain while constantly pursued by Chiang Kai-shek's forces. It was the longest – and fastest – infantry march made under combat conditions by any army in history.

Since the Red Army had no motorised transport, the Long March was indeed a march, every man afoot except Mao himself, who was so ill from malaria that he rode the army's solitary horse. When the terrain was too difficult for him to stay in the saddle, four soldiers would carry him in a wooden litter.

Every soldier had to march with his own supplies. According to Mao's chief artillery engineer, 'Each man carried five pounds of ration rice and each had a shoulder pole from which hung either two small boxes of ammunition or hand grenades, or big kerosene cans filled with our most essential machinery and tools. Each pack contained a blanket or quilt, one quilted winter uniform, and three pairs of strong cloth shoes with thick rope soles tipped and heeled with metal.'

The army had little ammunition, less food and virtually no medical supplies. Sometimes forced to go several days without eating, many fell by the wayside due to weakness while even more died of disease.

Almost insuperable obstacles barred the Red Army's progress. At Luting the soldiers had to haul themselves over a river on a chain suspension bridge from which all the wooden slats had been removed. Later they had to cross seven high mountain ranges crested with snow, and in the heat of August they tramped across the Grasslands of Chinghai, a high plateau that was boggy with rain and infested with swarms of malaria-carrying mosquitoes. The wet ground prevented the soldiers from making fires to cook the little food they carried, and many suffered from severe dysentery from eating raw rice and vegetables.

Although China's Communists were on the point of annihilation, the Long March not only provided a stirring example of revolutionary zeal and commitment, it also gave Mao time for the political situation to change. China had already been under attack from Japan, but Chiang Kai-shek had decided to cleanse the country of Communists as his first priority. The Long March showed that total victory against the Communists was unachievable, and by September 1937 the Kuomintang and the Communists had (temporarily) joined forces to fight the common enemy. Once the Japanese were defeated, however, the civil war was re-ignited almost immediately, and in 1949 Mao's armies took over the country, forcing Chiang to flee to Taiwan and amply demonstrating his famous maxim that 'political power grows out of the barrel of a gun'.

Also on this day

1632: English architect Christopher Wren is born * 1818: Britain and the United States agree on the 49th parallel as the boundary between Canada and the USA * 1854: French poet Arthur Rimbaud is born

21 October

Trafalgar

1805 Atop his column in London's Trafalgar Square stands one-armed Admiral Horatio Nelson, who won a battle and lost his life on this day in 1805 at the age of 47.

Nelson joined the navy at the age of twelve, so he had been serving for over twenty years before his years of greatness during the French Revolutionary and Napoleonic Wars. He lost an eye at Calvi helping to capture Corsica in 1797 and four years later his right arm at Tenerife. A year after that he destroyed Napoleon's fleet at the Battle of the Nile.

On this day Nelson, with only 27 ships, completely outmanoeuvred a French/Spanish fleet of 33 warships at Cape Trafalgar on the south coast of Spain. It was before this battle that he issued his famous signal, 'England expects that every man will do his duty.'

Nelson certainly did his. Ordering what amounted to a frontal assault on the French line, Nelson in his flagship *Victory* led one column of ships directly at and through the French fleet, raking the enemy's flagship with crippling cannon shot.

Even when *Victory* became entangled with a French warship, Nelson remained fully exposed to enemy fire, walking resolutely on the quarterdeck with his captain Thomas Hardy. At 1.15 in the afternoon a sniper's bullet fired from the rigging of the enemy ship caught Nelson in the shoulder, passed through his lungs and shattered his spine.

In indescribable pain, Nelson was carried below, to survive for another three hours. Knowing he was about to die, he beseeched Hardy 'to take care of my poor Lady Hamilton' (Nelson's mistress). At the end he murmured, 'Kiss me, Hardy.' The captain knelt and kissed his cheek, and the great admiral expired, according to legend dying with the famous words, 'Now I am satisfied. Thank God I have done my duty.'

The Battle of Trafalgar was one of the truly decisive naval encounters in history. The French lost 19 ships and 14,000 men killed or captured, including their admiral. British losses were only 1,500, and not a ship was lost. Napoleon's last hope of invading England had been denied for ever.

Nelson's body was brought back to England to receive an imposing funeral in St Paul's Cathedral. There he was buried in a coffin that he himself had ordered, made from timber taken from the French warship *Orient* that he had destroyed at the Battle of the Nile.

Also on this day

1680: Louis XIV signs a decree establishing the Comédie Française * 1760: Japanese printmaker Katsushika Hokusai is born * 1772:

English poet Samuel Taylor Coleridge is born * 1918: The Great Influenza Epidemic, which will kill 30 million people, begins * 1940: Ernest Hemingway's novel *For Whom the Bell Tolls* is published

22 October

The mad Emperor Commodus takes power in Rome

AD 180 Still only eighteen years old, in March Commodus had been campaigning on the Danube with his father the Emperor Marcus Aurelius when Marcus was carried off by plague. After arranging for burial and deification, young Commodus, now the most powerful man in the world, slowly travelled with his army the 700 miles to Rome, there to put his own malign imprint on history. Today in a spectacular triumphal procession he and his troops entered the Eternal City to take control of the government. He would rule supreme for the next twelve years.

Before Commodus's succession to power, Rome had enjoyed 83 uninterrupted years of peace and prosperity under five benevolent emperors, Trajan, Hadrian, Antoninus Pius, Lucius Verus and Marcus Aurelius. Initially Commodus, too, ruled generously and well, but the omens were unfavourable: born on 31 August, he shared a birthday with his psychotic predecessor Caligula.

Within five years Commodus began to show signs of the brutal insanity that would consume him. He assumed a lifestyle of enormous depravity and expense, organising orgies with his harem of 300 women and 300 boys and revelling in luxuries. Soon he was running short of money, a problem he resolved by executing rich senators on trumped up charges of treason, and seizing their property.

In 186 he executed one chief minister in order to placate the army, and three years later allowed the Roman mob to lynch another one. Meanwhile the unfettered power he enjoyed only fed his megalomania. He changed the name of Rome to Colonia

Commodiana (Colony of Commodus) and he renamed the months after the many names that he had given himself. Starting from January, they were now to be known as Lucius, Aelius, Aurelius, Commodus, Augustus, Herculeus, Romanus, Exsuperatorius, Amazonius, Invictus, Felix and Pius. He ordered that henceforth every Roman citizen should carry the name Commodianus.

Even more bizarre, Commodus began to imagine that he was Hercules. Dressed in a lion skin and bearing a club, he now entered gladiatorial contests against both men and beasts. According to the historian Herodian, 'He defeated his opponents with ease, and he did no more than wound them, since they all submitted to him, but only because they knew he was the emperor, not because he was truly a gladiator.' The animals he faced fared less well. Another historian, Dio Cassius, reports that he once killed five hippopotami in a single combat and also cut down various elephants, rhinoceroses, leopards, lions and deer, 'always killing them with a single blow ... he cleanly shot the heads off countless ostriches with crescent-headed arrows. The crowd cheered as these headless birds continued to run around the amphitheatre.'

Convinced that he was Rome's greatest gladiator, Commodus forced the gladiatorial fund to pay him 1 million sesterces every time he appeared in the arena. He also brooked no competition, once executing another gladiator merely for having skilfully killed a lion with a javelin.

This playing at gladiator scandalised the Roman people and appalled the Senate, as the arena featured condemned criminals and other dregs of society. The authority of the Emperor was draining away, while both senators and members of the imperial household lived in fear for their lives.

Inevitably, a plot against the Emperor developed. His chamberlain, his Praetorian Prefect and his favourite concubine Marcia swore to bring him down.

On the last day of AD 192 Marcia surreptitiously slipped poison in his wine, but Commodus's delicate stomach rejected the toxin. The conspirators then called in a professional wrestler named Narcissus, who strangled him in his bath.

Joyful at this unexpected end to Commodus's tyranny, the

Senate expunged his name from all state documents and ordered his statues destroyed.

Also on this day

1746: Princeton University receives its charter * 1797: French aeronaut Jacques Garnerin makes the first parachute jump, jumping from a hot air balloon and landing in the Parc Monceau in Paris * 1811: Hungarian composer and pianist Franz Liszt is born * 1906: French painter Paul Cézanne dies in Aix-en-Provence

23 October

America's first combat in the First World War

1917 At 6.05 in the morning on this day C Battery of the 6th Field Artillery fired a round from its French 75mm gun towards the German trenches a few hundred yards to the front. America had truly entered the Great War at last.

Ever since 1914 the Allied powers had attempted to persuade the United States to join in the conflict against Germany, and finally, on 6 April 1917, President Woodrow Wilson had declared war. But now American troops were for the first time actually engaging the enemy.

By the time the Germans collapsed seven months later the United States had increased the strength of the American Expeditionary Force to just under 2 million men, an incredible feat of planning and logistics. Commanding US forces in Europe was General John 'Black Jack' Pershing, aged 57 when he took command but still tough and energetic, as he proved on arriving in Paris when he took a 23-year-old French mistress.

Pershing was originally dubbed 'Black Jack' by fellow officers in a derisory reference to his command of a black cavalry unit, but later it came to represent his dark, hawk-like looks and stern discipline. He had climbed the ranks of the military in part through unimpeachable connections. He had become a great friend of Teddy Roosevelt when Roosevelt was Police Commissioner of

New York, and his father-in-law was the head of the Senate Military Affairs Committee. No doubt there was also tremendous sympathy for him because his wife and three daughters had all perished in a fire in San Francisco a few years before the war. Nonetheless he was a fine soldier, as he had demonstrated in searching out and almost killing the Mexican revolutionary and bandit Pancho Villa.

Pershing deserved and received much of the credit for the great fighting success of the American forces in Europe. In all they fought in thirteen battles and turned the tide of the war from stalemate to victory. Although light compared with the European nations that had fought since 1914, American casualties were still significant. In all over 116,000 were killed in action while another 200,000 were wounded.

Also on this day

42 BC: At the Second Battle of Philippi, Octavian and Mark Antony defeat Brutus and Cassius * 1642: Charles I defeats the forces of the English Parliament at Edgehill, the first battle of the English Civil War * 1707: The First Parliament of Great Britain

24 October

The end of the Thirty Years' War

1648 At last the Treaty of Westphalia was signed, and the Thirty Years' War – the most destructive in European history until 1914 – staggered to a close.

The Thirty Years' War was really a series of wars, fought chiefly over religious differences between Catholic and Protestant, but eventually broadened by grasping kings who saw in the chaos of war an opportunity to seize someone else's territory.

The war's prime instigator was Jesuit-educated Ferdinand II of Austria. Recognised as King of Bohemia by the Bohemian Diet, he started forcibly converting his predominantly Protestant population to Catholicism. By all accounts, he was a kind and gentle man, a roly-poly monarch who dressed as a Spanish courtier, but when it came to religion, his devotion to Romish absolutism was too much for his new subjects, who, led by the nobles, rose in open revolt and deposed him.

Following five years of armed conflict Ferdinand finally regained his royal authority, but by this time the war had spread, involving Poland, Russia, Denmark, Sweden, the Netherlands and dozens of the semi-autonomous German principalities over which Ferdinand had gained theoretical overlordship on becoming Holy Roman Emperor in 1619. In addition to the religious battle, the Thirty Years' War was exacerbated by the underlying struggle between the Habsburg Holy Roman Empire and France led by Cardinal Richelieu.

Most of the combat took place on German soil, and some 350,000 were slain on the field of battle, as the contending powers relied increasingly on mercenaries to do the fighting. Caring nothing for the civilians in their path, armies on all sides destroyed whole villages and ravaged the countryside as they went, burning, looting and sweeping it clean of farmers and food. Some 8 million people are thought to have perished.

The winners, if there were any, were France, now Europe's strongest power, the Netherlands, which had gained independence from Spain, and Sweden, which now dominated the Baltic. The biggest loser would have been the man who started it all, Ferdinand II, except that he had died eleven years before the end. But his cherished idea of a dominant Holy Roman Empire with an emperor at its head and the Pope at its heart was as dead as the hordes of people cut down by sword, famine and pestilence during the war.

Also on this day

1273: The first Habsburg emperor Rudolf von Habsburg is crowned at Aachen * 1537: English Queen Jane Seymour dies twelve days after the birth of the future Edward VI * 1725: Italian composer Alessandro Scarlatti dies in Naples * 1917: The Austrians rout the Italians at the Battle of Caporetto * 1929: Share values on the Wall Street stock market crash on 'Black Thursday', starting the Great Depression

25 October

Agincourt

1415 Shakespeare tells us that today was the feast day of Saint Crispin and Saint Crispian when an exhausted, bedraggled English army met a French force at least four times its size at Agincourt, a hamlet a little south-east of Boulogne amid the rolling countryside of Normandy. Here England's King Henry V achieved enduring fame in one of the great victories of medieval Europe.

Convinced that his Angevin inheritance entitled him to great swathes of France, Henry had resolved to invade in order to enforce his claims, knowing that France was in turmoil, ruled by mad King Charles VI. In early autumn of 1415 he led his army across the Channel.

In September he successfully captured Harfleur, but battle casualties and disease substantially reduced his strength to perhaps 6,000 men, and he turned to find shelter in English-held Calais. But before he could reach safety, a huge French force of 20,000 to 30,000 men caught up with him at Agincourt. Determined to redress the humiliating defeats at Crécy and Poitiers over half a century before, the French blocked the English line of retreat. There was no escape.

Henry positioned his slender force along a narrow, 1000-yard front, flanked by dense forest on both sides. At about eleven in the morning French men-at-arms advanced on the English line.

'Cry "God for Harry! England, and Saint George!"' called out the English King to inspire his men (or at least so says William Shakespeare).

And the line held, as English archers devastated the advancing enemy infantry. Then heavily armoured, dismounted French knights moved forward through the churned mud. Henry urged his men to one more effort:

Once more unto the breach, dear friends, once more:
Or close the wall up with our English dead!

So narrow was the field of battle that the French could not bring their superior numbers to bear. Soon the crush was so intense that the knights could scarcely raise their swords to strike. They became easy targets for English archers who, when not skewering the enemy with arrows, finished off fallen knights with axes and mallets.

In half an hour the battle was over, the French in full retreat. But now, fearing that he lacked the troop strength both to guard the prisoners taken in the battle and to withstand an expected renewal of the French attack, Henry ordered the killing of all prisoners. When his soldiers refused, he ordered his own guard of 200 to carry out the grisly massacre.

In all the French lost three dukes, 90 counts, over 1,500 knights and about 4,000 men-at-arms, plus an uncounted number of archers, servants and fighters of low station. France would remain at the mercy of the English until the miraculous appearance of Joan of Arc some fifteen years later.

Also on this day

1400: English poet Geoffrey Chaucer dies * 1825: Austrian composer Johann Strauss the Younger is born in Vienna * 1853: The Light Brigade charges during the Battle of Balaclava in the Crimean War * 1881: Spanish painter Pablo Picasso is born in Malaga

26 October

A date with a political orientation?

1759, 1879, 1916, 1947 Is it possible for a date to have a political orientation? It seems implausible, but consider this.

On this day in 1759 the great (and corrupt) French revolutionary Georges Jacques Danton was born in Arras in the Champagne country. A leader in overthrowing the monarchy, he voted for the execution of Louis XVI and later was head of the notorious Committee of Public Safety that rooted out anyone with even the smallest royalist (or indeed moderate) leaning. Towards the end of the Revolution he seemed to turn more conservative and paid for it with his head, disdainfully crying at his execution, 'Let me be led to death, I shall go to sleep in glory.'

Precisely 120 years later another dedicated revolutionary was born, this time in the Ukraine. His name was Lev Bronshtein, but he is better known to us as Leon Trotsky, a pseudonym he adopted from a forged passport when he escaped from a tsarist prison in Siberia when he was 23. Shortly afterwards he fled to London where he first encountered a certain Vladimir Ilich Ulyanov, who would adopt the pseudonym of Lenin.

When he returned to Russia, Trotsky became a leading member of Lenin's drive to overthrow the Tsar. Although he was in jail at the time, he was elected to membership of the Bolshevik Central Committee and later, after the Reds had seized power, became commissar of war. As number two man to Lenin, he was one of five charter members of the Politburo. Eventually, of course, Trotsky was undermined, toppled and exiled by yet another pseudonymous Russian, one Iosif Vissarionovich Dzhugashvili, who styled himself Joseph Stalin (derived from the Russian *stal*, steel). Like Danton before him, Trotsky was eventually consumed by the revolution that he had helped to create. On Stalin's orders an assassin buried the point of a pickaxe in his head while Trotsky was living in exile in Mexico in 1940.

While Trotsky was fomenting revolution in Russia, another wily left-winger was born. On this day in 1916 a stationmaster and his wife in Jarnac, France, celebrated the birth of a boy who would one day become his country's first Socialist president. His name was François Mitterrand.

As a socialist stalwart in the years before his presidential triumph, Mitterrand made much of his valour as a wartime member of the French Resistance. It emerged only shortly before he died that his time in the Maquis had been less than heroic and that he had previously laboured for the collaborationist Vichy government.

In Mitterrand's first foray into presidential politics he represented both the Socialists and Communists in opposing de Gaulle in 1965. By the time he had finally achieved office in 1981, his initial measures were to nationalise a large number of banks and key industries, most of which had to be reversed when the French economy stalled. He managed to avoid both execution and assassination, dying of cancer in 1996. But did Mitterand leave a birthday legacy? On the day that he became 31, when he had just become a cabinet minister in the Fourth Republic's coalition government, a girl named Hillary Rodham was born in Chicago.

Also on this day

1764: English caricaturist William Hogarth dies in London * 1860: Italian unification leader Giuseppe Garibaldi proclaims Victor Emmanuel King of Italy * 1881: The 'Gunfight at the OK Corral' takes place at Tombstone, Arizona * 1905: Norway and Sweden sign a treaty of separation, making Norway an independent state

27 October

A flaming cross inspires Emperor Constantine at Milvian Bridge

AD 312 Few battles are true turning points in history, but the one fought today at Milvian Bridge near Rome was one of them.

Early in the 4th century several rivals were jockeying (and fighting) for control of the Roman Empire. Two of the most powerful were Constantine, who held sway over Gaul, England and parts of Germany, and Maxentius, who was master of Italy, Spain and Africa. In 310 Constantine took over Spain and now was determined to seize the rest of Maxentius's territories. (The fact that the two were brothers-in-law apparently made no difference in their bloody rivalry.)

At noon on 26 October, the day before the battle, Constantine saw suspended in the sky a flaming cross brighter than the sun inscribed with the words *In hoc signo vinces*. (By this sign thou shalt conquer.) Understanding this as a message direct from God, he ordered a cross interwoven into the imperial standard and attached to the helmets and shields of his soldiers.

441

The following day the two contending emperors met at Milvian Bridge, where Constantine's inspired troops scored an overwhelming victory, and Maxentius was drowned in the Tiber when a bridge collapsed while he was fleeing the field. So convinced was Constantine that he had received divine aid that he immediately erected a triumphal arch in Rome which credits his success to the inspiration of God.

The first result of the Battle of Milvian Bridge was the eventual reunification of the Roman Empire under a single ruler (another regional Caesar, Licinius, still had to be overcome first, which he was in 324). But of far more lasting consequence was Constantine's confirmed commitment to Christianity. The year after the battle he and Licinius published the Edict of Milan that established toleration of Christianity throughout the Empire.

For the remainder of his reign Constantine actively and continually tried to Christianise his subjects. Numerous laws supported Christianity while (usually mildly) suppressing paganism. He abolished crucifixion as a punishment because of its symbolic significance and imposed the observance of religious worship on Sundays. He even went to war with a portable altar and commanded that his soldiers recite a special Christian prayer that he himself had written.

In 326 his mother Helena, long a committed Christian, travelled to Jerusalem where she discovered the Holy Sepulchre. Constantine ordered the construction of a great basilica on the spot.

It was largely through the efforts of Constantine that the Western world was converted to Christianity as early and as completely as it was. Oddly, the emperor himself waited until a few days before his death to be baptised into the Church.

Also on this day

1466: Dutch humanist Erasmus is born in Rotterdam * 1728: English explorer Captain James Cook is born * 1782: Italian composer and violin virtuoso Niccolò Paganini is born in Geneva * 1858: American President Theodore Roosevelt is born

28 October

Catherine de' Medici marries a future king

1533 Unmarked at the time, today was one of the most calamitous days in French history.

On this day the future Henri II, still a gangling fourteen, married a Tuscan orphan of the same age. Black-haired and bug-eyed, the bride's primary attraction was the temporal power of her uncle, Giulio de' Medici, now Pope Clement VII, and the eminence of her forebears, for she was the great-granddaughter of Lorenzo the Magnificent.

The Pope himself performed the wedding rites, which took place in Marseille, with King François I and his Queen in attendance. And so, if Florence lost a daughter, France gained a future queen, in the person of Catherine de' Medici.

Catherine spent the next 26 years playing second fiddle to her husband's famous mistress, Diane de Poitiers, who was nearly twenty years older than her lover. Despairing of attracting her own husband while he enjoyed Diane's favours, Catherine ingested a number of so-called magic potions, including mule's urine, a sure cure for sterility, to boost her sexual allure. When all else failed, she even drilled a spy hole in the floor so that she could watch Henri and Diane in action, in the hope of learning her rival's secrets.

But in 1559 when Henri died from wounds suffered in a joust, Catherine was quick to take control, ruling France for 30 years through the destructive incompetence of her three dismal sons. 'She had too much wit for a woman, too little honesty for a queen', said a contemporary, and even her closest foreign ally and son-in-law Philip II of Spain called her 'Madame la Serpente'. Indeed, her method of keeping tabs on her court was to establish a group of beautiful women (the *Escadron Volant* or Flying Squadron) who dallied with her friends and enemies alike to prise out their secrets.

Catherine's shallow intelligence, malevolent deviousness and lust for power combined to add fuel to France's terrible religious wars, culminating in the Massacre of St Bartholomew. Over this period the population was decimated and France reduced to a second-rate power.

Surprisingly, Catherine also made some positive contributions to her country. Tradition has it that she introduced the fork to France, the nation that today knows best how to use it, and she created one lasting monument for which all tourists to France have been eternally grateful, the exquisite château of Chenonceaux. Henri II had originally confiscated Chenonceaux from a rebellious baron and had given it to his mistress Diane, but when Henri died, Catherine forced Diane to relinquish it to her. It was Catherine who then built the remarkable gallery that crosses to the left bank of the Cher River, making Chenonceaux the most hauntingly beautiful of all the châteaux in the Loire Valley.

Also on this day

1636: Harvard University is founded * 1828: French novelist Victor Hugo is born * 1886: In New York, the Statue of Liberty is dedicated

29 October

Sir Walter Raleigh goes to the block

1618 'Fain would I climb, yet fear to fall', scratched Sir Walter Raleigh on a window pane with his diamond ring. His patroness Queen Elizabeth noticed the scribble and cut beneath it, 'If thy heart fail thee, climb not at all.'

In all the years that followed, Raleigh's heart never failed him, whether he was colonising Virginia, attacking the Spanish, exploring the Orinoco, battling for the Queen's favour or seducing ladies at court.

For 22 years Raleigh was supported by Queen Elizabeth (even though he was periodically banned from court for his misbehaviour). His only serious mistake was to impregnate and secretly marry one of Elizabeth's ladies of court, Elizabeth Throckmorton, for which both Raleigh and his wife were briefly confined to the Tower of London.

After the Queen died in 1603, Raleigh found himself at odds with her successor, James I, who had no interest whatever in Raleigh's swashbuckling adventurism. Worse, Raleigh's enemies spread false rumours that he was plotting to dethrone the King, so he was once more imprisoned in the Tower, where he spent some thirteen years. But even this second imprisonment failed to damp his spirit, for there he began his *History of the World*.

At last released in 1616, Raleigh was sent on another expedition to the Orinoco to search for gold, but with strict orders that no Spanish possessions must be molested.

Sadly for Raleigh, his co-commander defied orders and burned a Spanish town. Returning to England, Raleigh was immediately imprisoned and, on 29 October 1618, the 66-year-old courtier-poet-adventurer was led to the block in the yard of the Old Palace at Westminster. There, encircled by officials and some 60 guards, the Queen's favourite who had feared to fall, fell at last.

But even at the very end Raleigh's spirit did not desert him. Standing with the masked executioner, Raleigh reached to touch the axe and punned, ''Tis a sharp remedy, but a sure one for all ills.' Then, turning to the solemn witnesses, he addressed them with his final words, 'I have a long journey to take, and must bid the company farewell.'

In a gruesome coda to the execution, Raleigh's head was given to his wife in a red leather bag.

Also on this day

1628: French Cardinal Richelieu conquers La Rochelle, ending Protestant independence in France * 1787: In Prague, Mozart's opera *Don Giovanni* is performed for the first time * 1863: Swiss philanthropist Henri Dunant founds the International Red Cross * 1923: The Turkish Republic is proclaimed after the fall of the Ottoman Empire

30 October

John Adams, America's second president

1735 Among his enemies, from time to time he counted Benjamin Franklin, Alexander Hamilton, James Madison and Thomas Jefferson, a virtual galaxy of supernovae of the American Revolution. Yet he, too, was a revolutionary hero, America's first ambassador to Great Britain, his nation's first vice-president (a position that he derided as 'the most insignificant office that ever the Invention of man contrived or his Imagination conceived'), and America's second president.

He was John Adams, born today in Braintree (now Quincy), Massachusetts, the first child of Deacon John Adams and his wife Susanna.

Raised in a simpler time when the population of the American states was only two and a half million, Adams was a stout, irascible, round-faced man who was one of the last American politicians to eschew political parties on the idealistic if impractical belief that each member of government should simply do what he thought right for his country rather than support a particular faction.

As a 35-year-old lawyer, Adams demonstrated his determination to live by his own high principles when, in the face of popular outrage, he successfully defended British soldiers accused of murder during an incident known as the 'Boston Massacre'. Later, as President, he avoided a potentially ruinous war with France when the majority of congressmen were baying for blood.

Some of Adams's most valuable contributions to the building of an independent United States were seemingly minor actions with significant consequences: it was Adams who nominated George Washington for Commander-in-Chief of the revolutionary army; he also chose Jefferson to draft the Declaration of Independence.

Despite his success, during his long career in government Adams managed to rouse the ire of many of the nation's most influential leaders. Benjamin Franklin, who preceded Adams as American representative in Paris, thought him mentally unbalanced for his insistence on speaking his mind to his French hosts rather than kowtowing to advance American interests.

Adams and Thomas Jefferson had been firm allies during revolutionary days, but Jefferson and his great supporter James Madison were two great states-righters, who distrusted what they saw as Adams's belief in strong federal government, leading to an acrimonious break with Adams. On the other hand, Alexander Hamilton thought Adams not federalist enough, while Adams thought Hamilton to be planning a coup to make himself king.

Happily, after years of estrangement, Adams was finally reconciled with Jefferson and initiated a brilliant series of 158 letters between the two former presidents, who died on the same day, Adams with Jefferson's name on his lips.

Also on this day

1485: Henry Tudor is crowned as Henry VII of England, starting the Tudor dynasty * 1821: Russian novelist Fyodor Dostoyevsky is born in Moscow

31 October

The building of St Peter's inspires Luther to ignite the Protestant Reformation

1517 Today has been called the first day of the Reformation, when, on the eve of All Saints' Day, a 34-year-old Augustinian monk named Martin Luther nailed his famous 95 theses to the door of the Schlosskirche at the Saxon city of Wittenberg.

What triggered Luther's historic challenge to the Church of Rome was Pope Leo X's decision to complete the rebuilding of Rome's ancient and crumbling St Peter's Cathedral – or rather, how Leo proposed to pay for the work.

St Peter's had been one of Christianity's holiest places since the putative burial there of the apostle St Peter in about AD 67. The first known monument, an *aedicule* or shrine for a small statue, was constructed in around 170, and later Emperor Constantine built a basilica over the *aedicule*. Over the centuries several more churches were built there, but by the 15th century they had fallen into disrepair, and Pope Nicholas V determined to build a cathedral without rival to be named the Basilica of St Peter in honour of the founder of the Church.

Nicholas died in 1455, and construction on St Peter's began only in 1506 under the pontificate of Julius II, and when Leo X became Pope in 1513, the great building was still only partly finished. Leo resolved to continue the project, and with artists like Raphael to hand, he had only one problem – money. So, to raise the cash for the new basilica, he took to selling indulgences to deliver souls from Purgatory.

Leo's call went out to bishops throughout Europe, urging them to find buyers. One particularly energetic salesman was Johann Tetzel, a German Dominican friar who was assigned by the Archbishop of Mainz to get to work.

The Church had been awash with simony, nepotism, venality and corruption for a century, but when Luther, then a monk lecturing at the University of Wittenberg, learned of Tetzel's cynical sales programme, it was the final straw. In reaction to this last impiety, he hit back at the offending Church, starting with Tetzel, about whom he swore, 'God willing, I will beat a hole in his drum!' Then on this day he nailed his famous 95 theses to the church door at Wittenberg.

Luther's theses, written in Latin, only indirectly criticised papal policy, while emphasising spiritual life within the Church. Luther contended that divine grace cannot be easily acquired but must be gained through true belief and tribulation. But to ensure that someone beyond a junior acolyte would read the theses, he sent copies to the Archbishop of Mainz. Thanks to the recently developing art of printing, further copies were then circulated across much of Europe.

Thus it was that the building of its greatest monument touched off the blast that sundered the Catholic Church for ever.

Also on this day

1632: Jan Vermeer is born in Delft * 1795: English poet John Keats is born * 1902: The first telegraph cable across the Pacific Ocean is completed * 1940: The Battle of Britain ends * 1952: The United States detonates the first hydrogen bomb at Eniwetok Atoll in the Pacific

1 November

The pope who asked Michelangelo to paint the Sistine Chapel

1503 When Giuliano della Rovere was elected Pope on this day, he was a month short of his 60th birthday. In the eleven years of his reign, this headstrong and irascible pontiff achieved the worldly greatness of a Renaissance prince.

Giuliano's uncle was Pope Sixtus IV, who made him a cardinal and granted him nine bishoprics in Italy and France as well as numerous prosperous abbeys. While enjoying his riches and generally ignoring his flock, the sophisticated cardinal managed to father three illegitimate daughters. But in 1492 he was forced to flee to France when the spectacularly corrupt Alexander VI became Pope, whose election Giuliano had vigorously opposed.

Still trying to bring about Alexander's downfall, Giuliano twice joined foreign invasions of Italy, first with the French King Charles VIII and subsequently with his successor, Louis XII. Enraged, the Pope ordered the cardinal's assassination, but Giuliano remained in safety in the French court.

Alexander died in 1503, and after the seventeen-day reign of Pius III, Giuliano finally managed to buy enough votes to assure his own election, taking the name of Julius II. One of his first acts as Pope was to declare that in the future any papal election won by simony would be invalid.

During the next eleven years Julius fought two wars to strengthen the temporal powers of the Vatican, often taking the field himself, the last of the warrior popes. During the second of these he unsuccessfully attempted to force his former French allies to leave Italy. In spite of his own shady rise to power, he worked hard to cleanse the Church of much of its nepotism and corruption.

But Julius's greatest contribution was artistic. He ordered the construction or refurbishment of countless buildings and churches in Rome, and he laid the foundation stone for the new St Peter's basilica, commissioning Bramante and Michelangelo to work on it.

He was a patron of Raphael and formed a virtual partnership with Michelangelo in the creation of the great frescoes in the Sistine Chapel.

Pope Julius died on 21 February 1513 and lies buried in St Peter's, but the tomb he commissioned, never completed, is in the Church of San Pietro in Vincoli, guarded by Michelangelo's statue of Moses.

Also on this day

1500: Italian sculptor and jeweller Benvenuto Cellini is born * 1755: An earthquake destroys most of Lisbon, killing 80,000 people * 1757: Italian sculptor Antonio Canova is born * 1800: The White House becomes the residence of American presidents as John Adams spends the first night there

2 November

The prince in the tower who became the monarch with the shortest reign in British history

1470 Today was born the future Edward V of England, who twelve years later would inherit the throne and reign a mere 79 days, the shortest rule of any British monarch from William the Conqueror to Elizabeth II.

On 1 May 1464 Edward's father, 22-year-old King Edward IV, had secretly married a ravishing widow five years his senior named Elizabeth Woodville. The English court was appalled by this misalliance, as Elizabeth came from a family of only modest gentility, but the marriage seemed to work, in spite of the King's flagrant promiscuity. Six years later a son was born, shortly followed by another.

When the elder Edward died on 9 April 1483, young Edward inherited the throne. As he was still only twelve, his uncle Richard, the capable but ambitious Duke of Gloucester, was made protector of the realm.

In order to 'ensure their safety', Richard first moved the young King and his brother to the security of the Tower of London. Then, citing his brother Edward IV's licentious adventures and his secret marriage to Elizabeth, he persuaded the court that the marriage had in fact never taken place, making young Edward V illegitimate – and therefore not King at all.

On 25 June an assembly of lords duly declared Richard King Richard III, while Edward and his brother were still held in the Tower of London. And, as every schoolchild knows, neither of the young princes was ever seen again.

In all probability, in August that same year Richard's agents secretly smothered the two brothers in their room, but to this date debate has raged concerning their fate. Two centuries later the skeletons of two young boys were found buried in the Tower, presumed to be the princes, but historians still debate who killed them. Some claim it was their traitorous paternal uncle Richard, others nominate their equally unscrupulous maternal uncle, Richard's supporter Henry Stafford, Duke of Buckingham, while a few maintain it was the King who supplanted Richard III, King Henry VII.

Also on this day

82 BC: Roman general Lucius Cornelius Sulla marches on Rome to force the Senate to make him dictator * 1734: American pioneer Daniel Boone is born * 1755: Future French Queen Marie Antoinette is born in Vienna

3 November

Rome's April Fools' Day

BC In ancient Rome today was a festival called the Hilaria, a sort of Roman April Fools' Day when believers were permitted to play practical jokes on each other. It was a special holiday of celebration and gaiety observed by the cult dedicated to Isis and Osiris, two deities the Romans had adopted from their Egyptian colony. The Hilaria honoured the murdered god Osiris, who had been resurrected on 3 November.

The full tale was pretty grim stuff, and pretty confusing, too. Osiris, who was both the god of fertility and king of the underworld, married his sister Isis, a great magician. The two of them had a brother named Seth, who was a formidable fellow with a curved, fox-like snout, slanting eyes and a dog's body with a forked tail. He was also the god of storms, warfare and chaos.

Seth hated Osiris and was desperate to usurp his position as king of the underworld. One day he tricked his brother into climbing into a chest, slammed the lid shut and hurled the chest into the sea. He then sliced his drowned brother's corpse into fourteen pieces and scattered them all over Egypt. But Seth hadn't counted on Isis, who retrieved her husband's bits and buried them, all except for his penis. She then magically brought Osiris back to life and, no doubt with the help of that one unburied member, miraculously produced a son, Horus. Horus was a god who looked like a falcon, whose eyes were the sun and the moon. He spent most of his life fighting with his uncle Seth and finally defeated him, but during the battle he received a wound to his left eye. The injury accounted for the waning and waxing of the moon.

Also on this day

1870: Italian Reunification is completed * 1871: British-American explorer and reporter Henry Stanley finds Dr David Livingstone in the African bush * 1903: Panama declares independence from Colombia

4 November

Montgomery defeats Rommel at El Alamein

1942 Make sure you drink a Montgomery cocktail (recipe below), for today marks the completion of a tremendous two-week battle at El Alamein, Egypt, in which the British Eighth Army, under the command of General Bernard Law Montgomery, defeated the Italian-German Panzerarmee Afrika led by General Erwin Rommel.

If you were in England and read the next day's *Daily Telegraph*, you would have seen this headline: 'AXIS FORCES IN FULL RETREAT: OFFICIAL. Rommel's disordered columns attacked relentlessly. 9,000 prisoners; 260 tanks destroyed.' In America, on the eve of congressional elections, news of the victory swept politics off the front pages.

El Alamein was a most welcome feat of arms, coming as it did after the British debacles at Singapore and Tobruk, and went a long way to cement relations between the British and American military chiefs. Montgomery's victory saved Egypt and the Suez Canal. Churchill, in handsome overstatement, said, 'Before Alamein we never had a victory; after Alamein we never had a defeat.' In truth, the battle marked a turning of the tide of war, a shift that would be entirely confirmed three months later by the German defeat before Stalingrad.

Monty always had his detractors, however, who found his style of warfare too cautious and deliberate. Some years later in Harry's Bar in Venice, Ernest Hemingway invented the Montgomery cocktail, a martini made up of fifteen parts of gin to one of vermouth. This mixture, its inventor swore, was based on the ratio of his own troops to those of the enemy that Monty required before ordering an attack. Serve very cold.

Also on this day

1847: German composer Felix Mendelssohn dies in Leipzig * 1922: British archaeologist Howard Carter discovers the entrance to King Tutankhamen's tomb

5 November

Guy Fawkes

1605 London was smaller then, the population only a few hundred thousand, and November nights were cold and black, the only lighting seeping from a few unshuttered windows. But tonight there were bonfires in the streets, the crowds around them rejoicing to the sound of church bells ringing across the city. England's Protestant King James I and his young son Prince Henry had been saved from a murderous Catholic plot.

A nobleman named Robert Catesby, frustrated in his efforts to gain from the King greater tolerance for the Catholic faith, was at the heart of the conspiracy. Drawing together a group that finally included thirteen others, he planned to blow up the Houses of Parliament on their opening day on 5 November 1605, killing not only the King and his son but also virtually the entire parliament and the Protestant churchmen in attendance. Among the plotters was a certain Guy Fawkes, an English mercenary soldier just returned from the Spanish Netherlands after ten years of fighting Protestants. Fawkes was the group's technician; thanks to his military experience he knew how to build and detonate bombs.

In early 1605 one of the conspirators leased a house across the street from Parliament with a cellar that extended directly under the building. Soon the cellar was filled with 36 barrels of gunpowder, each weighing 100 pounds. After the explosion, Catesby would ride north to incite a Catholic uprising.

Ten days before the target date, however, probably in an attempt to save Catholic members of parliament, one of the plotters sent an anonymous letter to his brother-in-law warning of a forthcoming 'blow'. The brother-in-law promptly turned it over to the King, who proclaimed, 'It smells of gunpowder.'

King James now alerted his security services under the command of his redoubtable First Minister Robert Cecil. At exactly midnight on 4 November, the King's men pounced, catching

Fawkes in the cellar about to light an eight-hour fuse that would detonate the powder the following morning just as the King opened Parliament.

Taken to the Tower, Fawkes was first interrogated by the King himself, then tortured on the rack, soon revealing all he knew. Troops were dispatched to apprehend the other plotters, who were surrounded in a house in Warwickshire where they had fled on hearing of Fawkes's arrest. The soldiers shot down two. Then Catesby and one remaining ally, armed only with swords, charged out through the front door like Butch Cassidy and the Sundance Kid. His companion was killed immediately, but Catesby, wounded, managed to crawl into the chapel before dying.

The remaining conspirators were incarcerated in the Tower with Fawkes until their trial in Westminster Hall. Quickly found guilty, all were dragged through the streets on sledges to Old Palace Yard where they were hanged, drawn and quartered, their heads displayed on pikes around the Tower.

Remember, remember the fifth of November
Gunpowder, treason and plot.
I see no reason why gunpowder treason
Should ever be forgot.

So chant the children to this day, as the British light bonfires on the evening of 5 November, burning Guy Fawkes in effigy amid a celebration of fireworks commemorating the explosion that never took place.

Also on this day

1854: During the Crimean War British and French armies defeat the Russians at the Battle of Inkerman * 1955: French painter Maurice Utrillo dies

6 November

Russia loses Catherine the Great

1796 Catherine the Great died today, having lived for 67 years, Empress of Russia for the last 34 of them.

Catherine had been born in Germany and brought to Russia at the age of fourteen to marry the future Tsar, Peter III. By the time this ineffectual prince finally gained the throne, Catherine was 33 and entirely estranged from her husband. She had already taken at least three lovers, of whom one was probably the father of her son, future Tsar Paul I. Six months after Peter's succession, Catherine seized power and engineered her husband's murder by her current lover's brother.

From then on Catherine ruled as the most absolute monarch in Europe, while taking a succession of increasingly younger lovers whom she lavishly rewarded when she tired of their services. She had at least nine favourites while she was Empress, the youngest being twenty-year-old Alexander Lanskoy, whom she took up when she was 51.

It was rumoured that Catherine's lovers were all market tested by ladies of the court before being invited to attend the Empress. No doubt the candidates needed both stamina and imagination, since the licentious Catherine grew increasingly fat as she grew older. Her last paramour, Platon Zubov, must have been particularly resolute: he was only 22 when the Empress engaged him at the age of 60.

Although a scandal across Europe (Frederick the Great called her the Messalina of the North), Catherine changed Russia for ever. Claiming to be a liberal, in most things she was actually an extreme reactionary. She made the plight of Russia's serfs even worse by increasing the power of landowners, stripping the serfs of any state protection and strictly prohibiting any appeal for relief to the sovereign. She also imposed serfdom on the Ukrainians, who had hitherto been free.

Even so, she fancied herself an enlightened ruler, corresponding with intellectuals such as Voltaire and Diderot. She volunteered herself and her son for the first tuberculosis inoculations in Russia in order to set an example for her suspicious and recalcitrant people. She also enormously increased the size of her country by appropriating over 200,000 square miles of new territory, equivalent in size to California and New York State combined, and more than twice as large as Great Britain.

On 5 November 1796 Catherine was felled by a stroke. Like George II before her and Elvis Presley after, she was sitting in her privy closet when she was stricken. It took six strong men to carry her unconscious body to her bedroom, where, too heavy to be lifted onto her bed, she was laid on a mattress on the floor. In spite of the efforts of her doctors to revive her, she never regained consciousness, dying at 9.45 the following evening.

No sooner was Catherine dead than her son Paul had his putative father's body exhumed. He then turned Catherine's state funeral in the cathedral of Saints Peter and Paul into a double ceremony, the still fresh corpse of the bloated Empress lying beside the desiccated remains of the husband she had murdered 34 years before.

Also on this day

1860: Abraham Lincoln is elected 16th President of the United States * 1893: Russian composer Peter Ilyich Tchaikovsky dies * 1924: British Tory leader Stanley Baldwin is elected Prime Minister

7 November

The October Revolution – the Bolsheviks take over Russia

1917 Today one of the most improbable events in history took place. It was announced with this message at 10.00 a.m., composed by Lenin only minutes before: 'TO THE CITIZENS OF RUSSIA! The Provisional Government has been deposed ...' But what had occurred during the night was no glorious uprising of workers, no pitched battle in the streets, no storming of a Bastille, only a mild and bloodless coup carried out so quietly that almost nobody resisted and very few knew it had even happened. When it was over, however, the city of St Petersburg and the government of Russia lay in Bolshevik hands.

The slightest resistance might have saved the day. The Bolsheviks had taken over the instruments of power simply by walking in and dismissing those on duty: post offices, railway stations, banks, bridges and telephone centres changed hands without a shot. When morning came, only the Winter Palace remained under the control of the Prime Minister, Alexander Kerensky, and the Provisional Government.

Leaving his Cabinet ministers behind, Kerensky departed St Petersburg by car and in disguise, looking for troops who would defend the government. At Pskov he persuaded some Cossack units of the Third Cavalry Corps to accompany him, but when the soldiers discovered that no other units would join them, they quit two hours from the capital.

Lacking sufficient forces to take the lightly defended Winter Palace by assault, the Bolsheviks ordered the artillery of the Peter and Paul Fortress to fire on the building. Of 35 shells fired, two hit their target with minimum damage. The 'storming' of the Palace, later portrayed by Bolshevik historians as the epic event of a great popular rising (called the October Revolution because in Russia the old Julian calendar still prevailed), came about that night only after most of the discouraged defenders – teenage cadets – sensing that reinforcements were not going to turn up, had slunk away, and only then because, as George Kennan wrote, '... someone had inadvertently left the back door open'.

In the capital of Russia, at least, the first day of their bid for power ended successfully, if not heroically, for the Bolsheviks. In other places it was not always so easy – where there was resistance, it often prevailed – but authority, whether military or civil, showed little determination to save itself. So the improbable became reality. Within weeks, in most of the cities of central Russia, the Bolsheviks, with barely 25,000 members around the country, had taken power in the name of 100 million Russian people, most of whom had never heard of the Bolsheviks.

No one mourned the death of the Provisional Government. It had come to uncertain power in the vacuum left by the fall of the monarchy in February. It could not govern a Russia grown unmanageable under the multiple burdens of war, shortages, inflation, strikes and mutiny.

One eyewitness to the day's events was John Reed, who liked what he saw. Later, in *Ten Days That Shook the World*, he remembered how he felt the next morning: 'Now there was all great Russia to win – and then the world! Would Russia follow and rise? And the world – what of it? Would the peoples answer and rise, a red world-tide? Although it was six in the morning, night was yet heavy and chill. There was only a faint unearthly pallor stealing over the silent streets, dimming the watch-fires, the shadow of a terrible dawn grey-rising over Russia …'

Also on this day

1783: The last public hanging in England takes place when the forger John Austin is executed at Tyburn * 1805: Explorers Lewis and Clark become the first American men to travel across North America and reach the west coast * 1867: Polish scientist Marie Curie (née Sklodowska) is born in Warsaw * 1913: French philosopher and novelist Albert Camus is born

8 November

'O liberté! Que de crimes on commet dans ton nom!'

1793 'O Liberty, what crimes are committed in thy name!' The woman who spoke these famous words faced the guillotine today in Revolutionary Paris.

In 1780 25-year-old Manon de La Platière married an inspector of manufactures in Amiens named Jean-Marie Roland, who was twenty years her senior. Eleven years later, after the outbreak of the French Revolution, the couple moved to Paris, where she soon established a salon for like-minded liberals who eventually became known as the Girondins, a relatively moderate bourgeois faction that opposed the Revolution's most radical elements. Both striking and intelligent, Manon Roland, as she now was, masterminded her husband's career and helped him to rise to the post of Minister of the Interior.

In the early stages of the Revolution Manon Roland had sounded a bloodthirsty note, insisting that 'Il faut du sang pour cimenter la révolution.' (It takes some blood to cement the revolution.) Later, although still fervent democrats, both Rolands had become more moderate, and, at the instigation of his wife, Jean-Marie launched an attack on Danton and Robespierre before the Convention. Then, two days after the execution of Louis XVI, which he had vigorously opposed, he resigned his ministerial post.

Less than six months later Robespierre had become the most powerful man in France and expelled all Girondins from government. Then, in May 1793, began the awful butchery called the Terror. Jean-Marie fled, but on 31 May Manon was arrested and thrown into prison, where she occupied her time by writing her memoirs. After five months of incarceration she was led to the place de la Révolution for execution.

Ignoring the taunts shrieked by the brutal mob surrounding the scaffold, Manon hesitated before mounting the steps. Bowing in mockery in front of a giant statue of liberty at whose base stood the guillotine, she uttered her famous apostrophe.

Jean-Marie had evaded arrest, but on learning of his wife's execution, a week later he fell on his sword.

Also on this day

1656: English astronomer Edmond Halley is born * 1674: English poet John Milton dies * 1895: William Röntgen discovers X-rays at the University of Wurzburg * 1923: Adolf Hitler leads the unsuccessful Beer Hall Putsch in Munich * 1942: British and American forces commanded by General Dwight Eisenhower invade North Africa

9 November

Napoleon's coup d'état

1799 In revolutionary France, today was 18 Brumaire, An VIII, the first day of Napoleon Bonaparte's *coup d'état*.

Just back from his battles in Egypt, the diminutive Napoleon (he was just five feet six) was seen as a national hero. Backed by a few powerful members of government (notably Talleyrand), he donned his splashiest general's uniform – white breeches, blue coat with gold-embroidered lapels and a flamboyant red, white and blue sash at the waist – and paraded through the streets of Paris to tumultuous applause. He then entered the Tuileries to swear allegiance to one chamber of the government (the Elders) and next promptly sent 300 soldiers to 'protect' the other chamber, the Council of the Five Hundred.

The following day Napoleon boldly addressed each group, but the Council of the Five Hundred in particular turned on him savagely, and a pale and stammering Napoleon had to be accompanied from the chamber by four soldiers.

Having failed to charm the government with words, Napoleon did what he always did best. He sent in troops. His soldiers charged into the Orangerie, forcing the 500 members to flee through the windows.

On the evening of 10 November Bonaparte was declared First Consul; the Republican government known as the Directory was over. From that day until his abdication Napoleon held supreme power in France. Six years earlier to the day the revolutionary government had abolished the worship of God, and on that anniversary they instituted a replacement.

Also on this day

1918: Germany's Kaiser Wilhelm abdicates and flees to Holland * 1925: Adolf Hitler establishes the SS (Schutzstaffel or 'Protection Squad') as his personal bodyguard * 1965 Capital punishment is abolished in Great Britain

10 November

The US Marine Corps is born

1775 Today, just six months after the first shots of the American Revolutionary War were fired at the Battle of Lexington, the Continental Congress authorised the creation of the Continental Marines, now known as the United States Marine Corps. The first Marines signed up in the Tun Tavern in Trenton, New Jersey, and in March the following year they executed their first amphibious assault when they captured a British island in the Bahamas. Since then they have conducted over 300 amphibious landings on foreign shores.

Deactivated at the end of the war in 1783, the Marine Corps was re-instituted fifteen years later. Marines have fought in all of America's major wars, and in most cases were the first troops to see combat.

In the early 1800s Marines fought Barbary pirates from North Africa and crushed an enemy force in Tripoli, in what is now Libya. During the Mexican War they won a major victory at Chapultepec Castle, later fancifully referred to in a Marine Corps song as 'the halls of Montezuma'.

During the American Civil War the Marines' best-known assignment was a minor one, the apprehension of abolitionist John Brown at Harper's Ferry. Their commander was an Army general named Robert E. Lee. In 1898 28 Marines were among the 260 killed when the USS *Maine* blew up in Havana Harbour, igniting the Spanish–American War. During this same war the Marines established the American base at Guantanamo Bay in Cuba.

In the First World War the Marines' most famous battle occurred in 1918 when the 4th Marine Brigade attacked the German line at Belleau Wood. Both before and after that war, American presidents used the Marines to quell revolutions (and support American business interests) in the 'banana wars' of South and Central America.

During the Second World War the Marines were the country's

primary ground assault force in the Pacific, fighting in bloody battles such as Guadalcanal, Tarawa, Saipan, Guam and Okinawa. The bloodiest of all was Iwo Jima in early 1945, when the Marines suffered 6,000 dead and 17,000 wounded while killing some 20,000 Japanese defenders.

Marines played a prominent role in the Korean War, especially in MacArthur's surprise amphibious attack at Inchon. They were the first American ground troops to fight in Vietnam and saw combat in the Gulf War, Afghanistan and the war against Iraq.

Today the Marine dress-blue uniform still includes a standing collar, evolved from the leather one that was part of the original 18th-century uniform. From this distinctive if uncomfortable feature comes the Marine nickname of 'leatherneck'.

Marines like to think that 'Semper Fi', their shorthand version of the Corps motto 'Semper Fidelis' (always faithful), is their most famous slogan, but perhaps even better known is a word they coined during the Second World War, snafu, an acronym denoting confusion and chaos. It stands for 'Situation Normal, All Fucked Up'.

Also on this day

1483: Martin Luther is born in Eisleben, Saxony * 1697: English painter and caricaturist William Hogarth is born * 1759: German poet and dramatist Friedrich Schiller is born in Marbach

11 November

The eleventh hour of the eleventh day of the eleventh month

1918 At the eleventh hour of the eleventh day of the eleventh month an armistice, signed six hours before in French Marshal Ferdinand Foch's railway carriage at Compiègne, France, took effect between the Allies and the Central Powers, bringing the First World War to a close after four years, three months and nine days of fighting.

By July the Allied armies, greatly strengthened by 42 American divisions, had contained the German spring offensives and then launched a series of powerful counter-offensives that rolled the German army back towards the Rhine.

From far-flung fronts in Italy, the Balkans, Palestine, Mesopotamia and the Caucasus, and on the seas, the war news was at last favourable for the Allied cause.

For Germany, the news was correspondingly bad. During recent weeks, the Supreme Command had acknowledged that the war could not be won, the fleet had mutinied at Kiel, and revolution was in the streets. The Kaiser had fled to Holland the day before the Armistice, and the Reichstag declared a republic. Meanwhile, Germany's allies – Bulgaria, Turkey and Austria-Hungary – had all left the war.

Across the world, the news of the armistice was electrifying. Parisians sang and cheered in the boulevards. In New York 1 million people thronged Broadway. In London one observer recalled the event: 'I stood at the window of my room looking up Northumberland Avenue towards Trafalgar Square, waiting for Big Ben to tell that the War was over ... And then suddenly the first stroke of the chime ... From all sides men and women came scurrying into the streets. Streams of people poured out of all the buildings. The bells of London began to clash ... All bounds were broken. The tumult grew ... Flags appeared as if by magic ... Almost before the last stroke of the clock had died away, the strict, war-straitened, regulated streets of London had become a triumphal pandemonium.'

For all the celebration, the costs of the war were staggering. An estimated 65 million people were mobilised during the war, of whom 8.5 million had died, another 21 million had been wounded and 8 million were being held prisoner when the war ended. Another 6 million civilians also died.

As well as human beings, four imperial dynasties perished during or in the aftermath of the chaos. Had they tombstones they would read:

Habsburg 1282–1919
Hohenzollern 1415–1918

Romanov 1613–1917
Ottoman 1290–1922

For the Germans the end of the war brought still further losses. By the terms of the Versailles Treaty of 1919 they were made to relinquish large swathes of territory, their colonies and enormous quantities of war *matériel*. One of the few things the Germans gained during the peace process was the myth created by their generals that the German army were 'undefeated in the field' and had been 'stabbed in the back' by their own civilian government at the peace table. As the American commander General 'Black Jack' Pershing bitterly but presciently observed, 'They never knew they were beaten in Berlin. It will have to be done all over again.'

Also on this day

1821: Fyodor Mikhailovich Dostoevsky is born * 1855: Danish philosopher Søren Kierkegaard dies in Copenhagen * 1868: French Intimist painter Edouard Vuillard is born in Cuiseaux

12 November

Gustavus Adolphus takes the Swedish throne

1611 Gustavus Adolphus was still only sixteen when on this day he was crowned King of Sweden, having inherited the throne – and innumerable problems – from his unspeakable father, King Charles IX.

Charles had usurped the throne from his nephew, becoming a tyrant to his subjects, irascible, foul-mouthed and vicious. Worse, at the time of his death, he had involved Sweden in three wars simultaneously, against Russia, Poland and Denmark. But from this unpromising stock sprang Gustavus Adolphus, one of Sweden's very greatest kings.

The new king formed a remarkable partnership with his Chancellor Axel Oxenstierna. Together they not only reformed the government of Sweden but also had a profound impact on all of northern Europe through Sweden's decisive involvement in the Thirty Years' War.

Gustavus Adolphus first settled the wars he had inherited, largely through diplomacy but also through occasional battles. Here he first learned the art of war and then became the foremost European general of his generation.

Domestically, Gustavus Adolphus and his Chancellor radically modernised their government, making it more efficient than any other in Europe. Through his charm, good sense and more concrete economic benefits, he persuaded the Swedish nobility to serve the nation, even if it meant losing some of their ancient privileges. He also completely reformed the educational system of the country, supporting universities and virtually creating a new and superior system of secondary education.

Although Gustavus Adolphus had settled the wars inherited from his father, a new and much larger conflict, the Thirty Years' War, broke out in 1618 when the Holy Roman Emperor Ferdinand II tried to suppress the Protestant Reformation in the German principalities. For a dozen years Gustavus Adolphus watched and waited, no doubt hoping for a Protestant breakthrough that never materialised. By 1630 the Protestant cause looked all but lost as Ferdinand's great general Wallenstein recorded victory after victory.

When Gustavus Adolphus finally intervened, he launched a bold attack through northern Germany, almost immediately sweeping through Frankfurt and Mainz. That same year Ferdinand had made the cardinal error of replacing Wallenstein with Count Johann von Tilly, a highly capable soldier but no match for a military genius like Gustavus Adolphus. In September 1631 the two armies met at Breitenfeld, where the Swedes completely routed the imperial forces. They also roared through Bavaria, taking Munich, Augsburg and Nuremberg.

Only a year after Breitenfeld, in November 1632, Gustavus Adolphus defeated a recalled Wallenstein at Lützen, although the courageous Swedish King was killed during the action.

Gustavus Adolphus died just a month short of his 38th birthday.

Although the Thirty Years' War continued for another sixteen years, during the last two years of his life the great Swede had saved the cause of Protestant Reformation, with ramifications that are still with us today, almost four centuries later.

Also on this day

1035: King Canute dies at Shaftesbury in Dorset * 1840: French sculptor Auguste Rodin is born * 1948: Former Japanese Prime Minister Hikedi Tojo and seven other war criminals are sentenced to hang

13 November

Talleyrand finally calls it a day

1834 Today at last Charles-Maurice de Talleyrand, who had backed winning horses over six decades, resigned his last diplomatic post as French ambassador to Great Britain at the age of 80, thus ending the most spectacular and arguably the most successful career of all of history's diplomats.

This nimble careerist served first the Catholic Church, then the doomed monarchy of Louis XVI, followed by the Republic, the Emperor Napoleon, the restored monarchy of Louis XVIII, and finally the regime of King Louis-Philippe after the July Revolution of 1830.

Talleyrand entered the seminary of Saint-Sulpice in Paris at sixteen, received minor orders five years later and by 34 was a bishop. A year later, on the eve of Revolution, he was elected to represent the clergy at the National Assembly. Astutely reading the republican wind, he celebrated a Mass in commemoration of the fall of the Bastille and earned for himself the nickname of 'l'Evêque de la Révolution' (the Bishop of the Revolution). For this escapade, as well as for democratising the French Church, he was excommunicated by Rome and left the Church.

Talleyrand's next post was as envoy to Great Britain in 1792, representing the French monarchy in spite of his known republicanism. But the execution of Louis XVI and the failure of his peace mission left him no safe haven in either France or Britain, so he fled to the United States, where he spent two years.

By 1796 he was back in France, and a year later he was appointed Foreign Minister by the republican Directory. An early triumph was his negotiated peace with Austria after Napoleon's victories, taking home for himself over a million francs in bribes. He continued as Foreign Minister under Napoleon's Consulate, and in 1804 Napoleon, now Emperor, made him Grand Chamberlain. Even though he shortly resigned this office, he was pivotal in arranging Napoleon's dynastic marriage to Marie-Louise of Austria.

Alarmed by Napoleon's hubris, when the Emperor rashly invaded Russia Talleyrand began secretly negotiating with allied powers (most of whom were either emotionally or actively France's enemies) for the restoration of France's Bourbon kings. When Napoleon's first abdication led to the occupation of Paris, Tsar Alexander I stayed at Talleyrand's luxurious town house. (Talleyrand's easy change of loyalties caused Napoleon to refer to him as 'a shit in silk stockings'.)

In some measure due to Talleyrand's persuasive powers, the allies agreed to support the ageing Louis XVIII to replace the exiled Napoleon, and Louis expressed his gratitude by appointing Talleyrand once again as Foreign Minister. Sent to represent his country at the Congress of Vienna, he remained there when Napoleon escaped from Elba but returned to Paris after the former emperor's defeat at Waterloo. This time, however, Louis's ultra-royalist court forced him into retirement because of his revolutionary past.

By this time Talleyrand was 70, and the unwary believed he was retired, living in quiet luxury, writing his memoirs. But the old fox recognised Louis's successor Charles X for the reactionary bigot that he was, famously observing that the Bourbons 'have learned nothing and forgotten nothing'. He soon was scheming for Charles's removal, a job accomplished by the July Revolution of 1830, when Talleyrand, already in secret talks with Louis-Philippe, helped him to gain the throne. His reward? Once again to become an ambassador, this time to Britain, where he remained until his retirement on this day.

Also on this day

1312: Edward III of England is born * 1850: British novelist Robert Louis Stevenson is born in Edinburgh * 1868: Italian composer Gioacchino Rossini dies in Passy, France * 1903: French painter Camille Pissarro dies in Paris

14 November

How a Dutchman became King of England

1650, 1677 Today in 1650 in The Hague was born a brown-haired Dutch boy who was brought up speaking French and who would one day be King of England. His name was William of Orange.

Although of royal stock (he was the son of the Prince of Orange and Dutch Stadholder (Prime Minister elected by the States General), and grandson of England's Charles I), William's early years were difficult. His father died when he was just eight days old, and Dutch nobles, remembering his father's imperious ways, debarred the House of Orange from holding office. Meanwhile the bloodlines linking him to Charles I provided no help since Charles had been executed the year before William was born, leaving England in the tender care of Oliver Cromwell.

Perhaps what gave William his first boost to power came in 1671 when Louis XIV of France decided to invade the Netherlands. Appointed captain general, William led a band of largely untrained Dutch soldiers in combat against the French. Desperately searching for leadership that might halt the invaders, the States General shortly elevated him to Stadholder, and, although unable to overcome the French militarily, William managed to ally himself with Spain and the Holy Roman Emperor, thus bringing the conflict to a stalemate that could be settled by negotiation.

Now a man of consequence, on 14 November 1677, his 27th birthday, William married his cousin, Princess Mary of England, then a fifteen-year-old girl, daughter of the future James II.

In 1685 James inherited the throne on the death of his brother Charles II, but his militant Catholicism alarmed his Protestant subjects. In June 1688 the English Parliament invited William to invade their own country, and William landed at Brixham on the Devon coast on 15 November 1688, the day after his 38th birthday. By December the feckless James was in exile in France, and on 12 February 1689 Parliament invited William and Mary to become joint King and Queen, the only time in English history that a husband and wife have reigned together. Although Mary died after five years as Queen, William ruled until his death in 1702.

Also on this day

565: Byzantine emperor Justinian dies in Constantinople * 1687: Charles II's mistress Nell Gwyn dies * 1716: German mathematician Gottfried Leibniz dies in Hanover * 1840: French Impressionist painter Claude Monet is born in Paris * 1862: Lewis Carroll begins writing *Alice in Wonderland* * 1940: German bombers devastate Coventry, killing 1,000

15 *November*

Louis XIV opens Versailles

1684 Of all the palaces in the Western world, the most magnificent is surely Versailles, which took over half a century to build. Even twenty years after work had first begun, the palace was still being constructed by a force of 36,000 labourers and 6,000 horses. Within Versailles, surely the grandest room is the Galerie des Glaces, which on this day proud King Louis XIV opened to his court.

The Galerie des Glaces is 225 feet long, pierced by seventeen huge windows, each reflected by an equal-sized wall mirror. The hall was in its greatest glory at night, when it was lit by hundreds of candles glittering in 32 enormous silver chandeliers.

The Galerie des Glaces was often the scene of great events, like the marriage of the hapless Louis XVI to Marie Antoinette, but two centuries after its first opening, this great hall was used for a more sombre purpose. It was there that a victorious Bismarck proclaimed King Wilhelm of Prussia to be Kaiser of a united Germany after having humiliated the French in the Franco-Prussian War.

Louis XIV might have been better pleased half a century after that, however, when the Treaty of Versailles, humiliating the Germans at the end of the First World War, was signed in the Galerie on 28 June 1919.

Also on this day

1708: British statesman William Pitt the Elder is born * 1787: Austrian composer Christopher Gluck dies in Vienna * 1802: English painter George Romney dies * 1864: Union General William Sherman burns Atlanta during the American Civil War * 1908: Chinese dowager empress Tz'u-hsi dies

16 November

A king dies incarcerated in the Tower of London

1272 Henry III, son of the iniquitous King John and fourth Plantagenet king of England, breathed his last on this day in the Tower of London. He was 65 years old and had been King for 56 years, a record reign among European monarchs that would survive for 450 years until France's Louis XIV surpassed it with the all-time record of 72 years.

Sadly, length of reign was Henry's sole achievement. It is calculated that this ambitious but cowardly and incompetent monarch actually ruled during only 24 of the years that he was King. First he was dominated by his courtiers, then he was overthrown by the redoubtable Simon de Montfort, Earl of Leicester, and when Leicester was finally defeated and killed, Henry's son Edward I took over the reins of government from the now faltering and senile old King.

Although Henry's 56-year reign is impressive, two non-European monarchs before him had reigned longer, the Byzantine Emperor Basil II for 62 years in the late 10th–early 11th centuries and the Egyptian Pharaoh Ramses II for 66 years in the 13th century BC.

Today Henry ranks eighth in length of reign, surpassed not only by Louis XIV, Basil and Ramses but also by:

Louis XV – 59 years
George III – 60 years
Hirohito – 63 years
Victoria – 64 years
Franz Joseph – 68 years

Papal reigns of course cannot compete, as popes are invariably at least middle-aged when elected. But Pius IX lived until he was 88, Pope for a record 32 years.

In terms of longevity of title (if not of reign), queen consorts put the kings to shame. Elizabeth Bowes-Lyon, the Queen Mother of England, died at almost 102, a queen for 66 years (the last 50 of them a widow), and the remarkable Eleanor of Aquitaine managed 67 queenly years, 15 as Queen of France, 52 as Queen or Queen Mother of England, before dying at 82 in 1204. Napoleon III's consort Eugénie of France also managed 67 royal years, dying only in 1920, but the all-time champion was Zita von Bourbon-Parma, wife of Charles, the last kaiser of Austria and King of Hungary. She was titularly a queen for a magnificent 75 years, although she was widowed for 67 of them, dying in exile in Switzerland at 96.

Also on this day

42 BC: Roman Emperor Tiberius is born * 1632: Swedish King Gustavus Adolphus is killed at the Battle of Lützen * 1913: French novelist Marcel Proust publishes the first volume of *Remembrance of Things Past* * 1920: The last White Russian troops leave Sebastopol, ending the counter-revolution against the Bolsheviks

17 November

The Suez Canal opens for business

1869 The Suez Canal finally opened today, after ten years, six months and 24 days of backbreaking labour by Egyptian workmen led by a stubborn but charming and generous French aristocrat, Ferdinand de Lesseps. Attending the ceremony were a mixed lot of Middle Eastern potentates and European literati such as Théophile Gautier, Emile Zola and Henrik Ibsen, plus a smattering of royalty, including Austrian Emperor Franz Joseph and French Empress Eugénie, who happened to be a cousin of de Lesseps's.

De Lesseps was already 54 when he ceremonially delivered the first blow of a pickaxe to start construction on 25 April 1859. He had already pursued a successful diplomatic career, including several stints in the Middle East. But when he was only 27 he had been stationed in Alexandria, where he studied plans for a canal drawn up by one of Napoleon's engineers.

The Suez Canal connects the Mediterranean and Red Seas, but its real achievement is to allow ships to sail between the Mediterranean and the Indian Ocean and even on to the Pacific. Its route meanders for 101 miles, taking advantage of several lakes, instead of driving straight across the isthmus, a distance of only 75 miles as the crow flies. The original wedge-shaped canal was just 26 feet deep and 190 feet wide at the surface, reducing to 72 feet wide at the bottom. (In subsequent years it was significantly deepened and further widened.)

Originally the canal was jointly owned by the French and the Egyptian Khedive Isma'il Pasha, but in 1875 Benjamin Disraeli persuaded the British Parliament to buy out Isma'il Pasha, a purchase which inadvertently led to the Suez Crisis of 1956 when Egyptian President Gamal Abdel Nasser nationalised it.

The grand opening of the canal on this day should probably be called a grand re-opening. The first canal across the Isthmus of Suez had been built in the 19th century BC and subsequently restored by rulers such as the Egyptian Pharaoh Ptolemy II, the Persian King Xerxes and the Roman Emperor Trajan.

Also on this day

1800: The US Congress meets for the first time * 1912: Woodrow Wilson is elected twenty-eighth President of the United States * 1912: French sculptor Auguste Rodin dies in Meudon * 1922: Kemal Atatürk deposes the last sultan of Turkey

18 November

Urban II launches the First Crusade

1095 The huge crowd outside Clermont Cathedral in the Auvergne region of France shivered with cold, wept with religious fervour and smiled inwardly with greedy anticipation when Pope Urban II made his dramatic appeal today for a holy crusade.

'Jerusalem is the navel of the world,' declared the Pope, 'a land more fruitful than any other, a paradise of delights. This is the land which the Redeemer of mankind illuminated by his coming, adorned by his life, consecrated by his passion, redeemed by his death, and sealed by his burial. This royal city, situated in the middle of the world, is now held captive by his enemies ... It begs unceasingly that you will come to its aid.'

Such was the call to arms that today launched the First Crusade to reclaim Jerusalem from the heathen Muslims and return it (and all the riches between it and Constantinople) to Christian domination.

Urban had been strongly influenced by an ascetic monk called Peter the Hermit who had visited the Holy Land the year before. His descriptions of the miseries of the Christians and the sacrilegious insults offered to Jerusalem's holy Christian shrines inspired Urban to unite the faithful into one vast effort to overthrow the Seljuk Turks who controlled Palestine.

Offering remission of all penance for sin to all who helped the

Christians in the east, Urban provoked an immediate and overwhelming response. Soon a massive force of some 4,000 mounted knights and 25,000 infantry, principally from France, Italy and the Germanic states, was headed towards Constantinople en route to the greatest Christian adventure in history.

Wearing the symbolic white cross on their breasts, the crusaders were soon pillaging and sacking their way to the Holy Land, encouraged by their battle cry of 'Deus le volt!' (God wills it!)

In June 1099 the Christian army, which had dwindled to perhaps 1,500 mounted knights and 12,000 foot soldiers, reached Jerusalem. On 15 July the great walled city fell to the crusaders for a triumphant massacre and sack. The First Crusade had reached its jubilant conclusion.

Peter the Hermit, however, fared less well. He and another rabble-rousing friar, Walter the Penniless, led a 'People's Crusade' of unattached soldiers, fervent peasants, adventurous youths and unemployed criminals to Constantinople. Evicted from the city as a threat to its civilian population, this ragtag army was ambushed at Cibotus and annihilated by the Turks.

Jerusalem remained in Christian hands for less than a century, falling to Saladin in 1187. In all there were nine crusades aimed at conquering or retaining Jerusalem, the last in 1365.

Also on this day

1626: St Peter's in Rome is consecrated * 1789: French photography pioneer Louis Daguerre is born * 1820: American captain Nathaniel Parker discovers Antarctica * 1922: French novelist Marcel Proust dies

19 November

The second Medici pope

1523 Elected on this day as Pope Clement VII was that vacillating schemer, Giulio de' Medici, whom history remembers primarily for his refusal to allow England's Henry VIII to annul his marriage.

Giulio had been born both illegitimate and posthumously, for his father had been assassinated in Florence's great red-domed Duomo a month before his birth. Fortunately for Giulio, he was immediately taken into the household of his uncle, Lorenzo the Magnificent, where he learned the life of a Renaissance prince. He also grew up with his cousin, Lorenzo's son Giovanni, two years his senior.

Since Giovanni was Lorenzo's second son, he was destined for the Church, receiving his tonsure at the early age of eight. And as he rose in the hierarchy of Rome, Giulio followed in his footsteps.

By 1513 Giovanni had achieved his ultimate ambition of becoming Pope, taking the name of Leo X. Once enthroned, he lived (and spent) more like the prince he was than a man of the cloth. He wanted to elevate his cousin Giulio, but Giulio's illegitimate birth was a seemingly insurmountable barrier. First Giovanni/Leo gave his cousin a special dispensation and then he accepted a formal declaration that Giulio's parents had really been secretly married, therefore making Giulio legitimate. He then promoted Giulio to the rank of cardinal, all within his first year as Pope.

When Giovanni/Leo died at the end of 1521, the College of Cardinals turned to Adrian VI, history's only Dutch pope, no doubt believing that two Medici cousins back to back would be more than decency (or the papal treasury) could bear. But ten years later Adrian died, and at last Giulio was elected at the age of 51, taking the name of Clement VII.

During his eleven papal years Giulio/Clement used most of his energies grasping for temporal power for himself and his family while commissioning great artists such as Michelangelo and Raphael. He completely failed to come to grips with Catholicism's greatest challenge, the emergence of Protestantism. Although usually supporting Holy Roman Emperor Charles V, he once made the serious error of signing a treaty with Charles's rival, François I of France. Charles sent his army into Rome for its worst sack since Alaric over a millennium before, and Guilio/Clement escaped only by barricading himself in the Castel' Sant'Angelo. Later the Pope made amends by agreeing to crown Charles, making Charles the last Holy Roman Emperor ever crowned by a Pope.

Giulio/Clement's dependence on Charles caused one of his few historically important acts. When England's Henry VIII petitioned for an annulment of his marriage to Catherine of Aragon, Giulio/Clement turned him down, not for doctrinal reasons but because Catherine was Charles's aunt. The Pope's refusal was the trigger that forced Henry at last to break for ever with the Catholic Church.

Also on this day

1600: British King Charles I is born in Dunfermline Castle * 1828: Viennese composer Franz Schubert dies of syphilis at the age of 31 * 1863: American President Abraham Lincoln gives the Gettysburg Address

20 November

The death of Leo Tolstoy

1910 Today died the man once hailed as the greatest of all novelists, Count Leo Nikolayevich Tolstoy, famous, rich and probably unhappy.

Tolstoy was born at his aristocratic family's estate in Yasnaya Polyana, about 130 miles south of Moscow. As a young man he fought with the army both in the Caucasus and in the Crimean War, and later he married and fathered ten children who survived infancy.

Tolstoy wrote his first novel when he was 24, but he was over 40 when he published his masterpiece of realism *War and Peace*. In it the experience he had gained in battle served him well in describing scenes of combat. The British poet Matthew Arnold maintained that a novel by Tolstoy was not a work of art but a piece of life.

Eight years later saw the publication of Tolstoy's other undoubted masterwork, *Anna Karenina*. While he was at work on this book he began to suffer bouts of depression and even considered suicide. At this time he was also developing his own religious and moral beliefs that led him to part from the Russian Orthodox Church (in the end he was excommunicated). He became a dedicated pacifist and came to believe that he should abandon material possessions.

A noble who gave up his own riches, Tolstoy soon found himself giving up his large family as well, as his wife and children, except for one daughter, became estranged from this dogmatic man with the air of an Old Testament prophet. Thus he was to experience his own famous first line from *Anna Karenina*, 'All happy families resemble each other; but each unhappy family is unhappy in its own way.' After years of increasing hostility, he finally decided to leave home for good. On his travels he caught pneumonia and he finally succumbed to heart failure in the small railway station of Astapovo at the age of 82. His last words were a bewildered, 'The truth ... I care a great deal ... how they ...'

Tolstoy's great novels are still widely read, although modern critics tend to rate the works of his Russian contemporary Fyodor Dostoevsky more highly for their psychological insights. But Tolstoy's influence still lives with us today. Mohandas Gandhi put into practice Tolstoy's ideas about pacifism and passive resistance in ousting the British from India, and Gandhi's principles in turn influenced the thinking of Martin Luther King.

Also on this day

1818: Simón Bolívar declares Venezuela to be independent of Spain
* 1945: The Nazi war crime trials begin at Nuremberg

21 November

Man's first free flight

1783 Earlier in the year the Montgolfier brothers had sent the first unmanned balloon aloft near Lyon. A few months later the French physicist Pilâtre de Rozier became the first man to ascend with a balloon, but Rozier's flight had been in a balloon made fast to prevent free flight, and he had risen a mere 90 feet. (At the time even this ascent was considered so hazardous that local authorities decreed that two criminals sentenced to death should be forced to undertake it. Only the intervention of King Louis XVI allowed Rozier and a colleague, the marquis d'Arlandes, the honour of manning the first flight.)

But a few months later, on 21 November, Rozier and the marquis lifted off in Paris's Bois de Boulogne and floated free for 25 minutes, crossing the Seine and landing some five miles from the Bois. For the first time in history man had flown.

In the audience that day was the American ambassador to France, Benjamin Franklin. When asked by a friend what good a balloon flight would do, Franklin replied, 'And what good is a new-born baby?'

In 1785 Rozier and a colleague attempted to be the first to cross the English Channel in a balloon, but they unwisely used a hot-air balloon tucked under a hydrogen balloon. When this double balloon reached a height of about 3,000 feet, fire used to produce the hot air reached the hydrogen, and the upper balloon exploded, killing Rozier and his companion in the fall.

Also on this day

570: The Prophet Mohammed is born * 1620: After a 66-day Atlantic crossing carrying 102 Pilgrims, the *Mayflower* lands on Cape Cod at what is now Provincetown to establish the first permanent colony in North America * 1694: French writer Voltaire is born in Paris * 1898: Belgian Surrealist painter René Magritte is born * 1916: Austrian Emperor Franz Joseph I dies

22 November

Warwick the Kingmaker

1428 Today is the birthday of the man who was called by one of those magic names that echo down the centuries from medieval England: Warwick the Kingmaker, the man who made two men King of England.

The kingmaker's name was Richard Neville. The son of an earl, he attained his own earldom not by inheritance but by marriage to the richest heiress in England, daughter of the previous Earl of Warwick. Thus Neville gained not only a title but also the greatest fortune in the land, not excluding the King's.

Warwick's first venture at kingmaking came in 1461, when he stage-managed the defeat of poor Henry VI, as young Edward of York took over as Edward IV.

Warwick virtually ruled the country for several years, but when Edward showed signs of independence, he daringly switched sides and, in a matter of months, invaded England with a force from France and restored the hapless Henry to the throne.

Six months later, however, Edward gathered his own army and defeated Warwick at the Battle of Barnet on Easter Sunday 1471. At the battle's end two foot soldiers seized the fleeing Warwick. One forced open his visor with an axe, the other plunged in his sword.

Sadly, no likeness of Warwick remains, so we can only imagine the no doubt shrewd and forceful face of the most daring and adventurous man of 15th-century England.

Also on this day

1220: Frederick II is crowned Holy Roman Emperor * 1774: Robert Clive of India commits suicide * 1819: English novelist George Eliot (Mary Ann Evans) is born * 1869: French author André Gide is born * 1890: French general and President Charles de Gaulle is born * 1963: American President John F. Kennedy is shot

23 November

Queen Isabeau sends her lover to his death

1407 At first his subjects called Charles VI of France le Bien-Aimé for his kindly nature, but when he was 24 he suffered the first of the bouts of madness that continued throughout the rest of his life, and Charles the Well-Loved was now called Charles l'Insensé (Charles the Mad). Although he had occasional periods of rationality, his spells of insanity rendered him unfit to govern and thus loosed a bloody and ferocious power struggle for control of France.

The primary contenders were the King's brother, Louis, duc d'Orléans and his nephew, the powerful Duke of Burgundy, Jean Sans Peur (John the Fearless). But behind the scenes was Charles's wife, the beautiful, debauched and scheming Isabeau of Bavaria.

In the early years of Charles's madness, Isabeau had welcomed his brother Louis to her bed, and together they had ruled the kingdom. But it soon became clear that Jean Sans Peur had the support of most of France's powerful nobles, and Isabeau decided to switch sides.

On the evening of this day in 1407 the 36-year-old Queen invited Louis to sup with her in her apartments and then led him to her bedchamber. Suddenly the enraptured couple were disturbed by the arrival of an urgent summons from the King requiring Louis's immediate presence on the other side of Paris. He hurriedly dressed and left the Queen's quarters with a light escort to make his way through the darkened streets of the city.

Louis had ridden only a few hundred yards when he was suddenly attacked by a group of cut-throats who came at him from all sides. A sword severed his right hand as he held the reins.

'I am the Duke of Orléans', he shouted desperately. 'Just the one we wanted', came the reply, and Louis was knocked to the ground and savagely slain.

The next day it became clear that both the 'king's messenger' and the assassins had been sent by Jean Sans Peur, a charge the fearless duke readily acknowledged. His willing helper in the murder had been the heartless Isabeau, who had lured Louis to her boudoir to set the trap. Jean's position was now as unassailable as Louis's had been previously, for now he was sharing Queen Isabeau's bed as well as the rule of France.

For almost twelve years Jean Sans Peur remained a power in the land, but Louis's supporters had neither forgotten nor forgiven. In 1419 he was treacherously murdered during a diplomatic parley on a bridge in Montereau, about 50 miles from Paris.

As for Isabeau, she remained a power behind the throne until poor mad Charles died in 1422. Although her son Charles VII then became King, Isabeau found common cause with England's invading Henry V and married off her daughter Catherine to him. The fruit of that marriage was England's Henry VI, to whom Catherine passed on her father's feeblemindedness. Isabeau lived on until 1435, dying at the age of 64.

Also on this day

1863: The Union Army of General Ulysses S. Grant defeats the Confederates at the Battle of Chattanooga * 1874: Thomas Hardy publishes *Far from the Madding Crowd* * 1876: Spanish composer Manuel de Falla is born in Cádiz

24 November

Charles Darwin publishes On the Origin of Species

1859 Today Charles Darwin published the most important scientific work of the 19th century, *On the Origin of Species by Means of Natural Selection, or The Preservation of Favoured Races in the Struggle for Life*. In it he wrote, 'I have called this principle, by which each slight variation, if useful, is preserved, by the term of Natural Selection.' Although one reviewer called the book 'so turgid, repetitive, and full of nearly meaningless tables, that it will only be read by specialists', it sold 1,250 copies on the first day and has never since been out of print.

On the Origin of Species elicited admiration from scientists, dismay from God-fearing Christians and fury from the Church hierarchy, enraged at its denial of the story of Genesis and the creation of the world in seven days. But in this work Darwin focused primarily on the evolution of animals, only lightly touching on the implications of his hypothesis for mankind. Twelve years later he remedied this omission with the publication of *The Descent of Man and Selection in Relation to Sex*, which filled out his theory of evolution.

Here Darwin describes man's primordial ancestors as 'a hairy quadruped, furnished with a tail and pointed ears, probably arboreal in its habits'. He concludes his book with the claim that man 'still bears in his bodily frame the indelible stamp of his lowly origin'. The Church was hostile in the extreme, for, in positioning humans as descendent from other primates rather than created separately in God's image, the book specifically refutes the biblical account of man's origin. As Darwin's theories became more widely known, the public reacted with bemusement; one no doubt apocryphal story tells of a vicar's wife who, on hearing of Darwin's contentions, exclaimed, 'I hope it is not true that we are descended from apes, but if it is true, I hope it does not become generally known.'

A year after the appearance of *The Descent of Man*, Darwin published yet another contentious theory in *The Expression of the Emotions in Man and Animals*. Here he once again positioned human beings as simply a more highly developed form of animal, showing that animals experience many of the same emotions as human beings and use the same facial muscles to express emotions such as fear, anger, love and grief.

In spite of his conviction that his books revealed nature's truth, Darwin always felt somewhat guilty for his heretical theory, referring to himself as 'the Devil's Chaplain'. He declined to comment publicly on his own views on a Christian God, writing to a friend, 'I feel most deeply that the whole subject is too profound for human intellect. A dog might as well speculate on the mind of Newton.'

Darwin's angst about his own ideas manifested itself in extreme poor health that started about the time he first began to commit his theories to paper in 1837. For the next 35 years he suffered from a whole raft of unpleasant symptoms – nausea, heart palpitations and insomnia – and became a semi-invalid. No specific cause was ever diagnosed, and many believe his illnesses were psychosomatic, brought on by the stress of developing ideas so totally in conflict with the religious teachings with which he had been raised.

Darwin continued to write at his house in Kent, his last work the rather less controversial *The Formation of Vegetable Mould, Through the Action of Worms, with Observations on Their Habits*. He died at home on 19 April 1882 at the age of 73. Today virtually the entire civilised world has come to accept his revolutionary evolutionary theories, as Christians and Jews now accept the story of Genesis as symbolic rather than literal. But his brilliant discoveries are still denied in some backward parts of Borneo, the Congo, rural Pakistan and the United States.

Also on this day

1713: Novelist Laurence Sterne is born in Clonmel, Ireland * 1864: French painter Henri de Toulouse-Lautrec is born

25 November

A remarkable woman stages a coup

1741 Although Tsarina Elizabeth was the daughter of Russia's Peter the Great, it required sixteen years and the death of five sovereigns before she could gain the throne – and then she had to take it herself. On this day she executed a successful *coup d'état* while the reigning Tsar Ivan VI was still only a year old.

Elizabeth was just sixteen when her father died. By the standards of her day or any other, she was remarkably beautiful, with a beauty evenly matched by vanity. She dyed her hair and eyebrows jet black (she was actually fair), never wore the same dress twice and smothered herself in ostentatious jewellery. She reputedly owned 15,000 pairs of shoes, with dresses to match. She was also believed to be licentious in the extreme, preferring lovers from the lower social orders, including coachmen and household servants. In spite of her promiscuity (or perhaps because of it), she was extremely religious, attending Mass regularly.

By the time Elizabeth was 32, she had watched four rulers come and go – her father Peter the Great, his wife Catherine, his grandson Peter II, and his niece Anna. Now Anna's great-nephew, the year-old Ivan VI, was Tsar, under the control of his ferocious mother, another Anna.

But when the second Anna threatened to banish Elizabeth to a convent, Elizabeth displayed the ruthlessness she had inherited from her father. Gathering her allies in court, she imprisoned Anna and the infant Tsar and seized the crown for herself.

Elizabeth was a complex mixture of European sophistication and Tartar barbarism. She established Russia's first university and built St Petersburg's fabulous Winter Palace. She abolished the death penalty but did not shrink from torture. She once discovered a treasonous plot involving two noble women whom she hated anyway for their beauty. She spared their lives but had their tongues cut out.

Elizabeth ruled Russia for twenty years, leaving her weak-minded predecessor Ivan VI languishing in prison. On her death, although Ivan was still alive, the throne went to the first Anna's son Peter III, who made the colossal blunder of marrying a German princess named Sophia von Anhalt-Zerbst, known to history as Catherine the Great. In 1762 Catherine took over Russia in a *coup d'état*, and had her husband locked away and subsequently murdered in his cell. Two years later, poor Ivan, who had never been released, met the same grisly fate.

Also on this day

1562: Spanish dramatist Lope de Vega is born in Madrid * 1616: Cardinal Richelieu joins the French government for the first time * 1741: Peter the Great's daughter Elizabeth becomes Tsarina of Russia * 1875: The British government buys shares in the Suez Canal

26 November

George Washington proclaims Thanksgiving

1789 During his first year as President, George Washington proclaimed today a National Day of Thanksgiving in honour of the new American Constitution. In so doing he gave prominence to a holiday that Americans had first celebrated in 1621 and had continued to celebrate sporadically over the intervening years.

But Thanksgiving has always been a moveable feast. The famous first one was celebrated sometime in early October by the 56 Pilgrim colonists who still survived from the 102 who had landed with the *Mayflower* the previous November. They invited 90 members of the Wampanoag Indian tribe to join them in a three-day harvest festival.

During the ensuing years Thanksgiving was mostly not held at all, and when it was, it was a local affair on varying dates. In 1777 for the first time all thirteen of the nation's states agreed on a single Thanksgiving Day in October, but this was really to commemorate the American victory over the British at Saratoga the month before, rather than a harvest festival.

In spite of Washington's declaration, Thanksgiving did not become an official American institution, but in 1827 a 39-year-old New Englander named Sarah Josepha Hale initiated her tireless campaign to have it formally recognised. The next year she became America's first female editor of a magazine when she was asked to take charge of the *Ladies' Magazine* and, later, *Godey's Lady's Book*. She used both publications as forums for continuing her crusade (while on the side penning the children's verse 'Mary Had a Little Lamb', a poem that became so famous that in 1877 Thomas Edison recorded himself reciting it for the first public demonstration of his gramophone).

Finally, after 36 years of writing to presidents, governors and senators, Sarah Hale was rewarded when, in 1863, Abraham Lincoln made Thanksgiving an official national holiday, specifying that it should always take place on the last Thursday in November.

Even then there was one more change to come. In 1939 the United States found itself in the midst of a worldwide depression and wanted to boost consumer purchases. Therefore President Franklin Roosevelt proclaimed Thanksgiving Day a week earlier – on the fourth, not the last, Thursday of November – to give American consumers one more week of shopping before Christmas. It has been celebrated on the fourth Thursday in November ever since.

Also on this day

1252: French Queen Blanche of Castile dies * 1504: Queen of Castile and Aragon Isabella I dies at Medina del Campo in Spain * 1607: Founder of Harvard University John Harvard is born

27 November

Clovis, the first French king

511 Clovis, the Frankish king whom the French regard as the founder of France, died today in Paris at the age of 45. So revered was he that a derivation of his name – Louis – was used for eighteen future kings.

French claims notwithstanding, Clovis was really a Belgian, born a prince of the Salian Franks, whose capital was around Tournai and whose native language was Frankish German.

At only fifteen Clovis inherited his father's small kingdom and immediately set out to expand it. By his death he had quadrupled its size to form an 'r'-shaped realm that covered most of western France, south as far as Toulouse, east almost to the Rhône, and in the northern part, covering today's Belgium and parts of what is now western Germany.

Clovis's take-over of the Rhineland Franks was a good example of his cunning and ruthlessness. Knowing of bad blood between King Sigebert and his son Chlodoric, he persuaded Chlodoric to murder his father to put himself on the throne. After the assassination Chlodoric was searching through his father's treasure chest for a gift for Clovis when one of Clovis's knights crept up behind him and split his skull with an axe. Clovis then reported to the remaining Rhineland Franks that Chlodoric had murdered his father but had received a mortal blow in the process. Now leaderless, the gullible Rhinelanders then accepted Clovis as King.

Later he defeated his cousin Ragnacaire, the King of Cambrai, who was taken prisoner and brought before Clovis with his hands chained behind his back. 'Why', asked Clovis, 'have you permitted our blood to be humiliated by allowing yourself to be put in chains? Better that you should die.' Whereupon Clovis hacked his prisoner down. Then, turning to Ragnacaire's brother, who had also been taken prisoner, he said, 'Had you but helped your brother, they would not have chained his hands', and promptly executed the brother as well.

Clovis was the only French king ever to wed a saint. At about 30 he married Clothilde, the Catholic daughter of the King of Burgundy. At first he ignored her pleas to become a Christian, but in 496 he found himself threatened with defeat by the Alemanni. Desperate for help from any quarter, he offered a prayer to Christ for victory. After his triumph in the ensuing Battle of Tolbiacum, he led 3,000 of his army to Reims for a mass baptism on Christmas Day.

According to legend, just as the ceremony began it was discovered that the consecration oil was missing, but a dove descended from heaven with a full ampoule carried in its beak. This so-called Sainte Ampoule of Reims was miraculously preserved in Reims cathedral and used for the coronation of every French king from Philip Augustus in 1179 until Charles X in 1824, even though the cathedral itself burned down at the beginning of the 13th century, to be replaced by the one that stands there today.

After the baptismal ceremony the presiding bishop, St Remi, famously characterised Clovis's change from paganism to Christianity with the remark, 'Henceforth we must burn what we have worshipped and worship what we have burned.'

Although Clovis's decision to push his people towards Christianity changed the direction of religion in France for ever, his faith was manifested in some rather unchristian ways. After one battle a knight snatched a vase from a church, prompting the local bishop to plead for its return. Shortly Clovis met with his men at Soissons to divide the spoils of war. There he asked for the vase, but the knight refused, shattering it with his axe. Without a word the King took the pieces and returned them to the bishop.

A year later Clovis saw the same knight at a military assembly. Before the gathered warriors, the King accused him of carrying a dirty axe and threw it to the ground in front of him. When the knight stooped to pick it up, Clovis brought his own axe down on the offender's head, sneering, 'Thus didst thou serve the vase of Soissons.'

Later in his reign Clovis established Paris as his capital, a useful central location to keep an eye on his various conquests. There he and Clothilde built the church that ultimately became Sainte-Geneviève, where they were buried side by side. During the French Revolution their tomb was desecrated and their ashes scattered to the winds.

Also on this day

43 BC: Octavian (future Augustus), Lepidus, and Mark Antony form the second Triumvirate * 1582: William Shakespeare marries Anne Hathaway * 1770: Twelve-year-old Horatio Nelson enters the British Navy * 1953: American playwright Eugene O'Neill dies

28 November

The story of the 'Eleanor Crosses'

1290 Throughout 36 years of happy marriage King Edward I had been devoted to his wife Eleanor, and during that time she had borne him no fewer than seventeen royal children. So when she died this day of a persistent fever, the King was sorely stricken.

Although originally Spanish (her father was the King of Castile), Eleanor might just as well have been English. She married Edward (then still a prince) in Spain when she was only eight years old and immediately went with him to his lands in Gascony and then came to England, still only ten years old.

When Eleanor was 26 (and already married for eighteen years), she became Queen of England on the ascension of her husband. That same year she accompanied him on crusade. When the royal couple were at Acre an assassin nearly killed him by attacking him with a poisoned knife. Tradition has it that Eleanor saved his life by sucking the poison from the wound. Whatever the truth of the matter, when they returned to England Edward was more devoted than ever to his wife, who was a moderating influence on his sometimes arrogant and even brutal behaviour.

In 1290 the couple were visiting Harby in Nottinghamshire when the Queen fell sick and died. Edward had her body brought to London for burial, and as a special demonstration of his love, he ordered built a beautiful stone cross at each place along the way where her body had rested for a night.

In all, eleven 'Eleanor Crosses' were carved, a few of which are still standing. The last was placed at a town near London called Charing. The town is no more, nor is its cross, but the place where it stood is still known as Charing Cross.

Also on this day

1680: Italian sculptor and architect Giovanni Bernini dies in Rome * 1757: English poet and painter William Blake is born * 1820: German Communist philosopher Friedrich Engels is born in Barmen

29 November

Cardinal Wolsey dies just in time

1530 Cardinal Thomas Wolsey was the son of a butcher and cattle dealer in Ipswich, but had become the second most powerful man in England through intelligence, diligence and an uncanny ability to give Henry VIII what he wanted. He was a short, corpulent man of earthy humour who was known for his arrogance, his vanity and his greed. But he was an outstanding administrator, and such talent, combined with his all-consuming ambition, had helped him to run England successfully for almost twenty years.

But now Wolsey had been cast out from the court he served, charged with high treason and summoned for trial. His first mistake had been building Hampton Court and staffing it with over 400 servants. His master King Henry simply took it over as far too good for a cardinal but just about right for a king.

But Wolsey's fatal error was his failure to gain Henry an annulment of his marriage to Catherine of Aragon. The Pope sided with the Queen under pressure from her nephew Holy Roman Emperor Charles V, the most powerful man in Europe.

On 28 November Wolsey arrived at Leicester Abbey in the custody of Sir William Kingston, the lieutenant of the Tower. Sick at heart but also in body, he lamented his fate, 'Had I but served God as diligently as I have my king, He would not have given me over in my grey hairs.' He died the next day at the age of 55.

Also on this day

1226: Louis IX (St Louis) of France is crowned at Reims * 1314: Philip IV (the Fair) of France dies * 1780: Austrian Empress Maria Theresa dies * 1797: Italian composer Domenico Donizetti is born * 1864: American cavalry units kill over 150 disarmed Cheyenne and Arapaho Indians during the Sand Creek massacre * 1924: Italian opera composer Giacomo Puccini dies

30 November

Oscar Wilde's last quip

1900 At the turn of the 21st century in the rue des Beaux Arts on Paris's Left Bank is one of Europe's most sophisticated hotels, somewhat self-consciously called simply 'L'Hôtel'. Each room is different, each impeccable in its décor.

At the turn of the 20th century, however, the hotel that occupied the same site was a far more humble establishment, and it was here that a poor and demoralised Oscar Wilde took lodging.

Almost twenty years before, Wilde had established himself as England's leading wit and playwright, over the years producing masterpieces such as *Lady Windermere's Fan* and *The Importance of Being Earnest*. He was also an inveterate traveller, which provoked a typical Wildean witticism, 'I never travel without my diary. One should always have something sensational to read in the train.' He married at 30 and had two children.

But Wilde's sexual preferences were homosexual, and in one of the great scandals of the time, at 41 he was convicted of sodomy and served two years in jail, his career and reputation entirely destroyed.

So Wilde fled to Paris, weak and prematurely aged. No doubt he wondered about his famous claim that he put only his talent into his books but his genius into his life.

Installed in the rue des Beaux Arts, Wilde this day was dying and he knew it. But he kept his celebrated wit to the end. His last words were, 'Either that wallpaper goes, or I do.'

Also on this day

1508: Italian architect Andrea Palladio is born in Padua * 1667: Irish writer Jonathan Swift is born in Dublin * 1835: American writer Samuel Clemens (Mark Twain) is born * 1874: British Prime Minister Winston Churchill is born at Blenheim Palace

1 December

Lady Astor becomes the first woman to sit in the House of Commons

1919 In the 654 years since Simon de Montfort, Earl of Leicester, had organised the very first British parliament in 1265, not a single woman had been a member. Today that changed for ever when Lady Nancy Witcher Astor took her seat in the House of Commons as MP for the Sutton division of Plymouth, becoming the first ever woman MP. (As a measure of her achievement, women in England had only been given the vote the previous year, and in America they were not enfranchised until 1920.)

Born of the rich Langhorne family near the sleepy town of Danville, Virginia, Nancy married richer, divorced her first husband and married yet richer still, to Waldorf Astor of the fabulously wealthy Astor clan. Waldorf's American great-great-grandfather John Jacob had made most of the money, and in 1890 Waldorf's father William had moved to England. After giving generously to the British war effort during the Great War, William had been rewarded with a title in 1917.

Waldorf had been a Member of Parliament but had given up his seat in 1919 when he succeeded to his father's viscountcy. This opening inspired Nancy, then 40, to stand in his place. To the astonishment of many, she was elected by a wide margin, and so an American (by birth anyway) became the first female member of the British Parliament. When someone suggested that her marriage to an Astor had helped her, she jokingly retorted, 'I married beneath me. All women do.'

Intelligent, quick-witted and afraid of neither man nor beast, Nancy Astor had a particular interest in what today we would call women's liberation. 'We are not asking for superiority [to men],' she said, 'for we have always had that. All we ask is equality.' Once while visiting the Churchill family's ancestral home at Blenheim Palace she started to harangue Winston Churchill about her favourite cause, a subject Churchill considered much of an irrelevance.

After several minutes of disagreement, she finally exclaimed, 'Winston, if I were married to you, I would put poison in your coffee!' 'And if you were my wife,' the great man replied, 'I'd drink it.'

Nancy Astor served in Parliament for 26 uninterrupted years, retiring only when she was 66. (Or, as she once told a friend, 'I refuse to admit that I am more than fifty-two, even if that makes my children illegitimate.') She lived on in luxury for another nineteen years, to die in the bosom of her family. During her final illness she showed she had lost none of her wit. Waking to find her relatives grouped around her bed, she asked, 'Am I dying or is this my birthday?'

Also on this day

1135: Henry I of England dies 'of a surfeit of lampreys' * 1455: Death of Lorenzo Ghiberti, the sculptor who created the 'Gates of Paradise' bronze doors for the baptistery of the cathedral of Florence * 1521: The Medici Pope Leo X dies

2 December

American abolitionist John Brown is hanged

1859 It is said that fanatics make good martyrs, and John Brown, who was hanged today, was a perfect example. Hawk-nosed, hard-eyed and bearded, he even looked the part he played.

Born in Connecticut in 1800, he had failed at numerous trades: tanner, land speculator, drover and travelling salesman. Moving his large family from place to place, he became a fanatical abolitionist, once demonstrating his ardour by living in a free black community in New York State. Later he moved to the Kansas Territory and led a night-time guerrilla raid against a pro-slavery community in which five men were dragged from their cabins and beaten to death.

In October 1859 Brown led a ragtag bunch of sixteen whites and five blacks on a raid on Harper's Ferry, Virginia (today West

Virginia). After an early exchange of shots in which two bystanders were killed, he set up headquarters in the federal armoury that his men had captured. For two days and nights he holed up there with some 60 hostages, waiting for nearby slaves to rise up to claim their freedom. By then state militia had surrounded the armoury, and on the morning of 18 October a company of US Marines under the command of Colonel Robert E. Lee stormed it. A Marine lieutenant beat Brown to the ground with his sword, and ten of Brown's men were killed in the action, including two of his sons.

Brown was quickly taken to Charleston (now in West Virginia), tried, convicted of murder, treason against the state and inciting slave insurrection, and sentenced to be hanged.

About eleven o'clock this morning he was brought to the field of execution, where a crowd of 1,000 waited in anticipation, along with 1,500 soldiers. He arrived riding in a furniture wagon, sitting on his own coffin, his arms tied at the elbows.

The shabbily dressed prisoner was calm and courteous. He mounted the scaffold without resistance and offered his neck for the noose. His head was then covered with a white hood.

The sheriff asked Brown if he wanted to signal the drop himself by throwing a handkerchief, but the tired old man replied, 'No, I don't care. I don't want you to keep me waiting unnecessarily.' These were his last words, spoken civilly, without emotion. Then a hush fell over the crowd until there was total silence, and the sheriff cut the rope with a sharp blow from his hatchet.

Within eighteen months Brown's cause was vindicated; the Civil War had begun, and 'John Brown's Body' soon became a favourite marching song of Northern troops.

Also on this day

1547: Spanish conquistador Hernán Cortés dies in Seville * 1697: The newly rebuilt St Paul's Cathedral in London reopens * 1804: Napoleon crowns himself Emperor * 1805: Napoleon defeats the Austrians at Austerlitz * 1814: French writer, philosopher and pornographer the marquis de Sade dies * 1851: Louis Napoleon stages a coup d'état, to become dictator of France * 1852: The French Senate passes a resolution making Napoleon III Emperor

3 December

The first French dauphin

1368 Born on this day was King Charles VI of France, known as Charles l'Insensé for the 44 fits of insanity that he suffered during the last 30 years of his life.

King for 42 years, Charles was one of the longest reigning and most disastrous monarchs in French history. His madness – attacks that lasted up to nine months – permitted his greedy cousins, the Dukes of Burgundy and Orléans, to usurp his power while battling each other. Meanwhile his sensuous wife, Isabeau of Bavaria, was trying to gain influence for herself, simultaneously cuckolding the King with a legion of lovers. Into this chaos marched England's King Henry V, who smashed the French at Agincourt and became de facto co-ruler of the country.

Charles has one unique distinction. On his birth he was given as his apanage (the grant of land given by his father, Charles V) the Dauphiné, a region in south-eastern France, thus becoming the first royal dauphin, the title given to all subsequent heirs to the French throne.

Although the French word dauphin also means dolphin, the title has no real aquatic origins. It is a personal name that appears as early as the 4th century, apparently derived from a family's coat of arms featuring a dolphin (*dauphin* in French). In the 12th century a certain Guigues IV Dauphin was ruler of what was then called Viennois, and most of his successors also used the name until it became a title and the territory began to be called the Dauphiné.

Also on this day

1469: Leading Florentine citizens call on Lorenzo de' Medici to take over the rule of Florence * 1857: Polish-born English writer Joseph Conrad is born in what is now Berdichev, Russia * 1894: Scottish writer Robert Louis Stevenson dies of a stroke in Samoa

4 December

Death of the great Cardinal Richelieu

1642 Cardinal Richelieu, Duke and First Minister to King Louis XIII, had virtually ruled France for eighteen years. Brilliant, calculating, pragmatic and unrelenting, he had the clearest of visions of the greatness and glory that he thought his country deserved.

When he was still young, Pope Paul V had said of him, 'He will prove a great rascal.' At least in the eyes of Richelieu's adversaries, that prediction proved true, as the mighty cardinal crushed his enemies at home and confounded them abroad to make France the greatest power in Europe.

But the all-powerful Richelieu had a history of ill health. He had been afflicted with migraines since the age of 25 and also suffered from those classic symptoms of over-stressed executives, ulcers and haemorrhoids. Further, he had a tubercular osteitis on his right arm that was evidenced by a festering sore. His constitution was weak, and he was prey to frequent fevers.

By 1642 Richelieu was 57, sick and weary. In November he was stricken with pneumonia compounded by pleurisy. After persuading King Louis to appoint Cardinal Mazarin as his successor, the great cardinal waited for death in the Palais Cardinal. At midday on 4 December he summoned his favourite niece to bid farewell. She told him that she had heard of a vision that predicted that he would not die at this time. 'My niece,' said the cardinal who had dealt in worldly power his entire career, 'there are no truths except those in the gospel; it is only in them that you should believe.' He died that afternoon.

On hearing of Richelieu's death, the sceptical old Pope Urban VIII commented, 'If there is a God, Cardinal Richelieu will have much to answer for. But if not – well, he had a successful life.'

Also on this day

1154: The only Englishman to become Pope, Nicholas Breakspear, is elected Pope Adrian IV * 1795: Scottish author Thomas Carlyle is born * 1892: Spanish dictator Francisco Franco is born in El Ferrol

5 December

Requiem for Mozart

1791 At five minutes to one o'clock on this cold, damp December night died the composer many consider to be supreme in the history of Western music, Wolfgang Amadeus Mozart.

In the last months of his life Mozart completed some of his very greatest works. His clarinet concerto was published on 29 September, and the most loved of all his operas, *Die Zauberflöte* (*The Magic Flute*), premiered in Vienna the very next day. At the time of his death he was finishing his magnificent Requiem.

At the end of November Mozart had taken to his bed in his apartment in the Rauhensteingasse in Vienna, but he continued to work on his Requiem. The day before he died part of it was sung at his bedside. Undoubtedly aware of his coming end, the composer remarked, 'Didn't I tell you that I was writing this Requiem for myself?' He then slipped into unconsciousness.

The exact cause of Mozart's death is still debated. At the time it was attributed to 'severe miliary fever', but later diagnoses have included heart disease, rheumatic fever, typhus, trichinosis, kidney failure, broncho-pneumonia caused by a streptococcal infection and the fearful-sounding Schönlein-Henoch syndrome. Perhaps it was the uncertainty of the cause that immediately engendered speculation that his demise had not been so natural after all but the result of poisoning by the rival composer Antonio Salieri. One source maintains that in his final illness Mozart complained to his wife, 'Surely someone has poisoned me.' Most historians consider this no more than a plaintive description of how unwell he felt. Salieri, the Emperor's distinguished *Hofkapellmeister*, is said to have admitted to poisoning Mozart from professional envy, but at the time of the supposed confession he was already unhinged.

Mozart died two months before his 35th birthday. He was buried with scant ceremony in an unmarked multiple grave, and, at his wife's request, his Requiem was completed by the minor Austrian composer Franz Xaver Süssmayr.

Also on this day

63 BC: Roman consul Cicero denounces the agitator Catiline in the Roman Senate * 1926: French Impressionist painter Claude Monet dies * 1933: Prohibition is repealed in the USA after more than thirteen years of privation

6 December

The true story of St Nick

AD 343 Today in the small town of Myra on the Mediterranean coast of Lycia (now Demre in Turkey) a popular local bishop named Nicholas died, whose legend would enthral millions for centuries to come. Nicholas had been born a pagan in the Lycian seaport of Patara, but converted to Christianity in his youth. After travels in the Holy Land he returned to become Bishop of Myra, only 50 miles from his birthplace. There he was imprisoned during Emperor Diocletian's ferocious persecution of the Christians but released when Constantine came to power.

Nicholas gained a saintly reputation by generous deeds for the poor and despondent, including the miraculous reassembling and reviving of three small children who had been carved into pieces by a greedy butcher trying to pass them off as spring lamb.

His most famous charitable deed concerned three sisters who were on the point of being forced to sell themselves into prostitution because their father could not afford dowries. Hearing of their plight, Nicholas dropped bags filled with gold coins down their chimney, one of which landed in a stocking that had been hung up by the fireplace to dry.

When the good Bishop Nicholas died in 343, he was buried in Myra, where his tomb quickly became a shrine. We do not know if he was ever officially canonised, but nonetheless he was soon considered the patron saint of some seemingly conflicting groups: prisoners and judges, sailors and virgins, pirates and merchants, and charitable guilds and pawnbrokers. So celebrated was he that in 1087 some Italian sailors filched his bones and transported them to Bari on Italy's Adriatic coast. There they remain, enshrined in the Basilica di San Nicola, built especially to house them.

During the Middle Ages the cult of St Nicholas was widespread in Europe, where he was depicted with a full beard, wearing the red robes of a bishop. The cult gradually died away except in Holland, where he was known as Sinterklaas (a Dutch corruption of Saint Nicholas). The Dutch in turn took the tradition with them to the New World when they colonised New Amsterdam (New York) in the 17th century. There Sinterklaas soon evolved into Santa Claus.

Today in Great Britain and America Santa Claus still wears red, is still full-bearded and is known to drop down the chimney on Christmas Eve to fill deserving children's stockings hung by the fireplace. In much of Europe he appears on his feast day on 6 December, the anniversary of his death, when children put their shoes outside their bedroom doors in the hope that they will be filled with fruit and sweets.

In spite of the evidence from millions of small children around the world, some remain sceptical. In 1969 Pope Paul VI had the Feast of St Nicholas dropped from the Catholic calendar, citing the lack of documentation of St Nick's life and deeds.

Also on this day

1779: French painter Jean-Baptiste-Siméon Chardin dies * 1815: Napoleonic marshal Michel Ney is executed in the courtyard of the Palais Luxembourg in Paris on orders from Louis XVIII * 1882: British novelist Anthony Trollope dies * 1917: Finland declares independence from Russia

7 December

Cicero faces his executioners

43 BC 'At least make sure you cut my head off properly', he said to the soldier seconds before his death, and then leaned out of the litter in which he was being carried to offer his throat to his executioner. So on this day died 63-year-old Marcus Tullius Cicero, the Roman world's greatest orator, sometime philosopher, occasional poet, senator, consul and backer of wrong horses.

Cicero had been born in the Roman provinces of a rich and influential family. During his early years in Rome he became one of the city's greatest trial lawyers, when he perfected his rhetorical style. First a senator, later consul, Cicero was a strong believer in the old values of the Roman Republic at the very time when the expansion of the state was making its labyrinthine systems of checks and balances an unworkable way to run an empire. As consul he thwarted the Catiline conspiracy to overthrow the government and summarily executed some of the plotters, dramatically proclaiming their death to the waiting crowd with the single word *vixerunt* (they are dead). But some of the conspirators came from exalted families, and their relations never forgave Cicero for executing them without trial.

Later Cicero backed Pompey as representative of the 'legitimate government' in his fight against Caesar and survived Caesar's triumph only because Caesar spared all his opponents. But after Caesar's assassination, in which he took no part, Cicero praised the murderers, while repeatedly haranguing the Senate against the unrestrainedly ambitious Mark Antony, who claimed to be Caesar's political heir. In one fiery speech he blamed all of Rome's troubles on Mark Antony, calling him an embezzler and a criminal, a drunken lecher who spent his time with outlaws and prostitutes.

Worse, Cicero seriously underestimated Octavian (the future Augustus), suggesting to his colleagues that 'the young man should be given praise and distinctions – and then be disposed of'. When his remarks were reported, Cicero had gained another mortal enemy.

In 43 BC Mark Antony, Octavian and Lepidus formed an alliance against Caesar's assassins, taking the opportunity to cleanse the state of other undesirables as well. Cicero's name was added to the proscribed list, which stripped him of all property and meant that any Roman citizen could kill him without fear of state reprisal.

Cicero refused to flee from Italy, dramatically vowing, 'I will die in the country I have so often saved.' He headed south by boat to his estate in Formiae, on the Mediterranean coast about 90 miles from Rome, but his servants, aghast at seeing him in so much danger, forced him into his litter to escape. But they were too late. A force of Roman soldiers caught up with him on the road and dispatched the venerable statesman. His head and hands were cut off, to be nailed to the speakers' platform at the Forum in Rome, but not before Mark Antony's wife Fulvia had pierced his tongue with a long hairpin, symbolising the lies he had told about her husband.

Also on this day

1598: Italian sculptor and architect Giovanni Bernini is born in Naples * 1709: Dutch landscape painter Meindert Hobbema dies in Amsterdam * 1837: Benjamin Disraeli makes his maiden speech in the House of Commons * 1941: Japanese warplanes launch a surprise attack on the American base at Pearl Harbor

8 December

Horace the poet (and soldier)

65 BC Today in Venusia (now Venosa) in the ankle of southern Italy was born Quintus Horatius Flaccus – known to us as Horace – one of the greatest poets of the Roman world. He came from low estate (he was the son of a freed slave) but rose to become poet laureate and friend to the Emperor Augustus. Much of his success was due to his father, who was devoted to his son and gave him a first-class education, including a time in Athens, then the cultural capital of the world.

While Horace was a twenty-year-old student in Athens, Julius Caesar was assassinated by a cabal of Roman republicans who feared he would make himself king. Shortly two of the leading conspirators, Marcus Junius Brutus and Gaius Cassius, found themselves under attack from Caesar's vengeful heir Octavian and

Caesar's sometime protégé Mark Antony. Horace, then the young student liberal, hurried to enlist with the republican cause. Although short, podgy and unathletic, he radiated enthusiasm and was appointed *tribunus militum* (a junior officer) and given co-command of a legion.

The two armies met in Greece for the two battles of Philippi. Horace held his ground in the first battle, but when Brutus's army was overwhelmed in the second, the poet-to-be dropped his shield and ran from the field, an experience that may have temporarily slipped his mind when he later wrote, 'Dulce et decorum est pro patria mori.' (Lovely and honourable it is, to die for your country!)

Making his way back to Italy, Horace was broke and without resources, except for his poetical genius, which he used to earn a living. Fortunately, his brilliant work soon brought friendship with the established poet Virgil, who introduced him to Maecenas, a friend and political adviser to Octavian (soon to become the Emperor Augustus).

Maecenas not only became Horace's devoted friend but also bought him a country retreat near Tivoli. There he composed many of his greatest works, often reflecting his own buoyant nature and love of life. 'Misce stultitiam brevem: / Dulce est desipere in loco', he writes. (Mix a little foolishness with your serious plans: it's lovely to be silly at the right moment.) Most famously, he advises, 'Dum loquimur, fugerit invida / Aetas: carpe diem, quam minimum credula postero'. (While we talk, time will have meanly run on: Seize the day, don't count on the future in the slightest.)

In time Maecenas presented Horace to Augustus, against whom he had fought at Philippi. The open-minded Emperor admired his work and, on the death of Virgil, made him virtually poet laureate of the Empire.

Horace expired in Rome on 27 November in the year 8 BC, naming Augustus as his heir. Years earlier he had written, 'Non omnis moriar.' (I shall not die completely.) That we still enjoy his poetry to this day is proof that he was right.

Also on this day

1542: Mary, Queen of Scots is born, Linlithgow Palace, Scotland * 1813: Beethoven's Seventh Symphony is performed for the first time, with Beethoven as conductor * 1914: A British force sinks the German cruisers *Scharnhorst*, *Gneisenau*, *Nuremberg* and *Leipzig* in the Battle of the Falkland Islands * 1941: The US and Great Britain declare war on Japan

9 December

Gladstone becomes Prime Minister

1868 Today William Gladstone began the first of his four terms as Prime Minister, an office he held for fifteen years. About this man of lofty principles and stern moral probity, his great rival Benjamin Disraeli once commented, 'He has not a single redeeming defect.'

Gladstone was first elected to Parliament in December 1832 as a Tory but progressively moved to the left, claiming towards the end of his career that 'I will back the masses against the classes.' By the time he became Prime Minister in 1868, he was leading the Liberal Party. Although undoubtedly highly principled, he was seen by his enemies as humourless and sanctimonious, as demonstrated by his comment, 'I think [the clergy] are not severe enough on congregations. They do not sufficiently lay upon the souls and consciences of their hearers their moral obligations, and probe their hearts and bring up their whole lives and actions to the bar of conscience.'

Until he died in 1881, Disraeli was not only Gladstone's most formidable opponent but also a man of wit and charm. When asked to define the difference between a calamity and a misfortune, Disraeli innocently answered, 'If, for instance, Mr William Gladstone were to fall into the river, that would be a misfortune. But if anyone were to pull him out, that would be a calamity!'

A woman who happened to sit next to Gladstone one night at dinner and next to Disraeli the next encapsulated the difference between the two men: 'When I left the dining room after sitting next to Mr Gladstone I thought he was the cleverest man in England, but after sitting next to Mr Disraeli I thought I was the cleverest woman in England.'

Gladstone was on the side of history; he espoused a long list of liberal causes, almost all of which are common practice today. He fought for free trade, better working conditions for London dock workers, the admission of Jews to Parliament, reduced defence spending, Irish home rule, women's right to own their own property, free elementary education, and the secret ballot in voting. He was also highly influential in broadening the franchise to include a much wider range of working men.

Gladstone's reforming zeal extended even to his private life. He and his wife famously established a 'rescue' home for prostitutes and at night he would occasionally trawl the London streets for fallen women in an attempt to persuade them to take up a different life.

As Gladstone grew older, he became increasingly insufferable with his ponderous air of noble rectitude. Fellow politician Henry Labouchere once famously remarked that 'he did not object to the old man always having a card up his sleeve, but he did object to his insinuation that the Almighty had placed it there'.

Even Gladstone's wife occasionally seemed overawed by her husband's righteousness. On one occasion several guests at the Gladstone house found themselves in debate over the meaning of a biblical text. 'Well,' a guest commented, 'there is One above who knows all things.' 'Yes,' replied the earnest Mrs Gladstone, 'and Mr Gladstone will be coming down in a few minutes.'

When the Liberals won the general election of 1892, Gladstone became Prime Minister for the fourth time at the age of 82, a record among British Prime Ministers. Among those who both objected to his liberal policies and detested his demeanour was Queen Victoria, who complained that he 'addresses me as if I was a public meeting'. When she heard the results of the election she insisted that it was 'a defect in our much-famed Constitution to have to part with an admirable government like Lord Salisbury's for no question of any importance, or any particular reason, merely on account of the number of votes'. It was with great reluctance that the Queen, who was herself 73, entrusted the government 'to the shaking hand of an old, wild, incomprehensible man of eighty-two and a half'.

In 1893 Gladstone suffered the indignity of having the House of Lords reject his Irish Home Rule bill by a vote of 419 to 41, the greatest majority ever recorded. He then found himself in total disagreement with his own Cabinet over the navy's budget and resigned, using his failing hearing and eyesight as an excuse. Retiring to his country house in Wales, he developed cancer of the palate and died on 19 May 1898.

During Gladstone's last years in Parliament, Randolph Churchill had described him as 'an old man in a hurry'. His son Winston had a more acerbic summing up: 'Mr Gladstone read Homer for fun, which I thought served him right.'

Also on this day

1608: English poet John Milton is born * 1641: Flemish portrait painter Anthony Van Dyck dies * 1854: Alfred, Lord Tennyson publishes 'The Charge of the Light Brigade'

10 December

The abdication of Edward VIII

1936 If you had listened to the BBC this evening at 10.00, you would have heard a thin voice saying, 'You must believe me when I tell you that I have found it impossible to carry the heavy burden of responsibility and to discharge my duties as King, as I wish to do, without the help and support of the woman I love.'

It was the voice of the former King Edward VIII – the man who would *not* be King – speaking from Windsor Castle to inform a stunned nation that he was giving up the British crown. Just hours before the broadcast he had signed the instrument of his abdication in favour of his younger brother who was now King George VI.

Edward's reign had lasted 325 days, since the death of his father, King George V, on 20 January. At the end, he had to choose between marriage and the throne. He chose Wallis Simpson, whose two divorces, the second granted only weeks earlier, had rendered her unsuitable as a wife for a monarch, at least in the eyes of those in the British establishment who knew of the King's intention to marry her. Among the powerful opposition to the marriage were the King's mother, the Archbishop of Canterbury, the Prime Minister Stanley Baldwin, the Cabinet ministers, and the Prime Ministers of the largest dominions in the British Empire. At last it became clear to Edward that if he persisted in his plan to marry Mrs Simpson, the Government would resign, bringing on elections in which the main issue would be the King's personal affairs, with all the attendant damage to the monarchy such a debate would create.

Some hours after the broadcast, HMS *Fury* slipped out of Portsmouth harbour bearing the Duke of Windsor, as Edward would now be known, to France where Wallis waited. Of that moment of departure from crown and country, he later said, 'So far as I was concerned, love had triumphed.'

For many, however, it appeared that what love had triumphed over was duty, responsibility and national tradition. In Britain, where a press ban had kept the public ignorant of the events leading up to the abdication, the reaction was restrained, the mood one of regret, of shame for some. Among many people, there was resentment, not only towards the woman who had wooed away their King, but also towards the King who deserted them for her.

Edward married Wallis the following year in France shortly after her divorce decree became final. It was a small ceremony, held in the Château de Cande in the Loire valley, with only sixteen guests. Wallis became Duchess of Windsor, but in their displeasure at the marriage the British royal family had withheld from her the expected title of Her Royal Highness. Snubbed, the Windsors chose thereafter to live abroad, glamorous irrelevancies in luxurious exile.

Also on this day

1475: Florentine painter Paolo Uccello dies * 1848: Louis Napoleon is elected President of France * 1896: Swedish dynamite inventor Alfred

Nobel dies; the anniversary of his death has been used ever since for the presentation of Nobel prizes * 1898: Spain and the United States sign a peace treaty to end the Spanish–American War

11 December

James II flees from London, never to return

1688 On this day King James II of England hurried from St James's Palace in London to sail down the Thames before his son-in-law William of Orange and his daughter Mary could arrive and usurp the monarchy. As he raced down the river the enraged King petulantly dropped the Great Seal of England overboard, determined that no one but he should have this symbol of authority. No doubt his rage was even greater when he later learned that, by an incredible stroke of luck, a fisherman caught the Seal in his net and turned it over to William, now William III of England.

In his younger years James (the Duke of York at the time) showed both mettle and ability. When he was just fifteen, a year before his father Charles I was beheaded, James had evaded zealous Roundheads and escaped to France during the English Civil War. At 21 he joined Louis XIV's army under the legendary general Turenne, and proved to be an able commander, fighting in four campaigns. Later, when his brother Charles (II) gained the British throne to start the Restoration, James fought valiantly at the Battle of the Dunes. Then, back in England during Charles's reign, he became Lord High Admiral and planned the British seizure of New Amsterdam from the Dutch, renaming it New York in his own honour.

Although capable, James was stubborn, humourless and arrogant. Worse, he became a devoted Catholic during a period when Catholicism was virtually illegal in England. He had been admitted to the Church in 1669 but at first, on his brother's insistence, continued outwardly to practise Protestantism. But in 1673 he refused to take an anti-Catholic oath and the same year he married the staunchly (and publicly) Catholic Mary of Modena, causing near hysteria among the country's devout Protestants, who feared James's ascension should his childless brother die. Wild rumours grew that Catholics had developed a 'Popish Plot' to murder Charles so that James could inherit the throne.

Then, on 6 February 1685, Charles II did die (of kidney failure, not assassination) and James, Duke of York, became King James II.

High on principle but low on common sense, the haughty new King grandly informed his subjects that 'our Kings derive not their rule from the people but from God; that to Him only are they accountable, that it belongs not to subjects, either to create or censure, but to honour and obey their sovereign'. For just such sentiments had these same subjects removed the head of James's father some 39 years before. Worse, James started to bring Catholics into important government positions, formed new army regiments with Catholic officers and even directed that Magdalen College, Oxford, should be given over to Catholics. In the meantime, the always suspicious James became almost paranoid about real and imagined plots against him.

In late autumn 1687 what should have been joyful news proved to be the last straw for the country's uncompromising Protestants – the 30-year-old Queen was pregnant, and the British monarchy might soon have a Catholic heir. (Previously the direct heirs had been James's two daughters, Mary and Anne, who had been raised as Protestants on the insistence of their uncle, King Charles, but if the new baby was a boy, he would stand first in line to the throne.)

Then, in May of the following year, James ordered read aloud in churches throughout the kingdom a Declaration of Indulgence that, in effect, established freedom of religion for Catholics. Next, in June Queen Mary produced a young son (James Edward, in the future to be known as the Old Pretender). By the end of the month leading Protestants had written to William of Orange inviting him to invade the country and seize the crown. On 15 November William landed at Brixham, and after a month of desertions among his own army, James fled London, and was briefly intercepted in Kent but then allowed to leave for France on 23 December. That was the last

England would see of James II, the man whom his brother's mistress Nell Gwyn had mockingly christened 'dismal Jimmy'.

Also on this day

1475: Pope Leo X, the son of Lorenzo the Magnificent, is born in Florence * 1803: French composer Hector Berlioz is born * 1941: German dictator Adolf Hitler declares war on the United States

12 December

Robert Browning dies at 77

1889 'Fear death? – to feel the fog in my throat, / The mist in my face.'

So had Robert Browning evocatively described the coming of death, which came to him today in Venice, as he was struck down by what looked to be a simple cold but which the 77-year-old poet could not withstand.

The son of a clerk in the Bank of England, Browning was born and brought up in London, showed little interest in formal education and lived at home with his parents until he was 34, writing poems and plays. By most accounts he was attractive and entertaining, and he is praised by one biographer for 'the perpetual boyishness, the hearty enthusiasm, the noisy ebullience, the invincible optimism, the graciousness and personal charm' that everyone found in him.

In his early years Browning's poetry was only marginally successful. One of his better-known works was the narrative poem *Sordello*, which became famous for its obscurity. When the editor of *Punch* tried to read it while recuperating from an illness, he became so confused that he feared he had suffered brain damage. Later in life Browning was asked for the meaning of a particularly bewildering passage. The poet reread his own lines aloud and then replied, 'When I wrote that, God and I knew what it meant, but now God alone knows!'

When he reached 33 Browning was still a bachelor, but then he met the woman of his life. Living with her parents in Wimpole Street was a 39-year-old spinster named Elizabeth Barrett. Since the age of fifteen she had been a semi-invalid suffering from some sort of bone disease, but she was also a poet – in fact, a better-known one than Browning. But she had read some of his poems, and in her work *Poems* included words of praise for Browning. In January 1845, although he had still not met her he responded with a telegram saying, 'I love your verses with all my heart, dear Miss Barrett. I do, as I say, love these books with all my heart – and I love you too.'

A few months later they met and a romance developed, one that she was careful to keep secret from her autocratic father. Browning later related that he gained great encouragement from an unusual source. One day in his library he asked himself, 'What will be the extent of my love for her?' and took a book at random. Only then did he see that it carried the unpromising title of *Cerutti's Italian Grammar*. He looked down to see what text would meet his eye, hoping for a positive word like 'together' or even just 'mine'. To his delighted surprise he found himself reading a sentence in a translation exercise, 'If we love in the other world as we do in this, I shall love thee to eternity.'

In September 1846 the couple married clandestinely, and a week later decamped for Italy, where they lived in genteel poverty, mostly in Florence, surrounded by ex-pat English and Americans, largely ignoring the Italians.

Although there is no doubt that Browning was devoted to her, Elizabeth must often have been a wearisome companion. In spite of her invalidity, she continued to write sentimental and successful poetry ('How do I love thee? Let me count the ways'). But she also became impassioned with Italian politics and devoted to the French Emperor Napoleon III, whom, despite all the evidence, she obstinately saw as a champion of democracy. She also turned to spiritualism and the occult under the guidance of an American named Daniel Home, whom Browning denounced as a fraud. Furthermore, she became addicted to laudanum, a habit her husband attempted to cure by persuading her to drink Chianti instead.

Nonetheless, the couple lived contentedly, he showing a continued tolerance and good humour towards his difficult wife and towards others as well. Once he was waylaid at a party by a guest who insisted on questioning him endlessly about his poems. Desperate to escape, Browning apologised to his interrogator. 'But my dear fellow, this is too bad', he said, turning away. 'I am monopolising you.'

In the summer of 1861 Elizabeth, still only 55, came down with something resembling the flu and died. Just before leaving for Italy sixteen years before, Browning had written one of his more famous lines, 'Oh, to be in England / now that April's there'. Now, with his wife gone, he returned there and a few years later produced his finest work, *The Ring and the Book*, a lengthy dramatic monologue based on a 17th-century Roman murder trial. He became even more celebrated than his wife had been and when he died was buried in Westminster Abbey.

Also on this day

1800: Washington DC is established as the capital of the United States * 1821: French novelist Gustave Flaubert is born in Rouen * 1863: Norwegian painter Edvard Munch is born * 1915: American crooner Frank Sinatra is born in Hoboken, New Jersey

13 December

Samuel Johnson dies in London

1784 'When a man is tired of London, he is tired of life; for there is in London all that life can afford.' So believed Samuel Johnson, the greatest conversationalist of the 18th century, who may himself have been tired of life when he died this evening at 7.15 in the city he loved.

Son of a bookseller, Johnson was considered both a leading literary figure and a formidable eccentric during his time. In his youth he had contracted scrofula, which left him scarred on the neck and face. A great, lumbering man with an erratic temper, he is unforgettably described by Macaulay: 'The gigantic body, the huge massy face, seamed with the scars of disease, the brown coat, the black worsted stockings, the grey wig with the scorched foretop, the dirty hands, the nails bitten and pared to the quick.'

Johnson's most famous work was his *Dictionary of the English Language*, which he published in 1755 after eight years of work. It contains some 40,000 entries, all articulate, many arresting and some amusing. With self-deprecating humour, he defined 'lexicographer' as 'a writer of dictionaries; a harmless drudge'. And surely he had his tongue firmly in his cheek with his definition of 'network': 'Anything reticulated or decussated at equal distances, with interstices between the intersections.' Because of the success of this work, he came to be known as 'Dictionary Johnson'. Ten years after the publication of his dictionary Johnson received an honorary Doctor of Laws degree from Trinity College, Dublin, thus gaining the title 'Dr'.

Although he maintained that 'no man but a blockhead ever wrote, except for money', Johnson achieved only moderate financial success, as his passion was literature rather than financial reward.

In spite of the admiration of his many literary friends, Johnson suffered from frequent depression, experiencing two nervous breakdowns. A religious man who nonetheless feared death, he had his watch engraved in Greek with the memento mori 'The night cometh'. He was also in severe physical discomfort for most of his life, plagued by a constant swelling of his legs and chronic bronchitis.

A year before his death Johnson suffered a stroke, while still in continual distress from his other illnesses. Depressed but determined to soldier on, he wrote to an acquaintance, 'I will be conquered [by death]; I will not capitulate.' Conquered he was at the end of 1784 at the age of 75. Here is the account given by his great biographer, James Boswell, of Johnson's last moments: 'Having, as has already been mentioned, made his will on the 8th and 9th of December, and settled all his worldly affairs, he languished till Monday, the 13th of that month, when he expired, about seven o'clock in the evening, with so little apparent pain that his attendants hardly perceived when his dissolution took place.' He is buried in Westminster Abbey.

Much of our knowledge of Johnson comes from Boswell's monumental biography. Published seven years after the good doctor's death, *The Life of Samuel Johnson LL.D.* recounts many of Johnson's pithy epigrams such as 'Patriotism is the last refuge of a scoundrel', and provides an imperishable portrait of a literary man whose work is now largely unread but whose personality fascinates us still.

Also on this day

1250: Holy Roman Emperor Frederick II dies * 1466: Florentine sculptor Donatello dies * 1553: France's first Bourbon king Henri IV is born * 1642: Abel Tasman discovers New Zealand * 1944: Russian painter Wassily Kandinsky dies * 1961: American primitive painter Grandma Moses dies at the age of 101

14 December

George Washington dies hard

1799 Today at about ten in the evening George Washington, America's first president and its greatest 18th-century general, died quietly in his bed at the family home at Mount Vernon, the Virginia estate originally owned by his great-grandfather.

Washington was an active and robust man who delighted in the outdoors and horseback rides around his property. Two mornings earlier, after writing a reply to a letter from Alexander Hamilton on the subject of a military academy for the young republic, he rode for several hours in the damp cold of a snowy Virginia December, to return home frozen and exhausted. The next morning, suffering from a sore throat, he remained in the house to pursue farm business at his desk. Late in the afternoon, however, when the weather cleared, he went outside to mark trees for removal. At dinner he was hoarse and his cold had worsened, but he was cheerful and afterwards read aloud to his wife Martha from journals recently arrived. He refused the suggestion of medicine for his condition, preferring, he said, to 'let it go as it came'.

The next day he was unmistakably ill, suffering from fever and acute laryngitis, possibly with diphtheria. The local doctor James Craik ordered the former president to be bled and to gargle with a mixture of vinegar, butter and molasses.

By the morning of 14 December it was clear that Craik's prescriptions were ineffectual, for Washington was still in great pain and sinking fast. He knew his demise was imminent. For fear of being buried alive, he instructed his secretary, 'Do not let my body be put into the vault in less than three days after I am dead.'

Facing death with serenity, just before the end he murmured, 'I die hard, but I am not afraid to go.' His last words were, ''Tis well.' So departed the nation's Founding Father at the age of 67.

Also on this day

1503: French astrologer and charlatan Nostradamus is born in Saint-Rémy * 1861: Prince Albert dies of typhoid at Windsor Castle * 1911: Norwegian Roald Amundsen and his expedition become the first to reach the South Pole, 35 days before Captain Scott

15 December

Napoleon divorces Joséphine

1809 Perhaps it was because she had bought 524 pairs of shoes that year alone. Or perhaps it was because she was 46 while he was still only 40 – and he thought that a delicious Austrian princess of eighteen was available. Or perhaps it was really because she had borne him no children in over thirteen years of marriage, he needed an heir and he now knew he could father one, having recently impregnated his mistress. Whatever the true reason, on this day the

Emperor Napoleon divorced his wife Joséphine. 'I love you still,' he told her, 'but in politics there is no heart, only head.'

The ceremony took place in Napoleon's study in the Tuileries. First the Emperor signed the decree, then Joséphine. As soon as the witnesses had added their signatures, Joséphine fled from the room in tears, leaning on the arm of Hortense de Beauharnais, her daughter by her first marriage.

Joséphine moved to Malmaison, still on cordial terms with her ex-husband, but she died there only five years later, while he was in exile on the Island of Elba. Sadly, she never knew that her grandson, not Napoleon's, would one day rule France, for Hortense had married Napoleon's brother Louis. Their son was Napoleon III.

Napoleon died in 1821, but his body was returned to Paris in 1840, where a great funeral was held on the exact anniversary of his divorce.

Also on this day

AD 37: Roman Emperor Nero is born * 1640: Portugal gains independence from Spain * 1675: Dutch painter Jan Vermeer dies * 1734: English painter George Romney is born * 1791: The Bill of Rights' ten amendments become part of the US Constitution * 1832: Engineer and tower builder Gustave Eiffel is born

16 December

The Boston Tea Party

1773 The colonial Americans had just about had enough. Restricted by British law from many types of manufacturing, the colonies' sole role had been arbitrarily defined by the Parliament in London as purchasers of British manufactured goods and suppliers of raw materials – except for some, like wool, in which the British had their own interest.

Britain had also given the foundering East India Company a

monopoly of the colonial tea trade, including the sole right to transport the tea in its own ships.

In early December 1773 the ships *Dartmouth*, *Eleanor* and *Beaver* of the East India Company reached Boston Harbor, but a furious populace refused to allow the tea to be landed. In retaliation, the British governor Thomas Hutchinson, already hugely unpopular because of his repressive measures, commanded the ships to remain in the harbour and posted two warships to enforce the order.

Led by the radical propagandist Samuel Adams, some 2,000 Americans gathered at the wharf on the afternoon of 16 December. Then a smaller group of about 60 protestors, some disguised as Mohawk Indians, boarded the three ships and flung the cargo of 342 cases of tea into Boston Harbor.

The incident at Griffin's Wharf was not the protest of a mob but a carefully organised political response, a true act of revolution. It provoked Governor Hutchinson to close Boston Harbor, caused much suffering among the citizens of Boston, and pushed the colonies one step closer to revolution. In time, however, it became remembered as a slightly comic affair, fondly celebrated as the Boston Tea Party. For its centennial observance in 1873 Oliver Wendell Holmes wrote 'The Ballad of the Tea Party', which hinted at the radical spirit of the original day with these splendid, mocking lines:

An evening party, – only that
No formal invitation,
No gold-laced coat, no stiff cravat,
No feast in contemplation,
No silk-robed dames, no fiddling band,
No flowers no songs no dancing –
A tribe of red men, axe in hand,
Behold the guests advancing.

Also on this day

1653: Oliver Cromwell is declared Lord Protector of England * 1689: The British Parliament enacts a Bill of Rights * 1770: German composer

Ludwig van Beethoven is born * 1944: Germans launch a surprise attack against American positions in the Ardennes to start the Battle of the Bulge

17 December

Henri IV divorces the notorious Reine Margot

1599 Today, after 27 years, three months and 29 days of marriage, King Henri IV of France was free at last of his scandalously unfaithful wife Marguerite de Valois. Not that he had been a saint – between the two of them they had bedded a full measure of France's nobility. But now Pope Clement VIII finally granted the annulment that, despite her infidelity, the Queen had so vigorously opposed.

From the very beginning the marriage seemed ill-omened. In 1572 Henri was a Protestant, King of Navarre but not yet King of France. Princess Marguerite – universally known as Margot – was a Catholic, daughter of French King Henri II (long dead) and Catherine de' Medici, and sister of Charles IX of France. The marriage was supposed to shore up the tenuous peace between France's Catholics and Protestants, but only five days after the wedding the Catholic League launched the Massacre of St Bartholomew against France's Protestant Huguenots. The leader of this bloodbath was Henri, duc de Guise, one of Margot's many former lovers. (Guise himself was murdered fifteen years later on orders from Margot's brother Henri.)

Although only nineteen at the time of her marriage, Margot was already renowned for her beauty and her licentiousness. Soon she was taking new lovers, the first of whom, Joseph Boniface de La Molle, was decapitated for plotting against Charles IX. (Legend has it that Margot had his head embalmed as a keepsake. Later this romance was idealised by Alexandre Dumas in his famous *La Reine Margot*.) After La Molle came liaisons with Bussy d'Amboise, de Saint-Luc, Champvallon, Aubiac (who was executed by another of

Margot's brothers, Henri III, for more plotting), Vermont and Dat de Saint-Julien, who was murdered by Vermont.

In the meantime Margot's husband Henri acquired numerous mistresses for himself, and the couple lived largely apart. But in 1578 they were reunited, and a year later at Nérac they established a court that the French still remember for its gaiety and sophistication. Among those in attendance were the poet du Bastas and the essayist Montaigne, who was a particular favourite of Henri's. The court sparkled with parties, concerts, poetry reading and debates about love, all of which did not prevent more down-to-earth gallantries, to which both Margot and Henri turned a blind eye. Renowned throughout Europe, it became the setting for Shakespeare's *Love's Labour's Lost*.

But at length Henri tired of his faithless wife, and in 1586 he locked her up in gentle confinement in the Château d'Usson in the Auvergne, where she remained for the next eighteen years. During this period of semi-captivity she scandalised the local populace with her dissolute parties, heavy drinking and occasional trips through town riding a camel. But it was also at Usson that she wrote her famous *Mémoires*, full of anecdotal remembrances of her brothers Charles IX and Henri III and her husband, who in 1589 had become Henri IV of France.

While Margot was thus engaged, Henri found yet another glamorous mistress, Gabrielle d'Estrées, who bore him the children that Margot had failed to provide. There were many possible reasons for Henri to annul his marriage to Margot: consanguinity (they were cousins), duress and religious differences. But foremost in Henri's mind was his ardent desire to marry his mistress, legitimise their offspring, and put them in line for the throne of France. To this Margot swore she would never agree, and three-sided negotiations between Henri, Margot and the Pope dragged on until suddenly at Easter in 1599 Gabrielle died. Only then did Margot consent to an annulment. Pope Clement quickly invalidated their union, and Henri, with no Gabrielle to entice him, went on to marry the faithful but boring Marie de' Medici, whose enormous dowry would help resolve his debts. She also bore him six children to ensure the continuation of the House of Bourbon.

Free of her husband, Margot retained her title of Queen, was created Duchess of Valois and received large financial support from the King. In 1605 she returned to Paris, referred to herself as 'sister' to her ex-husband, and became a devoted friend to his new wife. There she lived for ten more years in ostentatious splendour in her *hôtel particulier* in the rue de Seine, still amorous but increasingly fat, a bizarre mixture of debauchery and piety, the subject of knowing snickers from Parisian society. Henri was assassinated in 1610, the fifth of her bed partners to have been either murdered or executed. Margot followed him to the grave on 27 March 1615 at the age of 61.

Also on this day

1830: South American liberator Símon Bolívar dies in Santa Marta, Colombia * 1843: Charles Dickens's *A Christmas Carol* is published * 1892: In St Petersburg the Russian Imperial Ballet performs Tchaikovsky's *The Nutcracker* for the first time * 1903: At Kitty Hawk, South Carolina, Wilbur and Orville Wright take man's first heavier-than-air flight, lasting 59 seconds

18 December

A new bride in the White House

1915 This afternoon in Washington, DC, Edith Bolling Galt, a widow, married Woodrow Wilson, a recent widower and 28th President of the United States. Her presence in his life had rescued him from the acute depression he suffered after the death of his first wife in August 1914. With Edith at his side, a revitalised Wilson ran for re-election in 1916 and won a second term.

In 1919 she rescued him once again, with very different consequences. With the war in Europe over, President Wilson embarked on a strenuous nationwide campaign to raise public support for the Versailles Peace Treaty and the League of Nations. In late September he collapsed from exhaustion. Back in Washington a week later, he suffered a massive, near-fatal stroke that left him partly paralysed and incapacitated. It was then that Edith Wilson, at the head of a loyal inner circle that included his doctor and his press secretary, directed one of the most remarkable cover-ups in American history.

For a month Wilson lay in the White House, completely disabled. Edith was the buffer between him and the world outside his sickroom. Encouraging medical bulletins were issued to counter rumours about his condition. Few visitors were allowed. Trusted advisors were turned away. Messages for the President went mainly unanswered, or his replies were relayed by Edith. Slowly, Wilson made a limited recovery, but he had become in one observer's description, 'an emaciated old man with a white beard'. He was allowed on his first drive in January but didn't attend his first Cabinet meeting until mid-April. Legislation passed in the Congress became law without his signature. The business of government, insofar as it depended on the President, came to a standstill.

Edith's 'bedside presidency' was meant to keep the President at the helm. Personal loyalty was placed above the national interest. When his doctor refused to certify the President's incapacity, the question of resignation in favour of the Vice-President, as the Constitution provides, was avoided. Seventeen months after his stroke, Wilson was still not strong enough to attend the inaugural ceremony of his successor Warren G. Harding.

Besides the President himself, the greatest casualty of the episode may have been the League of Nations, whose establishment was contained in the Versailles Treaty. The League – and United States membership in it – was Wilson's great cause. It represented his vision of global peace ensured by America's involvement in world affairs. But to the Republicans in the Senate, where they held a majority, the League entailed a threat to American sovereignty and the unwelcome prospect of the nation's entanglement in international affairs. There was room for compromise in the wording of the Treaty, and many members of both parties were anxious for it, but Wilson, diminished in mental acuity and shielded from the political realities outside his sickroom, refused to budge, or allow his Democratic supporters to do so in his name.

Knowledgeable observers believed that if Vice-President Thomas Marshall had become President, a solution allowing ratification could have been found. Without compromise, however, the Treaty – and the League – went down to defeat in the Senate, first in December 1919, then a final time the following March. In later decades, as war clouds gathered, many people speculated on how the course of 20th-century history might have changed had the United States joined the League of Nations in 1920.

Woodrow Wilson died in 1924. Edith Wilson lived another 37 years, long enough for her to attend the inauguration of President John F. Kennedy in 1961.

Also on this day

1638: The original Éminence Grise, Richelieu's aide Père Joseph, dies * 1737: Violin maker Antonio Stradivari dies in Cremona * 1941: Six hundred and ten American defenders surrender to 5,000 attacking Japanese on the island of Guam after a three-hour battle

19 December

The coronation of Henry II

1154 Medieval chronicles tell us that this Sunday was brilliantly sunny despite the season, symbolic of the great occasion that took place today, the coronation of England's Henry II, who had inherited the throne on the death of King Stephen the previous October.

The place was London's Westminster Abbey, where a throng of commoners waited with anticipation in the road outside, and a few sanctuary seekers who had claimed refuge inside were locked up in a side chapel for the duration of the ceremony.

First entering the church were the realm's most eminent nobles, walking solemnly and bearing the royal crown and the ring of Edward the Confessor, miraculously retrieved from the Holy Land a century after it was lost. Then came the men of the cloth –

bishops, abbots and priors, all in full vestment, followed by lesser persons of note, including simple knights and wealthy merchants. The Abbey was crammed with the great and good.

When all were in position, through the front door came Henry Plantagenet and his wife of eighteen months, the fiery Eleanor of Aquitaine. Still only 21, the King was sturdily built, with a leonine head of curly red hair cut short, a freckled face and blue eyes. He was dressed in a doublet and a short Angevin cloak, which would earn him the nickname of Henry Curtmantle. Eleanor wore white and gold, her head uncovered, her dark hair hanging in four plaits. Two pages carried her long train. Although eleven years older than her husband, she retained the beauty for which she was famed.

Henry would rule England for almost 35 years, during which time he would father five sons and three daughters, including two who would become kings of England, Richard the Lion-Heart and the conniving John.

His relations with Eleanor would be tempestuous, to say the least. She resented his string of mistresses, and the myth developed that she poisoned his favourite, Fair Rosamund Clifford. (No doubt she did resent her husband's inamorata, but Rosamund actually died in a convent.) She also foolishly schemed with her sons in their conflicts with their father. After encouraging a failed revolt in 1173, she tried to escape to France disguised as a nun, but on being apprehended, Henry locked her up in honourable and comfortable confinement at Woodstock.

Henry died in 1189, and Eleanor outlived him by fifteen years, but the Plantagenet dynasty they founded held the throne of England for 330 years, eight months and three days, until Richard III lay dead on Bosworth Field.

Also on this day

1562: The Huguenots and the Catholics fight the first battle of the French Wars of Religion at the Battle of Dreux * 1732: Benjamin Franklin publishes the first issue of *Poor Richard's Almanac* * 1783: William Pitt becomes the youngest British Prime Minister at the age of 24 * 1848: English novelist Emily Brontë dies * 1851: English Romantic landscape painter Joseph Turner dies

20 December

Vespasian becomes Emperor when his predecessor is lynched

AD 69 Today one of Rome's worst emperors was killed with appalling brutality, leaving the Empire in the hands of one of the best.

It had been a horrendous eighteen months. In June 68 the atrocious Nero had escaped capture and execution only by suicide, plunging Rome into the calamitous Year of the Four Emperors. In January 69, Nero's successor Galba was brutally murdered in the Roman Forum by soldiers supporting Otho. But by April Otho was dead, another suicide after his defeat at Cremona by the army of the next claimant, Vitellius.

Vitellius was a cruel, vindictive man who was reputed to have had his own rebellious son put to death. Immensely fat, he often ate four times a day, while relieving himself with emetics between meals. According to Tacitus, 'He was the slave and chattel of luxury and gluttony.'

After only four months of power, Vitellius learned that the Roman legions in the eastern provinces had abandoned him, acclaiming their general Vespasian as Emperor. Soon an army supporting Vespasian was on the march towards Rome, although the general himself remained in the east for another year.

On this day the insurgents arrived at the gates of the city. Realising that his cause was hopeless, Vitellius hid himself in the janitor's quarters in the imperial palace, but Vespasian's marauding soldiers quickly discovered him. Frog-marching him to the Forum, they put him to the torture of the little cuts and then slit his throat and threw his body into the Tiber. Now Vespasian was the only would-be emperor left standing, and a fine ruler he turned out to be.

Already 60 when he took power, Vespasian was the son of a simple knight and had spent most of his life as a soldier. He was known for his bluff, straightforward style and infectious if sometimes coarse sense of humour. As Emperor he initiated a tax on public urinals, to the dismay of his son Titus, who believed it beneath imperial dignity. Holding out two gold coins, Vespasian asked, 'Do these smell bad?' Relaxed and down-to-earth, he dispensed with the usual bodyguard and mixed freely with Rome's citizens.

After nearly ten years in power, Vespasian was nearing 70 when he caught a fever while visiting Campania. He then made matters worse by retreating to his summer residence in Reate and bathing in cold water. Suspecting that the end was near, the old emperor wryly referred to Rome's habit of deifying dead emperors with the remark, 'Vae, puto deus fio.' (Oh dear, I think I'm becoming a god.)

Vespasian tried to soldier on with his imperial duties, but on 23 June 79 he was seized with violent diarrhoea. Almost fainting, he struggled to remain on his feet, murmuring, 'Decet imperatorem stantem mori.' (An emperor should die standing.) He then fell dead into the arms of his attendants.

During his ten years as Emperor Vespasian followed a practice of reconciliation, dispensing justice with mercy. According to Suetonius, 'No innocent party was ever punished during Vespasian's reign.' He ended the civil war and probably saved the Empire from dissolution. He also embarked on an ambitious reconstruction programme in a country torn by war. Now of course the Roman Empire is long gone, as are most of its buildings, but one of Vespasian's monuments is still with us, the Flavian Amphitheatre (Flavius was his original family name), which we call the Coliseum.

Also on this day

1860: South Carolina is the first southern state to secede from the United States, leading to the American Civil War * 1894: Australian Prime Minister Sir Robert Menzies is born in Jeporet, Victoria * 1915: The ANZACS, Australian and New Zealand forces with British troops, are evacuated from Gallipoli

21 December

King Richard the Lion-Heart is captured in Austria

1192 Returning from his famous crusade in the Holy Land, England's King Richard the Lion-Heart was sailing home through the Adriatic when a storm forced him ashore near Venice. He then made the foolish decision to continue his journey on land through Austria, even though he knew that its ruler Duke Leopold could be counted among his enemies. When the Crusaders had conquered Acre, Richard had refused to give Leopold his share of the booty and had ordered his standard thrown from the city's walls into the dirt below. Leopold left in cold fury, vowing revenge.

Richard's one precaution as he entered Leopold's domains was to travel disguised as a wealthy merchant. But nearing the Duke's capital in Vienna, Richard made two further mistakes. Exhausted from his time on the road, he remained in the town of Ganina for three days and sent one of his pages to purchase supplies with a pocket full of gold coins.

On this day, Richard's last in Ganina, the page ambled through the market dispensing his gold and with one of the King's gloves bearing the royal insignia carelessly tucked in his belt. Sharp-eyed agents of Duke Leopold spotted and seized the insouciant page and quickly forced him to reveal that Richard and the rest of his entourage were staying at a nearby inn.

Leopold's soldiers instantly surrounded the inn and had no trouble capturing the English King, despite his attempt to disguise himself yet again, this time as a cook in the kitchen.

For the next fourteen months Richard was held prisoner in Leopold's castle at Dürnstein on the Danube. Tradition has it that he was found by his faithful troubadour Blondel, who wandered through Europe singing a ballad that Richard and he had composed together. When Blondel passed before the castle, Richard heard his voice and responded by singing a verse of the same ballad so that Blondel would know he had found the King.

In all likelihood, however, Duke Leopold kept no secret of his royal prisoner since the King's primary value was his ransom. Richard was finally released on 3 February 1193 for a payment of 150,000 silver marks, equal to 34 tons in weight. In 2004 that would have been worth a paltry £3,500,000, but in 1192 it was truly a King's ransom, a price that virtually bankrupted England.

Also on this day

1375: Italian writer Giovanni Boccaccio dies in Certaldo * 1804: British Prime Minister Benjamin Disraeli is born * 1879: Russian tyrant Joseph Stalin (Dzhugashvili) is born in Gori, Georgia * 1940: American novelist F. Scott Fitzgerald dies

22 December

Napoleone becomes a general after the Siege of Toulon

1793 Today Captain of Artillery Napoleone Buonaparte was promoted to the rank of brigadier general at the tender age of 24, rewarded for his heroic achievements during Republican France's victorious Siege of Toulon.

In late August French royalist counter-revolutionaries had treacherously welcomed an enemy Anglo-Spanish fleet under the command of Admiral Hood into the key French naval base of Toulon, just down the Mediterranean coast from Marseille. There the English had seized over 70 vessels, including 30 ships of the line, over half the French fleet. For reasons of both political prestige and military necessity, the Revolutionary government in Paris had resolved to wrest back the base and ordered a siege.

The siege began on 28 August. After several months of mutual cannonading, French soldiers at length captured the forts overlooking the port. Then, on the afternoon of 18 December, Buonaparte, still an obscure captain in charge of the French artillery, focused withering fire from the secured forts directly on the English ships moored in the harbour. Forced to evacuate, the English burned more than half the French ships on their way out. In the evening the revolutionaries reoccupied the city and shot several hundred royalists who had not fled with the English.

Based on his successful use of artillery, Buonaparte became a hero and was jumped half a dozen ranks to brigadier general. With supreme confidence he wrote to the Committee of Public Safety in Paris, 'It is the artillery that takes places; the infantry can only aid it.' But, as remarkable as it was, his dizzying rise was a bit less spectacular in 1793 than it would be today, given that Buonaparte was a trained and professional soldier. During this self-same siege of Toulon the attacking French force was commanded by three successive generals, men who before the Revolution had been, respectively, a painter, a sugar planter and a dentist.

Also on this day

1858: Italian opera composer Giacomo Puccini is born in Lucca * 1894: French officer Alfred Dreyfus is convicted of espionage and sent to Devil's Island * 1895: German physicist Wilhelm Röntgen makes the first X-ray

23 December

Champollion and the Rosetta Stone

1790 Today in the picturesque town of Figeac in the Midi of France was born Jean-François Champollion, one of history's greatest archaeologists, the man who deciphered the Rosetta Stone and thus discovered the key to understanding Egyptian hieroglyphics.

From an early age it was clear that Champollion was a child of exceptional ability. By five he could read without help and started learning Latin. At eleven he entered the lycée at Grenoble, where he astounded his teachers by translating Virgil and Horace. There he also studied Hebrew, Arabic, Syrian and Aramaic. By the time he was fifteen he had also learned Coptic and Ethiopian. Four years later, in 1809, he moved to Paris to study Sanskrit, Chinese and Persian.

In 1799 Napoleon had invaded Egypt, and on 19 July of that

year one of his retinue had been foraging near the town of Rosetta, 55 miles north-east of Alexandria. There he had discovered an ancient slab of black basalt over three feet long and about two feet across commemorating the deeds of the thirteen-year-old boy Pharaoh Ptolemy V Epiphanes, which dated the stone to 196 BC. The stone was covered in Greek and Egyptian inscriptions with the same text in three writing systems, Greek, hieroglyphics and demotic script (a phonetic form of Egyptian writing). Two years later the British chased the French out of Egypt and captured the stone in the process, bringing it back to the British Museum in London, but fortunately paper copies of the writing became available for study.

In 1809 Champollion, still in Paris, began to study the Rosetta Stone texts. After thirteen years he finally deciphered the hieroglyphics, the first to see that they include alphabetic and syllabic signs as well as pictographs. On 27 September 1822, he presented his findings to a special meeting of the Académie des Sciences et des Arts and within the next two years published *Egyptian Pantheon* and *A Summary of the Hieroglyphic System of the Ancient Egyptians*. At last the world could read a system of writing that had served the Egyptians for 3,500 years.

Also on this day

1823: 'A Visit from Saint Nicholas' ("Twas the night before Christmas …') by Professor Clement Clark Moore is first published in the *Troy Sentinel* * 1834: English economist and demographer Robert Malthus dies * 1948: Japanese General Tojo and six other military leaders are hanged for crimes against humanity * 1953: Soviet secret police chief Lavrenti Beria is shot for treason

24 December

Van Gogh and his famous ear

1888 North-west of Marseille on the sunbaked Camargue Plain on the Rhône River lies the ancient town of Arles, a place of culture and beauty since it was settled by Greeks in the 6th century BC. With its 1st-century amphitheatre and 12th-century Romanesque church, it should be the perfect retreat for any sensitive artist.

In February 1888 a supersensitive artist arrived there: 35-year-old Vincent van Gogh. Worn out by the winter gloom of Paris, he was seeking to explore nature through the explosive colours that he saw in his mind. He hoped eventually to surround himself with other Impressionists such as Toulouse-Lautrec and Gauguin, perhaps to form a sub-group of 'Impressionists of the South'.

Van Gogh had long showed signs of instability, and his art dealer brother Theo was anxious to provide him with some sort of companionship and support. Theo approached Paul Gauguin and offered to foot the bill for the trip if he would join Vincent in Arles.

On 23 October Gauguin arrived at Arles and soon was living with van Gogh in the yellow house that van Gogh made famous in his paintings, a small, cosy establishment with green shutters and no indoor toilet.

The two painters worked together for two months, occasionally strolling to the Café de la Gare around the corner for a glass of Pernod or making a quick visit to one of the town's many *poules*. But as the days went by they discovered they were artistically and temperamentally incompatible.

By Christmas Eve the situation was unravelling fast. During the evening van Gogh attacked Gauguin with a razor but failed to wound him. He then returned to his little yellow house and hacked off his own left earlobe to give to a favourite prostitute, a certain Rachel.

Gauguin fled from Arles the following morning, never to see van Gogh again. He soon installed himself in Brittany and then moved on to Tahiti and the Marquesas Islands, where he died in 1903.

Van Gogh stayed at Arles for just four months after that fateful Christmas Eve and then committed himself to an asylum only a few miles away at Saint-Rémy-de-Provence. A year later he finally returned to Paris, ravaged by loneliness and tormented by failure. There, on 29 July 1890, he put a pistol to his breast.

Also on this day

1167: King John of England is born at Beaumont, near Oxford * 1524: Portuguese explorer Vasco da Gama dies in Cochin, Kerala, India * 1822: English poet Matthew Arnold is born * 1888: Film director Michael Curtiz (*Casablanca*) is born in Budapest

25 December

Charlemagne is crowned Emperor

800 On Christmas Day Pope Leo III conducted the ceremonies in Rome. Charles, the great conqueror, devout Christian and King of the Franks, would be crowned Emperor with dominion over all the territories he had subjugated, which meant most of western Europe. Thus began a sort of revival of the Roman Empire that had lapsed in the 5th century. The new Emperor would be known in history as Carolus Magnus, Charles the Great, Charlemagne (or, if you're German, Karl der Grosse).

Charlemagne was the first Holy Roman Emperor to be crowned by the Pope. (Another Charles, the V, would be the last in 1530.) The empire he founded (or revived) would last over 1,000 years until the abdication of Franz II in 1806. His empire would first be described as 'Holy' by Emperor Frederick Barbarossa in 1157, and the full title, *Sacrum Romanum Imperium*, was first used in 1254. Even then it was a description, not a title, as the 'Holy Roman Empire' has in fact never existed as an institution but simply as a name used by historians.

Charlemagne was 48 at the time of his coronation, old for that time in history, but still the tall, athletic figure he had always been. Despite the French-sounding name by which he is known in the English-speaking world, his own language was German (although he had some Greek and Latin, too, and probably some of the Old French dialect spoken by his French subjects), and his capital was on the German side of the Rhine in Aachen, which the French persist in calling Aix-la-Chapelle.

As a ruler, Charlemagne was known for his personal leadership and excellent administration, and, although he could not write, his court was famed for the intellectuals it attracted from all over the world. Personally religious and a great supporter of the Church, he attempted to ban dancing throughout his empire because of its supposed pagan origins, but in this he was widely ignored.

Charlemagne also fiercely suppressed pagan German tribes, especially the Saxons, against whom he led his army into battle eighteen times over the years, but his conquests had more to do with building his empire than with promulgating his religion. In one rather unchristian moment, after a battle against the Saxons he ordered a mass beheading of 4,500 captured enemy warriors.

Charlemagne died in 814, leaving his empire to his son Louis I, but his Carolingian dynasty lasted only until 887.

Also on this day

AD 336: Christmas is first celebrated on 25 December * AD 496: French King Clovis is converted to Christianity * 1066: William the Conqueror is crowned * 1642: English physicist and mathematician Isaac Newton is born in Woolsthorpe near Grantham * 1883: French painter Maurice Utrillo is born in Paris * 1899: American screen icon Humphrey Bogart is born * 1983: Spanish painter Joan Miró dies at the age of 90

26 December

Washington crosses the Delaware to surprise the Hessians

1776 Today, like Lazarus raised from the dead, the Continental Army, widely dismissed as an effective fighting force after a series of defeats around New York, emerged from the early morning gloom in unexpected strength and total surprise to overwhelm the Hessian garrison at Trenton, New Jersey, and produce a timely and crucial victory in the American War of Independence, one of the most significant in the entire history of American arms.

Reports of the army's demise – from its friends as well as its foes

– seemed well founded by the late autumn. As its columns retreated southward through New Jersey, they were harried by the pursuing British and their progress was marked by increasing desertions and near-mutinies from troops who were weary, under-fed and defeated. It was a force reduced to 3,400 men, a 'shadow army' in the Commander-in-Chief's phrase, that Washington led across the Delaware River to Pennsylvania on 7 December.

Well satisfied with his own army's autumn operations, General Howe, the British Commander-in-Chief, went into winter quarters in New York City, leaving some 5,000 troops in forward positions in New Jersey, a force more than adequate, he thought, to keep the local population under control and deal with whatever attacks the rebel forces might mount.

At this blackest of times, with the enlistment periods of most of his regiments expiring at the end of the year, barely three weeks away, General Washington and his generals decided on a bold, do-or-die operation: they would lead the Continental Army back across the Delaware at night and attack the isolated British position at Trenton, held by three Hessian regiments.

From spies, deserters and British sympathisers, the British military expected American attacks against Trenton over Christmas, but assumed they would be no more than the usual patrol-sized, hit-and-run affairs. When, in fact, a rebel scouting party materialised and shots were exchanged on Christmas morning, Colonel Rall, the Hessian commander, supposed that he had met whatever the Americans intended. A raging northeaster bringing heavy snows that evening furthered the impression that the garrison was safe from raids, at least while the storm lasted.

On Christmas night, Washington and his regiments, numbering 2,400 men, began ferrying across the ice-swollen river nine miles above Trenton. It was slow, dangerous work, impeded by high winds, and the last of the artillery didn't get over until 3.00 a.m. The army marched over frozen roads in sleet, snow and freezing rain. The force divided at one point so that it would enter Trenton simultaneously from two directions. It was 8.00 when an outpost spotted the northern column advancing through the snow and shots were fired that roused the sleeping garrison.

It was a quick but bloody action as Washington's troops fought through the village of 100 houses. Captain Alexander Hamilton positioned the artillery pieces that enfiladed the streets in which the Hessians tried to form. Lieutenant James Monroe was wounded while leading a charge to capture Hessian cannon. By 9.30 the Hessians surrendered. American losses were light: four wounded, none killed. Of the Hessians, 106 were killed or wounded, and 918 taken prisoner. By noon the exhausted American army, with its large bag of prisoners, began returning to its positions across the river.

Washington's victory at Trenton – together with his brilliant follow-up successes a few days later at Assumpink Creek and Princeton – gave a tremendous boost to the American cause, breathing life into wavering patriots, restoring self-confidence to the army, and providing the Continental Congress with a glimpse of what its forces, poorly cared for as they had been, might after all accomplish.

Also on this day

1890: German archaeologist and finder of 'Troy' Heinrich Schliemann dies * 1891: American expatriate novelist Henry Miller is born * 1893: Dictator, mass murderer and founding father of the People's Republic of China Mao Tse-tung is born * 1944: American General George Patton's Third Army relieves the surrounded city of Bastogne in Belgium

27 December

Charles Darwin sets sail on the Beagle

1831 Today the refitted naval brig *Beagle* sailed from Plymouth on a voyage that would last five years and two days and change for ever our understanding of life on Earth. On board as an unpaid naturalist was Charles Darwin, not yet the balding, grey-bearded patriarch of later years but a clean-shaven 22 year old, cheerful and energetic, with an insatiable curiosity about the natural world.

Son of a wealthy doctor, Darwin showed little early indication of genius. He was so indifferent a student that his father once told him, 'You care for nothing but shooting, dogs, and rat-catching, and you will be a disgrace to yourself and all your family.' But after exposure at Cambridge to a circle of scientists and influenced by his beetle-collecting entomologist cousin, Darwin became fascinated by the natural world. Shortly after leaving university he accepted with alacrity the invitation to sail with the *Beagle* on an assignment to set up a series of time-keeping stations on the west coast of South America, the Galapagos Islands and in the Pacific.

During the next five years Darwin took every opportunity to go ashore wherever the *Beagle* docked. And every place he went he studied the flora, fauna, rocks, reefs and fossils, collecting specimens and assiduously taking notes. Particularly in the Galapagos Islands he noticed that birds seemed to have evolved differently to meet the varying conditions of each island. These observations would lead to his groundbreaking theory of evolution.

On returning to England, Darwin first published three books on geology. It was only seven years later, in 1838, that he began to complete his own evolutionary hypothesis on natural selection – the process by which 'favourable variations [in a species] would tend to be preserved, and unfavourable ones to be destroyed', leading to changes in the species.

As he refined his startling ideas, Darwin became increasingly aware of the hostile reactions most people would have to them, and so he continually deferred publication. Then, in June 1858, he received a letter from a younger colleague, Alfred Russel Wallace, which encapsulated in a single paper the principles that Darwin had been developing for the past two decades. Distraught, Darwin turned to his scientific friends for help.

Fortunately for Darwin, while Wallace's reasoning was correct, he lacked Darwin's extensive proof, and two friends arranged for a joint paper to be presented to the Linnaean Society of London on 1 July 1858. Darwin himself was not present at this first public unveiling of his earth-shattering theory, as he was attending the funeral of his youngest son, who had died of scarlet fever.

Sixteen months later, on 24 November 1859, Darwin at last

published his great work defining the process of evolution, *On the Origin of Species by Means of Natural Selection, or The Preservation of Favoured Races in the Struggle for Life*. The book caused instant controversy, hailed by the scientific community and renounced by the powers of the Church. It has never since been out of print and is now recognised as one of the greatest and most influential scientific works ever written.

Also on this day

1594: A Jesuit teacher's failed assassination attempt on King Henri IV leads to the expulsion of the Jesuits from France * 1822: French chemist and microbiologist Louis Pasteur is born * 1901: Singer and actress Marlene Dietrich is born in Berlin * 1927: Leon Trotsky is expelled from the Communist Party in Russia

28 December

The first true motion picture – cinema is born

1895 As you stroll up the boulevard des Capucines towards the Paris Opéra, you will pass the world-famous Café de la Paix, just a stone's throw from the spot where the Grand Café once stood. Here on this day Louis and Auguste Lumière demonstrated their new invention, the cinématographe, by projecting a short film clip that alarmed the café's customers with the image of an onrushing train as well as a longer film entitled *La Sortie des Usines Lumière* (Workers Leaving the Lumière Factory). It was the first true motion picture ever made and the birth of cinema.

Louis and Auguste had been born in Besançon in 1862 and 1864 respectively and brought up in Lyon. During their schooldays they exhibited both a taste and a talent for still photography, and when the elder brother was only eighteen he persuaded his father Antoine to bankroll him in establishing a photographic plate factory. It was such a runaway success that in a little over ten years the brothers were manufacturing 15 million plates a year.

Then, in 1894, father Antoine made a visit to Paris, where he saw a showing of Thomas Edison's Kinetoscope, a machine with which viewers could see a moving film, but only through an eyepiece. Returning to Lyon, he urged his sons to find a way to project a moving image.

Louis and Auguste combined two existing ideas, the projection of successive images, a concept already developed by Emile Reynaud, and Edison's use of sprocket-wound film. Their cinématographe was so successful that we have used its first three syllables – cinema – ever since. (The Lumières took their device's name from the Greek *kinema*, 'movement', which comes from *kinein*, 'to move'. Edison's 'Kinetoscope' derives from the same source. Although in English and all Latin languages the modern word starts with 'cine', the German word 'Kino' comes directly from Edison's contraption.)

The Lumières' machine had several clear advantages over Edison's apparatus: it could be used for both photographing and projecting, was quieter, smaller and lighter, and used less film. Furthermore, Edison's Kinetoscope showed images at 46 frames per second, but the Lumières understood that the human brain's illusion of continuous movement is created by images shown at any speed of more than 15 images per second. Therefore they reduced the rate of exposure to 16 frames a second, the rate still used in films today.

The brothers instantly patented their invention, and during the next four years made over 1,000 motion pictures. But, in spite of their technical brilliance, they proved less talented at predicting the future. Seeing their cinématographe as not much more than an oddity, they told a friend that it 'is an invention without a future'.

Also on this day

1065: Westminster Abbey is consecrated under King Edward the Confessor * 1734: Scottish freebooter and outlaw Rob Roy (Robert MacGregor) dies * 1836: Mexico's independence is recognised by Spain

29 December

Murder in the cathedral

1170 'What cowards have I about me', fumed an enraged King Henry II. 'Will no one rid me of this turbulent priest?' These hasty words spoken in anger triggered the most famous murder of the Middle Ages.

Henry Plantagenet had become King of England at only 21. Within a year he had appointed as Chancellor a tall, lean man with dark hair and a sallow complexion, fifteen years his senior. He was Thomas Becket.

The King and Becket were soon boon companions, perfectly complementing each other in court and enjoying each other's company while hunting or in the taverns of London. With his quick mind and astute understanding of Henry's will, Becket played a leading role in concentrating power in the King's hands at the cost of the feudal barons and the Church.

So pleased was Henry by Becket's performance that within seven years he appointed him Archbishop of Canterbury, second in power only to the King himself.

But then Becket began to change. His public style became more imperious, his arrogance more pronounced, his ostentation more insufferable. But privately he also changed, spending hours in prayer and becoming a vegetarian. Most critically, he increasingly came to support the old, medieval powers of the Church, especially when they ran counter to the claims of the crown.

The first signs of conflict came in January 1163 when Becket excommunicated one of Henry's senior barons. But the greatest dispute involved the trial of miscreant priests. Becket was adamant that all clerics suspected of crime be tried exclusively by canonical trial overseen by a bishop, but Henry insisted that they be subject to royal authority. The King also appropriated any income derived from vacant sees and banned the excommunication of court officials without royal consent.

So vehement were the arguments, so bitter the quarrel, that after

Becket had been Archbishop for just over two years he fled to the continent when Henry bitterly denounced him.

Six years later an uneasy truce was arranged, and on 1 December 1170 the Archbishop returned to England, but he immediately rekindled the fire by excommunicating three bishops appointed by the King. Henry was in Bayeux when he heard the news. Incensed, he barked out his famous exhortation.

Henry had spoken in a moment of temper and had no intention of ordering a murder, but in court were four impatient barons, Reginald Fitzurse, Hugh de Moreville, William de Tracey and Richard le Breton. Immediately they were riding hard for England, and although Henry sent out orders to stop them, the messenger failed to catch up with them.

On the afternoon of 29 December the barons reached the Archbishop's palace at Canterbury. Dressed in white cloaks over chain mail, they confronted Becket and demanded that he abandon England for ever. Contemptuously he replied, 'Not for living man, not for the King, will I fly!'

At the hour of vespers the Archbishop went to his cathedral. As he stood in the north transept the four armed knights strode in, accompanied by another knight named de Brock, with whom they had stayed the previous night. Becket moved to the altar as the men approached, trying to take him prisoner. But Becket resisted, crying out, 'I am prepared to die for Christ and for His Church.' At these, his last words, de Tracey struck at him with his sword, wounding one of the few clerics supporting the Archbishop but only grazing Becket's forehead. Then de Tracey and le Breton both hacked at the Archbishop, knocking him down, and de Brock placed his foot on his neck and sliced through his skull so that his brains spread out on the stone floor.

The arrogant Archbishop was finally dead. After the barons had fled, cathedral priests recovered the corpse and discovered that under his robes Becket was clothed in sackcloth and his body was scourged with the marks of a penitent.

As was usual in medieval times on portentous occasions, directly after the murder a violent storm broke out and lightning filled the sky. Becket's tomb instantly became a place of worship, and in less than three years he was canonised. King Henry came to Canterbury to do penance and receive absolution.

For four centuries Becket's shrine remained a goal of pilgrimage for the faithful, but in the 16th century Henry VIII had it ripped from the cathedral and destroyed. He had no patience with the priest who would defy a king.

Also on this day

1809: British Prime Minister William Gladstone is born * 1825: French painter Jacques Louis David dies * 1890: The last major battle between American Indians and US troops takes place at Wounded Knee, South Dakota * 1895: Cecil Rhodes's lieutenant Leander Starr Jameson leads an abortive raid to capture Johannesburg in the Boer Republic

30 December

Rasputin is murdered

1916 It was late in the evening of 29 December in St Petersburg when, accompanied by the jolly beat of *Yankee Doodle* playing on the gramophone, Prince Feliks Yusupov offered his guest two cakes laced with cyanide of potassium, along with a similarly doctored glass of Madeira. Yet despite a dosage theoretically 'enough to kill a horse', the intended murder victim, a bearded and brooding holy man, continued to chat calmly with his host.

After the clock chimed midnight Yusupov could wait no longer. Drawing a revolver, he shot his visitor in the back, knocking him to the ground. But instead of dying the victim rose to his feet and charged out into the garden. There another assassin waited. He shot the holy man twice, and then the two murderers rolled him up in a blue rug and pushed their grisly package through a hole they had carved through the frozen surface of the Moika Canal on the Neva River. When the body was recovered three days later, water was found in the lungs. The murdered man had finally drowned, after surviving both poison and bullets.

Such was the end of the sinister 'staretz', or self-styled mystic christened Grigory Yefimovich Novykh but universally known as Rasputin, Russian for 'debauched one'.

Rasputin had been born a peasant in Siberia in 1872. At eighteen he experienced a conversion to the Khlysty flagellant sect and developed the theory that he could achieve a state of grace through 'holy passionlessness', a condition best reached through the exhaustion of prolonged debauchery. Although illiterate, unkempt and unclean (he bathed but once a month), he found women susceptible to his sexually charged message from God.

For over a decade Rasputin wandered around Russia preaching and seducing and finally arrived in St Petersburg in 1903. There his reputation as a mystic grew until Tsar Nicholas and his neurotic wife Alexandra summoned him to attend their four-year-old son Aleksey, the Tsarevich, whose life was threatened by haemophilia. Miraculously, Rasputin seemed to help the boy, probably through his hypnotic powers, and his place at court was assured.

For the next ten years Rasputin continued his drunken orgies and faith-based seductions, claiming that any woman who had sex with him would purify her soul. But Nicholas and Alexandra refused to believe reports about him, considering them malicious and unfounded gossip, and his baleful influence grew, much to the distress of the country's nobility and even members of the imperial family. Then, in 1914, came war.

In August 1915 the feckless Tsar Nicholas decided to take personal command of his armies and left for the front, leaving the government in the hands of his wife Alexandra, whose spiritual and personal advisor Rasputin had become. Now the staretz could influence the choice of Cabinet ministers and even manipulate critical military decisions affecting the army.

This finally provoked Prince Yusupov and four other extreme conservatives to intervene to preserve the country, the monarchy and the power of the nobility. One, Vladimir Purishkevich, was a member of the Duma while another was the Tsar's cousin, Grand Duke Dmitry Pavlovish. Seeing the Tsar and Tsarina impervious to reason, they resolved to remove Rasputin by force and carried out the murder.

Hearing rumours of his impending assassination – the plotters were scarcely discreet about their intentions – Rasputin sent a last letter to the Tsar that may have proved him a psychic after all. 'I shall depart this life before the first of January', he wrote. 'If one of your relatives causes my death, then no one in your family, that is, none of your children or relations, will live for more than two years. They will be killed by the people of Russia.'

Just nineteen months later, on 16 July 1918, Communist insurgents shot Tsar Nicholas and Alexandra and their four children in a cellar at Ekaterinburg.

Also on this day

1865: British writer Rudyard Kipling is born * 1922: The USSR is established * 1924: American astronomer Edwin Hubble announces the existence of other galactic systems

31 December

Bonnie Prince Charlie

1720 Today Bonnie Prince Charlie, that quixotic Stuart prince who spent a lifetime in exile vainly trying to get his family and himself restored to the throne of England, was born in the Palazzo Muti in Rome.

Charlie was the grandson of the petulant and narrow-minded King James II, who in 1688 had been unceremoniously chased into exile for his fervent and unbending Catholicism. James had died in 1701, but his son, the unfortunate Old Pretender James Edward, twice tried and failed to invade the British Isles to regain the crown, resolutely refusing to convert to Protestantism for the chance to become the British heir. Then came the Bonnie Prince, a handsome, dashing young man who was determined to restore his father to the throne.

Charlie's first effort came when he was 24 and joined a French invasion fleet. But, just as it had with the Spanish Armada, a hurricane scattered the ships before they put the army ashore.

A year later Charlie mounted a second effort, this time on his own. In July 1745 he landed almost alone in the Hebrides. Reaching the mainland with only seven followers, he began rallying discontented Scots to his banner as he marched towards Edinburgh. By November he had attracted almost 6,000 supporters and headed for London. But soon a large English army was advancing towards him, and Charlie's officers and men started to trickle away, forcing him to retreat back across the border to Scotland.

In April 1746 the British army, now 9,000 strong, met Charlie's 5,000 men at Culloden Moor, six miles east of Inverness. The result was mass slaughter, as over 1,000 Highlanders perished during the battle to only 50 British.

What happened next is the stuff of legend. In a desperate attempt to escape his English pursuers, Charlie spent the next five months in what became celebrated as the 'flight through the heather'. In the Hebrides once again, he encountered Flora MacDonald, a brave young Jacobite sympathiser who disguised the prince as her serving maid and took him with her party across to the Isle of Skye. From there, still pursued, he wandered among the Highlands until he finally managed to get away to France. 'And so he left us,' wrote a bitter Scot, 'and he left us all in a worse state than he found us.'

Flora was temporarily incarcerated in the Tower of London for her treason but pardoned after a year. This adventurous tale became a popular classic after 1814 when Sir Walter Scott published *Waverley*, the account of Charlie's failed invasion and escape.

Bonnie Prince Charlie spent the next 42 years wandering around Europe, principally in Italy, gradually decaying into a drunken, self-indulgent wreck. Blindly committed to the theory of divine right, difficult and unapproachable, he styled himself Charles III of England. His wife, a woman 33 years his junior, called him 'the most insupportable man who ever lived, a man who combined the faults and failings of all classes, including the vice of lackeys, that of drink'. She went on to say that 'he rarely missed being drunk twice a day'. Such was the man who had once been the bonnie prince, who died one month after his 68th birthday in the Palazzo Muti, the palace where he had been born.

Also on this day

AD 192: The mad Roman Emperor Commodus is assassinated * 1869: French painter Henri Matisse is born in Le Cateau, Picardy * 1877: French painter Gustave Courbet dies at La Tour de Péliz, Switzerland * 1880: American general and father of the Marshall Plan George Marshall is born

Index

Carroll, Lewis 12 May 1820
Carus, Roman Emperor 4 September AD 476
Casca 15 March 44 BC
Cassius, Gaius 8 December 65 BC
Castel Sant'Angelo (Hadrian's Tomb) 8 August AD 117
Castelnau, Papal legate Pierre de 14 January 1208
Castillon, Battle of 17 July 1453
Castlereagh, Robert Stewart, Viscount, later 2nd Marquess of Londonderry 15 September 1814; 12 August 1822
Cataline Conspiracy 7 December 43 BC
Catesby, Robert 5 November 1605
Cathar 14 January 1208
Catherine I of Russia 25 November 1741
Catherine II of Russia (the Great) (Sophia von Anhalt-Zerbst) 25 November 1741; 30 May 1778; 22 April 1787; 6 November 1796; 23 March 1801
Catherine de Valois (wife of Henry V of England) 23 February 1421; 22 August 1485
Catherine de' Medici, Queen of France 24 September 1435; 28 October 1533; 24 August 1572; 17 December 1599; 9 July 1737
Catherine of Aragon, wife of Henry VIII 29 November 1530; 6 July 1535
Catherine of Siena, St (Catherine Benincasa) 29 April 1380
Catton, Bruce 7 April 1862
Cauchon, Pierre (Bishop of Beauvais) 29 May 1431

Cavell, Edith 12 October 1915
Cavour, Camillo Benso, Conte di 6 June 1861
Cecil, Sir Robert 5 November 1605
Cellini, Benvenuto 6 May 1527;
Cervantes, Miguel de 9 October 1547; 7 October 1571
Cesena, destruction and massacre 3 February 1377
Châlons, Battle of 20 June AD 451
Champollion, Jean François 23 December 1790
Charing Cross 28 November 1290
Charlemagne, Holy Roman Emperor 10 October 732; 2 April 742; 25 December 800; 28 January 814; 27 September 1389; 6 August 1806
Charles I of England 23 April 1661; 11 December 1688
Charles I of Spain See Charles V, Holy Roman Emperor
Charles II of England 2 February 1650; 23 April 1661; 6 February 1665; 4 November 1677; 6 February 1685; 11 December 1688
Charles II, duc de Bourbon 6 May 1527
Charles V of France 22 February 1358
Charles V, Holy Roman Emperor (Charles I of Spain) 25 December 800; 19 June 1369; 22 June 1478; 24 February 1500; 12 January 1519; 18 April 1521; 27 April 1521; 19 November 1523; 24 February 1525; 6 May 1527; 24 February 1530; 29 November 1530; 7 June 1914

Cleopatra, Queen and Pharaoh of Egypt 13 June 323 BC; 2 September 31 BC; 30 August 30 BC

Clive of India (Robert Clive) 8 June 1755

Clothilde, St 27 November 511

Clovis, King of the Franks 27 November 511

Cochise 3 September 1886

Coligny, Admiral Gaspard de 24 August 1572

Coliseum 20 December AD 69

Columbus, Christopher (Cristoforo Colombo) 3 August 1492

Comédie Française 17 February 1673

Commodus, Roman Emperor 7 March AD 161; 22 October AD 180

Conan Doyle, Sir Arthur 4 May 1891

Conrad IV, Holy Roman Emperor 25 June 1243

Constantine, Roman Emperor 29 February 45 BC; 27 October AD 312; 22 May AD 337

Cook, Captain James 18 January 1778; 17 April 1790

Coolidge, President Calvin 21 May 1927

Corday, Charlotte 13 May 1793; 13 July 1793

Corneille, Pierre 10 July 1099; 6 June 1606

Cornwallis, General Charles 19 October 1781

Corsica 15 May 1768

Cortés, Hernán 26 September 1513

Cranmer, Thomas (Archbishop of Canterbury) 21 March 1556;

Crimean War 15 September 1814; 12 May 1820; 10 March 1831; 4 October 1853; 20 November 1910

Cromwell, Oliver 23 April 1661; 4 November 1677; 6 February 1685

Crown of Thorns 11 August 1239

Crusade, First 18 November 1095; 15 July 1099

Culloden Moor, Battle of 31 December 1720; 16 April 1746

Dante Alighieri 15 March 44 BC; 8 August AD 117; 1 May 1274, 1283; 14 September 1321

Danton, Jacques Georges 26 October 1759; 17 April 1790; 13 May 1793; 8 November 1793; 5 April 1794

Darius I (the Great), Persian Emperor 21 September 490 BC

Darius III, Persian Emperor 1 October 331 BC

Darnley, Lord (Henry Stewart) 19 June 1566; 9 February 1567; 10 June 1688

Darwin, Charles 27 December 1831; 24 November 1859

Dauphin (origin of term) 22 August 1350

David, Jacques Louis 13 July 1793

Declaration of Independence, US 30 October 1735

Deladier, Edouard 10 March 1831

Descent of Man and Selection in Relation to Sex, The 24 November 1859

El Alamein, Battle of 4 November 1942; 14 October 1944

El cantar de mío Cid **(The Song of the Cid)** 10 July 1099

Eleanor of Aquitaine 25 March 1133; 18 May 1152; 19 December 1154; 27 March 1204; 25 November 1252; 16 November 1272

Eliot, T.S. (Thomas Stearns) 14 September 1321

Elizabeth (Sisi), Empress of Austria (Wittelsbach) 24 April 1854

Elizabeth I of England 22 August 1485; 8 February 1587; 19 April 1587; 29 July 1588; 24 March 1603; 29 October 1618

Elizabeth I of Russia 25 November 1741

Elizabeth II of England 29 June 1613

English Civil War 11 December 1688

Erasmus, Desiderius 6 July 1535

Escorial, El 10 August 1557

Este, Alfonso d' 23 June 1519

Estrées, Gabrielle d' 25 July 1594; 11 April 1599; 17 December 1599

Eugene of Savoy, Prince 12 September 1683; 11 September 1697; 13 August 1704; 11 September 1709; 16 August 1717

Eugénie de Montijo, Empress of France, wife of Napoleon III 29 January 1853; 17 November 1869

Eyck, Jan van 15 June 1467

Farewell to Arms, A 8 July 1918

Farragut, Admiral David 5 August 1864

Faust 28 August 1749

Fawkes, Guy 5 November 1605

Ferdinand I of Austria 12 January 1519

Ferdinand II, Holy Roman Emperor 12 November 1611; 24 October 1648

Ferdinand of Aragon, King of Spain 22 June 1478; 17 October 1483; 2 January 1492; 3 August 1492; 16 September 1498; 26 September 1513; 12 January 1519; 27 April 1521

Fillmore, President Millard 31 March 1854

First World War 15 November 1684; 10 November 1775; 10 March 1831; 18 January 1871; 9 May 1892; 13 January 1898; 13 March 1905; 28 June 1914; 12 October 1915; 9 January 1916; 21 February 1916; 5 June 1916; 23 October 1917; 8 July 1918; 8 October 1918; 11 November 1918; 19 May 1935; 20 January 1936; 14 October 1944

Flavius Silva 15 April AD 73

Foch, Marshal Ferdinand 11 November 1918

Fouché, Joseph, duc d'Otrante 13 May 1793

Francis of Assisi, St (Francesco Bernardone) 3 October 1226

Franco, General Francisco 24 July 1704; 26 April 1937

François I of France 1 May 1515–47; 2 May 1519; 24 February 1525; 11 October 1531; 28 October 1533

Manhattan 24 May 1626

Manstein, Field Marshal Erich von 31 January 1943

Manuel I of Portugal 27 April 1521

Mao Tse-tung 20 October 1935

Marat, Jean Paul 13 July 1793

Marathon, Battle of 21 September 490 BC

Marcel, Etienne 22 February 1358; 28 May 1358

Marcus Aurelius, Roman Emperor 7 March AD 161; 22 October AD 180; 15 September 1814

Margot, Queen (wife of Henri IV) See Marguerite de Valois

Marguerite de Valois (Queen Margot) (wife of Henri IV) 11 April 1599; 17 December 1599

Marguerite of Provence, wife of Louis IX 26 May 1234

Maria Theresa, Archduchess of Austria and Queen of Hungary and Bohemia 16 October 1793

Marie Antoinette, Queen of France 12 September 1683; 15 November 1684; 31 May 1785; 17 April 1790; 13 May 1793; 16 October 1793; 8 June 1795

Marie-Louise, Empress (wife of Napoleon I, later Duchess of Parma, Piacenza and Guastalla) 9 March 1796; 5 July 1809; 15 September 1814; 13 November 1834

Marignano, Battle of 11 October 1531

Marine Corps, United States 10 November 1775

Marius, Gaius 13 January 86 BC

Mark Antony (Marcus Antonius) 7 December 43 BC; 2 September 31 BC; 30 August 30 BC

Market Garden, Operation 17 September 1944

Marlborough, First Duke of (John Churchill) 6 February 1665; 11 September 1697; 13 August 1704; 11 September 1709

Martel, Charles 10 October 732; 2 April 742

Martin V, Pope (Oddone Colonna) 20 September 1378

Mary I of England (Bloody Mary) (Tudor) 4 August 1347; 22 August 1485; 12 February 1554; 21 March 1556; 7 January 1558

Mary II of England (Stuart) 4 November 1677; 4 February 1716

Mary of Burgundy (wife of Maximilian I) 12 January 1519

Mary, Queen of Scots 19 June 1566; 9 February 1567; 8 February 1587; 10 June 1688; 4 February 1716

Masada, siege of 15 April AD 73

Mata Hari (Margaretha Zella) 13 March 1905

Matilda 25 March 1133;

Maximes 17 March 1860

Maximilian I, Holy Roman Emperor 12 January 1519

Maximilian of Mexico 19 June 1867

Mayerling (Prince Rudolf's suicide) 30 January 1889

Mazarin, Cardinal Giulio (Mazzarini) 4 December 1642; 17 March 1680

McKinley, President William 15 February 1898; 1 July 1898

Mozart, Wolfgang Amadeus
5 December 1791; 26 March
1827
Murad II 3 May 1481
**Murat, Joachim, Marshal and
King of Naples** 15 August 1769;
5 October 1795; 21 August 1810
Murger, Henri 1 February 1896
Musset, Alfred de 10 March 1810
Mussolini, Benito 19 July 1848; 20
July 1944; 28 April 1945; 30 April
1945
Nanking, Treaty of 29 August 1842
Nantes, Edict of 14 May 1643
**Napoleon I of France (Napoleon
Bonaparte)** 25 June 1279 BC; 29
September 1273; 22 June 1527; 24
February 1530; 27 July 1675; 28
August 1749; 15 May 1768; 15
August 1769; 1 September 1785;
17 August 1786; 23 December
1790; 22 December 1793; 5
October 1795; 9 March 1796; 1
August 1798; 9 November 1799;
20 May 1802; 23 January 1806;
6 August 1806; 16 January 1809;
5 July 1809; 15 December 1809;
20 February 1810; 21 August
1810; 7 September 1812; 18
October 1812; 26 February 1815;
5 May 1821; 12 August 1822;
13 November 1834; 6 June
1861
**Napoleon III of France (Louis
Napoleon Bonaparte)** 23
January 1832; 29 January 1853; 19
June 1867; 1 June 1879; 1
February 1896
**Napoleon, Prince Louis (son of
Napoleon III)** 1 June 1879

Nasser, Gamal Abdel 17 November
1869
Navas de Tolosa (Las), Battle of
16 July 1212
**Neipperg, Adam Adalbert, Count
von** 26 February 1815
Nelson, Admiral Horatio 1 August
1798; 21 October 1805; 15
January 1815
**Nero, Roman Emperor (Nero
Claudius Caesar Augustus
Germanicus, original name
Lucius Domitius
Ahenobarbus)** 13 October AD
54; 18 July AD 64; 9 June AD 68;
20 December AD 69
Nerva, Roman Emperor 27 January
AD 98
**Nesselrode, Count (Graf), Karl
Vasilyevich** 15 September
1814
New Amsterdam 24 May 1626
New Orleans, Battle of 8 January
1815
Nicholas I of Russia 7 September
1812; 4 October 1853
Nicholas II of Russia 30 December
1916; 20 January 1936
**Nicholas V, Pope (Tommaso
Parentucelli)** 31 October 1517
Nicholas, Saint 6 December AD
343
Nicomedes, King of Bithynia 12
July 100 BC
Nicopolis, Battle of 25 September
1396
Nightingale, Florence 12 May
1820; 4 October 1853
Nika Revolt 17 January 532
Nile, Battle of 1 August 1798

Peter I of Russia (the Great) 18 March 1584; 15 May 1682; 25 November 1741; 22 April 1787

Peter II of Russia 25 November 1741

Peter III of Russia 25 November 1741; 6 November 1796; 23 March 1801

Peter the Hermit 18 November 1095

Petrarch 22 February 1358

Pharsalus, Battle of 9 August 48 BC

Philip I of Spain (the Handsome) 22 June 1478; 12 January 1519

Philip II (the Bold), Duke of Burgundy (Philippe le Hardi) 19 June 1369

Philip II of France (Augustus) 27 November 511; 6 March 1204; 23 June 1204; 7 January 1558

Philip II of Macedon 1 October 331 BC; 13 June 323 BC

Philip II of Spain 10 August 1557; 19 January 1568; 19 April 1587; 29 July 1588; 25 July 1593

Philip III (the Good), Duke of Burgundy (Philippe le Bon) 15 June 1467

Philip IV the Fair of France (Philippe le Bel) 19 March 1314; 5 June 1316; 3 February 1377

Philip V of Spain 24 July 1704; 13 August 1704

Philip VI of France 26 August 1346

Philippa, Queen of England (wife of Edward III) 4 August 1347; 22 August 1485

Philippa, Queen of Portugal 14 August 1385

Philippe Egalité 13 May 1793

Picasso, Pablo 26 April 1937

Pied Piper 26 June 1284

Pitt, William (the Elder) 17 April 1790; 23 January 1806

Pitt, William (the Younger) 24 June 1348; 23 January 1806; 12 August 1822

Pius II, Pope (Enea Silvio Piccolomini) 27 September 1389

Pius IV, Pope (Giovanni Angelo de' Medici) 10 April 1585

Pius IX, Pope (Giovanni Mastai-Ferretti) 16 November 1272

Pius XII, Pope (Eugenio Maria Giuseppe Giovanni Pacelli) 26 April 1937

Pizarro, Francisco 26 September 1513; 26 April 1937

Plantagenet, Arthur 3 April 1203

Plataea, Battle of 23 September 480 BC

Pliny the Elder 10 January 49 BC; 25 August 79 AD

Pliny the Younger 27 January AD 98; 25 August 79 AD

Plutarch 13 June 323 BC; 30 August 30 BC

Poincaré, President Henri 31 July 1914

Poitiers, Battle of 19 September 1356; 22 February 1358; 25 October 1415; 17 July 1453

Poltava, Battle of 22 April 1787

Polybius 2 August 216 BC

Pompeii 25 August 79 AD

Pompey the Great 9 August 48 BC; 7 December 43 BC

Ponce de León, Juan 3 March 1513

Portinari, Beatrice 1 May 1274, 1283

Stauffenberg, Colonel (Count) Claus von 20 July 1944; 14 October 1944

Stoke, Battle of 16 June 1487

Streltsy Rebellion 15 May 1682

Stuart dynasty, history of 4 February 1716

Stuart, James Francis Edward (the Old Pretender) 10 June 1688; 11 December 1688; 4 February 1716; 31 December 1720; 16 April 1746

Stuyvesant, Peter 24 May 1626

Suetonius 31 August AD 12; 19 August AD 14; 13 October AD 54; 18 July AD 64; 9 June AD 68; 20 December AD 69; 18 September AD 96

Suez Canal 17 November 1869; 7 June 1914

Suffragette 19 July 1848

Suleiman the Magnificent 10 October 732; 16 July 1212; 7 October 1571; 16 August 1717

Sulla, Lucius Cornelius 4 September AD 476

Sumter, Fort 12 April 1861

Tacitus 19 August AD 14; 20 December AD 69

Taj Mahal 22 January 1666

Talleyrand, Prince Charles-Maurice 11 April 1775; 9 November 1799; 7 September 1812; 15 September 1814; 13 November 1834

Tarawa, Battle of 10 November 1775

Tarik 16 July 1212

Tarquinius Superbus, King of Rome 4 September AD 476

Tartuffe 17 February 1673

Templars 19 March 1314

Tenniel, John 1 April 1815

Ternan, Ellen 7 February 1812

Terror (French Revolution), start of 13 May 1793

Thanksgiving 26 November 1789

Themistocles 23 September 480 BC

Theodora, Empress 17 January 532

Thermopylae, Battle of 20 August 480 BC; 23 September 480 BC

Thirty Years' War 24 October 1648

Tiberius, Roman Emperor (Tiberius Claudius Nero) 31 August AD 12; 19 August AD 14; 16 March AD 37; 9 June AD 68

Tilly, Johann Tserclaes, Graf von 12 November 1611

Titus, Roman Emperor 20 December AD 69; 15 April AD 73; 18 September AD 96

Toison d'Or, Ordre de la (Order of the Golden Fleece) 15 June 1467

Tolbiacum, Battle of 27 November 511

Tolstoy, Count Leo Nikolayevich 7 September 1812; 20 November 1910

Torquemada, Tomás de 17 October 1483; 16 September 1498; 26 July 1826

Tosca 8 August AD 117

Toulon, Siege of 22 December 1793

Tours, Battle of 10 October 732

Towton, Battle of 21 July 1403

Trafalgar, Battle of 21 October 1805; 23 January 1806

Trajan, Roman Emperor (Marcus Ulpius Traianus) 27 January AD 98; 8 August AD 117; 17 November 1869